THE WHICH? GUIDE TO

WEEKEND BREAKS IN EUROPE

THE WHICH? GUIDE TO

WEEKEND BREAKS IN EUROPE

Published by Consumers' Association
and Hodder & Stoughton

Which? Books are commissioned and researched by The Association for Consumer Research and published by Consumers' Association, 2 Marylebone Road, London NW1 4DF and Hodder & Stoughton, 47 Bedford Square, London WC1B 3DP

First edition October 1990
Revised edition May 1993

British Library Cataloguing-in-Publication Data
A catalogue record for this book is available from the British Library

ISBN 0 340 58727 X

Thanks for choosing this book . . .
If you find it useful, we'd like to hear from you. Even if it doesn't do the job you were expecting, we'd still like to know. Then we can take your comments into account when preparing similar titles or, indeed, the next edition of the book. Address your letter to the Publishing Manager at Consumers' Association, FREEPOST, 2 Marylebone Road, London NW1 4DF.
We look forward to hearing from you.

Cover, text design and illustrations by Paul Saunders
Cover photographs by *Holiday Which?*
Maps by David Perrott Cartographics
Typeset by Litho Link Ltd, Welshpool, Powys, Wales
Printed in England by BPCC Hazells Ltd, Aylesbury

Editor for this edition: Kim Winter

Contributors: Ros Belford, Sophie Butler, Val Campbell, Stephen Clues, Anna Fielder, Anne Harvey, Lindsay Hunt, Andrew Leslie, Frances Roxburgh, Adam Ruck, Nick Trend, Kim Winter

Additional research: Stephanie Barrett, Susie Casement, Lorna Dean, Natasha Ivanova, Helena Markusova, Polly Phillimore

CONTENTS

Introduction

We live in interesting times. As our last edition went to press, the Berlin Wall had been breached, heralding the reunification of the eastern and western halves of the city after a break of nearly 30 years. Elsewhere in the Eastern Bloc, equally tumultuous changes were heading towards division rather than unity: the Velvet Revolution in Prague, leading to Czechoslovakia's eventual split into the Czech Republic and Slovakia, and the loosening of the Soviet Union into the Commonwealth of Independent States.

Hyper-inflation, particularly in Russia, as the fledgling market economy struggles to find its feet, has caused hardship for locals and confusion for tourists. But there have also been opportunities, as new private enterprises, ranging from taxi services and tourist agencies to restaurants and beer halls, spring up and increase the range of choice and services on offer to everyone. Access is also becoming easier – there are more flights to Moscow and St Petersburg – though problems such as shortages of accommodation remain. But it's an exciting time to visit, if you're prepared to accept the pace and unpredictability of life there.

On the other hand, there's much to be said for a relaxing stay in a longer-established short-break destination – there may be as much pleasure to be got from tucking into *Sachertorte* in a Vienna café on a spring Saturday or spending a weekend out of reach of the British climate on the promenade at Nice. Whatever your reasons for wanting to get away, Europe's great cities lie in tantalising readiness to refresh, illuminate, entertain or indulge you. A short break in one of them – perhaps no more than a long weekend – can feel like a much longer holiday. And your purse doesn't have to be that deep. By taking advantage of the ever-increasing number of short-break package deals, of seats on charter flights, or of weekend reductions in the price of hotels, the informed break-taker can find some excellent bargains.

In this guide, we present 21 options for a short break in Europe. All are well served by scheduled flights and package tour operators. We tell you the advantages and drawbacks of each city, to enable you to make the best choice. All are quite different, a fact which is sometimes not obvious from the pages of holiday brochures, and some do not cater well for all tastes. For instance, if you shudder at a surfeit of sightseeing, or if you hate heat but have to travel in high summer, some cities will suit you better than others. The effects of weather should not be underestimated – you may be dismayed to find that 850 miles from home there can still be three times as many April showers as in London. Some cities are wonderful for leisurely strolling and window-shopping, others are hectic and traffic-ridden; some have their major sights concentrated in a compact area, others have them widely dispersed throughout the city. Nightlife options may include a quiet candlelit dinner, a night at the opera, or a dusk-to-dawn progression from one nightclub to the next; some cities offer all of these, others only a few.

Accommodation varies widely, too. For some cities, our hotel recommendations are the best (in various categories) that are available; for other cities (in particular, Paris) they are just a small selection of good places from among many. Where possible, we have included hotels favoured by tour operators as well as those used only by independent travellers; in some cities, there is an appreciable difference between the two categories, in others virtually none.

Package or independent?

Tour operator packages

A short-break package holiday is usually no more than an inclusive deal of transport and bed and breakfast accommodation: you don't travel with a group (Moscow and St Petersburg excepted) and there may be no rep to help you at the other end – although some operators do offer optional sightseeing tours and useful information packs. The main advantage of going on a package is that you can see the basic cost of your holiday at a glance in the brochure and can organise it with one phone call or visit to the travel agent.

If you choose to go on an inclusive package, remember that prices between operators can vary widely, even for stays in the same hotel. If you are likely to want to travel outside your city base, fly-drive packages offered by tour operators are often good value.

Going independently

Making your own arrangements is easy for the majority of cities in this guide. Information from the national tourist office and a competent travel agent (and *Holiday Which?* reports) are all you need. The exceptions are the Eastern European cities – Budapest, Prague, Moscow and St Petersburg – where acute shortage of accommodation is coupled with increasing demand. In these cities it's vital that you have a room booked in advance – and packages are still the easiest way to ensure this. The advantage of going independently is that you don't have to stay in the large and rather average hotels where tour operators get their biggest discounts. If you want a small hotel, a family-run *pension* or even a private room, you'll generally be better off booking your own holiday. You may also have more choice of times and days on which you can travel. (See *Practicalities*, page 10, for information on booking a flight.)

Impulse buy or advance planning?

Except at the most obviously busy times of year (Easter, Whitsun), short-break tour operators can usually cope with last-minute bookings, so there's usually little need to plan your city break months in advance. The exception is if you want to catch festivals or special events in European cities – Prague's Inter-national Music Festival, St Petersburg's White Nights or Venice's International Drama Festival, for example – where, if you leave things until the last moment, accommodation may be limited and tickets to concerts hard to come by. Of course, if you choose to go visiting cities like Florence, Venice or Nice in July and August, you'll be competing with intercontinental tourists and indigenous holidaymakers for space, and you may also find prices higher and the choice of accommodation limited.

If you are making your own arrangements, remember that the cheaper airfares are often sold in limited numbers, and that APEX fares need to be booked in advance (usually two weeks). Leaving things until the last minute may rule out the best bargains here.

Cities for all seasons

There are two good reasons for a winter jaunt to Europe – to escape the British climate and to escape other tourists. In Athens, Barcelona, Nice, Lisbon and Rome, winters may be as warm as an English spring. Madrid and Florence are a little cooler (around 10°C), as is Istanbul (which also has a great deal of rain). Winter is certainly the best season for sightseeing in Florence, and galleries will be pleasingly uncrowded in most cities. Some of the inland cities take on an extra sparkle in snow or hard frost – Salzburg and St Petersburg, for example. Charter flights designed for skiers can offer opportunities for city-breakers too. Round Christmas, shop window displays and street decorations add lustre to town-centre strolling.

Spring, though, is generally a more favourable time to up sticks for a short break, especially to those cities, such as Athens, Madrid, Rome and Florence, where the high summer temper-atures (often over 30°C) make life intolerable in July and August.

Flowers are at their best, too. Mimosa blossoms on the Riviera; Budapest is scented by lilac; flowering trees fill Paris with colour. Pre-Lenten carnivals are an added attraction in many European cities.

Summer is the most problematical time for choosing a city that is neither unpleasantly hot nor overrun by sightseers. The northern European cities come into their own now. The summer street life of Amsterdam and Copenhagen adds zest to those places (though Bruges is too small to cope with the crowds). Berlin and Prague are pleasant (though accommodation is scarce in the latter). Budapest can get pretty sticky. Paris empties of Parisians and Rome of Romans (in theory leaving a bit more room for everyone else, but many hotels and restaurants also take their annual break then, too).

Many cities can be lovely in autumn. By late October temperatures in southern Europe are dropping rapidly (19 to 24°C) and sightseeing becomes bearable again. Even the odd sleet shower in Berlin or Vienna does little to diminish the pleasure. And the crowds are on their way home again.

Practicalities

Finding the right airfare

Airfares inside Europe are still generally expensive, and full liberalisation seems as far away as ever. Currently, there is a bewildering variety of fares to choose from, and if you are prepared to seek out and cultivate a travel agent who knows the airfares jungle backwards, it will be well worth your while. Meanwhile, here are some general tips:

● **Compare prices:** It's no longer the case that all airlines on a given route always charge exactly the same. Don't let your travel agent trot out this excuse for not comparing prices, and remember that smaller airlines sometimes undercut the 'flag-carrying' airlines.

● **Check seasons:** Many of the fares offered by airlines vary according to the season (airlines can split the year into ten or more segments). August prices can be 30 per cent higher than in May, and prices can go up at weekends, too. If you have any flexibility about when you fly, it's worth checking to see if you can take advantage of a lower fare by altering the date of your outward flight.

● **Benelux and Dublin:** Routes between Britain and Ireland and Britain and the Benelux countries are fully liberalised. On these routes, make sure your travel agent does a thorough search for the best fare for you. Special deals are often available.

● **The Saturday-night rule:** The best bargains on scheduled flights (those which run to a regular timetable the year round) are available only if you are prepared to stay away for at least one Saturday night. Both APEX (advance booking and payment needed) and PEX or SuperPEX (no advance booking, but limited numbers) fares usually carry this requirement. If you can't stay a Saturday night, or if no APEX or PEX fare is available, look for a EUROBUDGET fare, which is likely to be the next cheapest.

● **Check charters:** Charter flights are run by tour operators to take holidaymakers abroad, so they don't necessarily run regularly all the year round. Otherwise, there's little difference nowadays between charter and scheduled flights (though in theory you are supposed to have bought accommodation as part of a charter package, and some countries still demand that you have a voucher to prove this). It's hard to book charter flights which will take you out and back inside a week. But if you are intending to stay exactly a week, don't neglect them. Because charter flights have never been subject to the same cartel agreements as scheduled flights, they can charge whatever prices they like for their tickets. This means that on many routes you can make considerable savings (though beware if you are taking children – there are few child discounts). In practice, there may not be much difference between charter prices and the cheapest scheduled fares to many of the nearer cities in this guide, but you should always check.

● **Discount fares:** Some travel agents specialise in finding cheap fares (usually sold off at a discount by airlines who can't sell all their seats at normal prices). These are usually much more widely available on 'long-haul' flights than on flights to European cities. Where they do exist, they are often on intercontinental flights making a stop in Europe. Deals may not be especially advantageous at the cheaper end, but if you want to travel in comfort, occasional bargains are to be found in discounted business or first-class fares.

Finding the right insurance policy

What happens if you urgently need medical treatment? The Department of Health leaflet *Health Advice for Travellers* gives details on getting free medical treatment abroad. However, there is often much bureaucracy involved, the time taken to deal with claims and reimburse expenses is often lengthy, and the state health provision in European countries varies greatly. There is also no provision for flying you back to the UK should the need arise. Nor should you rely entirely on the 'personal accident' cover provided by your credit card company. It's much better to take out adequate private holiday insurance which will cover every possible health hazard, as well as things like lost luggage or stolen money – by no means uncommon in the big cities.

Most holidaymakers buy an inclusive, ready-made policy. You should arrange insurance at the time of booking your holiday, so that you can claim reimbursement of the holiday cost if circumstances force you to cancel. Some people prefer a selective policy, which allows you to choose which risks you want to insure against, taking advantage of cover you may already have under an all-risks home contents policy, permanent health insurance or other policy. If you're taking your car abroad it's best to get a Green Card to ensure that your UK insurance covers you while driving overseas, and it's wise to arrange special breakdown insurance. If you're hiring a car, make sure you take out collision damage waiver to indemnify you against loss if the car is damaged or written off in an accident, but you won't need personal accident cover if you've taken out an all-in policy. Here are some tips in choosing the right policy.

● **Tour operator policies:** The insurance offered in the tour operator's brochure may not be the most competitively priced, or the most comprehensive available. It's worth shopping around to see if there's a policy that's better suited to your particular needs, or offers better value. Some operators make take-up of the insurance they offer a condition of accepting your booking, although many will back down if you can provide evidence of equivalent cover, or threaten to take your business elsewhere. Full policy details are not always included in the brochure, so ask the operator to send you them. If it refuses, complain – as the company would be breaching the statement of practice from the Association of British Insurers.

● **Main risks:** You need to insure against cancellation or curtailment of your holiday; medical expenses; loss of or damage to baggage, money and valuables; personal liability; and accidents causing death or disability. It's very important to scrutinise the small print carefully when choosing an insurance policy, as there are a large number of (varying) exclusion clauses which crop up under each section.

● **Medical expenses:** You should choose a policy which covers all reasonable medical, hospital and treatment expenses (including emergency dental work) incurred as a direct result of your injury, illness or death. Make sure you're covered for repatriation to the UK by air-ambulance. The limit of cover should be at least £250,000 in Europe.

● **Cancellation or curtailment:** You should look for a policy which will refund your deposit and other advance payments for your holiday if you have to cancel. And choose one that provides compensation and reimburses unexpected expenses (such as the cost of a scheduled flight home) if your holiday is cut short because of unforeseen circumstances. These should include: illness or death of yourself or of a close relative or business associate; being called to jury service or as a witness; redundancy; severe damage to your home by fire, flood or storm shortly before departure; your home or office being burgled, and the police requesting you stay. All the above points should apply to your travelling companion, too. Cover should be for the total holiday cost.

● **Personal belongings and money:** Policies cover loss or theft of, or damage to, all or part of your belongings or money. We recommend a minimum total limit of £1,500. You will need to check what the maximum amount per item is – usually £250. The minimum cover for money and documents, including travellers' cheques, passports and tickets, should be £400. The limit for cash is usually £250.

● **Personal liability:** Policies cover you for legal liability if you accidently injure someone or damage property. The minimum sum insured should be £1 million for Europe.

● **Other cover:** Many policies insure against other risks, including insurance for delayed luggage, delayed departure and alternative travel arrangements if you miss your plane.

HOTEL RECOMMENDATIONS

Hotels recommended in this book were chosen for their comfort, service and value for money.

Fire safety

Consumers' Association has long campaigned for an EC Directive on fire safety in hotels. At the moment there are agreed standards throughout the EC, but they are not legally binding, and standards vary from country to country.

One of the biggest dangers in a fire is smoke. When you arrive at a hotel, always:

● find out where the nearest fire exits to your room are and check that the exit doors will open easily
● find out where the nearest fire alarm point is and read the instructions
● find out how to open the windows in your room and look for ledges or balconies that might help you escape
● read any emergency information provided.

If a fire breaks out:

● do not panic
● report fire or smoke to reception immediately
● never use the lift
● never try to go through thick smoke.

A useful leaflet, *About Hotel Fire Safety*, is available free with an SAE from the Fire Protection Association, 140 Aldersgate Street, London EC1A 4HX.

Hotel prices

Symbols indicate approximate prices per room per night for a double room with bath. Many large hotels run special breaks which will work out far cheaper.

♦ = under £50; ♦♦ = £50 to £80; ♦♦♦ = £80 to £100;
♦♦♦♦ = £100 to £140; ♦♦♦♦♦ = over £140

Bedrooms have direct-dial telephone and colour TV unless otherwise stated. Hotels with 'baths in most rooms' have showers in the others unless otherwise stated. We also indicate whether or not a hotel has a restaurant. Credit and charge cards listed are Access (includes Mastercard and Eurocard), Amex (American Express), Diners (Diners Club) and Visa.

CHOOSING A CITY

What are your priorities? A stimulating cultural break to enlarge your knowledge and liven up your ideas? A self-indulgent shopping (or window-shopping) trip interspersed by leisurely coffee-and-cake breaks? An action-packed holiday with plenty of activities and nightlife? A gourmet weekend in luxury surroundings? We've prepared the chart below to help you make your choice of destination. Of course, almost all our cities have some opportunities for all the things listed in our headings – perhaps a particularly fine museum, a few excellent restaurants or cafés, good shops, musical or cultural events. We have awarded blobs only to those cities which excel in those areas.

	Outstanding food	Copious cafés	Atmospheric strolls	Great art galleries	Cultural events	Shopping
Amsterdam		●	●	●	●	●
Athens		●				
Barcelona	●		●			●
Berlin		●		●	●	
Bruges	●		●			
Budapest					●	
Copenhagen						●
Dublin			●			
Florence		●		●		●
Istanbul	●					●
Lisbon			●			
Madrid		●		●		●
Moscow					●	
Nice	●	●				●
Paris	●	●	●	●	●	●
Prague			●		●	
Rome		●		●		
St Petersburg				●	●	
Salzburg			●		●	
Venice		●	●			
Vienna		●		●	●	

AMSTERDAM

- Good for historical and cultural interest, with plenty of museums and art galleries to keep you occupied on a rainy day – which you're unlikely to be able to avoid
- One of the closest cities you can get to for a short break. Almost everyone speaks English and there's a casual, friendly atmosphere
- The combination of canals, medieval and seventeenth-century architecture and famous art galleries makes this a tourist's city *par excellence*
- Intriguing street life, ranging from the sleazy to the elegant. Lots of interesting window-shopping and plenty of backstreets to explore

AMSTERDAM began as a small medieval settlement on the River Amstel – the site is still the centre of the city. For centuries it was an insignificant fishing port, then gradually the settlement developed into a major trading centre. But it was war that made Amsterdam prosperous. When the Netherlands rebelled against their Spanish overlords in the seventeenth century, Amsterdam was on the fringes of the fighting, picking up trade when Antwerp, further to the south, was besieged. The 'Golden Age' of the city began when the Dutch broke the Portuguese monopoly on the trade in spices. The faster and better-equipped Dutch ships sailed home from Indonesia laden with pepper, nutmeg, ginger and cinnamon. They also brought tea and blue-and-white porcelain from China, and furs and whale oil from Spitzbergen. The Dutch East India Company, formed by Dutch ship-owners, soon became one of the most powerful companies in the world. Until well into the eighteenth century, the Dutch remained the most important traders in the world, and Amsterdam the greatest commercial and banking centre of Europe – with the Exchange Bank of Amsterdam at the heart of a vast network of credit transactions by foreign merchants.

The legacy of Amsterdam's Golden Age still exists. Opulent houses built by the wealthy merchants line the city-centre canals. Some houses have double frontages, richly decorated with dolphins, or Negroes bearing sugar cane; others are simple and look as if they have been squeezed into the space between their neighbours. Common features include the high windows, the strangely shaped gables, and the jutting beam at the top of the house to enable the owners to swing their furniture up from street level – for Amsterdam's staircases are often as steep as ladders.

In the art galleries are the paintings which were commissioned for town and guild halls and private homes. Without the traditional patronage of court, church or rich aristocracy, the Dutch School concentrated on portraits, land-, town- and sea-scapes, house interiors and still life. Rembrandt, the greatest of the Dutch Golden Age artists, was a rare exception, covering religious and mythological subjects too.

Amsterdam is an easy-going city: people stroll without urgency, seeming happy to linger over coffee or to spend time browsing in bookshops or watching the many jugglers, fire-eaters, buskers and puppeteers who provide street entertainment. Amsterdam's reputation for tolerance is almost as old as the city. Once it was a turmoil of competing religious sects – today it's better known for sex. Amsterdam's red-light district is a tourist attraction, and one of the closest 'sights' to the station is a sex museum.

It's a city that might have been purpose-built for idle wanderers. The canals curve gently and countless bridges link the tree-lined cobbled streets that run alongside. Most of the streets are too narrow for speeding traffic and, besides, many of them are constantly being dug up. Dodging canalside skips or waiting behind unloading lorries is a daily hazard for Amsterdam's drivers. From one street to the next you can pass from elegance to sleaze, from a medieval alley to a building site. Distances can seem deceptively short on a map and it is an easy city to lose your bearings in, as the uniform architecture and the similarity of the canals make it easy to confuse one location with another. But it's difficult to get seriously lost: navigate by the spires of Amsterdam's old churches and you won't go far wrong. Most of the sights lie within the four main canal rings: Singel, which encloses the medieval city, where the streets are narrow and the oldest houses tilt at the craziest angles; and Herengracht, Keizersgracht and Prinsengracht, constructed when the town's first major development took place in the seventeenth century. The narrow streets beside the four main canal rings hold most of Amsterdam's interesting shops and some of the best hotels. Beyond the canals to the west lies the Jordaan, one of the best areas to wander around; once home to Huguenot refugees, it is still an artisans' quarter, with small shops, workshops, street markets and cafés.

Dam Square is the commercial hub of the city: the austere and grandiose Royal Palace presides over this popular gathering place, which is linked by traffic-laden streets to Centraal Station. The northern side of the city is not particularly inviting. Damrak is broad and busy, full of snack bars and souvenir shops; the parallel Nieuwendijk is a pedestrianised shopping street. To the east lies the red-light district, around OZ Achterburgwal and OZ Voorburgwal. The tourist-friendly parts of this area merge with the student quarter and the old Jewish area. The northern part is one of Amsterdam's worst areas for hard-drug dealing.

South of Dam Square, pedestrianised Kalverstraat is the main downtown shopping street. Just to the west (and south of the Amsterdam Historical Museum) is the city centre's most peaceful retreat, the Begijnhof, a delightful grassy square surrounded by ancient almshouses. At the southern end of Kalverstraat is the decorative Munt Tower, a well-known landmark once part of the medieval city wall. Along the Singel, the broad canal just west of the Munt Tower, is the colourful and popular floating flower market. To the south-west, Nieuwe Spiegelstraat has antique shops and galleries, and Leidsestraat – lined with airline offices, boutiques and fast-food outlets – leads to the wide Leidseplein, a nucleus of activity with bars, restaurants and clubs and plenty of street entertainment in summer (in winter it becomes a skating rink). Here also is Amsterdam's best-known 'coffee-shop', the Bull Dog, where soft drugs are available. Avoid this and other 'coffee-shops' with henna leaves on the shop windows if you're not interested.

WHEN TO GO

The weather is as unpredictable as in London – and Amsterdam is even wetter and slightly colder throughout the year. In summer the streets are at their liveliest, and there are summer theatre festivals and carillon concerts, but some hotels charge

GETTING THERE

Going independently

By air The deregulated London to Amsterdam route is one of the busiest in Europe, with more than 20 flights leaving Heathrow alone on weekdays. You can also fly direct to Amsterdam from 20 other UK airports, as far afield as Belfast and Norwich, Southampton and Aberdeen. KLM (081-750 9000) and Air UK (0345 666777) have the largest number of UK departure points for Amsterdam. Services are generally geared to business travellers, though, and because of this they are more limited at weekends, with only one or possibly no flights back on Sundays into some of the smaller UK airports. The cheapest fares are almost always SuperPEX, and are very competitive. It's worth checking carefully, as you can pick up fares from around £80. Companies worth contacting for cheaper flights include Hamilton (071-287 2425), Holidaymaker (081-664 1234), Meridian Tours (071-499 0673) and Infocus Leisure (081-332 1221). Flights from London generally cost around £100 return, and you'll pay £5 to £30 more to fly from airports elsewhere in the UK. There is no seasonal variation in fares. The flight from London to Amsterdam takes about an hour.

Schiphol Airport Schiphol is one of the classier European airports (and among the busiest). There's an excellent range of shops (departure only), including delicatessens where packs of five baby cheeses or spiced cake are good souvenirs.

There's no bus to Amsterdam, but a train service runs every 20 minutes. You can go either to Amsterdam Centraal (Amsterdam CS, *see below*), or to a suburban station, Amsterdam Rai. (Beware, it's quite easy to get on the wrong service – check the indicator boards.) From Amsterdam Rai, catch a tram to the centre of the city: not advisable if you have a lot of luggage, otherwise the more interesting journey. Taxis are expensive. Many of the major hotels are served by a hotel bus.

higher rates. Easter is crowded, as is May – when the tulips are in bloom. In mid-November there's the big Christmas event of the arrival of St Nicholas in the city, with processions and activities for children.

MASTERING THE SYSTEM

Information The Netherlands Board of Tourism in the UK is at 25-28 Buckingham Gate, London SW1E 6LD, tel: (0891) 200277 for 24-hour recorded information. If you want to speak to someone, ring 071-931 0707 between 2pm and 4pm, Monday to Friday. You are now asked to make a voluntary contribution (£1.50 at time of

---

By sea Sea travel is well worth considering, even for a short break. Sealink (0233 647047), Hoverspeed (0304 240202) and National Express (071-730 0202), for example, have London to Amsterdam return fares – using combinations of ferry or hovercraft and train or coach – which start from around £50 return from London. British Rail return fares start from just over £60 from London.

The journey takes between 8 and 13 hours depending on the route and type of transport, but you can travel overnight. The most direct sea crossing is from Harwich to Hook of Holland (under seven hours, then a one and a half hour drive). The overnight ferry from Hull to Rotterdam takes 13 hours (and also a one and a half hour drive). The quickest sea crossing is Dover/Calais (35 minutes by hovercraft, 75 minutes by ferry); it's then about a four and a half hour drive to Amsterdam. The trains take about two hours from Hook, about an hour from Rotterdam. The tourist office in London has a brochure with details of ferry and coach companies.

Amsterdam Centraal Station This is an extraordinary neo-Gothic railway station built on three of Amsterdam's many artificial islands, in what used to be the main harbour on the River Ij. Stationsplein, the area immediately in front of the station, is the main tourist arrival point and the major tram terminus.

Tour operator packages

There's a huge variety of short-break packages to Amsterdam, using air, rail or coach and ferry travel. It's possible to fly from most British regional airports; rail and coach excursions usually use Hull, Dover or Harwich and start from London Victoria and London Liverpool Street. Hotels are rated from one to five stars: many won't be in Amsterdam itself, but on the fringes, or even some way out in the surrounding conurbation. If you want a city-centre hotel, you should ask before booking. A typical three-night package for a person in a three-star hotel sharing a twin room, leaving from London in high season, costs around £215 by air and £165 by rail/coach/ferry. Amsterdam is a very popular city for a short break; for a list of tour operators offering packages see page 385.

---

going to press) to cover postage and packing of standard brochures. In Amsterdam, there is a tourist office (known as VVV) outside the railway station in Stationsplein (open daily 9am to 6pm, and 9am to 11pm in summer, tel: 634034066), and another at Leidsestraat 106. Most of your needs can be supplied, though you may have to queue for some time. If you just want a map or leaflets, go straight to the cask desh (it's worth noting that there are fewer free tourists leaflets than in many other tourist information offices. Be prepared to pay if you load up). There's a hotel and theatre booking service, a good leaflet of 'What's on this month' variety, and a folder of four different shopping walks. The VVV can also advise on excursions outside Amsterdam. Fluent English is normally spoken here, as everywhere else in the city.

Maps If you buy a map, make sure it includes the tram routes and is big enough to show sights beyond the immediate centre. The free map from the tourist office is adequate.

Sightseeing tours Even if you don't normally like guided excursions, a trip in a perspex-roofed boat through Amsterdam's canal network is one you shouldn't miss. It's by far the best way to see the canalside architecture properly and to admire the ranks of bell, neck and step gables. Secondly, it's about the only way to get beyond the railway station and out on to the River Ij to catch a glimpse of Amsterdam's skyline. Trips start from about eight different points in the centre and are widely advertised. Variations extend to candlelit dinner cruises beyond the normal routes. The 'Museum Boat' operates as a shuttle to all the main museums near the canals.

Guided bike tours take place daily in summer, with visits to a cheese farm, an old windmill and an island in a lake.

Several operators run **excursions** into the countryside. Find out about them at the VVV, from your hotel, or by keeping an eye open for adverts in the station area. Good day-trip choices would be Delft, Haarlem, the flower auction at Aalsmeer (which involves a very early morning start), and the Mauritshuis art collection in The Hague. Marken and Volendam are pretty, popular and very touristy villages. Half-day excursions to the bulbfields operate from Easter to about the end of May. Excursions usually leave from the Centraal Station, but there are also pick-up points at several hotels.

When planning excursions don't underestimate the possibilities of touring by public transport, as the train service is excellent.

Changing money Banks open on weekdays from about 9am to 4pm or 5pm (sometimes later on Thursday nights). You can also change money at post offices and at the VVV on Stationsplein.

Opening hours and days Shops close on Sunday and slightly earlier than usual on Saturday afternoons (4pm or 5pm). Some close on Monday morning and are open until about 9pm on Thursday. Several of the major museums (including the Rijksmuseum and van Gogh Museum) close on Monday and on Sunday morning, but there are plenty that open daily.

GETTING AROUND

This city is easily covered on foot – Dam Square to Leidseplein takes under half an hour. But belligerent motorists, reckless cyclists, uneven pavements, awkwardly parked cars and dog dirt are just a few of the things you have to contend with.

Trams are the most convenient form of public transport (**buses** and **metro** are useful only if you're going out of the centre). Getting the hang of the tram system is quite easy. Most tram services start at Centraal Station, and a free map showing all public transport services, routes and stops is widely available. Tram stops have boards clearly indicating the tram numbers and the stops served from each one (bus stops look very similar). You can buy a single flat-fare ticket, strips of 10 or 15 (*stripkaarten*) which are based on a zonal system (you need to stamp the appropriate number of tickets according to how many zones you are crossing – two strips are usually ample for a city-centre journey), or a rover pass. Tram drivers generally sell only single or strip-tickets (valid for a single day only); you can buy passes and (cheaper) strip tickets from the office of the Amsterdam Transit Authority (GVB) opposite Centraal Station, or from post offices or tobacconists displaying the snake-like logo. Tickets must be stamped in the machine at the back of the tram and are then valid for an hour's travel which can include transfers to bus and underground.

Seaside-style pedalos or **water-bikes** are an entertaining way of exploring the city's waterways, though you have to steer clear of the canals used by boats. Suggested routes are provided, as are rainshields for wet weather and Chinese lanterns for romantic evenings. For a few pounds you can also rent an ordinary bicycle for a day, though a hefty deposit is required. VVV has a list of rental companies.

Taxis are generally found at a taxi stand, rather than by hailing. The central taxi telephone number is 677 77 77.

UNMISSABLES

The Rijksmuseum

A vast, red-brick, neo-Gothic building with more than 250 rooms houses this huge museum which contains outstanding collections of Dutch art from the fifteenth to nineteenth centuries, Delft porcelain, silver, pewter, glass, furniture and two splendid seventeenth-century dolls' houses. The most famous exhibit is Rembrandt's *Night Watch*, a great painting depicting (in life size) 29 civic guards emerging from their club house; only after the picture was cleaned was it clear that the scene did not take place at night, as was previously supposed. Frans Hals, Vermeer, Jan Steen and van Ruysdael are also well represented, their works giving a splendid insight into life in the Dutch Golden Age. Among non-Dutch works, it is worth seeking out Murillo's *Madonna* and El Greco's *Crucifixion*.

The Vincent van Gogh Museum

Large crowds seethe around the entrance to this wonderful gallery, but its spacious design means that large numbers are absorbed without trouble. The first and second floors contain most of the van Gogh paintings. They are supplemented by excellent information boards relating van Gogh's life to the paintings you see around you. His earlier works, sombre in tone and colour, are on the ground floor. The second floor shows the painter at his effervescent and frenzied best, with paintings full of the light and colour of southern France.

Anne Frank's House

Virtually in the shadow of Amsterdam's Westerkerk (West Church) lies the house where Anne Frank and her family hid from the Nazis for two years before they were betrayed. Anne and her sister were transported to the Bergen-Belsen concentration camp, where they died. The house is now a big tourist attraction, and the steep stairs and cell-like rooms behind the concealing bookcase become pretty crowded. If you've read *The Diary of Anne Frank*, the place will come to life immediately; if you haven't, an excellent series of information boards helps.

The red-light area

Part of Amsterdam's uniqueness is its willingness to turn its sleazy side into a tourist attraction. Both sides of the OZ Achterburgwal Canal and the streets surrounding the Oude Kerk (Old Church) are lined with sex shops, sex shows and sex emporia, with the odd incongruous greengrocer in between. Busloads of tourists mingle with sailors and businessmen during the evening. The red-lit windows with their inhabitants gazing languidly out on the passing rubberneckers are the more bizarre for being in the rooms of medieval houses where God-fearing traders once tucked into their herring and vegetable soup. This, too, is the area where the Dutch East India Company used to recruit its sailors. 'Six-day kings' they were called on their return – blowing a year's wages on hiring three separate carriages for hat, cane and self. Even in the eighteenth century, Amsterdam's 'music houses' were notorious: in those days the girls sang and danced and were fluent in all European languages; now most merely look bored.

If all you want is to wander around, don't venture too far north from the garish neon. The low life becomes very low indeed, and it's one of Amsterdam's worst areas for hard-drug dealing.

OTHER PLACES TO VISIT

Museums

Amstelkring Museum Many steps and creaking floorboards take you around a honeycomb of small rooms to a clandestine seventeenth-century attic church where Catholics worshipped in secrecy: an insight into Amsterdam's religious history.

Amsterdam Historical Museum This beguiling museum will remind you of the importance of Amsterdam as a trading port. The growth and decline of this industry is demonstrated by a variety of paintings, models and displays. You'll get a good idea of what the famous harbour with its forest of masts looked like in the seventeenth century. Photographs of the 'Hunger Winter' of 1944 are especially moving.

Moneybox Museum (Raadhuisstraat 12) Worth a look if you're passing, these piggybanks come in the worst and best of taste, from a 700 BC piggybank in the shape of a boat carrying papyrus, to a modern Batman.

Rembrandt's House A good collection of Rembrandt's etchings (displays change), together with paintings of his tutors and his pupils, but lacks atmosphere.

Scheepvaart Museum The Netherlands Maritime Museum contains an impressive collection of intricately worked models of ships from the sixteenth century to present-day battleships.

Stedelijk Museum This is Amsterdam's modern art gallery, with a major collection of Dutch and French art and sculpture from 1850 to the present, including Impressionists, Picasso, Chagall, Kandinsky, Klee, Mondrian, Ernst, Warhol, Rodin and Moore, as well as photos, posters and prints. The museum also puts on special shows and exhibitions.

Tropical Museum (Tropenmuseum) This museum of artefacts, collected from the Third World, and imaginative recreations of village life in Africa and India is often full of school parties.

Willet-Holthuysen Museum A visit here is a good way to see behind the elegant façade of the beautiful houses on the Herengracht. The interior lives up to expectations, and although most of the furniture is from the eighteenth century and doesn't belong to Amsterdam's heyday, the layout and the magnificence of the rooms are striking.

Other attractions

The Heineken Brewery Early morning and afternoon tours (Monday to Friday) take place around the large, now-defunct, brewery. It is largely a PR exercise but if you want to learn a little more about beer-making, sample the brew and meet other devotees – it's fun.

Aalsmeer Flower Auction In an undistinguished suburb of Amsterdam is the biggest flower mart in the world. Getting there while the action's on means an early start – you should be there by 8.30am at the latest. In a cavernous building, bigger than an aircraft hangar, you wander along a gantry slung beneath the roof. Beneath is a solid mass of flowers. The auction itself is fascinating, if baffling, and involves huge clock faces to indicate prices.

Excursions

Amsterdam is a small city in a small country, so it's relatively easy to get out and see the countryside and other towns. There are plenty of organised coach excursions on offer, including visits to the bulbfields, cheese markets and picturesque villages with windmills.

It's also easy (and generally cheaper) to organise your own excursion, using buses or the excellent train service. In this way you will be able to spend more time at interesting museums or sights, or visit villages which do not feature on the coach-tour itineraries. You can buy day excursion tickets – some of which include entrance fees – which cover bus, tram or boat connections: ask at the Centraal Station.

Attractive places to visit near Amsterdam include **Broek-in-Waterland**, a quiet canalside village with pastel-coloured wooden houses, and **Monnickendam**, a small town with lots more atmosphere than its neighbouring tourist-oriented villages of **Marken** and **Volendam**, which are very popular with tour parties and have streets lined with souvenir shops. The small and attractive towns of **Edam** and **Alkmaar** are famous for their cheeses. Market days are crowded and popular with tourists; other days are good for wandering around.

On the coast north of Amsterdam, the **Zuider Zee Museum** at Enkhuizen has a fine collection of houses and cottages from fishing villages around the old Zuider Zee. The history of the inhabitants of the various buildings is lovingly described in the excellent handbook, bringing more life to the cottages than any amount of period furniture.

South of Amsterdam, towards The Hague, are the justifiably popular bulbfields. In the middle of the tulip area, in Lisse near Haarlem, are the famous **Keukenhof Gardens**, open for about six weeks every year, and heavily visited. There are lakes, waterfalls and woodlands, and thousands of spring bulbs of every variety. Ranges of glasshouses hold further thousands, including rarities.

The Hague (Den Haag) is home of the Netherlands' Parliament, and the administrative capital. It's a good place to visit for its varied museums, particularly the **Mauritshuis**, which has an extremely fine art collection – notable for Rembrandt, Jan Steen and Vermeer. A short tram ride from the centre of The Hague lies **Madurodam**, a splendid miniature village with working models – including an enormous electric train system.

Delft is all you would expect from an old Dutch town – several extremely photogenic canals lined by old houses, some fine church towers with carillons and an open and bustling market place. It's like the prettiest bits of Amsterdam in miniature. Coachloads of tourists descend on the town to visit the porcelain factories: the most famous is De Porceleyne Fles, where you can buy hand-painted items at high prices. Tile devotees will find the Huis Lambert van Meerten Museum well worth visiting for its fine collection of seventeenth- and eighteenth-century tiles and other Delftware.

SHOPPING

Amsterdam has few large department stores and it doesn't have the kind of concentrations of glamorous shops that you might expect. However, it's a wonderful place for curio-lovers and window-shoppers, with masses of small specialist shops selling everything from dolls' houses to sculpture, from posters to kites. The small streets running between the canals and, to the west, the old artisan area of the Jordaan are the best places in which to browse. Many shops are tucked away in strange corners and you run across them by chance rather than by design.

Kalverstraat is the main pedestrianised shopping street – it's rather bland and smells of fast food, but a lot of people come here for leisure clothes or shoes. P C Hooftstraat and Van Baerlestraat, just north of the museum quarter, are the most exclusive streets, with boutiques, art galleries and interior design shops. Nieuwe Spiegelstraat also has galleries, antiques and jewellery shops. The best department store is the stylish Bijenkorf, on Dam Square. The new Magna-Plaza shopping centre near Dam Square, once the head post office, is very smart.

Amsterdam is one of the world's major diamond centres and you'll see notices everywhere inviting you to workshops to see the cutting and polishing. Van Moppes at Albert Cuypstraat is one of the most popular workshops.

For more down-to-earth purchases there are tulip bulbs (from the floating flower market on Singel), cigars, hand-made chocolates and cheese. Modern hand-printed Rembrandt etchings make attractive souvenirs – from Rembrandt's house or the Rijksmuseum.

With more than 20 markets, Amsterdam is a haven for the bargain-hunter in search of curios. One of the largest markets is the Albert Cuypmarkt in the street of the same name; for everything from cowbells to dentists' chairs (and a lot of rubbish in between) go to the Waterlooplein. The tourist office can give information on times and places.

EATING AND DRINKING

Go to any established Dutch restaurant and you're likely to find food that's overpriced and uninventive. But if you keep to street snacks, bar meals and *eetcafés* (something between a café and a bistro) you may be pleasantly surprised, by both quality and price.

At street stalls you can find anything from rolls to *sate* pork skewers; even vending machines sell surprisingly good snacks. *Poffertjes* – baby pancakes served with butter and coated with icing sugar – are very popular. *Broodjeswinkels* – sandwich shops – usually have an excellent selection of rolls and sandwiches.

French-style restaurants are the best bet for gourmet meals, but the city offers an enormous variety of ethnic food. Most interesting of all is Indonesian cuisine with its elaborate *rijsttafel* – as many as 20 little dishes of meat and vegetables, varying from spicy to sweet or sour, served with steamed rice.

Dutch food is often wholesome and heavy, with an emphasis on potatoes and thick soups. Fish is usually more interesting than meat – there's a large choice, including raw herrings, smoked eel and salmon. For authentic national cooking look out for the *Neerland Dis* restaurants, chosen by the tourist board for their 'honest, down-to-earth' fare (though not always at down-to-earth prices).

Some of the best-value meals are served in 'brown cafés' (or bars) which are good places in which to observe everyday city life. Some of the nicest are along the main canals, the Spui and in the Jordaan. Distinctive features include wood-panelled walls, thick oriental rugs spread over tables, reading desks with (Dutch) newspapers, chess and dominoes, and sawdust on wooden floors. Many brown cafés serve home-made soups, including the Dutch specialities: pea (*erwtensoep*) and red kidney bean (*bruine bonensoep*). *Uitsmijter* – open sandwiches topped with fried eggs – and dishes of the day are also generally available.

Wine is usually expensive. *Jenever* (known as Dutch gin but in fact a form of schnapps), drunk on its own or as a chaser, costs much the same as beer, variations include the sweeter and smoother *oude* and the more powerful *jonge*. Serious drinkers might like to try a 'tasting house', where the emphasis is on local spirits and liqueurs. A good place is Admiral, at Herengracht 319.

NIGHTLIFE

Amsterdam is a late-night city and there is no shortage of things to do, with something to suit almost all tastes. The Concertgebouw (Concert Hall), home of the leading orchestra of the same name, has top performers and brilliant acoustics; there are occasional free lunchtime concerts. The striking Muziektheater at Waterlooplein is the home of the national opera and ballet companies, and has seasons featuring the avant-garde Nederlands Danstheater and international companies. Churches frequently open for organ recitals (admission sometimes free); and modern music, particularly jazz, flourishes in concert halls, clubs and cafés throughout the city.

English-language films (with Dutch subtitles) are common, and there are usually plays being performed in English, too. There are plenty of cafés, coffee-shops and bars of all kinds – most stay open late. The Leidseplein is well supplied with discos and nightclubs (entrance to discos is usually free but drinks are quite a bit more expensive than in bars).

A visit to the red-light district around OZ Achterburgwal is an almost essential part of a stay in Amsterdam. Tourist groups can be amused by the window displays of prostitutes, and for the committed there's everything from porno supermarkets to live sex shows.

HOTELS

Hotels are scattered throughout the centre of Amsterdam, so it's well worth choosing one for its setting as well as for its quality. The station area and the main streets are best avoided in favour of the smaller roads bordering the canals, where many of the hotels look out on to the water. Up by the Vondelpark, near the museums, another clutch of hotels inhabits the quiet villa-lined streets – a peaceful area, and not too far from the centre. Many city-centre hotels have steep staircases, and lifts are the exception rather than the rule.

Hotel prices Symbols indicate approximate prices per room per night for a double room with bath. Many large hotels run special breaks which work out far cheaper. (See page 14 for further details.)

♦ = under £50; ♦♦ = £50 to £80; ♦♦♦ = £80 to £100;
♦♦♦♦ = £100 to £140; ♦♦♦♦♦ = over £140.

AGORA ♦♦
Singel 462, 1017 AW   *Tel: 627 22 00*   *Fax: 627 22 02*

This hotel is on the Singel, seconds from the flower market. There are comfortable armchairs in the glass-fronted reception area, and a twisting staircase runs past basic but comfortable bedrooms. An air of friendly formality and quiet reserve pervades this unpretentious hotel. The breakfast room also serves as a lounge: low ceilinged, with plenty of fresh flowers.

Bedrooms: 15, most with shower/WC, some with bath/WC, some with neither   **Credit/charge cards accepted:** All

AMBASSADE ♦♦♦
Herengracht 335-353, 1016 AZ   *Tel: 626 23 33*   *Fax: 624 53 21*

Combining eight seventeenth-century merchants' houses, this is a very attractive hotel with individually decorated bedrooms. There are beautiful bird prints on the walls and some rooms overlook the canal. The parquet floor, fine grandfather clock, backlit china cabinet and Regency furniture of the first-floor lounge create an atmosphere of casual grandeur complementing the fresh elegance of the adjacent breakfast room.

Bedrooms: 46, all with bath/WC; hair-dryer; safe   **Facilities:** Lift   **Credit/charge cards accepted:** All

AMSTEL INTER-CONTINENTAL ♦♦♦♦♦
Professor Tulpplein 1, 1018 GX   *Tel: 622 60 60*   *Fax: 622 58 08*

This grand hotel reopened in September 1992 after a major face-lift. Opulent and luxurious rooms are mostly decorated in Delft blue or Makkum red. Facilities are excellent: the main restaurant is open 24 hours a day. The hotel is on a canal and sightseeing boats can be picked up from the landing stage.

Bedrooms: 79, all with bath/shower/WC; mini-bar; some with whirlpool bath   **Facilities:** Lift; restaurant; swimming-pool; health and fitness centre; boat service   **Credit/charge cards accepted:** All

ASTERISK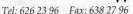
Den Texstraat 14-16, 1017 ZA   *Tel: 626 23 96   Fax: 638 27 96*

A little way out of the centre, but near the museums, this hotel is a good, reasonably priced option. It offers not only quiet, comfortable rooms but also studios with modern kitchen facilities. The breakfast room is light and clean, with whitewashed walls and displays of interesting aerial views of Amsterdam.

Bedrooms: 25, most with shower/WC, some with bath/WC, some with neither; all with safe   **Facilities:** Lift; self-catering   **Credit/charge cards accepted:** Visa

BORGMANN
Koningslaan 48, 1075 AE   *Tel: 673 52 52   Fax: 676 25 80*

The colour co-ordination of oranges, pinks, blues and greens in the breakfast room combines with the view over the lake and trees of the Vondelpark to produce an imaginative and relaxing atmosphere in this elegant hotel. Although a tram ride from the sights, it compensates for its position by having a peaceful location – guests may sit out in the garden. The bedrooms are feminine, floral and well equipped.

Bedrooms: 15, most with bath/WC; some with shower/WC; all with hair-dryer; trouser-press; most with mini-bar   **Facilities:** Lift   **Credit/charge cards accepted:** All

THE CANAL HOUSE
Keizersgracht 148, 1015 CX   *Tel: 622 51 82   Fax: 624 13 17*

Behind the heavy wooden front door of this well-situated hotel awaits a feast of interesting antiques. You may find a bedpan on your wall, heavy wooden headboards and elegant stand-up mirrors in your room. The focal point of the breakfast room is a grand piano, but the only sound you'll usually hear is the ticking of the grandfather clock.

Bedrooms: 26, all with bath/shower/WC; none with TV   **Facilities:** Lift   **Credit/charge cards accepted:** All

OWL   ♦♦
Roemer Visscherstraat 1, 1054 EV   *Tel: 618 94 84   Fax: 618 94 41*

This hotel is in a residential street affording peace and quiet, but close to the park and to museums. The green décor and fresh flowers offset by low lighting in the public room create a relaxing venue, and the breakfast room looks on to a grassy garden through huge french windows. Some of the front bedrooms have charming 'turret' corners made into desk areas.

Bedrooms: 34, some with bath/WC, some with shower/WC   **Facilities:** Lift **Credit/charge cards accepted:** Amex, Visa

PULITZER   ♦♦♦♦♦
Prinsengracht 315-331, 1016 GZ   *Tel: 52 3 52 35   Fax: 627 27 67 53*

An expensive but superb option ideally located and with excellent facilities. Twenty-four buildings from the seventeenth and eighteenth centuries have been carefully converted, retaining characteristic features including beams and a wonderful wooden staircase; the result is a warren of charming bedrooms, many with good views of the canals. The houses circle a bricked garden with a glass-covered walkway and flowerbeds.

Bedrooms: 232, all with bath/WC; mini-bar; hair-dryer; safe   **Facilities:** Lift; restaurant; self-catering   **Credit/charge cards accepted:** All

---

Hotel prices Symbols indicate approximate prices per room per night for a double room with bath. Many large hotels run special breaks which work out far cheaper. (See page 14 for further details.)

♦ = under £50; ♦♦ = £50 to £80; ♦♦♦ = £80 to £100;
♦♦♦♦ = £100 to £140; ♦♦♦♦♦ = over £140.

ATHENS

- An archaeologist's dream – the city's greatest attractions are the ancient sites of its Golden Age
- Polluted, grubby and chaotic as Athens undoubtedly is, it is also a refreshingly down-to-earth place
- A place for enjoyable evenings in the company of ouzo-drinking Athenians accompanied by bouzouki music
- Easy access to islands and coasts means that you can quite easily escape the summer heat

ON a map, Athens resembles an ink blot, its urban sprawl halted only by the sea and the mountains that encircle it. Approaching the city from the airport, traffic-choked roads are lined with high-rise blocks, tawdry billboards, dusty building sites and gleaming car showrooms – none of which give any intimation of the city's extraordinary architectural heritage.

The relics of ancient Athens stand at the heart of the modern city: some, such as the Acropolis, on top of one of the hills that peek up from the chaos of concrete and cars; others, such as the Olympeion Temple, the first ancient site as you enter central Athens from the airport, embedded in it.

There is no relationship between the ancient and modern cities, for Athens has developed in fits and starts. It reached its zenith in the fifth century BC, the age of Socrates, Sophocles and Euripides, and of the building of the Acropolis. This Golden Age was short-lived, however, for in AD 431 Athens tumbled into the long Peloponnesian War with Sparta, a drain on morale and resources from which it never recovered.

The history of its next 2,000 years is of a series of occupations: Macedonians were followed by Romans, Romans by Franks, Franks by Turks. The city's temples were converted into mosques, gunpowder stores and even harems, and by the time Greece won its independence from Turkey in 1832 Athens was little more than a shabby village. Despite this, Greece's first king, Otto, decided to make it his capital, and immediately launched an ambitious building programme. Many of Otto's ostentatious neo-classical buildings have survived, such as the Royal Palace on the main square, Syntagma, and the grandiose university buildings on Panepistimiou; but the city as a whole had little chance to become a grand European capital. In the 1920s all Greeks living in Asia Minor were forced to return to a 'homeland' most of them had never seen. Greece had to absorb over a million new people, most of whom ended up in squalid shanty towns around Athens which grew into the dreary suburbs that surround the city today. After the Second World War these immigrants were joined by droves of rural Greeks seeking work in the new factories. Today, holding almost one-third of the country's population and 70 per cent of its industry, Athens is one of the most polluted and overcrowded cities in Europe.

It is, of course, to have a taste of ancient Athens that most people come. But while the city's sights and museums remain its greatest attractions, it would be a mistake to ignore, or merely put up with, the reality of modern Athens. It is, in places, a quite primitive city, where elements of the Orient and Third World co-exist alongside the pizzazz of the modern.

Athens is also a remarkably easy-going city, its people rather laid-back, not worried by image or pressures of time. The atmosphere is relaxed so leave your smart clothes at home – shorts and T-shirts are acceptable even in luxury hotels. True, Athens has its designer shops and upmarket restaurants, but these are somewhat at odds with what the city is really about.

Although there are quarters for enjoyable wandering, the heat and crowds make the city tiring for sightseeing on foot. The centre of town is Syntagma Square, traffic-congested and surrounded by large hotels, banks and airline offices. Overlooking it is the neo-classical Parliament building, guarded by goose-stepping soldiers in stiff white kilts and pom-pom shoes. Backing on to the square, the National Gardens are cool and shady; and running along its northern edge is Vasilissis Sofias, lined with grand neo-classical embassies and some of the city's smaller museums. The exclusive Kolonaki quarter climbs up from here to the foot of Lykavittos Hill.

To the west of Syntagma, the parallel streets of Stadiou and Panepistimiou (officially known as Venizelou) lead to Omonia Square, north of which is the National Archaeological Museum. The Acropolis is south-west of Syntagma, most pleasantly approached through the mazed streets of the Plaka – the picturesque old working-class quarter, now heart of touristy Athens, bordered by Ermou, Amalias and Areopagitou. Overlooking the Acropolis is Philopappos Hill. Singrou, the continuation of Amalias, leads out of the city to the coast and airports.

WHEN TO GO

Athens is cool and dull in winter, and hot from June until September, reaching an unbearable peak in August. Even June and September can be sweatily uncomfortable, for the encircling hills trap the heat as well as the traffic fumes, and you should bear in mind that you will be doing a lot of walking. Consequently, spring and autumn are the most pleasant times to go.

GETTING THERE

Going independently

By air It's just over three and a half hours by air to Athens from London. Olympic Airways and British Airways have direct scheduled flights every day from Heathrow. BA also flies daily from Gatwick, and Britannia Airways once a week from Gatwick. SuperPEX fares are the cheapest bookable and vary according to the season; you'll pay slightly more if you travel at weekends.

London to Athens is also a busy charter route, particularly between April and October, and there are charter flights from several regional UK airports, including Manchester, Birmingham, Newcastle and Glasgow. But most charter flights are geared to 7- or 14-day holidays, and don't give the same flexibility as scheduled flights. Companies to try for charter fares (some have discounted scheduled fares, too) include Euro Express (0444 235678), Thomson (081-200 8733), Olympic Holidays (071-359 3500), Falcon Flights (061-831 7000), Cresta (0345 056511), Avro Elite (081-543 5833), Flightfile (071-323 1515) and Data Travel (0424 722394).

Ellenikon Airport The airport is on the coast, some seven miles from the city centre, outside the resort of Glyfada. There are two terminals, about 1½ kilometres apart: the West terminal takes Olympic Airways flights, all other airlines use the East terminal. The West terminal building is basic, functional and often grubby; the food is unappetising, the seating uncomfortable and the souvenir shops poor. The East terminal, particularly the departure area, is more modern, with adequate seating, coffee-shops and a duty-free shop. There are hotel and excursion booking offices and car-hire desks at both terminals; though their staffing is erratic. The tourist information office at the East terminal should be open 24 hours (but is not always). Most banks are open from 7am to 11pm; the Agricultural Bank of Greece at the East terminal is open 24 hours.

Express buses to the main central squares, Syntagma and Omonia, are supposed to leave from both terminals at intervals of every 20 minutes between 6am and midnight, and every hour between midnight and 6am, but industrial action can jeopardise the reliability of this service. Taxis are cheap, as long as you insist that the meter is switched on: if you haven't too much to carry, you may find it quicker to take the bus into Syntagma and a taxi from there to your hotel.

Tour operator packages

Prices can vary considerably between operators, even for packages using the same hotels, so shop around. Going independently is unlikely to work out cheaper unless you can get a good deal on a scheduled or charter flight. Packages generally use scheduled flights and three-, four- or five-star hotels. In 1992 a three-night break B&B in a three-star hotel cost from £239 in low season to £339 in high season, including transfers to and from the airport. For a list of tour operators see page 385.

MASTERING THE SYSTEM

Information The National Greek Tourist Office is at 4 Conduit Street, London W1R 0DJ, tel: 071-734 5997. The most convenient EDT tourist offices are located at 2 Karageorgis Servias Street at Syntagma Square on the ground floor of the National Bank of Greece (tel: 32 28 475) and at 1 Ermous Street off Syntagma Square (tel: 32 52 267). There are also branches at both airport terminals. The headquarters of the National Greek Tourist Office is at 2 Amerikis Street (tel: 32 23 111/9). The Syntagma office should meet most needs – free maps which show bus and trolley bus routes, a *What's On* booklet and fact-sheets with museum opening times, bus routes and times, ferries, etc.

Changing money Banks are generally open Monday to Thursday 8am to 2pm and Friday 8am to 1.30pm. The National Bank of Greece in Syntagma Square is open until 8pm and also opens on Saturday and Sunday. The National Agricultural Bank at the East terminal of the airport is open 24 hours, and the National Bank of Greece at the West terminal daily from 7am to 11pm. A cashcard machine on Syntagma Square takes Visa Connect cards.

Opening hours and days Many sites and museums are closed on Monday, but the Acropolis is open daily and the Benaki Museum closed on Tuesday. The tourist office has up-to-date lists of opening times. Shops are usually open Monday, Wednesday and Saturday from 8.30am to 3pm, and Tuesday, Thursday and Friday from 8.30am to 2pm and 5.30pm to 8.30pm. Exceptions do exist in the Plaka area, where many tourist shops remain open until late. In July and August many shops close during the afternoon and then stay open late at night.

Sightseeing excursions Athens is not an immediately appealing city, and if it's your first visit taking a city tour can be an effortless introduction. It is also worth making the effort to escape for a day – the island of Aegina and the Temple of Apollo at Sounion are easily accessible, but you could venture further afield to the islands of Hydra or Poros, to Delphi or to such sites as Mycenae and Epidavros on the Peloponnese.

Organised excursions, whistle-stopping through some of the most spectacular scenery and famous sites in Greece, are generally expensive and not usually recommended. Hiring a taxi for a full day, especially if there are more than two of you, can work out almost as cheap, and will be infinitely more relaxing and enjoyable. Alternatively, you could hire a car or use the long-distance buses. There are two bus stations: buses to southern and western Greece and the Ionian Islands leave from terminal A at 100 Kiffisou Street; buses to northern and eastern Greece and

Evia Island leave from terminal B at 260 Liossion Street. The stations are connected to Syntagma, Omonia and the airports by express buses A or A-slash and B or B-slash respectively.

For destinations in Attica, buses to the Byzantine monastery at Daphni leave from Deligiorgi, to the sanctuary of Elefsis from Plateia Eleftherias and to Sounion from 14 Mavromanteon.

For ferries and hydrofoils to the Argo-Saronic Islands, take the subway to Piraeus; the main harbour, for all ferries and hydrofoils to Aegina, is a short walk. Hydrofoils to other islands leave from Zea Marina, connected to the subway station by bus.

GETTING AROUND

Public transport is extremely cheap, with a flat-rate fare. A route map, available free from the tourist office, is essential. There's just one **underground** (metro) line, stretching from the port of Piraeus to the suburb of Kifissia; the most useful central stations are on Omonia and Monastiraki Squares. Tickets are from automatic machines which take only the exact fare. **Buses** and **trolley buses** are slow, hot and crowded. Tickets for buses can be bought individually or in packs of ten at most kiosks throughout Athens or at the main bus stops. On boarding, use the ticket punch machine. Each ticket costs 75Drs and is valid for one trip. **Taxis** are cheap and using them saves time, energy and stress. Fares double between 1am and 5am.

UNMISSABLES

The Acropolis
Excursion coaches stand bumper to bumper at the foot of its hill; souvenir vendors and unofficial guides pester you as you walk up the slippery marble path to the entrance; and swarming over the most famous ruins in Europe are tourists from all over the world.

For thousands of years, the Acropolis Hill, although considered sacred to the goddess Athena, was used as a fortress by the rulers of the city. Then in the sixth century BC the Delphic Oracle decreed that it should be inhabited only by the gods, and the building of temples began. These first temples were destroyed in 480 BC when the Persians invaded Athens. The monuments you see today date from the mid-fifth century, when Pericles put the great architect and sculptor Pheidias in charge of a massive rebuilding programme. That any of his monuments survive at all is something of a miracle. They have been used as brothels, mosques and arsenals; have been bombed, struck by lightning and pillaged by rapacious classical scholars; and now acid rain and visitors are eroding the buildings – each year 4.5 million tourists visit the rock on which they stand.

Saving the Acropolis is now a battle against time, and until the current restoration work is completed you should be prepared to find some of the temples encased in scaffolding.

Access to the site is through the monumental **Propylaia**. The central and widest passage was used only during the annual Panathenaic procession, and its steps, now protected by wood, are shallow so that the beasts being led to sacrifice could climb them easily. Only one corner of its coffered ceiling, which once glittered with gilded stars, has survived. The rest of it was destroyed in the seventeenth century when the building exploded while being used as a gunpowder store.

Perched above the Propylaia is the miniature **Temple of Athena Nike**. It was taken to pieces by the Turks to make room for a gun emplacement, but has been carefully reconstructed.

The most stunning, famous and photographed monument on the Acropolis is the **Parthenon**, temple of Athena, virgin goddess of wisdom and city-patron. Its designers, Pheidias and his co-architects Iktinos and Kallikrates, realising that straight columns appear concave when seen against a bright background, corrected the optical illusion by making the columns and the platform on which they stand slightly convex.

In the nineteenth century, Lord Elgin carted off much of the sculpted decoration to the British Museum. In addition, well-meaning restorers attempted to strengthen the temple by inserting iron rods into the columns. The acid rain has now corroded them and they are cracking the marble.

Across the road from the Parthenon is the **Erectheion**, the most remarkable feature of which is the southern portico, supported by six caryatids. They are, in fact, copies: the originals have been removed to the Acropolis Museum for safe keeping.

The **Acropolis Museum** also contains statues, pottery and architectural fragments from the site. Most striking are the sculpture of a beautiful youth known as the *Kritian Boy* and a relief of *Wingless Victory*.

Scooped out of the hill below the Acropolis (entrance on Areopagitou) is the **Theatre of Dionysos**, on whose circular stage the tragedies of Euripides, Aeschylus and Sophocles were first performed in the fifth century BC.

Twenty-five of the sixty-four tiers of stone benches added in the fourth century BC survive today, as does a section of a Roman frieze of Dionysos and Sileni along the stage front. The Romans made other modifications – the fourth-century BC drainage channel was covered with perforated slabs which could be plugged when they wanted to flood the arena for aquatic games, and the stone barrier was erected to protect the audience during blood sports.

Further towards the Acropolis entrance is the Roman **Odeion of Herodes Atticus**, now used for the Athens Festival; there is a good view from the south path up to the Acropolis. It has been heavily reconstructed and has little atmosphere except when full. It is open only for performances.

The Agora

After centuries of sackings, scavengings and rebuildings, only foundations remain of Athens' ancient market-place, and the site is consequently confusing. It can, however, be fascinating, as long as you visit the excellent Agora Museum first and arm yourself with a plan.

The Agora was the political as well as the social and commercial centre of town, and the Athenians would come here for news on the latest lawsuits, to see whether they'd been called up for military service, and to check on the agenda for the regular meetings of the citizens' assembly.

Socrates spent much of his time in the Agora: there's the foundations of Simon the Cobbler's shop where he engaged in dialectical arguments; the foundations of the Royal Stoa in which he was condemned to death on a charge of insulting the gods and corrupting the young; and the foundations of the prison in which he spent his last days before taking a fatal draught of hemlock.

Overlooking the site is the best-preserved temple in Greece. The **Hephaisteion** lacks the grace and delicacy of the Parthenon, but it does retain its coffered ceiling and many of its metopes, carved with the *Labours of Herakles and Theseus*. It is named after the god Hephaistos, the patron of metal workers.

The **Agora Museum** is housed in the completely reconstructed Stoa of Attalus. It is in this museum, more than any other in Athens, that the everyday life of the ancient Athenians becomes a reality. Here you can see the rules of a library forbidding the 'borrowing' of books, a water-clock used to time speeches in court, shards of pottery inscribed with names used in the annual ostracism vote, and even a sausage griddle, portable clay oven and child's terracotta potty.

National Archaeological Museum

The most important archaeological museum in Greece is crammed with textbook treasures, most of which are unimaginatively displayed. Highlights include the vast Mycenaean collection (though this is to be moved when its own purpose-built museum at Mycenae is complete), beautifully preserved 1500 BC frescoes from the island of Thera, and exquisite white marble figurines from the Cyclades. You could also trace the development of ancient sculpture from the stiff, two-dimensional statues of the seventh century BC through to a fluently sculpted and perfectly balanced bronze *Poseidon* dating from the fifth century BC. The ceramics collection is likewise extensive, starting with simple Proto-Geometric pots and progressing to the sophisticated black-and-red figure pots covered with mythological scenes.

The Plaka

Below the eastern slopes of the Acropolis a labyrinth of cobbled streets wind through a haphazard cluster of neo-classical villas, shack-like souvenir shops, tacky sixties villas, antique shops and the occasional Byzantine church or neglected mosque.

There are also a couple of relics of Roman Athens: **Hadrian's Library**, founded by the emperor in 132 BC, whose Corinthian columns rise from a tangle of undergrowth below Aiolou; and the nearby colonnaded **Forum** with its ingenious water-clock, the **Tower of the Winds**. Water was channelled down from a spring on the Acropolis Hill into the tank at the back of the tower, from where it steadily trickled into a cylinder inside. The time was indicated by the water level, and the door always left open so that people could consult it.

The Plaka is pleasant at any time of the day: bustling at lunchtime and night, peaceful in the mid-afternoon and morning, an ideal retreat from the chaos of the rest of the city. You can eat outside in lively squares or secluded courtyards, or inside in folksy dining-rooms or noisy smoky cellars.

OTHER PLACES TO VISIT

Museums and galleries

Benaki Museum This is a vast, varied and sumptuous collection of oriental and western jewellery, textiles, costumes and religious artefacts. The museum has been closed for periods recently while extension and renovation work have been taking place, but should be fully open by late 1993 when rearrangement of the exhibits has been completed. The Benaki's shop is an added attraction, with reproduction jewellery, records of folk music and an excellent range of postcards and greetings cards.

Byzantine Museum The only museum in Europe to concentrate exclusively on Byzantine art, this nineteenth-century villa has rooms laid out like churches, with collections of icons, frescoes and sculpture, and cases of lavishly embroidered textiles and intricately incised and gem-encrusted metalwork.

Cycladic Museum This small and well-presented museum is a favourite for many visitors, with its collection of beautifully preserved, white marble female figurines dating from between 3200 and 2000 BC, discovered on the Cyclades. Their virtually abstract forms, in particular their almond- or lyre-shaped heads and elongated noses, may seem familar, for they influenced many twentieth-century artists, notably Picasso, Modigliani and Henry Moore.

Upstairs, there is a small but almost equally interesting collection of ceramics, gold, bronze, glass and marble work, spanning almost 2,500 years. Finally, the shop sells high-quality reproductions of the sculptures and tasteful ceramics and jewellery.

Museum of Greek Folk Art A small, well-displayed collection of regional crafts and costumes has the occasional quirk – like the wine jugs emblazoned with couplets on the delights and dangers of drinking.

War Museum The (1967-74) Junta's one contribution to the cultural life of Athens is a celebration of Greek military prowess from the age of the bow and arrow to the era of the machine-gun.

Other attractions

Lykavittos Hill Ascend by a funicular railway tunnelled into the rock from the top of Ploutarchou for sweeping views of the city. Looking down on the Acropolis from the viewing platform outside the small chapel of Agios Giorgios is an odd sensation for, seen from above, the Acropolis looks rather insignificant. Most people come in the evenings for the performances in the red and yellow tubular steel amphitheatre.

Kerameikos The Kerameikos cemetery in downtown Athens was in use from the twelfth century BC until the Roman era, and examples of graves from most periods have been unearthed. The highlight is the funerary avenue on which the wealthiest Athenians were buried in the most elaborate graves.

Excursions

There are several major sights quite close to Athens that can be visited on half-day trips. The **Temple of Poseidon** at **Sounion** ranks among the most sensational sights in Greece, which means it's inevitably busy – especially at sunset. Sixteen creamy-white marble columns stand 60 metres above the sea on the southern-most tip of Attica. There are hourly buses from 14 Mavromanteon. The journey takes one and a-half hours.

A 20-minute ride by bus or taxi west of Athens centre takes you to the eleventh-century monastery of **Daphni**, which contains wonderful Byzantine mosaics.

If you have a full day to spare, there are many more places to visit. Particularly enjoyable is a trip to one of the islands in the Saronic or Argolic Gulfs. There are organised day cruises which take in Poros, Hydra and Aegina, but these leave little time for seeing the islands. A more pleasant alternative is to select one island and go there by hydrofoil (*Flying Dolphin*) from the central harbour at Piraeus (for Aegina) or the nearby harbour of Zea Marina (for Hydra and Poros). There are also ferries to all islands from the central harbour at Piraeus – cheaper, but considerably slower.

Poros and Hydra, off the Argolid coast of the Peloponnese, are both extremely picturesque. The waterfront at **Poros** is over-looked by well-kept buttermilk-washed houses with pantile roofs and wrought-iron balconies.

Hydra is an altogether more upmarket place, with whitewashed and stone-built mansions spread over two hills above a sheltered harbour. Cars are not allowed on the island and donkeys carry luggage from the port to the hotels. The only swimming is from a small rock on the edge of the harbour, where the strong currents are exacerbated by the wakes of motor boats.

Aegina, closest to Piraeus, is less picturesque than Hydra and Poros, and has a more workaday feel, although it gets very busy at weekends. The sightseeing highlight of the island and the target for numerous excursions is the well-preserved and beautifully sited **Temple of Aphaia** (to get there take a ferry from Piraeus – or a bus from Aegina town – to the busy island resort of Agia Marina, from where there are buses or taxis).

Mainland sights suitable for a day excursion include Delphi and the sites of the Argolid on the Peloponnese. The extensive ruins of the Oracle of Zeus at **Delphi** are spread over the foothills of Mount Parnassos overlooking a steep gorge. There's also an excellent museum, while the modern village of Delfi has cafés, with terraces overhanging the gorge.

Organised one-day excursions are offered to the Argolid. Sights visited include the beautifully preserved theatre at **Epidavros**, the pretty coastal town of **Nafplion**, and the forbidding fortress at **Mycenae**.

SHOPPING

The obvious first place to head for gift shopping is the Plaka. Leather goods are reasonable, especially if you haggle over prices; there's a heavy concentration of leather shops on the main street, Adrianou, while the most famous sandal maker is Stavros Melissinos at Pandrossou 89, who numbers John Lennon and Jackie Onassis among his former customers.

The range of jewellery is wide (though it can be very pricey) – from the traditional filigree earrings and shell and coral necklaces available in scores of shops to unusual designs in silver. There is also an increasing number of upmarket shops selling gold and silver jewellery. Most of the ceramics on sale in the Plaka are gaudy copies of the museum pieces featuring glittery Homeric heroes, but there are good-quality reproductions in the Cycladic and Benaki museum shops.

Kolonaki, a distinctly smart residential area, has a sophistication that lures visitors to its florists, bookshops and boutiques. The shops along the well-paved, tree-lined streets reflect this ambience both in the quality of the goods for sale and their prices.

Despite the burgeoning number of international designer shops in the streets above Kolonaki Square, Athens is not a good city for clothes shopping. Look out, though, in the Plaka for the heavily embroidered ethnic clothes and the exquisite handpainted silk scarves, dresses and purses.

For more down-to-earth shopping head for the streets around Omonia: tiny old-fashioned shops on Sofokleos sell olive oil, pulses, herbs, spices and loofahs; and Zinonas resembles a market, with stall-like shops laden with everything from freshly roasted and ground coffee to electric fans and cassettes of Greek and Arabic music.

On Sunday mornings the streets around Monastiraki Square, on the fringes of the Plaka, are packed with stalls selling everything from machine parts and rusty flat irons to digital watches and pornographic videos. You shove and elbow your way through the crowds, and watch the Athenians haggling over prices, consulting a roadside herbalist over their latest ailment, and catching up on the week's gossip. There are more conventional souvenirs – such as jewellery, scarves and friendship bracelets – along Pandrossou and Adrianou. February and August are particularly busy times, with month-long sales.

EATING AND DRINKING

Greek food does not lend itself to being fancified in luxury restaurants; nor does it taste right in a rarefied atmosphere where the talk is subdued, service slick and waiters attentive. Although the Plaka tavernas are touristy, many have a good atmosphere and are laid out in creeper-covered courtyards.

Greeks eat late and lingeringly, staving off hunger pangs with familiar starters like salad, *hummus*, *taramasalata* and *tsatsiki*, and more unusual concoctions with aubergines, pulses or seafood. Main courses are heavily meat based, featuring kebabs (*souvlakia*) and grilled or roast lamb, steak, pork or veal, almost invariably served with lukewarm chips. The best fish and seafood is served on the yacht harbour at Mikrolimani, near Piraeus, a half-hour taxi ride from Athens.

Athens has a selection of tea-houses and coffee-shops, some of them open from breakfast until the small hours, but ideal for tea-time indulgences. The chocolate cake at the long-established Floca on Korou off Stadiou is sinfully rich, and there's a wide range of intricate little cakes and pastries to nibble in the restrained atmosphere of another Athenian institution, Zonar's on Stadiou, just off Syntagma. For trendier surroundings, try the Italianate Café Mazi in the arcade at Stadiou 40.

NIGHTLIFE

Athens is a late-night city: there's no better way to get a feel of the place than by watching ouzo-flushed Athenians pacing and swaying to the sinuous rhythms and undulating melodies of mournful *rebetika*, a sound far removed from the synthetic *bouzouki* piped in many a restaurant.

More conventional ways for tourists to spend their evenings include the Athens Festival from June to mid-September – plays, ballet and music perfomed either at the reconstructed Roman Herodes Atticus Theatre below the Acropolis or in the modern amphitheatre on Lykavittos Hill. The tourist office on Syntagma has programmes, and tickets are sold at the box office in the arcade at Stadiou 4, open Monday to Saturday 8.30am to 2pm and 5pm to 7pm, and Sunday 10am to 1pm. Make sure you queue at the window marked with the appropriate venue. There's another theatre on Philopappos Hill: it looks down on the Acropolis and you can go for a sound and light show or, better, to see the prestigious Dora Stratou company performing traditional dance. It's cheaper to go independently than to take one of the 'Athens at night' tours. Athens also has its fair share of discos: one of the best is the hi-tech Stadiou above the modern Olympic stadium.

HOTELS

Athens has several modern luxury hotels but only a handful of tastefully decorated small hotels. A room with air-conditioning should be seen as a necessity rather than a luxury in summer. The Kolonaki quarter below Lykavittos Hill, and Kefalari, in the garden suburb of Kifissia, both provide havens from the chaos of the city centre. The main sites are a good walk from Kolonaki. Kefalari is a half-hour taxi ride (or 15-minute walk and half-hour subway ride) from the centre; however, with its park and stylish 1930s hotels, it's a lovely place in which to stay.

Closer to the heart of things are the hotels on the fringes of the Plaka, in the quiet quarter below the Acropolis, and around Omonia Square (many of these are noisy). Finally, and only because the hotel is good, we recommend one hotel on Singrou, one of the main approach roads into the city.

ATHENAEUM INTER-CONTINENTAL   ♦♦♦♦♦
89-93 Singrou, 117 45   *Tel: 90 23 666   Fax: 92 43 000*

Set back from one of the main approaches to the city, about ten minutes' drive from the centre, is this expensive hotel. The lobby is vast, with an irregular polygonal well, its ceiling supported on tubular scaffolding, with transparent lifts. Clusters of comfortable sofas with traditional-style upholstery are overlooked by statues. Rooms are spacious, colour-co-ordinated and divided into sleeping and sitting areas by a trellis; most have good views of the Acropolis and Lykavittos. There's a roof garden with café and swimming-pool, and four restaurants.

Bedrooms: 560, all with bath/WC; air-conditioning; mini-bar
Facilities: Lift; restaurants; outdoor pool; gym; sauna; hairdresser; private parking   **Credit/charge cards accepted:** All

ATHENIAN INN
22 Haritos, 106 75   *Tel: 72 38 097   Fax: 72 42 268*

Sited on a quiet residential street three minutes' walk from Kolonaki plateia, this is reckoned by Lawrence Durrell to be the ideal Athenian hotel. Behind the spotless whitewashed façade is a quarry-tiled lobby with a small sitting area and bar/breakfast room adjoining – simple, plain and clean. Rooms have whitewashed walls, polished dark wood furniture and small but well-designed tiled bathrooms. Some rooms have balconies with tables, chairs and plants. Service is personal – the hours of the bar vary, depending on the guests' requirements.

Bedrooms: 28, 12 with bath/WC, 16 with shower/WC; air-conditioning; none with TV   **Facilities:** Lift   **Credit/charge cards accepted:** Amex, Diners, Visa

DIVANI PALACE ACROPOLIS
19-25 Parthenonas, 117 42   *Tel: 92 22 945   Fax: 92 14 993*

A modern, luxury hotel on a steep, quiet residential street below the Acropolis. Copies of classical statues stand in large, airy and sumptuous public rooms, with furnishings reflecting the hues of the marble floors. The ground-floor bar opens on to a creeper-covered courtyard holding a swimming-pool. The roof garden, where there's live music most evenings, has unbeatable views of the Acropolis. Rooms are comfortable and elegant, with marble floors, rugs, dark wood furniture and spacious bathrooms, but not all have views.

Bedrooms: 260, all with bath/shower/WC; air-conditioning; mini-bar **Facilities:** Lift; restaurant; outdoor unheated pool   **Credit/charge cards accepted:** All

DORIAN INN
17 Pireos, 105 52   *Tel: 52 39 782   Fax: 52 26 196*

Just off Omonia Square on a busy four-laned road, the Dorian Inn is at the bold, lively and tacky heart of Athens. The hotel itself has been refurbished and is tastefully decorated: the small lobby has a marble floor, ceramics on the wall and a white marble bench with traditional woven upholstery. The roof garden has views of the Acropolis, and a paddling pool adjoins the smallish swimming-pool. Rooms are fairly simple, with balconies; there's street noise in those facing Pireos.

Bedrooms: 146, all with bath/shower/WC; air-conditioning **Facilities:** Lift; restaurant; outdoor heated pool; roof garden; private parking   **Credit/charge cards accepted:** All

ELEKTRA PALACE ♦♦
18 Nikodimou, 105 57   *Tel: 32 41 401*   *Fax: 32 41 875*

One of the few 'A' class hotels on the fringes of the Plaka, the Elektra Palace has a roof garden, with a smallish swimming-pool, and cool, airy bedrooms – though some of the bathrooms are rather cramped. There is not much atmosphere, but the facilities and the quiet, convenient location compensate.

Bedrooms: 106, all with bath/shower/WC; air-conditioning; mini-bar; hair-dryer   **Facilities:** Lift; restaurant; outdoor unheated pool   **Credit/charge cards accepted:** All

---

HERA ♦
9 Falirou, 117 42   *Tel: 92 36 682*   *Fax: 90 25 752*

A well-kept, appealingly arcaded and whitewashed building tucked away behind Singrou, at the foot of the quiet quarter south of the Acropolis. The reception area, chequered with black and white marble, has a small seating area and bar, and opens on to a courtyard – pleasant, despite being overlooked by the ugly backs of buildings. The breakfast room is tastefully decorated with fresh flowers on tables and Impressionist prints on the walls. Rooms are fairly small, with whitewashed walls, and, at the front, large balconies with fine views up to the Acropolis.

Bedrooms: 49, all with bath/shower/WC; air-conditioning; none with TV
Facilities: Lift   **Credit/charge cards accepted:** None

NEFELI ♦
16 Iperidou, 105 58   *Tel: 32 28 044*

A small, modern, unpretentious and well-maintained hotel on a pedestrianised street very close to the heart of the Plaka. Rooms are simple, spotless and tasteful, with whitewashed walls, wood fittings and botanical prints; service is friendly.

Bedrooms: 18, most with shower/WC; some with bath/WC; ceiling fans; none with TV   **Facilities:** Lift   **Credit/charge cards accepted:** None

> ♦ = under £50; ♦♦ = £50 to £80; ♦♦♦ = £80 to £100;
> ♦♦♦♦ = £100 to £140; ♦♦♦♦♦ = over £140.

PENDELIKON
66 Degliani, Kefalari, Kifissia   ♦♦♦♦

Tel: 80 80 311 Fax: 80 10 314

On a quiet street in the garden suburb of Kefalari, behind the Semiramis (*see below*), is this extremely elegant and sumptuously decorated 1930s hotel, cream with wrought-iron balconies and set in a luxuriant garden. Public rooms are palatial, with antique furniture among the marble floors and columns of the reception area, an arcaded restaurant with festoons of fabric on the ceiling and a piano bar with hand-painted flowers on the walls. Bedrooms are simpler, but similarly tasteful.

Bedrooms: 43, all with bath/shower/WC; air-conditioning; mini-bar
Facilities: Lift; restaurant; outdoor unheated pool   **Credit/charge cards accepted:** All

---

ST GEORGE LYCABETTUS
2 Kleomenous, 106 75   ♦♦♦♦

Tel: 72 90 711 Fax: 72 90 439

This hotel stands at the foot of Lykavittos Hill in the quiet residential suburb of Kolonaki, within walking distance of good restaurants and shops. On the grey marble floor of the spacious reception area plants stand in copper pots and comfortable sofas look down on the palms, oleanders and olives outside. The rooms are restful, simple and elegant, with marble bathrooms. Prices depend on the view: Lykavittos, the Acropolis, or nothing. The summery café has plants and a fountain, and the main restaurant is plush, with a panoramic view of Athens. The roof garden, looking up to Lykavittos, has a good-sized pool and a bar.

Bedrooms: 162, all with bath/shower/WC; air-conditioning; mini-bar
Facilities: Lift; restaurant; outdoor pool   **Credit/charge cards accepted:** All

---

SEMIRAMIS
48 Charilaou Trikoupi, Kefalari, Kifissia   ♦♦♦

Tel: 80 88 101 Fax: 80 88 106

In the garden suburb of Kefalari, a 15-minute walk from Kifissia metro station and a 30-minute taxi ride from the centre, is this shuttered 1930s hotel standing in an elegant garden overlooking a verdant park, with smart cafés and restaurants close by. Antiques and a tapestry in the reception area, and the old-fashioned dining-room and bar, create an elegant and intimate atmosphere. The rooms are simply decorated in serene shades of blue.

Bedrooms: 42, all with bath/WC; air-conditioning; mini-bar
Facilities: Lift; restaurant; outdoor unheated pool   **Credit/charge cards accepted:** All

BARCELONA

- Good for museums and art galleries, with an emphasis on modern art and local history
- A great place to potter around, enjoying the colour and vitality of the Ramblas and the narrow streets of the Gothic quarter
- The bizarre architecture of Antoni Gaudí is strangely compelling. Be sure to visit the Sagrada Família and Parc Güell to see his extraordinary imagination given free rein
- After the successful 1992 Olympics brought the city to the attention of the world, Barcelona is settling down once more

THROUGHOUT its history Barcelona – the capital of Catalonia, and Spain's second city – has tended to go its own way, looking beyond the Pyrenees for inspiration and cultural stimulation. There's a continental feel in Barcelona that's not found anywhere else in Spain.

It was the Romans (who colonised more successfully here than elsewhere in Spain) who recognised the potential of Barcelona's geographic position and began to develop the port that was to be the key to the city's future prosperity. Their successors in occupation, the Moors, were evicted several centuries before their expulsion from the rest of Spain and by AD 874 the conquering hero, Wilfred the Hairy, had established himself as the first of the powerful, independent Counts of Catalunya. He created a flourishing principality which became famous for its seafaring, mercantile and commercial skills.

A golden age followed from the twelfth to the fourteenth centuries, and Catalonia forged an alliance with Aragon by which it retained its own language, laws and customs. But imperial adventuring strained the state coffers and caused a banking collapse in 1381 which precipitated the city's decline. Catalonia was absorbed into the unitary Spanish state, which was, for a time, the world's greatest power.

Spain's earliest industrialisation was centred in Catalonia and the Basque country and, as the city's population grew (quadrupling between 1850 and 1900), with widespread immigration from other parts of Spain, socialist and separatist ideas took root, leading to conflict with Madrid. A literary revival promoted the Catalan language, which became a vehicle for nationalist sentiment and aspiration.

The medieval city walls were demolished in 1858 and a smart New Town (the Eixample) designed by Idelfons Cerdà was laid out on a regular grid pattern with wide streets, which contrast starkly with the narrow, twisting lanes of the Gothic quarter. Such mathematical precision could be stifling, but studded throughout the chessboard matrix of the New Town are stunningly flamboyant works by the modernist architect Gaudí, a riot of colour and undulating form which animates the whole area.

An autonomous Catalan republic was declared following the plebiscite called after the fall of the dictator Primo de Rivera in 1931, and throughout the Civil War years (1936-9) Barcelona was a bastion of the Left. As Franco's troops kept Madrid under heavy attack, the Spanish Republican government transferred its capital to Barcelona in October 1937. The city held out until January 1939.

Franco exacted terrible revenge on the Catalans – political murders were commonplace, autonomous status was rescinded and use of the Catalan language banned. The *sardana*, the national dance, was outlawed, place-names changed to Castilian Spanish, and street names reflecting aspects of Catalan life replaced with names that honoured Franco's victory.

Some concessions followed in the 1940s, but the language continued to be proscribed in the most important areas of everyday life – in newspapers, schools, on the radio and, later, on television. Only after Franco's death in 1975 were the Catalans able to reassert their claims to home rule and secure equal status for their language. Since 1981 Catalonia has been an autonomous territory within Spain (although separatists continue to seek greater independence from Madrid), and a sense of national pride assails you wherever you go.

Barcelona has a secure industrial and commercial base, and is Spain's economic powerhouse. Currently it's basking in the glory of the success of the 1992 Olympic Games, and the characteristic bustle and vitality is even more in evidence.

Given its economic importance the city centre is surprisingly small and divides naturally and conveniently into manageable quarters. You can while away your time in a carefully balanced timetable of relaxation and self-improvement in the city's excellent museums.

The narrow medieval alleys of the Barri Gòtic are the place to find the great Gothic cathedral, shabby palaces, idiosyncratic museums, and lively *cava* bars where you can nibble at fishy *tapas* and quaff very acceptable fizz at a fraction of the price of French champagne. North-east of the Via Laietana, beyond the arty quarter around the Picasso Museum, you'll find the Parc de la Ciutadella, where speed-mad young boys career around on hired BMX bikes, while the more sedate wander around the large zoo or museums devoted to modern art, geology and zoology.

Stretching up from the seedy port to the grand Plaça de Catalunya, the Ramblas is a succession of wide, shop-lined streets where horn-tooting cars pass by on either side of a central pedestrianised boulevard. Quite apart from the famous flower stalls, news-vendors and pet salesmen, a whole carnival of charlatans sets up shop, ready to part you from your cash. Keep a firm grip on your sense of humour, your scepticism, and your wallet or purse, find a perch with a good view for a lingering cup of *café con leche* and let the pervasive charm wash over you.

Beyond the Plaça de Catalunya, an elegant recreational square, the straight, wide streets of the nineteenth-century New Town, the Eixample, open out. Take away the pavement cafés and you almost feel that you could be in one of Britain's great Victorian cities – Glasgow, perhaps – until you stumble across one of

Gaudí's modernist fantasy buildings, with pliable rippling forms or dazzling primary colours quite at odds with the sober linear blocks that surround it.

Away from the city centre, the hill of Montjuïc, reached by funicular railway and cable-car, rises steeply above the harbour, and a park on its slopes houses a series of buildings erected for the International Exhibition of 1929. The famous illuminated fountain that fronts the magnificent façade of the Palau Nacional is currently boarded up, suspended by the city fathers following a long period of drought. You can easily spend a day wandering around museums devoted to subjects as diverse as Romanesque art, ethnology, archaeology, military history and hardware, and the modern painter Joan Miró. When all that gets too much there's a funfair, the Parc d'Atraccions, with a giant Ferris wheel.

WHEN TO GO

Barcelona is at its hottest in July and August, when the average maximum temperature is a sticky 28°C. July is drier, but the city is quieter in August, when a lot of locals are on holiday. The main drawback is that many restaurants close down for the month, too.

It's particularly pleasant to visit in spring and early autumn. Barcelona's main fiestas are Sant Antoni, with parades and fireworks in January, religious processions around Holy Week and the feast of Corpus Christi, Sant Jordi (St George) on 23 April, and the June fiesta in the Poble Espanyol at Montjuïc. In September there's a lot of pomp and circumstance to mark Catalonia's national day on the 11th, and on the feast of the Verge de la Mercè there are free concerts, fireworks, death-defying human towers and papier mâché giants on the march.

MASTERING THE SYSTEM

Information The Spanish National Tourist Office is at 57/58 St James's Street, London SW1A 1LD, tel: 071-499 0901. Local tourist offices are called Oficinas de Información Turistica. The main office is at Gran Via de les Corts Catalanes 658, tel: 301 7443. It is open Monday to Friday 9am to 7pm and Saturday 9am to 2pm. The airport office is open Monday to Saturday 8.30am to 8pm; it's also open on Sunday 8.30am to 3pm. Generally, the offices are not particularly helpful and are curiously ill-informed about the location and opening times of other tourist offices, but they can give you maps, information on guided tours and some useful literature.

Maps The free map from the tourist office is detailed enough for most purposes, with an overview of the city, a more detailed map of the Barri Gòtic and a plan of the underground system. It has the added advantage of showing street names in Catalan.

GETTING THERE

Going independently

By air You can fly direct to Barcelona on any day of the week with either Iberia (071-437 5622) or British Airways (081-897 4000) from London. There are also daily flights from Manchester with Iberia and Birmingham (not Thursdays) with BA. The cheapest bookable fare is the SuperPEX, which varies according to the time of year; you'll also pay from around £10 to £30 more if you travel at weekends. Both Iberia and BA have regular special offers on fares and good discounts on tickets – it's worth checking to see if there are any around.

Charter flights to Barcelona are also available although, like Madrid, this is not one of the busiest Spanish charter destinations, and you may find it's worth paying the extra to give yourself the flexibility of a daily scheduled flight. It is worth checking with, for example, Davies & Newman (071-827 9620), Hamilton (071-287 2425), Holidaymaker (081-664 1234), Iberian Services (081-968 9855), Marsans International (071-224 0504) and Meridian Tours (071-499 0673).

El Prat Airport This is a hub of Spain's transport system, and is large and well equipped by Spanish standards, with an exchange bureau, cash dispensers, car-hire desks, bars and cafeterias, souvenir shops and news-stands, a hamburger bar, a hairdresser, and a large duty-free shop. A glitzy new terminal was opened in 1991.

Trains to the city centre (about eight miles) are very cheap, run every 30 minutes (20 minutes during the summer), and the journey takes about 20 minutes. There is also a bus service every 15 minutes. The taxi journey takes about 20 minutes and costs considerably more.

Tour operator packages

Tour operators offer a good quality and good price range of hotels, situated mostly (though not entirely) in the Eixample, and generally in refurbished three- or four-star hotels. Expect to pay around £300 for a three-night package in a three-star hotel in high season. Hotel rates don't vary enormously according to season, but airfares do.

As a general rule, packages tend to cost less than independent travel in the summer. During the winter it may be cheaper to make your own arrangements. For a list of tour operators that offer packages to Barcelona, see page 385.

Sightseeing tours Most of the fun of exploring Barcelona comes from wandering around at your own pace. If you're a first-time visitor a city tour might be worth while to identify areas to probe more thoroughly on foot later; this usually covers the cathedral, Barri Gòtic and Montjuïc in the morning, and the Picasso Museum and the works of the architect Gaudí in the afternoon.

Alternatively (and much more cheaply), bus 100 tours the city in 90 minutes in the summer months, and you can hop on and off as you please. It leaves from the Plaça de Catalunya every 45 minutes during the day between June and the end of September.

There are popular excursions to the heavily commercialised but wonderfully located monastery at Montserrat – home of the Black Madonna, the most potent symbol of Catalan nationalism, and to the resorts of the Costa Brava. Organise your own trip, skip the hideous Lloret de Mar, and make for the prettier resorts of Tossa de Mar and Calella de Palafrugell, or go to nearby Sitges on the Costa Dorada. Sarfa buses leave for the coast from Plaça Antoni Lopez, near the post office at the foot of Via Laietana.

Changing money There is an astonishing number of banks on the Passeig de Gràcia and around the Plaça de Catalunya. They're open 8.30am to 2.30pm Monday to Friday and many open 8.30am to noon on Saturday. Many have cash dispensers which accept Access, Visa and American Express cards – a good way to get money outside banking hours.

Exchange rates at some bureaux de change are unfavourable and it's worth trying to avoid changing money at your hotel – commission can be as high as five per cent, and rates poor. Credit cards are widely accepted in hotels and restaurants, but carry cash if you want to leave tourist-oriented places and explore backstreet *tapas* bars.

Opening hours and days Most shops are open 9am or 9.30am to 1pm or 2pm Monday to Saturday and 4.30pm or 5pm to 8pm or 8.30pm Monday to Friday. The huge department store El Corte Inglés, on Plaça de Catalunya, and its rival Galerías Preciadas, on Avinguda Portal de l'Angel, stay open from 10am to 8pm.

With museums the general rule is that those near the Barri Gòtic close during the siesta, while those at Montjuïc stay open, although there are exceptions. Most museums are closed on Monday and many close at 2pm on Sunday.

If you want to see as much as possible, think about going to Montjuïc, to Gaudí's Parc Güell or to the extraordinary Temple Expiatori de la Sagrada Família in the afternoon.

Restaurants are usually open for lunch from around 1pm and dinner is served from around 9pm.

It's worth doing some research on local holidays when

planning your trip. If you're unlucky enough to come up against a local holiday followed by a national one (the intervening day is called a 'bridge') your sightseeing plans could be sabotaged.

GETTING AROUND

The **underground** (metro) is the fastest and cheapest way to make your way around the city. There's a flat fare but a ten-journey 'T2' travelcard is a bargain and also allows you to use the train to Tibidabo and the funicular railway to Montjuïc. For a little more you can get a 'T1', which is also valid on buses and blue trams. Trains run from 5am to 11pm (6am to 1am Saturdays, Sundays and the night before public holidays). Buy the travelcards in metro stations. Five lines cover most of the city and connect with the funicular. The trains are clean and almost graffiti-free, and an illuminated indicator and a synthesised voice announce the name of the next station as you approach.

Most city **buses** can be picked up at the Plaça de Catalunya, but if you're unfamiliar with the layout of the city it's probably better to stick to the metro. **Taxis** are black with yellow stripes, plentiful, cheap and metered. Most journeys to tourist sites from the Plaça de Catalunya cost less than £5. Small tips are welcomed, but not demanded as of right. Taxis available for hire display a green light, or a sign reading *lliure* in the windscreen.

UNMISSABLES

The cathedral

Called La Seu by locals, this superb Gothic church is strangely deceptive. Its most striking, apparently medieval, features – the ornate façade and the soaring spire – are actually nineteenth-century additions, built in accordance with the original plans and financed by a wealthy industrialist. Outside the ornate doors stand blind beggars with outstretched palms. Inside, a remarkable carved choir stall screens off the nave, enlivened by the coats of arms of the Knights of the Golden Fleece who assembled here in 1519.

Outside in the cathedral square, Peruvian musicians play guitars and pan-pipes and during Advent the site is transformed into a colourful Christmas market with dozens of stalls selling tinsel, tree decorations, bunches of mistletoe tied with ribbon in the Catalan colours and appallingly kitsch nativity cribs. Come on a Sunday morning, or on a Saturday between 5pm and 6pm, and watch the locals form a closed circle and dance the *sardana* to curiously infectious oompah-style music.

Picasso Museum

This isn't the best collection of the modern master's works but it's the best in Spain (although the epic *Guernica* is in Madrid). Barcelona was Picasso's adopted city, and the thirteenth-century Aguilar Palace (closed Monday) has been magnificently restored to house this collection, exceptionally rich in early figurative works and bolstered by gifts from Jacqueline Picasso. The best-known works displayed are the Meninas sequence, studies on a theme of Velázquez, and studies from the famous Harlequin sequence. There's an extensive giftshop which does a roaring trade in postcards, posters, books and T-shirts, and a cafeteria.

The Ramblas

Somerset Maugham believed that the Ramblas was the world's most beautiful street, and the Andalucian poet and dramatist García Lorca declared it to be the only street in the world he wished would never end. It's the experience of the Ramblas, rather than its physical appearance, that makes it so special. A lot of rather dreary souvenir shops line the central boulevard on both sides, and the end by the port has a liberal sprinkling of sex shops. At this end there are market traders offering leather goods and colourfully embroidered waistcoats; nearby, regiments of stout Barcelonan matrons perch on kitchen chairs, their tarots laid out on card tables before them, ready to disclose what the future holds (in Catalan, Spanish or French). You'll pass caricature artists, or students bent industriously over the pavement, reproducing the *Mona Lisa* in chalk; and while you are overwhelmed by the charm of it all, the locals jostle their way into the state lottery office and cram into McDonald's or Kentucky Fried Chicken.

Further up, towards the Plaça de Catalunya, there are lots of news-stands selling maps, T-shirts, postcards, guidebooks – and whole libraries of soft-core porn magazines. As you progress along the streets, past stalls decked with hanging baskets of flowers and plants, and chirruping caged birds, shoe-shine boys appear, ready to spring into action. Crowds gathered round a little table effectively conceal a sleight-of-hand merchant, bidding the gullible to 'Find the Lady'. Political activists offer books, badges and T-shirts; the less organised invite you to choose a scarf from a rainbow assortment spread out on a sheet on the ground. At night prostitutes wait ready to accost you – whether you're accompanied or not – and in the early hours outrageous transvestites parade past.

And don't forget the side-streets. Down at the port end there are tiny antique shops, jammed full of interesting clutter, and off to the right the Boquería market is full of locals buying bread, shellfish, skinned rabbits and exotic fruit.

Gaudí buildings

The most exciting sights in the New Town are the works of the architect Gaudí, and of these the most stunning is the unfinished (after more than 100 years) **Temple Expiatori de la Sagrada Família**, an almost surreal building, responsibility for which Gaudí assumed from a more conventional colleague in 1884, and which obsessed him until his death in 1926. Its four spires topped by coloured ceramic caps soar over 100 metres high above the city like giant skewered cigars and its porches have stalactite-like canopies which somehow make the tortured stone look like dripping wax. To visit is to find yourself in a building site for, haphazardly funded, work goes on in accordance with Gaudí's final plans. You can take an elevator up one of the spires and see the extraordinary detail of the work. There's a small museum with an interesting audio-visual on his work.

It's a building you'll either love or hate. In *Homage to Catalonia* George Orwell pronounced it to be 'one of the most hideous buildings in the world' and found its spires to be 'exactly the shape of hock bottles'.

There are two examples of Gaudí's domestic architecture on the Passeig de Gràcia. The contours of the **Casa Milà**, whose strangely undulating forms seem to flow around a corner, are said to be inspired by Montserrat, the saw-toothed mountain that is almost sacred in Catalan folklore and religious life. Because of its resemblance to an eroded rockface its nickname is *La Pedrera*, the rock quarry. **Casa Batlló**, four blocks down towards the Plaça de Catalunya, has a colourful ceramic façade and strangely mask-like balconies. The startling gingerbread-house-type roof is repeated in **Parc Güell**. Originally intended as a smart housing development, only the astonishing gatehouse and Gaudí's own house were completed, but the concept is a theme park ahead of its time. There's a definite Hansel and Gretel feel, with a strange hall of columns like a sinister grotto, a giant decorative lizard, enormous mosaic benches and weird steps which flow like lava.

Museum of Catalan Art, Montjuïc

This stunning collection is centred on Romanesque works from the eleventh and twelfth centuries, and Catalan religious paintings. Dozens of frescoes transplanted from small churches in the Pyrenees show wide-eyed figures framed in brilliant colours. The panel from the apse of San Climent de Taüll displaying Christ sitting in majesty is particularly memorable. Ask at the door for the (returnable) English language notes.

OTHER PLACES TO VISIT

Museums and galleries

Frederic Marès Museum You'll find this wonderfully eccentric museum just around the corner from the cathedral in the heart of the Barri Gòtic. There's an incredibly extensive and somewhat awe-inspiring collection of religious artefacts – particularly sculptures of the Crucifixion and of the Madonna (the founder, Marès, was himself a sculptor). Such an accumulation of depictions of suffering throughout the ages verges on the creepy but light relief is at hand. Marès was also an inveterate collector of secular items and his assembly of items in the upstairs **Museu Sentimental** includes all sorts of ephemera, such as cigarette cards, tarot cards, matchboxes and unusual clay pipes, as well as dolls, walking sticks and penny-farthings.

Modern Art Museum (in the Parc de la Ciutadella) Most of the works on display date from the late nineteenth and early twentieth centuries. The big names of modern Catalan art, Dalí and Miró, are barely represented, but there is some wonderful furniture by Gaspar Homar, and a strange 1927 indoor sculpture park by Josep Guinovart which can't fail to raise a smile.

Montjuïc The hill of Montjuïc, crowned by a castle, rises over 600 feet above the harbour, and is the setting for a large park which houses a number of museums and an old-fashioned funfair; it is also the site of the main Olympic stadium. It's a good place to spend a day enjoying the gardens, the views of the city and the variety of the attractions on offer, especially the Miró Foundation. To get there, take the metro to Plaça d'Espanya and walk up Avinguda de la Reina Maria Cristina, or take the funicular railway from Paral-lel metro station. This interconnects with a cable-car which will take you from the amusement park to the castle, home of the **Military Museum**. Here, as well as one of the biggest collections of model soldiers you're ever likely to meet, is a large collection of armour, weapons and uniforms as well as an imposing statue of General Franco on horseback.

The **Miró Foundation** is a fine white building endowed by the artist himself, with an extensive collection of his works, including paintings, drawings, bulbous sculptures and three-dimensional tapestries in brilliant reds, yellows and blues. If you hate modern art, stay away – it will confirm all your worst prejudices. If you don't, go with an open mind, and have fun.

Other attractions

Poble Espanyol Also on Montjuïc Hill is a collection of repro-duction buildings from all over Spain, assembled on an enormous site for the 1929 International Exhibition and maintained as a permanent attraction. The buildings range from Castilian castles to simple white houses from Andalucian *pueblo blanco*. There are artisans at work here, and you can buy good-quality souvenirs, especially glasswork, but expect to pay for the privilege. With bars and restaurants around every corner, and a red London bus to bring visitors from the city centre, it's something of a tourist trap, but it's an easy way to get something of the feel of Spain beyond Catalonia.

Zoo If you're tired of museums and galleries take a walk through the city park (Parc de la Ciutadella) to the zoo. Only the big cats are caged. There's a fine collection of primates and a detailed family tree that shows the success of the zoo's programme of breeding in captivity. There's also a dolphinarium, with perfor-mance times widely posted, but the real star of the show is the enormously photogenic Snowflake, the only albino gorilla in captivity, who literally 'plays to the cameras'.

Excursion

Montserrat The most heavily touted excursion from Barcelona (and the Costa Brava) takes coachloads of tourists up the spectacular sandstone, saw-toothed rockface to the monastery and hermitages of Montserrat, 40 kilometres north-west of the city. Tour guides feed their clientele legends. The famous image of the Virgin, discovered in a mountain cave amid celestial music and ecstatic visions in AD 880, had reputedly been hidden there by St Peter (this inspired Wagner's *Parsifal*).

The figure of the Madonna, set high above the altar and blackened by centuries of candlesmoke, is the centrepiece of the sixteenth-century basilica. The faithful, their ranks swollen by numerous curious tourists, queue patiently along the stairs to process past the Madonna. The famous Escolania Boys' Choir sings daily at around 1pm.

The cult of the Madonna is an important focus of Catalan nationalism, but if you're seeking spiritual uplift you're likely to be disappointed. There's a huge commercial operation at work, with coach parks, cafeterias full of sticky cakes, and gift shops with replica Madonnas. But the views and the mountain walks to the hermitages, plus the spectacular approach with views of the Llobregat Valley, are enjoyable. Get the best views by coming on the funicular railway and cable-car. The Ferrocarrils Catalans leaves from below the Plaça de Espanya (at 9.10am, 11.10am, 3.10pm and 5.10pm, returning at 1.20pm, 3.20pm, 5.20pm and 7.40pm) and connects with the aerial cable-car.

SHOPPING

Shopping is fun in Barcelona. Wander down Avinguda Portal de l'Angel and see the constant stream of customers for the religious statuary shop, admire the brightly coloured hand-carved wooden mobiles, ideal for the nursery, sold at little stalls in the narrow cobbled streets behind the cathedral in the heart of the Barri Gòtic, or choose a keyring (from a selection of 5,000) in an eccentric little shop called El Món del Claver at Carrer de l'Hospital 33, just off the Ramblas. Continuing the theme of monomania, there's even a shop – Pino 4, on Plaça del Pi – almost entirely devoted to clothes-hangers.

Market stalls at the bottom of the Ramblas and around the cathedral (on Thursdays) have a wide choice of heavy, calf-length brocade skirts and colourful embroidered waistcoats. The maze-like streets of the Barrio, especially Carrer Banys Nous, have dozens of little antique shops. Heavy Spanish furniture predominates, but you might find some art nouveau curios. Sundials make unusual gifts.

Designer names flash at you on the wide streets of the Eixample. You'll find Dior, Armani and Loewe around Passeig de Gràcia and the Diagonal. You'll also find well-made fashionable clothes at El Mercadillo on the pedestrianised Carrer de la Portaferrissa, between the cathedral and the Ramblas.

There's lots of scope for rummaging around in the assorted markets that are scattered around the city. There's a flea market, called Els Encants, at Carrer Dos de Maig, all day Monday, Wednesday, Friday and Saturday. On Sunday mornings coin and stamp stalls are set up in the Plaça Reial; books and comics can be found between Carrer Mansò and Carrer Comte Urgel, just off the Parel-lel. There's a wonderful selection of Catalan foods with colourful displays of unusual fruit, vegetables and sausages at the Mercat de Sant Josep, just off the Ramblas.

Ceramics make good souvenirs, as do bottles of local *cava*. You can browse among beautiful fans at La Cubana at Carrer de la Boquería 26 or flip through modern art prints in the shops near the Picasso Museum on Carrer de Montcada.

EATING AND DRINKING

You'll see lots of locals eating *ensaimades* (turnovers) on the hoof, especially on the Ramblas at lunchtime. Wander the backstreets and find queues at *sandvitxerías* and pâtisseries while many restaurants are virtually deserted. Tourists with a bit more time can have a filling *menú del dia* at a fairly anonymous place for around £5.

If you want a snack, but prefer more stylish surroundings, have a drink and a sandwich in the splendid green and white belle époque Café de l'Opéra, opposite the Liceu, the opera house on the Ramblas. Other good places for light meals on the Ramblas include the fast-food Viena and the terrace of the Café Zurich, at the Plaça de Catalunya end. In the Eixample, the cool, design-conscious La Jijonenca, at Rambla de Catalunya 35, is a stylish ice-cream parlour, with geometric black and white fittings, Dalí prints and a good-value *menú del dia*, which makes it a popular choice with apparently incongruous elderly patrons. The Cerverzeria d'Or on Carrer del Consell de Cent is another good choice.

When it comes to more substantial fare, menus are heavily weighted towards fish. There is a host of seafood restaurants around the Passeig Nacional near the port in the Barceloneta area. The rough and ready Restaurante Paris, Carrer Maquinista 29, is good value. Los Caracoles, at Escudellers 14 (just off the seedy section of the Ramblas), is a Barcelonan institution. Mysterious men from Moscow were said to haunt its labyrinth of rooms during the Civil War. Signed photographs of less publicity-shy patrons such as Sacha Distel line the walls. Strings of red peppers hang from the rafters and musicians serenade you at your table. Also in the Barri Gòtic, La Bona Cuina, Carrer de Paradis 4, is expensive and touristy but has excellent meat and fish.

Around the Picasso Museum try the *truita catalana* at the unpretentious Nou Celler at Princesa 161 and Barri de Ferro 3. Near the port the more expensive Restaurante 7 Portes on

Passeig de Isabel II is popular with locals and tourists, particularly on Sunday nights, when much of the opposition is closed. The food is competent but not outstanding, the menu is in Catalan (there's a translation on display outside). Oysters and *cava* are specialities.

For a splurge take yourself to La Puñallada, Passeig de Gràcia 104. It's expensive, particularly the starters, but the salads are big enough for two, the chicken cooked to perfection, the *butifarra* (sausage) and mushrooms delightful and the service is extremely solicitous. Also in the Eixample, Ca La Marion, Carrer d'Amigó 53, offers excellent Spanish nouvelle cuisine at reasonable prices.

If you want to break away from the orthodox three-course meal, do what the natives do: go to the bar and order *tapas*. The word means 'lid', and traditionally *tapas* was a small portion of appetisers served free to accompany a drink. From there the idea developed and today you can fill up on a succession of interesting nibbles, usually small pieces of fish or meat. Often you'll see an array of trays set out below a counter, buffet-style. Typical *tapas* include *anchoas* (anchovies), *chorizo* (spicy sausage), *pimientos* (peppers), *gambas* (shrimps), *calamares* (squid) and *tortilla Espanola* (Spanish omelette). If you want a larger portion ask for *raciones*. A good place to experiment with *tapas* is the satisfyingly ethnic unnamed bar opposite La Pizza Nostra in Carrer de Montcada, near the Picasso Museum.

Cava is Spanish sparkling wine made in accordance with the *méthode champenoise* (the secondary fermentation takes place in the bottle). It's cheap and often excellent quality and an ideal accompaniment to *tapas*.

NIGHTLIFE

Young citizens stroll smooching along the Ramblas or stand locked in more or less passionate embraces in cinema queues. Film-going is very popular and there are a number of cinemas throughout the city. Most films are dubbed but if a Hollywood or British film is labelled 'VO' it's in English with subtitles. Check the weekly *Guía del Ocio* or the newspaper *La Vanguardia* for what's-on listings covering cinema, theatre, opera, dance, music and ideas on bars and restaurants.

Music, dance and plays are staged at the Greek theatre on Montjuïc and at the Parc de la Ciutadella during the summer. The Gran Teatre de Liceu on the Ramblas, an opulent orgy of gilt and velvet, is one of the world's leading opera houses, with a formidable reputation for its Wagnerian productions. You'll find jazz in several bars, particularly at weekends. A bit off the tourist trail, try the bar at Carrer de la Fussina 6, in Barceloneta, around midnight.

Much of the city's heavy-duty nightlife is centred on the Eixample, in the streets around Aribau and the Diagonal, where there are a number of smart cocktail bars. The classic gin and vermouth brigade will enjoy drinking at the Dry Martini Bar, Aribau 162, a veritable temple to the granddaddy of them all; the pleasant, ship's clubroom-styled Ideal Cocktail Bar at Aribau 89 has a kilted Highlander logo and international awards for its dry Martinis. Altogether more bizarre is Il Nostro Raco at Aribau 101 where tarot cards (a Barcelona obsession) are read in the vestibule, tight-jeaned youths shoot pool in the backroom and, in curiously bordello-like surroundings, *cava* and orange juice cocktails are served in specimen bottles.

If you want to join the smart set and dance in a nightclub till dawn, try Up and Down, Carrer Numancia 179, or Otto Zutz, Carrer Lincoln 13.

HOTELS

In town the hotels are clustered around the Ramblas (the smarter ones are up towards Plaça de Catalunya, where it's advisable to forgo the view and stay in a quieter back room) and the Barri Gòtic, where you'll find the majority of *pensions* and cheaper hotels, which are almost universally unenticing. In the Eixample, which is slightly less convenient, the hotels are around the Passeig de Gràcia and the Diagonal.

A typical hotel used by tour operators can be found either on the Ramblas or around Passeig de Gràcia; a turn-of-the-century building with a marble-floored reception could promise more than it delivers, as the interior may be slightly less inspiring.

Hotel prices Symbols indicate approximate prices per room per night for a double room with bath. Many large hotels run special breaks which work out far cheaper. (See page 14 for further details.)

♦ = under £50; ♦♦ = £50 to £80; ♦♦♦ = £80 to £100;
♦♦♦♦ = £100 to £140; ♦♦♦♦♦ = over £140.

ASTORIA

Carrer Paris 203, 08036

Tel: 209 8311   Fax: 202 3008

Next to a cinema in the heart of the Eixample, the Astoria is in a fairly quiet and convenient position. It has an airy, neo-classical style with a white marbled and pillared reception. Dark leather armchairs and sofas add to the smooth feel of the sitting-room. The bedrooms are light, with black and white chessboard floors, built-in pine cupboards and good bathrooms with twin basins.

Bedrooms: 114, all with bath/WC; air-conditioning   **Facilities:** Lift
Credit/charge cards accepted: All

COLÓN

Avenida de la Catedral 7, 08002

Tel: 301 1404   Fax: 317 2915

Situated in the heart of the tourist area of the Barri Gòtic, the hotel looks on to the thirteenth-century cathedral across a pedestrian thoroughfare lined with souvenir shops. The hotel was built in 1951, but blends well with its ancient surroundings. The panelled reception is warm and busy; an ante-room and bar off it are relaxed and tasteful. Bedrooms are carpeted and comfortable, with flower-patterned bedspreads and armchairs. Ask for a room with a terrace overlooking the cathedral.

Bedrooms: 147, most with bath/WC; all with air-conditioning; some with mini-bar   **Facilities:** Lift; restaurant   **Credit/charge cards accepted:** All

CONDES DE BARCELONA

Passeig de Gràcia 75, 08008

Tel: 484 8600   Fax: 216 0835

The hotel is in the art nouveau Casa Batlló building. Tiles and wrought-iron railings adorn its exterior. Off the reception is a bizarre gallery surrounded by small columns and arches ascending five floors to a large skylight. The hotel is elegant and modern, with a marble floor in reception, slick black stools and chairs in the bar, comfortable grey and yellow sofas in the sitting-room. The bedrooms are attractive and inviting, and the 'Condal' bedrooms extremely spacious.

Bedrooms: 100, all with bath/WC; air-conditioning; mini-bar   **Facilities:** Lift; restaurant   **Credit/charge cards accepted:** Amex, Diners, Visa

---

♦ = under £50; ♦♦ = £50 to £80; ♦♦♦ = £80 to £100;
♦♦♦♦ = £100 to £140; ♦♦♦♦♦ = over £140.

GRANVIA ♦♦
Gran Via de les Corts Catalanes 642, 08007   *Tel: 318 1900   Fax: 318 9997*

A small nineteenth-century palace converted into the most original and cosy hotel in the city centre, near Plaça de Catalunya. The unassuming and rather dirty exterior is deceptive: a swirling red-and-green-patterned carpet, and arches and pillars greet you in the reception. The fusty sitting-room is straight out of the last century with rather formal furniture. Panelled corridors lead to rooms with more modern furniture, rugs on parquet floors and old-fashioned bathrooms.

Bedrooms: 54, all with bath/WC; air-conditioning; mini-bar   **Facilities:** Lift
Credit/charge cards accepted: All

LE MERIDIEN ♦♦♦♦♦
Ramblas 111, 08002   *Tel: 318 6200   Fax: 301 7776*

Formerly the Ramada Renaissance, Le Meridien is a stylish establishment on the Ramblas in the heart of Barcelona. The hotel is spotless. The peach-coloured exterior is adorned with old-fashioned wrought-iron lamps. The reception has a shiny white marble floor, and you can relax in a deep, modern, upholstered armchair. The bar has brown curtains and glass-topped tables, and the restaurant's centrepiece is an impressive food display. The bedrooms, though not special, are attractive and of a good size.

Bedrooms: 208, all with shower/WC; air-conditioning; hair-dryer; mini-bar   **Facilities:** Lift; restaurant   **Credit/charge cards accepted:** Amex, Diners, Visa

ORIENTE ♦♦
Ramblas 45-47, 08002   *Tel: 302 2558   Fax: 412 3819*

An ex-Capuchin convent, the Oriente is a romantic place that's seen better times. The large sitting-room, with pillars that look like Victorian lampposts, is eccentric; stranger still is the octagonal restaurant above it, with dainty chandeliers and an art deco skylight, but plain, cheap furniture. The bedrooms are adequate: light and clean with decent bathrooms. For a quiet night ask for one not facing the Ramblas.

Bedrooms: 142, all with bath/WC; none with TV   **Facilities:** Lift; restaurant   **Credit/charge cards accepted:** All

RITZ ♦♦♦♦♦
Gran Via de les Corts Catalanes 668, 08010   *Tel: 318 5200   Fax: 318 0148*

By far the most stylish hotel in town, the Ritz opened in 1919 and has retained its belle époque elegance. A large oval sitting-room with mirrored walls, a marble floor and numerous sofas and armchairs occupies the centre of the building. The restaurant is also oval, dominated by large pillars, crystal chandeliers and a blue-patterned carpet. The rooms are large and comfortable even if some are a bit plain. The Ritz is on the corner of the main street running through the Eixample, less than ten minutes' walk from the top of the Ramblas.

Bedrooms: 161, all with bath/shower/WC; air-conditioning; mini-bar
Facilities: Lift; restaurant; hairdresser   **Credit/charge cards accepted:**
Amex, Diners, Visa

RIVOLI RAMBLAS ♦♦♦♦
Rambla dels Estudis 128, 08002   *Tel: 302 6643   Fax: 317 5053*

This refurbished art deco building is on a salubrious section of the Ramblas, opposite stalls selling twittering caged birds. The reception is smart, with modern columns painted with classical scenes. A white marble staircase leads to a pine-floored restaurant and a bar overlooking the ground floor. The bedrooms are decorated in grey and reds and are well equipped. There's also a fitness centre, and a terrace for relaxing.

Bedrooms: 87, all with bath/WC; air-conditioning; hair-dryer; mini-bar
Facilities: Lift; gym; sauna; solarium; whirlpool bath   **Credit/charge cards accepted:** Amex, Diners, Visa

Hotel prices Symbols indicate approximate prices per room per night for a double room with bath. Many large hotels run special breaks which work out far cheaper. (See page 14 for further details.)

♦ = under £50; ♦♦ = £50 to £80; ♦♦♦ = £80 to £100;
♦♦♦♦ = £100 to £140; ♦♦♦♦♦ = over £140.

BERLIN

- The speed at which changes have occurred in Berlin since 9 November 1989 has been astonishing; and it is impossible to predict what further changes may occur in the near future
- Though no longer divided, the city's eastern and western halves are still very different
- Berlin is enormous: the western half alone is four times as big as Paris. It is a major industrial city, and no longer beautiful after its wartime battering, but large areas of parks, forests and lakes still exist
- There's an excellent selection of splendid museums

DESPITE its unassuming beginnings as a medieval trading town, Berlin's development has been anything but ordinary. As the Hohenzollern dynasty consolidated its power from the fifteenth century onwards, Berlin flexed its muscles in the fields of architecture and art, commerce and industry. In 1871 it emerged as the capital of a united, increasingly militaristic Germany, which Bismarck and Kaiser Wilhelm steered towards the First World War. Berlin bore the brunt of Germany's post-war ignominy, with food shortages, economic chaos and political unrest. But the 1920s were brilliant years of social and artistic change. It was the era of Brechtian satire, Schönberg's atonal music, outrageous cabaret and Marlene Dietrich's début in *The Blue Angel*.

'Decadent,' said Hitler, and replaced the new ideas with some of his own. Berlin was Hitler's political springboard, capital and wartime HQ. After seeing virtually all of it destroyed by bombing, he committed suicide as the Second World War drew to an end. Berlin was divided by the Allied Powers into four occupied sectors. The Western Allies grimly resisted Soviet attempts to incorporate Berlin in a new communist Germany.

The Wall went up in 1961, sealing West Berlin in a concrete capsule a hundred miles inside East Germany. The Wall was an attempt to staunch the flow of highly skilled workers fleeing East Germany for richer pickings in the West. West Berlin clung to its separate, peculiar identity at great expense, regarding its anomalous and precarious position with studied indifference.

Strangely, even at the height of the Cold War, when the frontier was most fiercely guarded, West Berlin didn't feel like a claustrophobic city: the Wall was built to restrict the East, not the West. There are large areas of parks, forests and lakes which seem surprisingly like open country, and there are even sandy beaches and quiet farms. Twenty years ago West Berlin had the drab, makeshift feel of a hastily rebuilt city. Today, with the Wall down, the rebuilding is smart, confident reconstruction, fuelled by massive amounts of money. The central area in particular, since reunification, is like one huge building site, as property speculators move in to develop the land.

Kurfürstendamm, known as 'Ku'damm', is western Berlin's most famous street, glitzy at one end, seedy further down. The nearer you are to the zoo and the black plate-glass slab of the Europa-Center at the top end, the smarter it becomes. The wide pavements are studded with glass display kiosks of jewellery, handbags and designer clothes. As you saunter down the Ku'damm, it becomes less glamorous. Prostitutes loiter and cinemas show programmes of soft porn.

The Kaiser Wilhelm Memorial Church is the Ku'damm's most noted building, the spire bombed to a jagged stump and left as a permanent reminder of the horrors of war. The simple 1960s shapes of an octagonal tower and a blue glass church stand in sharp geometrical contrast by its side.

Charlottenburg is an enormous area containing a university, Hitler's 1936 Olympic Stadium, a vast Congress Center where Berlin hosts many international events, a 500-foot radio mast and a great number of dignified residential streets. Most visitors head for Charlottenburg to see the reconstructed Prussian baroque palace and its museums.

The former hunting forest of Tiergarten is now a park of spindly post-war trees. Around it are some striking buildings. There's a blue and pink steam engine (the Hydraulic and Ship Engineering Institute), a yellow tent (the Berlin Philharmonic's concert hall) and the white sails of the Bauhaus-Archiv. Designed by Walter Gropius, this startling building contains documents and drawings of the Bauhaus School, which briefly made a home in Berlin before being harried across the Atlantic by the Third Reich.

The section of Berlin known as the Hansaviertel suffered terribly in the war, and was completely devastated. In the International Architectural Exhibition of 1957, 48 world-famous architects were invited to design new housing projects for the area. The results meant that the Hansaviertel has many different and some very distinguished examples of modern architecture.

Kreuzberg, a quarter near the now dismantled Checkpoint Charlie, has become home to many immigrants, and is a popular meeting point. Architecturally there's an odd mix of bleak tower blocks and beautiful terraces, carefully rebuilt after bomb damage. The area has a slightly Bohemian, subversive flavour and is particularly lively at night, with bars, café-theatre and ethnic restaurants.

Eastern Berlin still feels quite different to the west, despite the 'growing together' since unification. In places it's an unremarkable provincial German town where respectably dressed burghers order coffee and cakes. Some areas have been clinically restored to pre-war elegance. A few streets away there are spectacular towers, insanely wide streets and howling squares. It's bleak, often ugly.

But it's no longer a subdued and drab counterpart to the west – the neon lights, shop windows and advertising hoardings have spread fast. Traffic has also increased, though the small boxy 'Trabbis', wheezing like bronchitic lawnmowers and emitting clouds of fumes, are seen less often.

The centre of the former capital of Prussia and the Third Reich was pounded to rubble in the war, but has largely been rebuilt in the 'old' style. The showpiece street, Unter den Linden ('under the limes'), fades from ponderous neo-classical buildings to drab 1950s blocks. Soldiers used to goose-step past the Doric columns of the Neue Wache (New Guard) every afternoon, as part of a tourist attraction. Unter den Linden now peters out near the Wall by Berlin's most celebrated monument, the Brandenburg Gate, open once more to buses and taxis. Before long, the street may be restored to its former glory as a major thoroughfare in the heart of Berlin.

Alexanderplatz belongs to a more brutalist school: tower blocks overlook acres of bleak, windswept paving and in the middle is the East's most striking landmark, the television tower – a spike stuck through a golf ball.

If you have time, you might take a trip to the suburbs of Kopenick (old town houses and a seventeenth-century castle, now a museum), or Rahnsdorf village on the Muggelsee Lake. Well off the tourist track you can find some less familiar aspects of Berlin in the streets off Prenzlauer Allee, a working-class district of the old Berlin of the 1920s north of Alexanderplatz, colonised at night by artists and intellectuals in smoke-filled bars.

After a gruelling day's exploration you may find yourself in need of a drink. Try the restored St Nicholas quarter near the Red Town Hall for a coffee or a beer (it was a sort of Eastern Bloc Covent Garden). Or finish up in the smart café of the Grand Hotel just off Unter den Linden, five minutes' walk from Friedrichstrasse.

WHEN TO GO

Berlin has colder and drier winters than London, and slightly warmer and wetter summers. There are always plenty of cultural activities – including a film festival in late February/early March, a summer music festival in July and August, with open-air jazz concerts, an international festival of opera and music in September/October, and a jazz festival in October/November.

MASTERING THE SYSTEM

Information The German National Tourist Office is at Nightingale House, 65 Curzon Street, London W1Y 7PE, tel: 071-495 3990.

In Berlin, the central tourist office (Verkehrsamt Berlin) is in the Europa-Center at the top of the Ku'damm (tel: 2626031). English is spoken. There is a hotel reservation service for a small charge. Leaflets on city tours, hotels, local events, public transport, sights and entertainment are available.

Maps It's advisable to supplement the free tourist office handouts with a good street map which also plots bus and underground routes and stopping points. The folding map produced by Falk-Verlag is excellent.

Sightseeing tours A good way to find your bearings is to take one of the city bus tours. Several companies run very similar tours of Berlin, some in English. These are easy to find and book; most start near the Europa-Center. A cheaper alternative is to take bus No 100 from the Zoo to Alexanderplatz. You can also take a tour to Potsdam – a full-day and expensive tour. (*See 'Other places to visit' section for how to get to Potsdam independently*.) In summer there are boat-trips on the Havel and Tegel Lakes, and along Berlin's canals.

Changing money There are many banks around the central area (open Monday to Friday 8.30am to 1pm and 2.30pm to 4pm (5.30pm Thursday), closed weekends). Exchange offices at the airport and railway station stay open longer (6am to 10pm); one office, at Bahnhof Zoo, is open seven days a week; another in the Europa-Center six days.

Changing money is painless, but some banks charge commission. Hotels, travel agencies and the central post office will also change money (at less favourable rates). Large shops, restaurants and hotels take travellers' cheques, and credit cards are now much more readily acceptable in Germany than they once were.

Opening hours and days Berlin wakes up very early. You can have breakfast at 6.30am in most hotels, be at the tourist office by 7.30am, and out sightseeing by 8am, if you're keen. The biggest museums and galleries open from 9am, others from 10am. Monday and Tuesday may be closing days. Check with the booklet *Berlin Turns On* (free from the tourist office) for a detailed list of current opening times. For such a cosmopolitan and consumerist society shopping hours are surprisingly limited at weekends. Many shops shut at 2pm on Saturday (4pm on the first Saturday of the month), and all day Sunday. On Thursday most shops in the centre are open until 8.30pm. Flea markets often operate at weekends.

GETTING THERE

Going independently

By air British Airways, United Airlines and Lufthansa all offer daily flights to Berlin from Heathrow. There are also scheduled and charter flights from Gatwick, Edinburgh and Birmingham. The cheapest scheduled fares are APEX (book 14 days in advance), and there's no seasonal variation in fares. It's worth trying the following companies for discounted flights: Avro Elite (081-543 5833), Data Travel (0424 722394), Cresta Holidays (061-929 9995), GTF Tours (071-792 1260), German Travel Centre (071-379 5212) and DER Travel Services (071-408 0111).

Tegel Airport This is about five miles from the city centre. Bus No 109 takes you into town for a fraction of the price of a taxi; the journey takes about half an hour.

By rail UK rail services connect with the Harwich-Hook ferry and a direct train to Berlin. The journey takes about 21 hours and a second-class return costs almost as much as the APEX airfare.

By road From London there are regular weekly coach services to Berlin, with the journey taking about 24 hours.

Tour operator packages

Berlin is a popular weekend destination, and several tour operators offer packages. In 1992 a three-night B&B package at a three-star hotel ranged from £270 (low season) to £432 (high season). A few coach operators offer good-value breaks, but the journey takes about 24 hours. See page 385 for a list of tour operators. By taking a cheap flight and finding your own accommodation you can probably save a few pounds on most packages. But hotel beds are in short supply during major events and at certain times of year. To be sure of a particular hotel, always book ahead. Most of the large hotels used by tour operators are high-quality if uninteresting modern buildings. Traffic noise can be a problem in central areas.

GETTING AROUND

Most parts of Berlin are accessible by an excellent public transport system. The **U-Bahn** (underground) is fast and frequent. The **S-Bahn** (urban railway) is older and slower, but you see more of the city on the overground trains. Single fares are expensive. It's nearly always worth getting one of the special inclusive tickets. A 24-hour Berlin Ticket is the best type to buy for the bus, U-Bahn and S-Bahn network. Have your ticket stamped on your first trip, then afterwards just show it on request. You can also buy *Sammelkarten* (multiple tickets) in groups of five, six-day cards, family cards (for weekend travel), and short-journey tickets (for about five stops). You can buy tickets from machines in the stations, and must have them validated before you travel. The system operates largely on trust, but there's a sharp fine if you're caught without a valid ticket.

Bus routes need a little research before you tackle them, but are basically straightforward with the help of a good map. The drivers are taciturn, anxious to keep to their schedules, and don't like giving change. **Taxis** are easy to find in central Berlin but quite expensive (the meter starts running at well over £2).

Walking Berlin has a large number of dogs, not all of which have the best pavement manners. Also, the red sections of some pavements are used as bicycle lanes: walking along them will provoke agitated bell-ringing from the rear.

Driving As Berlin is so large and the road systems so efficient, driving is more of a pleasure than in many cities. Parking in the city centre is difficult. Illegally parked cars are often towed away. If you have to bring a car to the centre the large multi-storey car-parks charge around £5 a day. But as the public transport system is excellent it is scarcely necessary.

UNMISSABLES

The major museums are grouped in three complexes: two in the west, one in the east.

Dahlem
Berlin's best-known museums are housed in an enormous complex in the same modern building. Take the U-Bahn to Dahlem Dorf (Line 2). Entrance is free and there are good information sheets in English for each museum. It's a gruelling day's expedition to see them all properly, but both contents and displays are superb. There's a pleasant café downstairs when you tire. Here are just a few of the highlights.

Museum of Oriental Art (Ostasiatische Kunst) Melon-breasted Indian goddesses and swirling arms are interspersed with exquisite miniatures and intricate woodcarving. Upstairs there's Central and South-East Asian art and a copy of the frieze from the Cambodian temples of Angkhor Wat.

Museum of Ethnology (Volkerkunde) Superbly imaginative collections from Africa, Asia and the New World are displayed: South American gold, Eskimo art and boats from the South Seas.

Picture Gallery (Gemäldegalerie) Halls of European fame which are strong on Italian, medieval German, Flemish and Dutch Schools – including a couple of Bosch's waking nightmares, and a self-portrait of a handsome Rembrandt at 28.

Museum of Islamic Art (Islamische Kunst) Iridescent geometric patterns on silk and wood are displayed in this collection.

Charlottenburg

The elongated, repetitive façade of Frederick the Great's monumental residence (reached by bus No 145 from the Zoo) is an enlargement of an earlier and more charming summer palace built for Queen Sophie Charlotte in the 1690s, reconstructed after war damage. Today it houses a museum of indifferent paintings, sparse furniture and superb porcelain. See the bleaky grand Golden Gallery, encrusted with twirls of rococo gilt, and the Porcelain Room. The prize exhibit in the **Egyptian Museum** (opposite the palace) is a bust of Queen Nefertiti, and there are some wonderful animal carvings. Opposite the Egyptian museum, the **Museum of Antiquities** is crammed with Attic vases and bronzes and has a sparkling treasure-trove of silver downstairs. The underrated **Brohan Museum**, next door, has a fine collection of early twentieth-century decorative arts.

Museum Island

Museum Island is an assembly of several museums on an island in the River Spree. The **Bode Museum** (entrance on Monbijou Bridge) contains the Egyptian Museum (with a papyrus collection), the Museum for Pre- and Early History, and the fine Early Christian and Byzantine collection. There's a wonderful life-size horse and rider sculpture in the entrance hall.

Don't miss the **Pergamon**. One of the greatest museums of Greek, Roman and Mesopotamian antiquities in the world, its contents are so enormous that the building had to be constructed around them. There are three outstanding set-pieces on a mammoth scale: the temple frieze and altar from second-century Pergamon, a Babylonian processional way, and a gate from Miletus. Fierce lions and mythical beasts stride along towering walls of brilliant blue tiles. The museum also houses the fine Islamic and Far Eastern collections.

The Wall

At the present rate of progress you will find hardly any remains of what used to be Berlin's most startling tourist attraction. After German reunification, international investors speedily bought up the land around the Wall. So what was left by souvenir-hunters after attack by hammer and chisel was pretty well finished off by bulldozers. Touts sell pieces of the Wall all over Berlin, especially round the Brandenburg Gate (the best souvenirs are the bits of coloured concrete with graffiti on them). The thrill of watching the barriers close behind you at Checkpoint Charlie and wondering if you'll get back again has gone for ever.

If you didn't see Berlin before the Wall came down, it is hard to imagine what an extraordinary phenomenon it was. With the Great Wall of China in mind, the Berlin version may have come as rather a disappointment. It zigzagged round West Berlin for 99 miles, but was only about 13 feet high, and dwarfed by the tall buildings on either side. It was a dreary slab of concrete with a rounded top, smothered with graffiti on the Western side. In some parts of the city it was a high, electrified fence rather than a wall. It was only when you looked over the wall from one of the special viewing platforms that you could see what a daunting barrier it was.

A strip of raked sand, concrete and grass separated the Wall from its partner on the Eastern side. Between it armed border guards stared from white watchtowers bristling with search-lights. To get across, you had to brave dog-runs, electrified tripwires, tanktraps and landmines. For many people, the challenge was irresistible. The **Checkpoint Charlie Museum** gives a vivid, if partisan, history of the Wall, with accounts of many audacious and ingenious escape schemes. By the Reichstag a line of simple crosses commemorates the escapees who didn't make it.

If you want to see parts of the original Wall there is still one section remaining opposite the Hauptbahnhof (main railway station) in eastern Berlin. This part has been preserved because of its unique graffiti and paintings – for example, Gorbachev kissing Honecker!

OTHER PLACES TO VISIT

Tiergarten There are several interesting museums near the Berlin Philharmonic Orchestra's home at the east end of the Tiergarten park, only a short distance from Potsdamer Platz. In the **National Gallery** there's a fine permanent collection of nineteenth-century art, including Impressionists, and modern exhibitions upstairs, all housed in a streamlined building by Mies van der Rohe.

The **Arts and Crafts Museum** (Kunstgewerbemuseum) has an extensive and impressive array of decorative arts: ceramics, gold and silverwork, tapestries, furniture, glass, and so on. The

Musical Instruments Museum is connected to the nearby home of the Philharmonic.

Grunewald and the Wannsee (Take the S-Bahn to Wannsee) Beaches, islands, marinas and forests come as a surprise in Berlin's circumscribed territory. The playgrounds on the western flank of the city are lakes and woods. Wide bits of the River Havel attempt a seaside illusion with imported sand and ocean-going boats. You can take boat trips on the lakes and visit the islands. Peacock Island has a small eighteenth-century folly and landscaped gardens (open April to October).

Carefully marked paths lead through the woods, where there are wild boar and rabid foxes. But mostly all you see are earnest joggers. Over the stern iron struts of the Glienicke Bridge the spies of John Le Carré novels (sometimes real spies too) used to come in from the cold.

Spandau The prison that once made this part of Berlin famous was demolished when Rudolph Hess died in 1987. You can still see the sixteenth-century citadel and part of the castle keep and a few remnants of the old town, a rare glimpse of what Berlin was like before the bombs fell.

Lübars An old village of half-timbered houses lies on the northern outskirts of Berlin. Here you can walk or ride (there are stables everywhere) through open fields and meadows.

Excursion

Potsdam This small town is now effectively the federal capital of Brandenburg. It's outside the city boundary, about 12 miles to the south-west, in former East Germany. There are guided coach tours or you can take the S-Bahn.

Potsdam used to be the summer retreat of the Prussian kings, and, although it was damaged during the war and suffers from depressing concrete socialist architecture, there are still many old houses and villas that are now being renovated.

The star attraction on all the tour itineraries is Frederick the Great's eighteenth-century **Sans Souci Palace**, with its wonderful ceilings of spider's-web gilding, marquetry work and wood carving. Even better is the grotto of the **Neue Palais**. The walls and ceilings are covered with thousands of different minerals and millions of shells clustered in fantastic swathes, festoons and sea monsters. Both palaces have fine furniture and ceramic displays.

SHOPPING

Berlin's biggest department store is KaDeWe, near the Europa-Center. What looks like a million different types of sausage are on sale in the delicatessen section. There's plenty to buy on or near the Ku'damm – including clothes, antiques, porcelain, cutlery, linen, toys and records – but many shops are expensive and touristy.

Berlin has several interesting markets. On Sunday mornings the open-air flea market is in full swing on Strasse des 17 Juni. You need plenty of Deutschmarks for the trench-coats, art nouveau glass and porcelain, mild erotica and Turkish rugs on sale, but the spectacle is lively.

In eastern Berlin many shops have been refurbished and are now under the aegis of West German companies selling Western consumer goods.

EATING AND DRINKING

Among Berlin's enormous range of restaurants, only a handful are actually German in style. Berlin's home-grown speciality is an *Eisbein*: a large piece of boiled pig embedded in a layer of pallid fat. It usually appears with sauerkraut or mushy peas and dumplings, but tastes a little better than it sounds. *Königsberger Klopse* are meatballs in a cream and caper sauce. Other dishes to ring the changes are *Schnitzels*, chops, steaks and stews, often drenched in thick, creamy sauces, with noodles or *Rösti* on the side. There's excellent Italian food at Ponte Vecchio, Spielhagen-strasse 3 (dinner only).

Berlin's bars (*Kneipen*) have an authentic German flavour. Beer *vom Fass* (on draught) is much cheaper than bottled beers, and there's a huge range. Chasers of *Schnapps* and *Apfelkorn* (apple liqueur) are a popular variation. For a local tipple you might try a *Weisse Berliner mit Schuss* – beer with a dash of raspberry juice. The casual but civilised SpreeGarten, in Uhlandstrasse, has Jacobean-style blackened panelling with barley-sugar pillars and grotesquely carved figures, and serves a huge array of beers and well-prepared food.

If you're happy with fast food you can eat reasonably cheaply in Berlin. A snack of the excellent local *Bratwurst* and beer or *Glühwein* (mulled wine with spices) at a stand-up *Imbiss* bar is easy on the pocket. The German idea of a hot dog is a world away from ours. There are masses of fast-food cafés and bars in the

Europa-Center (Mövenpick has a good reputation for ice-cream and buffets). The food in the restaurant at the top (i-Punkt) is unremarkable, but the views are splendid.

Coffee and cakes are not cheap, but are an ideal excuse to rest your feet after a tiring afternoon's sightseeing. The Kranzler Café, on Ku'damm, is a pre-war institution which moved to its present site from an original home in the East. It serves expensive coffee and cakes, and full meals, in smart surroundings.

NIGHTLIFE

At night there's still more than a hint of *Cabaret* about Berlin. Drag-shows, café-theatres and ephemerally modish bars are the places to be seen in. You can find everything from classical music to the most avant-garde in films, fashion, design and architecture, and some pretty sleazy stuff besides. Berlin's cosmopolitan, heterodox population and traditional radicalism produce a steady hum of new ideas. If you're interested in the traditional variety theatre made famous by Berlin in the 'wild' 1920s, see the splendid show in the Wintergarten in Potsdamerstrasse.

Opera is a highlight. There are over 30 theatres, some firmly on the fringe. Berlin is a great place for films, as its International Film Festival (in February) indicates. You can see films in English in some of the Ku'damm cinemas, though most are dubbed. The Odeon on Hauptstrasse is a specialist English-language film cinema.

HOTELS

Because the city is so large, and the sights so spread out, try to stay somewhere within walking distance of a U-Bahn or S-Bahn station. In western Berlin, most hotels are close to the busy Kurfürstendamm and Zoo, the liveliest, smartest but most expensive bit of the city. Traffic noise can be a problem. The quieter side-streets offer pleasant *pensions* and smaller hotels with some character.

Hotel beds are in short supply at certain times of year, especially during the Film Festival and other major events. The tourist office can usually find you a room with a Berlin family.

ALSTERHOF RINGHOTEL
Augsburger Strasse 5, 30　　　　　*Tel: 21 24 20　Fax: 21 83 949*

No beauty from outside, but inside the Alsterhof is quiet and comfortable; modern but less impersonal than many Berlin hotels. The ground floor has terracotta décor and subdued ceiling spotlights. Downstairs is a smartly designed modern restaurant and bar area, with a pleasant glazed conservatory letting in the light from a courtyard. Rooms are super clean and well equipped, if conventionally furnished.

Bedrooms: 136, half with bath/WC, half with shower/WC; all with mini-bar; trouser press　**Facilities:** Lift; restaurant; indoor heated pool; sauna; solarium; guarded parking　**Credit/charge cards accepted:** All

BRISTOL KEMPINSKI
Ku'damm 27, 15　　　　　*Tel: 884 34 734　Fax: 884 34 870*

This is the poshest of Berlin's hotels, on the Ku'damm corner of smart Fasanenstrasse. It's part of an international chain, with all that that implies. The atmosphere is hushed and serene, as the hotel is shielded from the traffic noise by careful insulation. The furnishings in the plush-carpeted public rooms are conservative, suave, in places almost stern. The bedrooms, renovated in 1992, include many suites, all comfortable enough to use as sitting-rooms if the lounges seem too formal for total relaxation. There are two international restaurants.

Bedrooms: 315, all with bath/shower/WC; air-conditioning; mini-bar
Facilities: Lift; restaurants; private parking; indoor heated pool; gym; sauna; massage; solarium; hairdresser; beauty salon　**Credit/charge cards accepted:** All

DITTBERNER
Wielandstrasse 26, 15　　　　　*Tel: 881 64 85*

The Dittberner is a quaint, old-fashioned, upper-floor *pension* down a side-street off the Ku'damm, reached by a creaking lift. This is a delightful unpackaged experience of Berlin, run by Frau Lange with character, style and sophistication. It is full of interesting pictures, plants and mementoes of a much-travelled life. Furnishings are traditional and many period features of pre-war Berlin are still intact. Bedrooms vary greatly in style and size.

Bedrooms: 21, some with shower/WC, some with bath/WC, some with shower only, some without bathroom; 3 with TV　**Facilities:** Lift
Credit/charge cards accepted: None

MARITIM GRAND

Friedrichstrasse 158-164 Tel: 232 73 500   Fax: 232 73 221

This luxury hotel is very expensive, but very comfortable, a clever pastiche of nineteenth-century elegance – chandeliers, marble and an eye-catching airy stairwell. Even if you're not staying, the hotel is a good place to rest your feet.

Bedrooms: 349, all with bath/WC; air-conditioning; hair-dryer; mini-bar
Facilities: Lift; restaurants; indoor heated pool; sauna; masseur; whirlpool bath; hairdresser; beauty salon; private parking   **Credit/charge cards accepted:** All

RESIDENZ BERLIN

Meinekestrasse 9, 15 Tel: 8 84 43-0   Fax: 882 47 26

At the far end of a central but quiet side-street branching off the Ku'damm, a bit of Berlin that survived the war is the site of Residenz Berlin. The fine exterior of balconies and tall windows still leaves you unprepared for the splendid and startling art nouveau ceiling decorations in the entrance hall. The dining-room, just off the reception area, is particularly elegant in blue, gilt and white, with huge textured mirrors reflecting flower displays. Period details are carefully preserved throughout. There's a small attractive bar area with limited seating; otherwise no lounge. Staff are pleasant, easy-going and speak English.

Bedrooms: 88, most with shower/WC, some with bath/WC; all with air-conditioning; mini-bar   **Facilities:** Lift; restaurant; bar   **Credit/charge cards accepted:** All

SCHWEIZERHOF INTERCONTINENTAL

Budapester Strasse 21-31, 30 Tel: 2 69 60   Fax: 2 69 69-00

At the top end of the package price range, but still good value, this hotel is central, a stone's throw from the Ku'damm, but on a quieter street behind the zoo. The lobby leads into a series of spacious lounges and bars with pianists where smart folk linger over cocktails. Beyond is a cheerful and less awesome *Bierstube* in rustic style. There are two formal restaurants. In one a vast array of buffet dishes makes breakfast last a long time. Bedrooms are exceptionally well thought-out, comfortable and sensibly equipped.

Bedrooms: 430, all with bath/shower/WC; air-conditioning; mini-bar
Facilities: Lift; restaurants; indoor heated pool; gym; masseur; private parking   **Credit/charge cards accepted:** All

SEEHOF ♦♦♦♦♦
Lietzensee-Ufer 11, 19 *Tel: 3 20 02-0 Fax: 3 20 02-251*

A smart, comfortable and stylish hotel in a quiet side-street near the
Congress Center in Charlottenburg. The blue-and-white chequerboard
exterior may not entice, but once you're inside, the atmosphere is
civilised and peaceful. Back bedrooms and the pink, light restaurant
overlook a terrace, where you can dine in summer, and a small lake
beyond. Transport links to the centre are good. A couple of small single
rooms have no bath or shower, which means you will have to shower by
the swimming-pool! Berliners, however, are unmoved by such things.

Bedrooms: 78, most with bath/WC, a couple with no bathroom (*see text*);
all with mini-bar   **Facilities:** Lift; restaurant; indoor heated pool; sauna;
solarium; private parking   **Credit/charge cards accepted:** All

AM ZOO ♦♦♦♦♦
Ku'damm 25, 15 *Tel: 8 84 37-0 Fax: 8 84 37-714*

A well-kept central hotel, in an excellent position on the Ku'damm. It has
style – a modern, slightly arty touch – and bedrooms are very comfortable
and sensibly equipped. It makes an excellent base for a short-break visitor
who wants to try local restaurants rather than hotel food. The breakfast
(included in the room price) is a good way to stoke up for a hard day of
Berlin sightseeing. Despite its location a surprising number of rooms have
interior views over a tidy little courtyard, and no traffic noise.

Bedrooms: 136, some with bath/WC, rest with shower/WC; all with
hair-dryer; mini-bar   **Facilities:** Lift   **Credit/charge cards accepted:** All

Hotel prices Symbols indicate approximate prices per room
per night for a double room with bath. Many large hotels run
special breaks which work out far cheaper. (See page 14 for
further details.)

♦ = under £50; ♦♦ = £50 to £80; ♦♦♦ = £80 to £100;
♦♦♦♦ = £100 to £140; ♦♦♦♦♦ = over £140.

BRUGES

- This is a showpiece little Belgian city where, within the central walls, the medieval character has been well preserved. A view of the gabled rooftops from the Belfry is a must
- Waffles, chocolates and lace – the Brugean specialities – sum up the more frivolous aspects of the city
- Whether you travel by foot, bicycle, canal boat or horse and carriage, most of the sights can be seen in two or three days
- There are many very high-quality restaurants in the city centre, though they're not cheap

TWENTIETH-CENTURY Bruges is a city stuck in a time-warp. As you wander through the cobbled streets, the carefully preserved enchantment of the Middle Ages surrounds you like a sanitised theme park reconstruction. The skyline bristles with slim wrought-iron crosses on spindly church spires, and fairy-tale turrets with fish-scale tiling and spiky crenellations decorate the roofs of the Town Hall and the Courts of Justice. In the central streets of Dijver and Gruuthusestraat the houses are built of narrow, red, medieval brick; and arched bridges solidly straddle the ancient waterways. Blinkered horses pull carriages from Burg Square, their hooves sparking on the cobbles, and small open-topped motorboats carry tourists on the canals. A busker dressed as a medieval jester juggles or plays the violin and the carillon in the Belfry strikes a cheerfully haphazard quarter-hour.

Bruges was originally built as a ninth-century fortress on the present site of the central square called the Burg. In Blinde Ezelstraat (Blind Donkey Alley), you can see the remains of a hinge – part of the gate that once enclosed the tiny town. As the city prospered, it expanded around the central stronghold. The medieval maps of Bruges, on display in the Town Hall, show a circular walled city with six gates, surrounded by a double canal. It is not so very different today. You can trace the oval shape of the old fortifications (although the walls no longer exist) now defined by the canals that girdle the city. Four of the old town gates can still be seen, and the Ghent Gate and Blacksmith's Gate still act as entry points for traffic coming into and out of the city. The River Reie, which flows through the city, once connected with the now silted-up River Zwin, which linked Bruges to Damme – formerly a thriving port – and the North Sea.

The fourteenth and fifteenth centuries saw the golden age of Bruges. Skills in manufacturing high-quality cloth led to the growth of Bruges as a trading centre on a route between northern Italy and England, with a population as big as London's. By the early fourteenth century, the people of Bruges ceased travelling to sell their wares abroad and found they could make a good living by staying at home and specialising in warehousing and brokerage between foreign merchants visiting their city. When the powerful Dukes of Burgundy gained control over large areas of the Low Countries, Bruges reached its greatest prosperity, and echoed the splendour of the Burgundian court, which was the envy of all Europe. In 1430 Philip the Good founded in Bruges the famous Order of the Golden Fleece as a symbol of the power of the House of Burgundy. The heyday of Flemish art – which produced masterpieces by Jan van Eyck, Rogier van der Weyden and Hans Memling – was Burgundian court art.

Each merchant or nobleman wanted a house that was more impressive than his neighbour's – and so every building is different: a triangular gable next to a stepped one, an imposing square house with elegant windows next to a tall narrow one, each storey jutting out a little further into the street. To the east, in the Jan Van Eyckplein and along the Spiegelrei, the jumble of façades reflects in the still water of the canal.

In the quiet residential areas of Snaggaardstraat and Carmersstraat, further north, houses are just as varied: some have window boxes laden with geraniums, others have decorative roundels or bird motifs – pelicans or swans with beaks of gold – and some the heraldic shields of local trade guilds. Statues of the Madonna appear high on street corners, in glass boxes and in tiny alcoves. Curtains of local lace, with intricate flower designs, decorate windows.

To the south of the two central squares, the Burg and the Markt, lie the oldest houses, their walls made mossy by the canals that lap them. Formerly made of wood, the façades were replaced by brick after continual fires led to a ban on the use of wood for building. To get an idea of the thin slatted planks that were used originally, visit No 7 Genthof (it's marked, like other historical buildings, with a small blue and white symbol).

A folk museum has been created in a smartened row of tiny almshouses (*Godshuizen*), which were set up for the poor and elderly and run by the citizens and trade guilds. Many of these *Godshuizen* still house the tiny communities, such as the one in Noordstraat. Leafy squares to hunt out include Huidenvettersplein and Simon Stevinplein.

Like Venice, Bruges was simply neglected because there was no money for modernisation after its slow financial decline after the sixteenth century. Unlike Venice, Bruges is not dependent on tourists for its survival. With the digging of the Boudewijn Canal and the development of Zeebrugge at the end of the nineteenth century, trading links were revived. However, the old-world atmosphere is strenuously preserved and even reconstructed by the citizens of Bruges for themselves and their visitors. Modern street lighting has been replaced by romantic, old-style lamps, and Tarmac by cobbles. Today, houses are mostly built in a faithful imitation of medieval style. Draped down the shopping streets of Steenstraat and Noordzandstraat running westwards from the centre are colourful banners, a reminder of the medieval custom of addressing houses not with numbers but with pictures: a windmill, a rose, a swan, a fleur-de-lis. In the central Markt, once the scene of gallows and guillotine, the outsize Belfry overlooks flags depicting rampant lions in reds and yellows.

Occasionally in winter the canals freeze over and skaters take to the ice. With the pale light and bare trees the scene is reminiscent of a Bruegel painting. This is a popular time for tourists, who can enjoy the many museums without the summer crowds. But even in high season it's possible to escape the crush: in the quiet backwaters of the Pottenmarkersstraat, or the canal-backed gardens. To the south, the Beguinage entices the tourists into the spiritual peace of its shaded garden; and nearby, the open spaces of the city – the Minnewaterpark and Koningin Astridpark – are excellent picnic spots.

WHEN TO GO

Bruges is popular almost all year round, and if the weather is bad there are plenty of museums to visit. A few hotels close in January or February. From March onwards Bruges becomes crowded, and in summer it can be packed. An attractive time to visit is in early spring (when there are daffodils in the Beguinage) or in autumn. Bruges has many festivals, including the Festival van Flanderen (classical music), which is held at the end of July and beginning of August. On Ascension Day, the lively and colourful Procession of the Holy Blood commemorates the triumphal return of the Count of Flanders from the Crusades.

MASTERING THE SYSTEM

Information The Belgian Tourist Office in the UK is at Premier House, 2 Gayton Road, Harrow HA1 2XU, tel: 081-861 3300, Monday to Friday 9am to 5pm. The main tourist office in Bruges is at 11 Burg, tel: 448686, in the central square; there's also a smaller one at the railway station. For a few pence you can buy a useful tourist map which indicates the main sights and gives practical information. The tourist office can supply tickets for various summer festivals and events, and there is a reservation desk for on-the-spot hotel bookings (you pay a deposit which is refunded when you pay your hotel bill). It's worth getting the free monthly news-sheet *Agenda Brugge*, and guidebooks to Bruges (in English) are sold too.

Maps The Bruges tourist office provides an excellent street plan of central Bruges with all the main tourist attractions marked and briefly described. A large-scale street map (1:7,000) by Geocart is

GETTING THERE

Going independently

By air Brussels is the nearest airport to Bruges; it's only an hour away by rail and there are trains at least every hour from Brussels Nord and Central Stations. The single train fare to Bruges costs around £6. Flying to Brussels is easy, with a good choice of direct flights from 11 UK airports. British Airways and Sabena each have several flights a day from Heathrow. As the route is primarily a business one, however, there is a much-reduced service at weekends, and not all airports have flights coming back from Brussels on Sunday. APEX fares (book 7 or 14 days in advance) or SuperPEX fares are generally cheapest, and you can fly from London to Brussels and back for less than £100 (fares from regional airports are higher). There's no seasonal variation in fares. It's worth checking fares with Euro Express (0444 235678), Holidaymaker (081-664 1234), Air UK (0345 666777), Hamilton (071-287 2425) and Infocus Leisure (081-332 1221).

By sea The shortest sea crossing is the Dover/Calais route: 35 minutes by hovercraft or Sea Cat or 75 minutes by ferry. Hoverspeed's City Sprint service (081-554 7061) by hovercraft or Sea Cat and coach is much cheaper than flying (£50 at the time of writing). The main road from Calais (70 miles to Bruges) is busy in high season. Bruges is only 15 miles from Ostend and 9 from Zeebrugge. The Dover/Ostend route takes four hours; Felixstowe/Zeebrugge just under seven. P&O's 72-hour and five-day short-stay fares for the Felixstowe crossing are good value (from just over £30 for a foot passenger five-day return) and give you enough time to see the sights. For around £20 more you can take the comfortable jetfoil service (it doesn't take cars) from Dover to Ostend, which cuts the sea crossing to 100 minutes. The Belgian ports of Ostend and Zeebrugge are both only a 15-minute train ride from Bruges.

Bruges Station This is on the southern outskirts of the city, and you won't see anything of your destination until you leave the confusing maze of roads that surrounds it. There are taxis and frequent buses (marked 'Centrum') to the centre.

Tour operator packages

Bruges is a popular city for short breaks and is included in many brochures. Typical packages are for two, three or four nights with travel by scheduled flights, although some operators also offer the cheaper options of getting to Bruges by rail and ferry, hovercraft or jetfoil. Packages using flights from regional UK airports are available, too. High season is usually April to October, but prices on the whole don't vary greatly throughout the year. Typical cost in 1992 for three nights' B&B in a three-star hotel was around £150 by rail/coach and from under £200 by air. These prices include the return rail fare from Brussels Airport to Bruges. For a list of tour operators see page 385.

called *Bruges* (£4.50). A map of the whole city by Falk, again called *Bruges* (1:15,000), also has an inset of central Bruges (£4.95).

Museum tickets If you plan to visit lots of museums it's worth buying a museum card. A blue card allows you entry into the big four – the Groeninge, Memling, Gruuthuse and Brangwyn museums – and saves you around 15 per cent. The combination ticket is available from the tourist office or the museums. Labelling of exhibits in English is often poor or non-existent, so it's worth being equipped with a guidebook.

Sightseeing tours A half-hour **canal boat** tour is recommended (daily March to November, weekends and holidays December to February, 10am to 6pm). The pick-up points are marked with an anchor on the tourist office map and there are plenty of boats which depart as soon as enough tourists turn up. Guides speaking many languages give a cursory guided tour. Evening trips are sometimes arranged for groups. **Walking tours** leave from the main tourist office at the Burg in July and August (around £2 per person). You can also hire an official guide for an independent ramble around the city (just under £20 for two hours).

Short sightseeing trips (50 minutes, £6) by **minibus** leave the Markt in front of the Belfry every hour (10am to 7pm in summer, 11am to 2pm in winter); the commentary is in seven languages.

Changing money Most banks are open Monday to Friday, 9am to noon, 2pm to 4.45pm; some are open on Saturday morning. Bureaux de change are open longer (some until 10pm in the summer).

Opening hours and days Shops are generally open from 9am to 6pm (late-night shopping is Friday). Market day is Wednesday (7am to 1pm on Burg Square). During the winter (beginning of October to the end of March) the main museums are closed on Tuesday, and the Memling Museum and the Museum of Our Lady of the Potterie are closed on Wednesday, too. Museums also have shorter admission periods than in the summer. Most close between noon and 2pm throughout the year. Visitors are not allowed into churches during Sunday services. Details of admission times and prices are included on the tourist office map.

GETTING AROUND

The best way to see Bruges is on foot – it's important to have a sturdy pair of walking shoes, as most of the streets in the centre are cobbled. There are many little back streets which are delightful to walk along and are relatively crowd-free.

Horse-drawn cabs are a romantic way of seeing the town. The cabbies are generally fluent in English and point out the historical parts of town as you trundle along. A circular tour of about half an hour costs around £13 per cab; longer trips can also be made.

Bicycles can be hired from Het Koffieboontje, Hallestraat 4 and from Eric Popelier, Hallestraat 14. On the green embankments that mark the outer limits of the old part of the town, you can escape the bone-shaking cobbles. There are also two companies that organise bicycle tours of Bruges and the surrounding Flemish villages. Ask at the tourist office for departure points.

UNMISSABLES

The Burg
A visit to Bruges should begin in the Burg, the central pedestrianised square. The ninth-century fortress was built here, and this site is still the city's nerve-centre, housing the Town Hall, Courts of Justice and former Recorder's House. Groups of camera-clicking tourists gather on the cobbles to admire the Gothic façade of the fourteenth-century **Town Hall** (the oldest in Belgium). Inside, you can visit the council room and admire the superb wooden Gothic ceiling with five hanging arches. There is a small minstrels' gallery and nineteenth-century wall paintings depicting medieval scenes of Bruges. A tiny museum displays early maps and seals of the city.

In the south-west corner of the square lies the **Basilica of the Holy Blood**. Its lower chapel is a fine example of early Romanesque architecture, with a twelfth-century stone relief showing the Baptism of Christ. The predominantly Gothic upper chapel has an unusual globe-shaped pulpit carved in 1728 from a piece of oak. An adjacent room displays religious treasures.

All over Bruges you will see fine fireplaces, but none as large and impressive as that in the **Brugse Vrije Museum**, which forms part of the Courts of Justice. An elaborately carved tribute to Charles V, it is so vast that there are copper rings for people to hang on to when warming themselves.

The Belfry
Climbing the 366 winding stairs of the Belfry, which stands incongruously high above the old market halls of the central **Markt** square, is one way to keep fit. Fifty-five steps take you to the treasury room, where thirteenth-century official documents were contained in heavy chests and locked behind intricate

wrought-iron gates. Each gate had nine locks, so the burgomaster and the eight deacons of the trade guilds – each with one key – had all to be present when the documents were removed.

Two hundred and seventy-eight steps later, now in the wooden part of the tower, you will arrive at the drum of the carillon – like the giant innards of an old music box – which consists of 47 bells producing a four-octave range. It works purely by weights. A *carillonneur* gives recitals three days a week (four in summer) – best heard from the Dijver canalside.

The Groeninge Museum

The main art gallery of Bruges is set in a pretty garden (on the site of an Augustine convent), and houses notable collections of Flemish paintings, including many masterpieces of the fifteenth century. Jan van Eyck's *Madonna with St Donatian and St George* includes a masterly and realistic portrait of the donor, Canon van der Paele. *The Judgement of Cambyses* by Gerard David depicts skinners stripping the leg of the corrupt judge Sisamnes with unmoved concentration. An altarpiece, *The Last Judgement* by Hieronymus Bosch, has grim scenes of grotesque deaths. Other artists well represented include Hans Memling, Jan Provoost, Peter Pourbus and Pieter Bruegel the Younger. The collections also include nineteenth- and early twentieth-century works.

The Memling Museum

Six of Hans Memling's paintings are displayed in the fifteenth-century chapel of the Hospital of Saint John. Born in Seligenstadt, Memling – like other artists – was attracted to the prosperous city of fifteenth-century Bruges with its many wealthy patrons, and spent 30 years working there. It is said he was nursed at the hospital after being wounded during wars in France and donated several of his pictures in thanks. Today, the collection includes the famous *Reliquary of St Ursula*, an oak casket on which her life is portrayed in a series of intricate miniature panels.

The thirteenth- and fourteenth-century former hospital buildings consist of large halls where patients were confined in three-sided beds. Old portraits and photos of stern-faced nurses suggest it was run with a firm hand. The former dispensary was in use until the 1970s.

The Church of Our Lady

The early Gothic Onze Lieve Vrouwekerk has the highest spire (122 metres) in the city, and its light interior houses some fine works of art, in particular a sculpture of the *Madonna and Child* by Michelangelo, carved from a single block of white marble. It is one of the artist's early pieces (dating from the same period as his *David*). Set against a black background, it is a moving sight: the Madonna – her faraway expression reminiscent of the famous *Pietà* in Rome – guards against the baby slipping off her lap with a gently restraining maternal hand.

You can visit the tombs of Charles the Bold and his daughter, Mary of Burgundy, in the main choir. On the walls of the tombs are simple but bold frescoes, like children's drawings of the Crucifixion.

The Beguinage
The horse-drawn carriages wait by the horse's-head fountain, while visitors walk past the weeping willow that trails over the bridge leading to the peaceful Beguinage. It was founded in the thirteenth century as a convent community of beguines, a religious order for women, and is now inhabited by Benedictine nuns. At the door, a notice requests visitors to keep a 'worthy and reflected attitude'. The tree-shaded, grassy courtyard surrounded by attractive whitewashed houses still retains a spiritual atmosphere. By the entrance is a tiny museum which depicts the life of a beguine: you can see an old kitchen with Delft-tiled fireplace, and a little garden, its path in the shape of a cross.

OTHER PLACES TO VISIT

Folklore Museum Here is a nostalgic record of times past, with faithful reconstructions of various shops (apothecary, barrel-maker, grocer, shoemaker) and a schoolroom with slates and abacuses. There's even an old-world bar where you can have a drink at the end of the visit.

Gruuthuse Museum The museum is housed in a large fifteenth-century mansion built by Louis de Bruges, lieutenant-general for Charles the Bold. In the fine rooms are badly labelled displays of furniture, musical instruments, lace, weapons, irons and enough spinning wheels to make Sleeping Beauty shudder. From the south wing a private prayer gallery overlooks the choir of the Church of Our Lady.

Lace Centre (Kant Centrum) Lace-making is one of the oldest of Bruges' industries. Before you buy a lace souvenir, visit the Lace Centre: here you can see the huge variety of traditional lace patterns, each with a name like 'Chantilly' or 'Valenciennes', as well as having an introduction to the modern art of lace-making. After you've seen the end product, pay a visit to the lace school (around the corner in Balstraat), where children and adults pore over their bobbins, seemingly oblivious to the curious tourists wandering in and out. For the really enthusiastic, there is a lace shop (at No 11) where you can buy your own kit.

Church of Jerusalem While you're in the area, try to see this unusual fifteenth-century church, built to the plan of the Church of the Holy Sepulchre in Jerusalem. There's some fine stained glass, and a striking altarpiece from which a skull gapes, surrounded by instruments of torture.

Organ Museum Exhibits range from the humble wind-up gramophone, through electric pianos, to monstrous organs the size of lorries, lavishly decorated with sickly motifs. If you're lucky, you'll catch one playing a fairground waltz. Don't be surprised to see elderly visitors from a coach tour whirling around the wooden dance floor.

Excursion

Damme Once the important foreport of Bruges, now humbled into making money from waffle-hungry tourists, Damme still makes a good outing, even if it's just a brief visit. The little there is to see is in the Kerkstraat, which cuts a cobbled line through the centre. There is a tourist office (tel: 353219, near the Gothic town hall) which can direct you to the Church of Our Lady, the St John's Hospital Museum or the Til Uilenspiegel Museum. But most visitors just come for lunch. A steamboat runs between Bruges and Damme (35 minutes) daily in summer (April to end September).

SHOPPING

Bruges has many tempting shops; the most obvious souvenirs are the delicious hand-made Belgian chocolates and Bruges lace. This is traditionally cream or white and comes in many shapes and sizes, from tiny butterflies, bookmarks and handkerchiefs to lacy blouses and formal tablecloths. It's highly priced, although you can appreciate why it's expensive once you've seen the lace-making demonstration at the Lace Centre. Cheaper items are likely to be Far Eastern imports. The Lace Centre sells hand-made lace, as do many specialist shops in the centre of town.

The main shopping streets, with many smart shoe and clothes shops, radiate from the Markt. Off the Zuidzandstraat and Steenstraat there are shopping galleries, too. For more local food shops, as well as some antique shops, try the Langestraat and St Jacobstraat.

On Saturday, there is a large market on 't Zand selling vegetables, fruit and flowers, as well as clothes and leather goods.

EATING AND DRINKING

Eating out in Bruges can be a costly business. There are many restaurants from which to choose and they generally look appealing and comfortable with an old-world cosiness, but the food can be monotonous and average. At the top end of the market there are a few excellent and beautiful, though expensive, places.

Rather than typically Brugean dishes you'll find a large variety of Flemish specialities, and some rich French cooking making much use of butter and cream. Mussels and eels are popular and usually very tasty; fish is plentiful. Flemish stews such as *waterzooi* (chicken or fish boiled with herbs and vegetables), *hutsepot* (hotpot) or *carbonnade flamande* (beef stewed in beer) are usually good; other specialities include chicory and smoked ham.

For traditional starched tablecloths and candlelight glowing in copper pots on the walls, try De Postiljon at Katelijnestraat 3. They serve good unfussy food, and you sit among locals as well as tourists.

Other restaurants worth trying for a romantic, bistro-style atmosphere are Breydel De Coninck at Breidelstraat 24, where the house speciality is mussels served in a large saucepan; or De Visscherie, Vismarkt 8, not surprisingly, famous for fish.

At the top of the range, De Karmeliet, Jeruzalemstraat 1, is very formal, serving excellent and highly original *nouvelle cuisine* in generous portions; and Vasquez, Zilverstraat 38, is similar in style and set in a fine fifteenth-century house – with a small courtyard for drinks. The elegant Duc de Bourgogne (*see 'Hotels'*) has a beautiful waterside location.

You can find delicious snacks. The great Belgian national dish – chips and mayonnaise – is widely available. In the centre there are plenty of street cafés and tea-rooms in which to recover from sightseeing. They offer a mouthwatering variety of pancakes, waffles and diet-wrecking cakes.

Beer is taken extremely seriously in Bruges, as in the whole of Belgium. If you ask to see the list of available brews in a café, it may take you a while to read it. Try Het Brugs Beertje at

Kemelstraat 5, where there are more than 300 different types of beer available. Locally brewed beers include the light Straffe Hendrik and Brugges Tipfel.

NIGHTLIFE

Nightlife in Bruges centres around a meal and a stroll on the cobbled streets and floodlit canals. For anything livelier, the Fiermarkt offers discos and crowded bars. On summer evenings, four times a week, there's an hour-long carillon performance. From Easter to October the Bruges puppet theatre in St Jacobstraat presents evening performances of famous operas.

HOTELS

Central Bruges has many small hotels, all within walking distance of the main sights, shops and restaurants. Canalside hotels are attractive, although front rooms can be noisy because of traffic on the cobbled roads. Most hotels serve breakfast only, but there are many restaurants scattered throughout the centre of the city. Most of the hotels mentioned are within the inner ring of canals.

AZALEA   ♦♦♦
Wülfhagestraat 43   *Tel: 33 14 78 Fax: 33 97 00*

The Azalea is a converted fourteenth-century house. The lobby is dominated by a superb wooden staircase with wrought-iron handrails, which winds up to the higher floors with no apparent means of support. The bedrooms are modernised but have antique furniture. The front sitting-room is an elegant period room with tapestry upholstered chairs. Outside, a garden patio shaded by trees faces the canal. A smart hotel with a homely feel, close to the Markt.

Bedrooms: 25, all with bath/shower/WC **Credit/charge cards accepted:** All

---

> ♦ = under £50; ♦♦ = £50 to £80; ♦♦♦ = £80 to £100;
> ♦♦♦♦ = £100 to £140; ♦♦♦♦♦ = over £140.

DE CASTILLION ♦♦♦
Heilige Geestraat 1   *Tel: 34 30 01   Fax: 33 94 75*

This hotel is named after the fifteenth Bishop of Bruges, who lived in the building in 1743. It lies in the shadow of St Salvator's Cathedral along a narrow cobbled street between the t'Zand and the Markt. Much of the hotel is modernised but certain period rooms have been preserved: the Gothic bedroom is a particular favourite with visitors. The art nouveau sitting-room is classic and stylish with gold woodwork, peacock-green furnishings and a stuffed peacock blending into the background. It is predominantly a business hotel.

Bedrooms: 22, half with bath/WC, half with shower/WC; all with mini-bar **Facilities:** Restaurant; gym; sauna; solarium   **Credit/charge cards accepted:** All

DUC DE BOURGOGNE ♦♦♦
Huidenvettersplein 12   *Tel: 33 20 38   Fax: 34 40 37*

Behind the Burg and on the side of the canal, the Duc de Bourgogne faces a square where artists frequently congregate to sell their paintings and tourists queue for boat trips. The hotel is quite dark inside, with wood panelling and old oil paintings. The seventeenth-century restaurant juts out into the junction of two canals, so diners can watch the ducks and boats. Some of the bedrooms are small, but the hotel complements the antique atmosphere of Bruges. A charming hotel in a central location.

Closed: Jan and Jul; restaurant closed Mon, Tue lunch   **Bedrooms:** 10, all with bath/WC; none with TV   **Facilities:** Restaurant   **Credit/charge cards accepted:** All

GROENINGE ♦
Korte-Vuldersstraat 29   *Tel: 34 32 55   Fax: 34 07 69*

Situated in a quiet back-street, the hotel building dates from 1856. The décor in the lounge is formal, with red velvet chairs, brass candelabras, ornate antique mantelpiece clocks and oil paintings on the wall. The bedrooms have overpowering flowery wallpaper in pinks, greens, blues or browns. Only a short distance from the main shopping area and reasonably priced, this is a peaceful retreat from the bustle of the crowds.

Closed: Jan   **Bedrooms:** 8, all with bath/WC; none with TV   **Credit/charge cards accepted:** Access/Mastercard, Amex, Visa

JACOBS ♦
Baliestraat 1 Tel: 33 98 31 Fax: 33 56 94

On the corner of Baliestraat opposite St Gilliskerk, a couple of streets away from the Markt, is the Jacobs Hotel. Its exterior has the typical Brugean small red-brick and stepped gables. The bedrooms are clean, plain and functional. One, on the upper floor, has a bathroom which faces the Belfry and, according to the landlady, has 'one of the best views from the loo in the centre of Bruges'. It is a family-run hotel and the management is very friendly. A good budget option for families or couples.

Closed: Jan **Bedrooms:** 26, most with bath/WC **Facilities:** Lift **Credit/charge cards accepted:** Access, Amex, Visa

RELAIS OUD HUIS AMSTERDAM ♦♦♦
Spiegelrei 3 Tel: 34 18 10 Fax: 33 88 91

Converted from two rambling seventeenth-century houses, this is an elegant canalside hotel with many sitting-rooms that have been kept in their original style. A small garden to the rear of the hotel has modern statues, and garden furniture set out for evening drinks. The bedrooms are large with antique or modern furnishings. It is a moderately expensive hotel with old-world charm.

Bedrooms: 17, all with bath/shower/WC **Facilities:** Lift **Credit/charge cards accepted:** All

PANDHOTEL ♦♦♦
Pandreitje 16 Tel: 34 06 66 Fax: 34 05 56

Mrs Dewaele takes pride in her hotel and, with knowledge gained from many years as a tour guide in Bruges, she has devised special weekend packages including visits to the main sights. The hotel is a fine old town house in a quiet tree-lined street. Great care has been taken to co-ordinate furnishings throughout; bedrooms are individually decorated, and have modern conveniences. A buffet breakfast is served in a bright garden-style room decorated in green, white and yellow.

Bedrooms: 24, some with bath/WC, some with shower/WC; hair-dryer; mini-bar **Facilities:** Lift **Credit/charge cards accepted:** All

PRINSENHOF
Ontvangersstraat 9

Tel: 34 26 90   Fax: 34 23 21

The Prinsenhof is a small, luxurious hotel only a couple of minutes' walk from the Markt, away from the main shopping streets. Antique pieces clutter the small lounge off the reception area. The bedrooms are large and have modern, co-ordinated furnishings in deep blues and pinks. The breakfast room is small but bright and has tasteful period furnishings. The hotel is a member of a group selected for their peaceful and calm atmospheres.

Bedrooms: 16, all with bath/shower/WC; hair-dryer; mini-bar
Facilities: Lift   **Credit/charge cards accepted:** All

DIE SWAENE
Steenhouwersdijk 1

Tel: 34 27 98   Fax: 33 66 74

Voted one of the most romantic hotels in Europe, the Swaene earns its reputation. The hotel overlooks the canal behind the Burg and has a quiet secluded garden to the rear. Bedrooms tend to be large, some packed with antiques. One has a four-poster bed covered in creamy lace. Piano concerts are held downstairs in the lounge where the Tailors' Guild used to meet. The walls are draped in tapestries and the wooden surround of the door is embossed with the arms of local guilds.

Closed: Restaurant closed last two weeks Jan, first two weeks July, Wed and Thurs lunch   **Bedrooms:** 24, all with bath/shower/WC; mini-bar
Facilities: Lift; restaurant   **Credit/charge cards accepted:** All

TER DUINEN
Langerei 52

Tel: 33 04 37   Fax: 34 42 16

A modern-style hotel converted from a late nineteenth-century town house overlooking the canal. Each room is bright and airy and furnished in co-ordinated pastels. Double glazing in the front rooms cuts down the noise of traffic and early-rising ducks. Bedrooms at the back of the hotel are much quieter, the upper-floor rooms have a view of the rooftops. Buffet breakfast is served in an elegant high-ceilinged dining/drawing room. It's a ten-minute walk from the Markt and main shopping areas.

Bedrooms: 18, all with bath/WC   **Facilities:** Lift; restaurant   **Credit/ charge cards accepted:** All

T'VOERMANSHUYS ♦
Oude Burg 14   *Tel: 34 13 96   Fax: 34 23 90*

This is a small family-run hotel situated on a quiet cobbled street. The rooms are plainly furnished with no extra frills; the prices for such a central location are reasonable. Breakfast is served in a bright, street-facing room with a Brugean fireplace made of small red bricks, and Flemish etchings hang on the wall. At the weekend, evening meals can be enjoyed in the restaurant in the sixteenth-century cellar below the hotel.

Closed: Restaurant closed Sat and Sun   **Bedrooms:** 11, most with bath/WC; some with TV   **Facilities:** Lift; restaurant   **Credit/charge cards accepted:** Access, Diners, Visa

---

Hotel prices Symbols indicate approximate prices per room per night for a double room with bath. Many large hotels run special breaks which work out far cheaper. (See page 14 for further details.)

♦ = under £50; ♦♦ = £50 to £80; ♦♦♦ = £80 to £100; ♦♦♦♦ = £100 to £140; ♦♦♦♦♦ = over £140.

BUDAPEST

- Budapest has something to satisfy most tastes – historic sights, hill walks, grand opera, cream cakes in cafés, steam baths and gypsy dances
- By Western standards, the cost of food, shopping and transport is low. Hotels, however, charge Western prices and many demand Western currency – but you can always find private accommodation with a Hungarian family
- German is the second language, but most staff in the bigger hotels and restaurants speak English

UNTIL recent events in Eastern Europe, Hungary was regarded as the most liberal of the Warsaw Pact countries – a place where ruling socialism and backdoor *laissez-faire* capitalism seem to co-exist without too much antagonism. So the trains are clean and run on time, and the platforms and escalators are peppered with advertisements. Fashion on the street – mostly made locally or imported from Poland – wouldn't look out of place in Western Europe, but there are still queues outside the hard-currency Adidas shop.

Budapest was originally two separate towns – Buda and Pest – separated from each other by the Danube. The two were not united politically until 1873, and their diverse historical development means that the two parts still feel very different. The hillier landscape of Buda on the west bank, offering the better defensive position, means that this part developed earlier and so has more of the historical sights. Celtic tribes fortified Gellért Hill in the third century BC, and in the first century AD the Romans set up a military base there. Today the ruined streets, mosaics and baths of Aquinum can still be seen among the flyovers and modern housing blocks of Óbuda, north of Buda.

The Hungarians themselves didn't arrive until the end of the ninth century, after several other tribes, including the Vandals and the Huns, had been, seen, and conquered. King Stephen, Hungary's first king, accepted Christianity and was later canonised – his equestrian statue stands today in front of Matthias Church on Castle Hill in Buda.

Two hundred and fifty years and one Mongol invasion later, King Béla IV began to build the Royal Palace on Castle Hill. He also founded the Church of Our Lady, better known today as the Matthias Church because it was King Matthias who restored the church (in the fifteenth century), added the royal oratory, and married Beatrice of Aragon there. He also expanded the Royal Palace, bringing in Italian artists to complete the decoration, and Buda prospered as a centre of Renaissance culture. After Matthias's death the Turks took advantage of internal squabbles to march in and occupy Buda. Today's public baths – such as Király – are one of the few remaining traces of their 145-year rule.

Liberated from the Turks in 1686 after a series of sieges by Christian allied forces, Hungary then fell under the power of the Habsburgs. Despite widespread dissatisfaction and two unsuccessful wars of independence, both Buda and Pest made great economic progress. Buda was declared the capital of Hungary, Pest's town walls had to be demolished as its population expanded, and in the 1840s the Chain Bridge (Széchenyi Bridge), the first permanent link between the two towns, was built across the Danube (by an English architect, and an English builder, Adam Clark, whose name survives in the 'Clark Ádám' square at the Buda end of the bridge). In 1873 Buda merged with Pest to become the Austro-Hungarian Empire's second capital.

Today, Pest is almost entirely a legacy of the drastic reconstruction that took place in the run-up to Hungary's millennium celebrations in 1896. Inspired by Parisian boulevards, the town planners tore everything down and started again. Nagykörút, or the Great Boulevard, sweeps in a great semi-circle, connecting Margit Bridge in the north to Petőfi Bridge in the south. Kiskörút, or Little Boulevard, links Széchenyi Bridge in the north to Szabadság Bridge in the south. The two remaining relics of the ancient core of the inner city are the Inner City Parish Church, with its baroque façade and Gothic chancel, and the Százéves (Hundred Years) restaurant, which is actually over 150 years old and the oldest restaurant in Budapest. But most of the grand apartment blocks lining the Great Boulevard date from the end of the nineteenth century: 251 were pulled down and replaced by 253 much larger blocks, with plaster ornamentation and inner courtyards.

During the Second World War both Buda and Pest suffered extremely serious damage when the 'liberating' Soviet army ousted the occupying Nazi troops. All the bridges across the Danube were demolished, and only one in four buildings survived intact. Both the Matthias Church and the Royal Palace had to be extensively reconstructed. In the Jewish quarter in Pest around Király utca you can still see the bullet holes in the walls of the apartment buildings.

For tourists, the main sightseeing area is around Castle Hill in Buda. From the museums and grandiose bronze statues in the stately Royal Palace you can stroll along cobbled streets lined with restored ochre and cream medieval and baroque houses to Szentháromság tér (Trinity Square). Here the Matthias Church stands, part of a grouping that includes the glass-clad Hilton Hotel and the Disney-ish turrets and walkways of the Fishermen's Bastion – apparently built to commemorate local fishermen who helped defend the hill in the eighteenth century. Despite the numbers of visitors, Castle Hill retains an air of serenity – probably because most traffic is banned from the area. Away from the main sights the streets become less crowded and you can wander in peace round the Music History Museum housed in a mansion at Táncsics Mikály, and admire the view from the Vienna Gate or from Tóth Árpád Sétány.

Pest, on the other hand, offers a more bustling view of more recent history. The heart of the inner city, enclosed by the Little

Boulevard, is Vörösmarty tér, with Gerbeaud's pâtisserie a reminder of café society days. Today the chandeliered rooms are filled with tourists rather than dowagers and their daughters, but the cakes are just as impressive. The nineteenth-century hotels that once lined the bank of the Danube have been replaced, too, by the uncompromisingly modern forms of the Duna and Forum Hotels, but the Corso is still perfect for a promenade, with views of Buda. There are some sights – the huge, domed Basilica, the Westminster-like Houses of Parliament – but the most absorbing thing to do in Pest is to wander down its grand nineteenth-century boulevards gazing at individual examples of interesting architecture – the porticoed, colonnaded State Opera House on Andrássy út, the delicate iron and glass structure of the Western Railway Station (Nyugati Pályand var), designed by the Eiffel company and dominating Marx tér, or the Moorish synagogue on Dohány utca. When you tire of that, everyday life can be just as interesting: restaurants, cafés, and shops – from dog grooming salons to folk art – and the endless chess battles in the parks or the mineral waters of the Széchenyi Baths Strand.

WHEN TO GO

Budapest's peak summer season (July and August) is hot and crowded, with both local and foreign tourists. From November to February the weather can get extremely cold, with temperatures barely rising above freezing, and sheets of ice appearing on the Danube. Tourists are fewer, though in the run-up to Christmas the cafés are full of Viennese in town to do their Christmas shopping. Some of the museums may be closed for refurbishment, but there's still plenty to do and see. Budapest's Film Festival takes place in February, and its Spring Festival of music, drama and dance is held in March. Art Weeks in September and October start the winter concert season. National Day, on 20 August, sees a regatta on the Danube followed by a firework display.

MASTERING THE SYSTEM

Information This can be obtained from Danube Travel, 6 Conduit Street, London W1R 9TG, tel: 071-493 0263. IBUSZ, the Hungarian tourist organisation (Felszabadulás tér 5, tel: 1181-120, open Monday to Friday 8am to 5pm, Saturday 8am to 1pm), arranges sightseeing tours and accommodation. There is also an IBUSZ office open 24 hours a day at Petöfi tér 3 (opposite the Duna

Intercontinental Hotel, tel: 1184-842). If you need practical information about sights and opening hours, go to Tourinform, V, Sütö utca 2, near Deák tér, tel: 1179-800, open daily 8am to 8pm. It can also provide copies of *Programme*, a monthly listings publication, and *Budapest Week*, the local English-language newspaper.

Districts Budapest is divided into 22 districts, each designated by a Roman numeral. Addresses give the number of the district first, followed by the street name and number, for example, V, Petöfi tér 3. Many street names have changed since 1990, so beware of old maps!

GETTING THERE

Formalities Visas are no longer required for British passport-holders. You must have a full 10-year passport.

Going independently

By air British Airways and the Hungarian airline, Malév, fly direct daily to Budapest from Heathrow. Two fares worth looking out for are the Budapest Weekend ticket (depart Thursday/Friday/Saturday, return Sunday/Monday/Tuesday) or the SuperAPEX (book 14 days in advance). Try Regent (0272 211711) or Danube Travel (071-493 0263).

If you want to combine your visit with a trip to Vienna, British Airways and Austrian Airlines fly daily from Heathrow to Vienna. There are daily flights from Vienna to Budapest or, in season (April to early October), you can take the hydrofoil down the Danube (about 4½ hours). The train also takes about 4½ hours.

Ferihegy Airport Budapest's airport is split into two: modern terminal 2 is reserved for Malév flights only, while terminal 1 is used by all other airlines. There are plenty of currency exchange and information facilities, a reasonable duty-free shop and rather a dingy buffet.

The journey from the airport to the city centre takes about half an hour. Use the LRI Airport Passenger Service minibus, which will drop you at any city-centre hotel or private address for a set fare of about £4. Airport buses run at half-hour intervals between 6am and 10pm and drop you at Erzsébet tér bus station in central Pest. Buy your ticket on the bus. A taxi to the city centre costs about eight times as much.

Tour operator packages

Unless you plan to stay in private accommodation, which is very cheap, it is almost certainly cheaper to take an inclusive package arranged by a tour operator. A typical price for three nights in peak season, in a three-star hotel, is £370.

For a list of tour operators offering short breaks to Budapest, see page 385.

Maps You can get a very basic free map of the city centre from Tourinform or your hotel. Alternatively, you can buy a *Budapest Guide and Atlas* from bookshops or kiosks: it shows the districts and gives useful addresses and brief descriptions of the main sights. Make sure it has the new street names – usually labelled *új utcanerekkel*.

Sightseeing tours Guided tours are offered by several companies, including the state tourist organisation IBUSZ, and are usually advertised in *Programme*. Payment is usually in hard currency. Half-day coach tours lasting about three hours are a useful introduction to the structure of the city. Guides give rapid descriptions of the main sights in several languages. There's also a stop at the Hilton coffee-shop for coffee and cakes. During the summer there are sightseeing trips by boat on the Danube. There are also tours of Budapest by night, folklore and goulash evenings, and trips to the theatre can be arranged. If you want to see the inside of the Parliament building you must go on a tour, when Parliament isn't sitting.

Further afield, you can visit Lake Balaton or the horse shows in Kecskemét. But if you have time the best day-trip is to the Danube Bend to see the historic towns and ruins of Szentendre, Esztergom, and Visegrád (*see pages 110-11*).

Changing money Banks are open Monday to Thursday 8.30am to 3.30pm, but usually close at 1pm on Friday. Tourist offices and hotels are open longer and offer the same rate of exchange. The rate is officially changed on Tuesday each week. Most places don't charge commission.

You are not allowed to take more than 100 forint out of the country, so do not change too much at a time. You will receive many offers on the street to change money on the black market at rates as high as 60 to 80 per cent above the official rate. Be warned: the black market is illegal and you face the risk of being cheated or caught by undercover police.

Tipping Always keep small change handy for tips; tipping is a way of life in Budapest and cloakroom attendants are quick to remind you if you forget to hand over the obligatory ten forint. Taxi drivers expect at least 10 per cent, and often round up the fare to the nearest ten forint. For personal attention from a gypsy violinist in restaurants, it's customary to leave 100 to 200 forint.

Opening hours and days Shops are generally open from 10am to 6pm during the week and close at Saturday lunchtime. Thursday is late-night shopping, when some shops and department stores are open until 8pm. Major food stores are also open on Sunday mornings. The shops also open on the three Sundays before Christmas (known as 'bronze', 'silver' and 'gold').

Museums are usually open Tuesday to Sunday, 10am to 6pm, though in winter they close as early as 4pm. They are generally closed on the day after a public holiday. Admission on Saturday is often free.

Several medicinal baths are open every day. Those that do not have separate baths for men and women usually admit different sexes on alternate days. Opening hours are generally about 6.30am to 6pm or 7pm, Monday to Friday; usually mornings only on Saturday and Sunday.

GETTING AROUND

Public transport is very cheap. Tickets must be purchased in advance and punched in the machines on the vehicle or, on metro lines 2 and 3, as you enter the station. You can buy tickets from newspaper kiosks as well as the ticket offices in the stations. You pay a flat-rate fare for tickets valid on trams, trolley buses, the metro, buses and HEV (suburban train) up to the city boundary. Daily and weekly passes are also available.

The Budapest **underground** (metro) is cheap and efficient. Advertising posters line the escalators, and traders sell bunches of flowers and Chinese silk dressing-gowns in the stations. There are three metro lines, numbered, 1, 2 and 3, which all intersect at Deák tér in central Pest. The trains are clean, fast and run at regular intervals of a few minutes between 4.30am and 11.10pm.

Trams run from 5am to 11pm; **buses** from 4.30am to 11pm and the stops are quite far apart. A useful night bus (6É) runs round the Great Boulevard every 15 to 20 minutes.

Taxis are still cheap: a journey across town costs around £3. Make sure that the meter is switched on and starts at not more than 50 forints.

UNMISSABLES

Castle Hill

Most of the better-known historical sights are in Buda, on or around Castle Hill. The funicular travels from Clark Ádám tér to the northernmost wing of the Royal Palace. Next to the terminal a bronze statue of the legendary Turul bird hovers on its plinth overlooking the Danube. On the left stands the Royal Palace with its three museums and imperious bronze lions; and cobbled streets lead to Szentháromság tér, or Trinity Square, location of the Matthias Church (*see below*) and starting point for horse-drawn tours of the hill.

In front of the Matthias Church is the **Fishermen's Bastion**. Named after the site of a medieval fish market on which it was built, this weird conglomerate of assorted walkways and towers, built at the beginning of the century, provides the best view of the Houses of Parliament opposite. It's also a popular site for Hungarian peasant women to market their embroidered lace tablecloths. The seven towers are said to symbolise the seven tribes which conquered Hungary, while the shape of the towers apparently resembles the shape of the ninth-century nomads' tents.

Although Castle Hill is only four streets wide, surprisingly few tourists seem to venture beyond Trinity Square. The quiet, oft-rebuilt streets, lit by the glow of yellow gas lamps, make for a delightful half-day's wander. Arched doorways with recessed benches (*sedilia*), baroque courtyards and monument plaques galore are testimony to Buda's multi-layered history.

The Matthias Church

The reconstructed neo-Gothic spire and glazed tiled roof, like a beaded pencil case, dominate the skyline of Buda. Inside, every wall and pillar is covered in murals or red and blue geometrical motifs leading up to the braided vaulting and trefoil-windowed galleries. The museum contains replicas of the crown jewels and various religious relics, including a blackened bone of St John.

The Royal Palace

This great neo-baroque building on the southern tip of Castle Hill, now home to three museums, has been rebuilt several times, though its origins lie in the fourteenth century. Excavations on the western side of the hill continue; medieval passages and fortifications previously discovered have been incorporated into the structure of the **Budapest History Museum**. Starting on the ground floor and basement with the Roman remains of Aquinum found in Óbuda, the exhibition continues underground through the medieval vaulted Albrecht's cellar to Stephen's Tower. There's a small art gallery on the first floor and an exhibition of archaeological finds on the second.

In the **National Gallery**, Hungarian painting is represented on the first and second floors – nineteenth century on the first, twentieth century on the second. The third floor usually has temporary exhibitions.

The palace's third museum, the **Museum of Contemporary**

History, houses temporary exhibitions and the Ludwig Museum for International Modern Art, which includes works by Hockney, Rauschenberg, Picasso, Baselitz and Warhol, and even American graffiti art.

Gellért Hill

Named after an Italian missionary responsible for bringing Christianity to Hungary, Gellért Hill offers many good vantage points. Look out over the Erzsébet Bridge from the bronze statue of Gellért himself, surrounded by colonnades and located on the spot from where the saint is supposed to have been thrown into the river by some die-hard pagans. Climb up to the Citadel, built by the Austrians to control the city after the War of Independence (1848-9). From here and the nearby Liberty statue are great views in all directions.

Hungarian National Museum

Standing back from the road in its own gardens, this neo-classical building is best-known for its display of the crown jewels, including St Stephen's crown and the royal sceptre. After being smuggled out of the country by Nazi allies during the Second World War, they were stored in Fort Knox in the United States for 30 years before being handed back to Hungary in 1978.

Other impressive exhibits include three carved ivory saddles, wooden pews engraved with the coats of arms of Matthias and his queen, and a parapeted Renaissance bookshelf.

Museum of Fine Arts

Flanking dramatic Heroes Square (Hösök tere), is an extensive collection of Italian Renaissance art, and a remarkable Spanish collection, including seven El Grecos. The small twentieth-century gallery includes a couple of Kokoschkas and a Chagall. The Egyptian section, with its black mummified crocodiles, cats and snakes, is ghoulishly fascinating.

OTHER PLACES TO VISIT

Museums and galleries

Museum of Agriculture This extraordinary fairy-tale castle is a catalogue of the various architectural styles found in Hungary before the First World War, from Romanesque to Renaissance-baroque. It was originally built in wood, cardboard and corrugated iron as an exhibition centre for Hungary's millennium celebrations in 1896.

Inside, exhaustive exhibitions cover the breeding of pigs, sheep, poultry and horses, the development of the plough and tractor, and conservation in Hungary.

Museum of Applied Arts Furniture, textiles and costumes are housed in a Secessionist (Hungarian art nouveau) building.

Museum of Music History Historical musical instruments are displayed together with a fascinating exhibition of Bartok's work.

Museum of Ethnography A wide-ranging, permanent collection of Hungarian folk art and culture, including gypsy photos, paintings and implements, and Carpathian embroidery. All are housed in a grand building that used to be the seat of the Supreme Court, opposite the Parliament building.

Museum of Transport Popular with children, this hangar-like museum contains ancient steam engines and carriages, old motor bikes and cars (including a 1934 Austin 7), dredging ships, Danube barges and old trams.

Other attractions

Basilica The biggest church in Budapest has a dome exactly matching in height the dome on the Parliament building – 96 metres. Apparently this figure was deliberately chosen to commemorate 896, the year of the Magyar conquest.

The treasury contains gold monstrances and relics of St Stephen, and in a side chapel lies the mummified right hand of the saint in a gold and silver case. Make a quick detour along nearby Hold utca to see the idiosyncratic savings bank designed by Ödön Lechner, master of Hungarian art nouveau.

Houses of Parliament These bear an uncanny resemblance to the Houses of Parliament at Westminster. Tours of the interior are restricted to groups, and must be organised through IBUSZ.

Steam baths The radioactive water from the Buda Hills is said to have medicinal properties, capable of curing and preventing various ailments. The bath house tradition goes back as far as the Romans at Aquinum, but it was after the Turkish invasion in the sixteenth century that the habit really took off. The most famous baths are those beside the Gellért Hotel, housed in a remarkable art nouveau building. Confusing corridors lead to the beautiful swimming-pools – a small hot pool and a large, gently shelving rectangular pool – surrounded by columns, palms and spouting dolphins.

The Király Baths date from Turkish times and the domed exterior still flaunts the Turkish crescent. Inside, the sanatorium atmosphere is overlaid with strong sulphurous fumes. Beyond an unpromising sauna lies a series of stone-lined domed baths, with coloured shafts of light streaming through the star-shaped apertures in the roof (open for men till 6pm Monday, Wednesday, Friday; for women till 6pm Tuesday, Thursday, and till noon Saturday).

The Széchenyi Baths (City Park) have a hot outdoor pool as well as steam rooms. After a swim in cooler waters you can wallow in 38°C temperatures and watch the chess players submerged in the hot pool.

Excursions

Buda Hills and Children's Railway The forests of the Buda Hills make a relaxing change from the bustle of the city. To get there, take the cog railway (opposite the Hotel Budapest) up to Széchenyi-hegy terminal. The journey takes 15 minutes and a normal tram ticket is valid. At the top you can wander along one of the hiking trails or make for the five-kilometre-long Children's Railway. This is a narrow-gauge railway run by schoolchildren, who act as conductors, ticket sellers and signal switchers. Only the driver is an adult. If you prefer not to continue to the terminus at Hüvösvölgy (quite possible, considering the discomfort of the hard, non-sprung seats), you can get off halfway at János-hegy (or at any of the six stations on the way). From the summit there's a chairlift back down into town.

Danube bend North of Budapest the Danube, flowing east from Vienna, turns abruptly south before entering Hungary's capital. Along its west bank at this point are the three historic towns of Esztergom, Visegrád, and Szentendre. If you wish to make your own travel arrangements there are frequent trains and buses from Budapest and, in summer, boats from Vigadó Pier (*see also* '*Sightseeing tours*' *under* '*Mastering the system*').

If you have time to visit only one of the three, **Szentendre**, the closest to Budapest, is the one to choose. This eighteenth-century town, with its numerous art galleries, craft shops and churches, verges dangerously close to being picturesquely twee. The clean, cobbled streets lead between the curving lines of the gold and cream houses, up to Templom tér with its huge Roman Catholic Parish Church and the Czóbel Museum's post-Impressionist collection. The town's most famous collection, however, is the work of Hungary's best-loved ceramist, Margit Kovács. Her stylised, naive folk style produces expressive, tubular, round-headed figures and effective relief work.

The palace at **Visegrád**, once the royal seat of King Matthias, has been excavated and is open to visitors; historical pageants are held there during the summer. Guided tours are available.

Esztergom's most famous landmark is its Basilica, the largest church in Hungary. Built on a hill by the Danube looking across into Slovakia, the Basilica's 100-metre cupola is easy to spot. The restrained baroque interior contains the beautiful red marble Bakócz Chapel.

EATING AND DRINKING

Hotel breakfasts are continental style, usually laid out as a serve-yourself buffet. Bread, cold meats and cheese, jam, and tea or coffee may be supplemented in the fancier hotels with eggs, bacon and sausages, cereal, yoghurt and watery bottled fruit.

Hungarian cooking is rich, based as it is on *rántás*, a roux of flour and pork lard, spiced with paprika. Strongly influenced by the French, heavy sauces using wine and cream dominate. Meat is mostly pork, veal, poultry or game; dishes featuring goose, venison and wild boar are also common. Not surprisingly for a landlocked country, practically all fish is freshwater: mainly pike and carp. Foie gras and caviare crop up on all menus in the most expensive restaurants, at prices lower than in the West.

Hungary's specialities are cakes and desserts. The most famous dessert, named after a famed restaurateur, is *Gundel palacsinta*: pancakes filled with nuts and raisins, smothered in a chocolate and rum sauce, and flambéed. And pâtisseries are packed with tourists replenishing their strength by stuffing themselves with wonderful sticky cakes at ridiculous prices (30p to £1). Gerbeaud (V, Vörösmarty tér 7), a throwback to the café society of the past, is probably Budapest's best-known pâtisserie. With its stuccoed trellised ceiling, red and green flock wallpaper, green velvet swags and marble floor and tables, it's an opulent place in which to sit and recover from a morning's shopping. But you won't be alone – every Viennese tourist will be there with you.

If you prefer your indulgence to be more discreet, two pâtisseries on Andrássy út offer similar delicacies: Müvesz at 29 and Lukács at 70. In Buda, the tiny Ruszwurm (I, Szentháromság utca 3) is the place to aim for.

The most famous and most beautiful café in the golden days of the first three decades of the century – when Budapest boasted about 500 cafés – was the Hungaria. Frequented by writers and journalists, it held 'all the dailies and arts journals of the world', and stayed open day and night. Now the clientele has changed, and it's rather too well known by tourists to be chic; but it still has plenty of atmosphere, and retains much of its exuberant décor.

By Western standards eating out in Hungary is reasonably cheap, even in the top restaurants. The Silhouette restaurant in the Forum Hotel is (relatively) expensive and classy, and has a pianist instead of the more usual gypsy violinist. The more informal restaurant in the Hotel Erzsébet – folk embroidery on the walls and smaller groupings of tables – has friendly and efficient service, and a menu which may offer chilled raspberry and cream soup and stuffed cabbage garnished with frankfurters and dill sauce.

The best cuisine in Budapest (at London prices) is at the exclusive Légrádi Testveret (V, Magyar utca 23). Or try the very reasonable Múzeum Kávéház (VIII, Múzeum krt 12), where large helpings come on even larger plates, all in beautiful surroundings.

You can eat and drink cheaply (£3 to £7) and well in small, non-touristy restaurants, though you may have problems translating the menu. Claudia (V, Bástya utca 27), a small brick-vaulted beer cellar down an unpromising dark alley, is popular with young people and students. There is an English menu and bar staff speak a little English. Or try the unpretentious Bóhemtanya (VI, Paulay Ede utca 6) just off Deák tér – but it's only open till 10pm.

The main feature of the more expensive tourist-oriented restaurants is the inevitable gypsy fiddlers. In the small Százéves (Hundred Years Restaurant), with a medieval atmosphere and candlelit tables, a gypsy band is tucked in a corner and occasionally forays round the tables hoping for further tips. It gets livelier as the evening wears on. Main courses might feature goose liver, venison and sirloin of beef.

Hungary's famous Bull's Blood wine (*Egri bikavér*), its quality having declined over the years, doesn't seem to taste any better in its country of origin. The sweet *Tokaji aszú*, however, is worth trying. Its sweetness is indicated by the number on the label (the sweetest, at number 5, is also the most expensive). Other Hungarian specialities are its fruit brandies (*palinka*): pear (*körte*), apricot (*barack*), cherry (*csereszny*), and plum (*szilva*).

SHOPPING

Hungary's headlong rush into the free market is reflected in its shops: no queues (except outside shops selling specialised Western goods such as Adidas) and supermarkets with well-stocked shelves.

For shopping, Pest is your best bet. Pedestrianised Váci utca is Budapest's Bond Street, with many classy shops accepting credit cards and hard currency. Around this area are Benetton, McDonald's and Adidas, selling imported goods at high prices. There's also a foreign-language bookshop, Idegennyelvü Könyvesbolt, which sells Penguin classics and glossy art books.

If you're interested in folk art, check out the range of wares and prices at the state-run Népmüvészeti Bolt on Váci utca before buying anything from the tourist shops on Castle Hill. It sells a wide selection of souvenirs, including linen-covered embroidered sewing boxes and shawls, ceramic vases, hand-painted eggs, furniture and rugs.

There are also shops selling folk art from other Eastern European countries: Népmüvészek Szövetkezete, on Kecskeméti utca, sells carved Russian chess sets, ceramic pots and embroidered toilet bags; the Polish cultural centre on Andrássy út has amber jewellery and woven rugs with pictures of the Pope; the Bulgarian centre, also on Andrássy, has carved candles and records of Bulgarian folk music.

Records and cassettes are a bargain, with classical recordings under the Deutsche Grammophon label selling for about £3. A boxed set of Domingo and Berganza singing *Carmen*, for example, sells for about £7. CDs sell at Western prices.

Visit at least one supermarket to stock up on food and drink souvenirs. The Skála Metro, opposite the striking West Station, has some lovely pear, cherry, peach and plum liqueurs, with fruit floating in the bottle. There are also boxes of hand-made chocolate cherry liqueurs for less than £2. You'll also find foie gras for £9 to £10, a good range of salami, and bottles of Russian champagne for £8.

There are also several delicatessens selling presentation packs of dried paprika, fruit liqueurs and Hungary's famous sherry-like Tokaji wine, and even tins of kangaroo soup. Try the Kalocsa on Régiposta Street, opposite the Duna Intercontinental Hotel.

For fresh food and local colour, visit some of the markets. Ropes of garlic and paprika adorn many stands, and in summer the air smells of apricots and raspberries. If the hangar-like indoor market on Vámház krt is still closed for repair, try further along the embankment on Közraktár utca, or across in Buda at the Fény utcai piac.

The easiest flea market to reach is held at weekends outside the youth centre, or Petöfi Csarnok, in the City Park of Varosliget. For a small entrance fee you can wander through a maze of stalls selling everything from brand-new Commodore keyboards and antique china to Russian badges and soft-porn magazines.

NIGHTLIFE

The state tourist organisation IBUSZ organises tours of Budapest by night (ending up in a nightclub with floor show), folklore evenings and goulash parties. If you prefer to take an active part in the stamping and clapping, there are several folk-dancing clubs that teach beginners; look in *Programme* or *Budapest Week* for details.

For a glimpse of the high life in Budapest, spend an evening at the Italianate Hungarian State Opera House, VI, Andrássy út 22. Here, where the most expensive ticket is less than £10 (though it may be more in summer), you get a chance to drink Russian champagne and rub expensively clad shoulders with the richer members of Hungarian society. Mozart, Puccini, Wagner and Verdi are all represented, as well as opera by Hungarian composers. If you can't get tickets for the State Opera House, try the modern Erkel Theatre (VIII, Köztársaság tér 30). Traditional ballet and modern dance are also performed here.

During the summer both opera houses are usually closed and opera performances are given on the open-air stage on Margaret Island. If you prefer something a little lighter, the Operetta Theatre, VI, Nagymezö utca 17, puts on a mixture of classical operettas and musicals. You can get tickets at the box offices of the individual theatres or from the Central Theatre Booking Office, VI, Andrássy út 18.

Budapest has no shortage of concerts for classical music fans. Venues include the grand Pesti Vigadó, V, Vörösmarty tér 1; the Ferenc Liszt Academy of Music, VI, Liszt Ferenc tér 8 and the Budapest Convention Centre, XII, Jagelló út 1/3. Tickets are sold at the Országos Filharmónia, V, Vörösmarty tér 1.

HOTELS

Hotel rates are usually quoted without the 15 per cent tourist tax which needs to be added. If you're going only for a weekend it's quite important to be centrally based – in areas I, V, VI, VII or VIII. There are clusters of hotels in both Buda and Pest; most are very well connected to the central areas by public transport. Accommodation can be difficult to find in the summer; IBUSZ can help book a hotel if you're stuck, or can book you into private accommodation. The IBUSZ office opposite the Duna Intercontinental Hotel can arrange this. Prices are charged per person, not per room – normally about £7 per night, but you may end up out of town; and you will have to wait for your host to return from work to let you in on your first night.

ASTORIA
Kossuth Lajos 19, V, 1053   *Tel: 1173-411   Fax: 1186-798*

The Astoria is very centrally placed near Deák tér in Pest, from which all metro and tram tours radiate. It's on a busy junction, but the atmosphere is calm. It's a well-kept *fin-de-siècle* building and a famous one, with an excellent and highly rated restaurant. In the reception area is a civilised little sitting-room – firmly traditional, in shades of green. The restaurant is finely proportioned and formally furnished. The bar resembles a gentleman's club, with dark wood furniture and a hushed air. Bedrooms are again highly traditional, with sombre but good quality furnishings.

Bedrooms: 130, most with bath/WC; all with mini-bar   **Facilities:** Lift; restaurant; nightclub   **Credit/charge cards accepted:** All

ERZSÉBET
Karolyi Mihaly 11-15, V, 1053   *Tel: 1382-111   Fax: 1189-237*

Erzsébet is a modern renovation of an 1872 building in a small side-street of Pest's oldest quarter. The outside is brash with neon signs. The rooms are smallish and functional, but comfortable, with the dark brown squashy leatherette chairs typical of Budapest's newer hotels. Folk embroidery on the walls and banks of greenery give the restaurant an informal air. Service is efficient and friendly. The Janos Beer Cellar in the basement is the bit many visitors head for; the ground-floor bar is rather cramped. Well located for exploring the city on foot.

Bedrooms: 123, all with shower/WC; mini-bar   **Facilities:** Lift; restaurant   **Credit/charge cards accepted:** All

Hotel prices Symbols indicate approximate prices per room per night for a double room with bath. Many large hotels run special breaks which work out far cheaper. (See page 14 for further details.)

♦ = under £50; ♦♦ = £50 to £80; ♦♦♦ = £80 to £100;
♦♦♦♦ = £100 to £140; ♦♦♦♦♦ = over £140.

GELLÉRT ♦♦♦♦
Szt. Gellért tér. 1, V, 1111   Tel: 1852-200   Fax: 1666-631

This is the famous spa hotel, with its palatial vaulted hall leading to the thermal baths. The price includes use of these. It's a faded wedding cake of a building at the foot of Gellért Hill, by the Szabadság Bridge. The hotel is grand, if not quite elegant: the spacious circular foyer has columns, rugs and plants, but other public areas are only average. The colour-schemes are somewhat peculiar.

Bedrooms: 239, most with bath/shower/WC; all with mini-bar, some with air-conditioning   **Facilities:** Lift; restaurant; thermal baths and pool; sauna; nightclub; hairdresser; beauty salon   **Credit/charge cards accepted:** Amex, Diners, Visa

HILTON ♦♦♦♦♦
Hess Andras tér. 1-3, V, 1014   Tel: 1751-000   Fax: 1560-285

The Budapest Hilton commands Buda Hill and has superb views. It is a moderately unobtrusive low-rise construction, incorporating part of an abbey and a Dominican church in an otherwise modern design. Medieval turrets reflect in the rosy plate-glass at the rear. The interior is smart and fairly sophisticated; bedrooms are stylish, spacious and well equipped. There's a wine bar tucked into the old walls of the abbey, and a casino. For a splurge, this is the place to come.

Bedrooms: 323, all with bath/WC; air-conditioning; mini-bar
Facilities: Lift; restaurant; hairdresser; beauty salon; casino   **Credit/ charge cards accepted:** All

CITY HOTEL NEMZETI ♦♦
Jozsef Krt. 4, VIII, 1088   Tel: 1339-160   Fax: 1140-019

This is a pretty, frivolous blue building on a busy corner near the metro and one of Pest's main shopping streets. Inside it has some period charm – pillars, arches, stained-glass ceilings, wrought-iron balconies – but the effect is not always sustained throughout. The restaurant has recently been redecorated. There is some nightlife. The welcome is friendly and staff speak English. It makes an inexpensive and central base.

Bedrooms: 76, all with bath/WC; mini-bar   **Facilities:** Lift; restaurant
Credit/charge cards accepted: All

RADISSON BÉKE
Teréz Krt. 43, VI, 1067   *Tel: 1323-300   Fax: 1533-380*

This is a smart modern revival of an imposing nineteenth-century building in an established part of Pest. It is well run and well thought out, but not intimate. Clubby red chairs furnish the darkish acres around the reception foyer. Go upstairs to two smart restaurants and a pleasant, upmarket coffee shop with potted palms, chandeliers, newspapers on poles, and bronze busts over the green marble fireplace. The restaurants have bizarre decorative effects, but are quite comfortable. Bedrooms are smooth and well furnished, with excellent bathrooms.

Closed: Restaurant closed Sun   **Bedrooms:** 238, all with bath/shower/WC; mini-bar   **Facilities:** Lift; restaurants; indoor heated pool; gym; solarium; masseur; casino   **Credit/charge cards accepted:** All

Hotel prices Symbols indicate approximate prices per room per night for a double room with bath. Many large hotels run special breaks which work out far cheaper. (See page 14 for further details.)

♦ = under £50; ♦♦ = £50 to £80; ♦♦♦ = £80 to £100;
♦♦♦♦ = £100 to £140; ♦♦♦♦♦ = over £140.

COPENHAGEN

- While Copenhagen has none of the magnificence of Paris or Vienna, and its sights and museums cannot compare with those of London or Rome, it's much more relaxing than most other European capitals. The city's charm lies in its small scale
- The city is ideal for those who aren't too keen on doing much sightseeing. A stroll through the old town, a boat trip and an excursion will keep people happy and will do justice to the major attractions
- Much of the city centre is traffic free, so you can enjoy the shops and sights in relative peace
- For such a small city, there's a surprising amount of nightlife – particularly in the Tivoli Gardens, which offer smart restaurants, serious concerts, hot dogs and traditional fairground fun

ONCE upon a time when the waters of the Øresund were full of herrings, a little fishing village called Havn grew up to become København, the merchants' port. The shoals eventually disappeared ('dead as a herring,' say the Danes) but not before Copenhagen had become a very prosperous trading centre. Until 1417 it belonged to the bishops of Roskilde – Danish kings being mostly on the move, empire-building in Norway and Sweden, Iceland and Greenland, the Faröes and Schleswig-Holstein. The stalwart Bishop Absalon built a fort, which was reconstructed as the royal castle when the medieval monarchy settled in and started to take an interest. Christian I was crowned king in Copenhagen in 1449, and the founding of the university (1479) ennobled Copenhagen as Denmark's cultural centre.

Of the alternating Christians and Frederiks who followed, the most notable was Christian IV, who between 1588 and 1648 was responsible for building most of the gilded and copper-green highlights of Copenhagen's decorative skyline and for doubling the city's size with the possession of the island area of Christianshavn. He left the city flat broke after several wars with Sweden, which the Danes lost, but is nevertheless remembered as the 'Builder King'. Renewed hostilities led to a two-year Swedish siege of Copenhagen, so famously resisted by its citizens that they and Frederik III entered into a happy relationship at the expense of the nobility – trading privileges and tax advantages for the burghers, under an absolute monarchy which lasted from 1660 to 1848. This Frederik's engineers built Castellet, the citadel at the northern end of the harbour channel, and extended the sweep of the city ramparts. Seventeenth-century Copenhagen gained a grid of long straight streets east of its medieval centre, the canal inlet of Nyhavn and the square called Kongens Nytorv, 'the King's new market', with magnificent surrounding buildings in Dutch baroque-style.

Moneyed elegance to the north, the cheerful university quarter to the west, and commerce and popular recreation to the south is still roughly the pattern radiating from Christiansborg Slot, the Royal Palace, now the seat of the Danish Parliament (lengthy guided tour available in English). The surrounding channel, complete with sightseeing boats, gives the city centre a touch of Amsterdam, but Copenhagen actually needed no extended canal system. Clean salt air straight off the sound makes this the most invigorating of cities to walk in; and the Danes were pioneers of traffic-free strolling when they linked five streets to form Strøget, 'walking street', the main pedestrianised tourist artery. Copenhagen's well-remembered 'happy sixties' linger on in the form of constant music, 'happenings', placards, politics and peaceful street chess. The careless youths hanging about in the various squares are as likely to be hippie as punk. Away from Strøget's ambience the streets are either one-way or generously wide with cycle lanes – this is a city where a cycling population has real parity with those who drive. The biggest, busiest open space is the Town Hall Square (Rådhuspladsen), an unavoidable tourist centre where Strøget, bus routes and coach tours converge and crowds pass west to the railway station, Tivoli Gardens and the Glyptotek Museum. Everything else lies to the east.

Depending on your mood and the weather you can fill two or three relaxed days by wandering along the open waterfront, quiet medieval backstreets or the entertaining Strøget to find more museums, churches and the palaces. The most elegant open space is Amalienborg, a symmetrical assembly of four rococo mansions to which the Danish royal family transferred after their palace at Christiansborg was destroyed – twice – by fire. The changing of the guard at noon is a protracted ceremony, involving much marching across the cobbled expanse to relieve the occupant of each little sentry box.

The great thing about Copenhagen is the leisurely pace; enjoy the distractions of cafés and bars, the alluring shops, the attractive detail of architecture and ornament and the ambience of Danish good humour. Like friendliness, cleanliness is a national virtue: litter, which only foreigners are ill-mannered enough to drop, is rapidly cleared up with ingenious stab-and-grip devices. And if in spite of your map and the well-displayed street names you need to ask your way, your only language problems will be pronouncing your destination, since Copenhageners respond to your tentative approaches in totally, shamingly, taken-for-granted fluent English.

WHEN TO GO

From May to mid-September is the best time to visit Copenhagen. Summer temperatures are very similar to London but Copenhagen has more hours of sunshine. It's often wetter than London in late summer, though. You should avoid the weekend of the Copenhagen Carnival (normally in May) if you're only taking a short break – it's very colourful and great fun but you can't see or do anything else while it's on. There's also a ten-day jazz festival in mid-July.

GETTING THERE

Going independently

By air There are frequent scheduled flights to Copenhagen from Heathrow with British Airways (081-897 4000) and SAS (0345 090900), and you can also fly direct from Aberdeen, Birmingham, Dublin, Gatwick, Glasgow and Manchester. Maersk Air (071-333 0066) has two daily flights to Copenhagen from Gatwick, and British European Airways (021-782 0711) also flies twice daily from Birmingham. APEX fares are generally the cheapest (book 14 days in advance). It's worth checking fares with NSR Travel (071-930 6666), Holidaymaker (081-664 1234), Scantours (071-839 2927) and Hamilton Travel (071-287 2425). Return scheduled fares in 1992 were on offer from £130. The flight takes one hour 45 minutes.

Copenhagen Airport The airport, six miles from the city centre, has excellent facilities, including banks, cafés, restaurants and shops. Scandinavian Airlines runs a bus service which leaves the airport every 15 minutes. The journey to the central railway station takes 20 minutes.

By rail From London via Harwich and Hook of Holland or Esbjerg, or via Dover and Ostend, or (in summer) from Newcastle to Esbjerg, the trip to Copenhagen by train and ferry takes 26 hours and costs from £79 low season economy return per person with Scandinavian Seaways (0255 240240). Flying is probably the best choice for a short stay.

Central Station is great fun. Escalators smoothly separate the platforms from the muffled hubbub of the concourse, with dark-beamed roof-vaults high above a resilient red-tiled floor (backpackers seem happy to sit about on it). There are shops and stalls, bars and permanently open cafés, and an appealing model railway (coin-operated) in a glass-cased Gothic landscape.

Tour operator packages

Several tour operators run short-break packages of three days to Copenhagen. Prices for three nights in a three-star hotel are about £290 in low season and £320 in high season. For a list of tour operators, see page 385. Given the high prices of Copenhagen hotels, a package is a sensible option, but you should most certainly check how far from the centre your hotel is, and be prepared (in the lower price ranges) to stay somewhere fairly bland.

MASTERING THE SYSTEM

Information The Danish Tourist Board is at 169/173 Regent Street, London W1R 8PY, tel 071-734 2637. The staff are extremely helpful. The *Wonderful Copenhagen* brochure is full of practical information. In Copenhagen, the tourist information office is at Bernstorffsgade 1 (by the main entrance to the Tivoli Gardens) and is open 9am to 6pm daily in summer. It covers all Denmark, not just Copenhagen, and is very busy, so you generally have to queue.

Maps These generally cover the whole urban area, spreading into suburbs six times larger than the historic part of the city. Blown-up inserts are on the small side and rather hard to read. The free tourist office version is as good as any: its 'central' insert is flanked by a street index and a key to sights and museums, and also includes bus route numbers.

Sightseeing tours There are several tours of the city. City sightseeing buses with guide depart from Town Hall Square and take between one and a half and two and three quarter hours depending on the visits included. If you don't want a running commentary, use the HT Sightseeing Bus: it stops at nine key points, and you can get on and off the half-hourly service as often as you like on a day ticket.

Canal trips start from Gammel Strand and Kongens Nytorv. A hour's cruise takes you through the canals of the old town, across the inner harbour to the old seamen's quarter of Christianshavn, then out to the main harbour to visit the Little Mermaid, and finally back to Nyhavn, where the hydrofoils from Sweden moor in the heart of the city centre. English-language **walking tours**, each about two hours in length, meet at various points and cover the city more intimately – motto 'Rain or sun, we hope to see you! (The weather may be worse tomorrow.)'

Changing money Banks are open Monday to Friday, 9.30am to 4pm (6pm on Thursday). There are currency exchange offices at the Central Station, at Tivoli, and at the airport, all of which open outside normal banking hours.

Opening hours and days Shops are open from about 10am to 5.30pm, Monday to Thursday, and to 7pm or 8pm on Friday. They are closed on Saturday afternoon and Sunday. (In summer, most shops remain open until 5pm on Saturday.) Many sights, including some of the major ones in winter, are closed on Monday; closing times are usually 4pm (Rosenborg Castle 3pm), or 3pm in winter. The Tivoli Gardens are open end April to mid-September, 10am to midnight.

GETTING AROUND

The centre of Copenhagen is relatively small. However, the **bus** system radiating from Town Hall Square can be useful. Fares operate on a zonal scheme. **S-trains** cover the suburbs of the city and beyond.

Taxis are run by private companies, but are subject to official rates. Tipping is not necessary.

Cycling is a popular way of getting around and there are special cycle lanes on many roads. Ask for information at the Cykelcentret at Central Station. You can hire a bicycle from Københavns Cykelbørs, Reventlowsgade 11; Oesterport Cykler, Oslo Plads 9 or Danwheel, Colbjornsensgade 3.

UNMISSABLES

Rosenborg Castle

Located in Copenhagen's oldest and loveliest park, this brick baroque extravaganza began life as a mock-fortified summer-house and was then extended to become a family home under Christian IV. By the eighteenth century the royals seldom used it, and in 1883 – its contents re-ordered chronologically – it opened as a museum of the Royal Collections. So densely packed with treasures are its rooms that it should be overpowering, but its almost absurd excesses are enchanting. The rooms appear small, except in the Long Hall, where near-life-size silver lions lie round a pair of thrones. On the route up you negotiate rooms of marble and tapestry, lacquer and painted panels, massed bibelots of amber and crystal, silver-gilt and porcelain. There's a walk-in collection of Venetian glass which has not been rearranged since 1714, where you hardly dare breathe, and many other royal idiosyncrasies – Frederik IV enjoyed both the scientific and the erotic possibilities of his mirror-cube room. Below, stoutly guarded, is the Treasury: a contrastingly stark 1970s concrete setting for glass-encased crowns and regalia.

Ny Carlsberg Glyptotek

Entering from the busy street you are immediately drawn towards the centre of this museum – the uplifting contrast of a palmy winter garden with a cool white statue. Around it are arched vistas of superbly coloured spaces, holding the fine classical collections – Greek, Roman, Egyptian and Etruscan work – assembled by the founder of the Carlsberg Brewery, Carl Jacobsen. The front of the building and its smaller upper galleries hold French and Danish art: most of Rodin's bronzes and all of Degas's statuettes are here, and a richly representative assembly of French nineteenth-century paintings includes many works by the Impressionists and Gauguin. The golden, but less familiar, age of Danish painting is another pleasure to explore.

Tivoli

This immensely popular pleasure park has been a national institution since it opened in 1843 on the site of some demolished city ramparts. It spreads over 20 city-centre acres, entertaining the public with music and theatre, food and drink, and the funfair of stalls and swooping, looping, stomach-churning rides, all set among flowerbeds, tall trees, fountains and a lake. Four million visitors a year find it a magical experience, and even to hardened cynics it's irresistible after dark, when each gaily lit event stands out from the anonymous crowd in a colourful chiaroscuro.

The Round Tower (Rundetårnet)

The attraction of the Tower is the view from the top, achieved after a walk up the wide spiralling ramp inside. The spiral itself is pleasing too: yellow-grey brick beautifully laid underfoot and whitewashed vaulted curves of wall and ceiling, lit from arched windows complete with seats. The roofscape of the city, devoid of ugly modern architecture, is notable for its lovely spires. Christian IV had the Tower built for the University's astronomers, whose equipment was trundled up the ramp to an observatory. Peter the Great rode up in 1716, followed by his Tsarina in a carriage, and it was first conquered by motor car in 1902. Half-way up is the door to what was the University Library, a long and lofty room over the adjacent students' church. All was gutted in Copenhagen's catastrophic fire of 1728 – the church, however, was decoratively rebuilt in 1731, a rococo fantasy of white and gold with a splendid deeply ticking clock opposite the pulpit. Exploring the precincts of the Tower you come across the courtyard of Regensen, off Store Kannikestraede: it's almost filled by its lime tree, planted in May 1785 and annually given a birthday celebration by the students.

OTHER PLACES TO VISIT

Fountains and statues

Copenhagen revels in sculpture. The works of **Bertel Thorvaldsen** (who made his name in Italy and came home in triumph on a Danish battleship) occupy a whole museum on Slotsholm. The disused Nikolas Church displays colourful modern pieces, the spire of the Stock Exchange building is a fanciful twist of dragons' tails, and over a gable in Strøget an incidental *Mercury* on tiptoe looks about to topple rather than take flight.

Town Hall Square (Rådhuspladsen) The **Lur Blowers** on their slim column raise two curved horns and indicate the starting point for tours and taxis. Across the façade of the Town Hall the **Dragon Fountain** has the beast writhing in combat with a bull, while **Hans Andersen** sits nearby with child-polished lap and a rather fatuous expression on his face.

Strøget area Gammeltorv is the oldest square in the city and its **Caritas Fountain** dates from 1610. The feat of balancing golden apples on its jets is still attempted on the monarch's birthday (16 April). The **Storkespringvandet** is a pretty little fountain in Amagertorv, where hippies have congregated since the 'sixties; but in Gråbrødretorv (Greyfriars Square) off to the west a lumpish modern work of Swedish granite is the only unpleasing feature among café tables and coloured 'fire houses' built after the 1728 conflagration. Near the canal at the bottom of Hodjbro Plads a rearing horse bears a splendidly militant Bishop Absalon, and much less prominently, across Gammel Strand, a stout little figure of a fisherwoman recalls the long tradition of fish-selling.

Langelinie In this area of gardens round the old citadel the **Little Mermaid** (Den Lille Havfrue) has sat modestly on the shoreline since 1913, vandalised and repaired once or twice, and exercising a fascination over visitors which reputedly baffles the Danes. Copenhagen's mascot is at its best lit by the morning sun. *En route* to the Mermaid you pass the best fountain of all: it's the goddess **Gefion**, who turned her sons into oxen in order to win all the land she could plough in a day and a night. Her huge plunging beasts snort spray from their nostrils with quite spectacular vigour.

Equestrian kings are dotted all over the city. Christian V in Kongens Nytorv, portrayed in flattering Roman mode, needed a bronze replacement for his 1687 horse of lead, whose legs gave out. Frederik V dominates Amalienborg, superbly sculpted by Saly of France in 1771 for a price exceeding the cost of the four palaces around him. And in Sankt Annæ Plads, Christian X sits sombrely as befits his dates – 1912 to 1947 – spanning Denmark's poverty in the First World War and German occupation in the Second.

Other attractions

Carlsberg Brewery The entrance to the famous brewery in Ny Carlsbergvej (at 'Elephant Gate' – for it's flanked by two elephants) proclaims *Laboremus pro patria*. Certainly, the Carlsberg Foundation has long played a large part in Danish cultural life, as is explained on the conducted tour. But the main point of the visit is generally to have a free tasting of the famous brew.

Christiansborg Palace This early twentieth-century building is now the seat of Parliament. There are conducted tours of the grand Royal Reception Chambers.

National Museum Centrally situated in the old Prinsens Palace, this very large museum has recently reopened after a major three-year modernisation. It contains several fine collections, covering (among other things) Danish culture from the Ice Age to the nineteenth century. The Nordic pre-history and ethnographical collections contain memorable items – including a Bronze Age sun chariot, an exhibition of Eskimo culture and a room of rune stones and unearthed bog people.

Excursions

Open-Air Museum, Lyngby About five miles north of the city, the Frilandsmuseet is an 86-acre rural site with faithfully reconstructed seventeenth- to nineteenth-century cottages and farmhouses – all painstakingly furnished in appropriate style. You can walk around the museum (two miles to cover it) or take a horse-drawn carriage. It's easy to reach by public transport – take either a bus or S-train to Sorgenfri Station.

Zealand's Castles and the Louisiana Modern Art Museum Coach excursions from Copenhagen include day trips to the castles of North Zealand. More expensively, you could hire a small car and tour the area, as within easy range of the city there is a variety of interesting places to visit.

Frederiksborg Castle is the outstanding attraction on Zealand. The ornate seventeenth-century castle stands on an island in a lake near the town of Hillerød and now houses the Museum of National History. Not far away is **Fredensborg Castle** – a comparatively modest baroque palace, with a delightful park leading down to the shores of Esrum So (the palace is open to the public when the royal family is not in residence; the park is always open). The third, and most famous, of Zealand's castles is on the coast north of Copenhagen, guarding the modern ferry port of Helsingør. This is the **Elsinore** castle of Shakespeare's play, and although no Prince Hamlet ever watched from its battlements, the castle was actually constructed during Shakespeare's lifetime. The principal rooms house several museum collections. Just south of Helsingør, at Humlebæk, is the **Louisiana Modern Art Museum** – an internationally famous gallery with a beautiful sculpture garden.

Roskilde An easy excursion by train (it's 19 miles west of

Copenhagen), this little town on its long fjord is Denmark's oldest, and is where Viking Harald Bluetooth first built a wooden church in about 980. A thousand years on, Roskilde is modestly municipal, a centre of research and education with the feel of an extended market village. But at its heart is the equivalent of Westminster Abbey and by its shore a unique museum. The red-brick **Cathedral** begun by Bishop Absalon in the 1170s is a massive stylistic mix of Romanesque, Gothic and neo-classical. Below soaring brick arches and white basilica, every space and surface is filled with decorative detail – flower-scattered fresco, intricate woodcarving, exquisite gilding.

The **Viking Ship Museum** is a pleasant rural walk from the Cathedral. Here, in a modern building with a glass wall facing the sea, are displays of the five assorted Viking vessels which in the eleventh century were filled with stones and deliberately sunk to create a barrier to prevent passage up the fjord; the story of their retrieval is portrayed in an excellent film, in a room below the display hall.

SHOPPING

The five streets of pedestrian shopping, starting north from Town Hall Square, are Frederiksberggade, Nygade, Vimmelskaftet, Amagertorv and Østergade. Very roughly it becomes more upmarket as you move eastwards, but even the massed rows of T-shirts are interspersed with interesting specialities – foodstuffs, porcelain, glass, jewellery and bookshops with English stock. Den Permanente, a centre where you can both admire and buy, is on Frederiksberggade; Illums Bolighus is a design-oriented department store on Amagertorv, and off Kongens Nytorv (at the head of Østergade) is the big Magasin. Illum, also on Østergade, is another large department store with good places to eat during the day. Royal Copenhagen Porcelain and Bing and Grøndahl, the two porcelain specialists, are both in Amagertorv; the Danish Handicraft Guild – for traditional embroidery kits – is on Vimmels-kaftet; and Georg Jensen, silver specialist, is on Østergade.

Pedestrian shopping is not confined to Strøget, but extends north from Amagertorv towards the Round Tower. In the streets of the university quarter (try Skindergade) you'll find a range of foreign shops from Italian to Indonesian, books, music and 'alternative' style. Parallel with Strøget to the south, Kompagni-straede and Laederstraede combine to form a thoroughfare of ancient houses with many antique shops and antiquarian booksellers; and further east Bredgade and Store Kongensgade have some exclusive luxury shopping.

Practically everything in Denmark costs more than in Britain, and MOMS (VAT) is 25 per cent. As a tourist, you can avoid most of this by having your purchases sent direct to your home address. Many shops also display the red and white Tax Free sign: if you spend a minimum of Dkr 4,700 you can take your goods with you and the MOMS will be remitted when you leave Denmark, or refunded to your home address. Porcelain, amber and Danish craft and design are the most seductive souvenirs.

EATING AND DRINKING

Copenhagen's 2,000-odd restaurants span most international cuisines, from first-class French to the branches of 'Mongolian Barbecue'. You can spend a lot on dinner, particularly if dining seems incomplete without a bottle of wine (it costs from £8 a bottle). The most effective way to economise is to develop a taste for beer with your meals.

The good news is that there is a huge daytime choice of cafés, bars and friendly cellar lunch places (*frokorestaurants*), with dishes chalked up daily (*dagensret*). Here you can sample the cold cuisine that is Denmark's speciality – herring (*silt*), shrimps and other fish variously pickled and spiced, salads, and of course *smørrebrød*. These succulent open sandwiches are also staple street food, displayed in huge and artistic variety in the sandwich bars. More familiar fast food for hungry tourists includes pizza and pancakes, hamburgers and hot dogs.

Two areas with an attractive choice of eating places are Nyhavn, whose old canalside houses have cellar bars decorated with scrubbed pine and pretty tiles, and Gråbrødretorv, with its leafy French-style terraces.

NIGHTLIFE

From May to September, Tivoli is the main venue for evening entertainment. As well as pantomime and pop, its concert hall has a resident symphony orchestra and visiting ballet and modern dance companies. As Tivoli closes, the season opens at the Royal Theatre in Kongens Nytorv, whose three stages offer drama, opera and the Danish Royal Ballet. Copenhagen also has two English-language theatres, and international films are sub-titled, not dubbed.

There are a number of jazz clubs and bars in the city. De Tre Musketerer has New Orleans-type jazz and a traditional knees-up atmosphere. Jazzhus Montmartre has modern jazz and folk, some international stars and lots of atmosphere. The Copenhagen Jazz Festival is a ten-day July bonanza.

The best source of 'what's-on' information is in *Copenhagen This Week*, which also tells you about the jazz, folk, rock and pop music scene and the discos, nightclubs and trendy late-open cafés dotted round the city centre. Striptease and topless waitresses can be found to the west, beyond the railway station, in Istedgade and Halmtorvet.

HOTELS

Copenhagen's hotels are expensive, thanks largely to the 13.1 per cent service charge and 25 per cent MOMS (VAT). It's not easy to find a double room in a central position for much less than £80, and paying £100 per night is the norm rather than the exception. Even so, the hotels lack character: clean, bland and functional with plenty of facilities seem to be the most desirable elements. The bulk of the tourist hotel trade is clustered around the station. It's not the best of areas, being some distance from the centre and rather seedy in character. Luckily, some of the nicest hotels are outside this area – but it's certainly the place to start looking if you are simply in need of a not-too-expensive room.

Room rates aren't necessarily fixed: you may be offered a considerable discount on the printed price. All in all, though, you'll save most on accommodation by going on a package to Copenhagen. But beware: hotels used by some tour operators are a long way from the city centre, and it may be a considerable slog in (unless you have a car).

Hotel prices Symbols indicate approximate prices per room per night for a double room with bath. Many large hotels run special breaks which work out far cheaper. (See page 14 for further details.)

♦ = under £50; ♦♦ = £50 to £80; ♦♦♦ = £80 to £100;
♦♦♦♦ = £100 to £140; ♦♦♦♦♦ = over £140.

ADMIRAL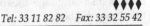
Tolbodgade 24-28, DK 1253   *Tel: 33 11 82 82   Fax: 33 32 55 42*

This hotel is an old, fortress-like warehouse with a black-stained sandstone exterior, a cannon and flags guarding its entrance. The lobby runs the entire length of the ground floor, with seating at one end and a nautical bar dominated by a figurehead at the other. The huge structural beams and trusses convey an inescapable sensation of being deep inside a ship. Bedrooms are smart, with startling abstract lithographs. The approach to the rooms is along a corridor with some stone arches running down the middle – it's like walking beside an aqueduct.

Bedrooms: 366, all with bath/shower/WC   **Facilities:** Lift; restaurant; sauna; solarium; nightclub   **Credit/charge cards accepted:** Access, Amex, Visa

CHRISTIAN IV ♦♦♦♦
Dronningens Tvaergade 45, DK 1302   *Tel: 33 32 10 44   Fax: 33 32 07 06*

This hotel is some distance from the centre but is in a pleasant area of interesting shops, with a French restaurant next door. It's a clean, five-storey white building with attractive blue canopies over the windows. There are high-quality bedrooms but no public rooms apart from a rather cramped breakfast area. Nevertheless, it is good value.

Bedrooms: 42, all with shower/WC; mini-bar   **Facilities:** Lift   **Credit/charge cards accepted:** All

EXCELSIOR
Colbjornsengade 4, DK 1652   *Tel: 31 24 50 85   Fax: 31 24 50 87*

A laid-back family hotel in the station area. In the lobby, you are faced by an area scattered with chunky modern chairs and tables in art deco colours. Behind the lobby is a more restful garden area with plants in pots and seats to flop in. Bedrooms are large and bright with abstract murals and slightly rudimentary bathrooms. The Excelsior is different from the run-of-the-mill tourist hotels in the area – it advertises with careful photographs of its breakfasts, not its rooms. Service is friendly.

Closed: Chr   **Bedrooms:** 105, most with bath/WC, rest with shower/WC; mini-bar; safe   **Facilities:** Lift   **Credit/charge cards accepted:** All

KONG FREDERIK
Vester Voldgade 25, DK 1552   *Tel: 33 12 59 02   Fax: 33 93 59 01*

This is a big, white, nineteenth-century building on a busy street, convenient for shops and relatively close to the Strøget. The lobby is decorated with dark wood, green carpet and brass – a little gloomy perhaps – but there's a pub bar in much the same style. The central courtyard is a bright contrast and it's a quiet and relaxing place to eat. The bedrooms and bathrooms vary in size, but all are attractive, with dark wood furnishings, blue carpets and prints of hunting scenes.

Closed: Chr to New Year   **Bedrooms:** 110, all with bath/WC; hair-dryer; mini-bar   **Facilities:** Lift; restaurant   **Credit/charge cards accepted:** All

MISSIONSHOTELLET HEBRON
Helgolandsgade 4, DK 1653   *Tel: 31 31 69 06   Fax: 31 31 90 67*

As spartan as it sounds, but by no means dingy and uncomfortable, the building is uncompromisingly institutional. The lobby, with drinks machines and functional seating, is not a place to relax in, but there are plenty of other hotels, bars and restaurants nearby to slip out to. Bedrooms are spotless, if rather old-fashioned, and have all the facilities you need. No frills, but probably the best value in central Copenhagen.

Closed: Chr   **Bedrooms:** 106, most with shower/WC, some with bath/WC; not all rooms have TV   **Facilities:** Lift   **Credit/charge cards accepted:** All

71 NYHAVN
Nyhavn 71, DK 1051   *Tel: 33 11 85 85   Fax: 33 93 15 85*

This old warehouse is right at the end of Copenhagen's old harbour area, and well away from the rows of tourist cafés a little further up. It's a stern-looking building, built in 1804 of red brick with small, cell-like windows. Inside, it has been extremely well converted, though the size of the rooms is severely constrained by the original warehouse layout. Timber baulks prop up the ceilings, and nautical equipment and paintings decorate the lobby. The atmosphere is quietly formal, though families should feel at home too.

Bedrooms: 82, most with shower/WC, some with bath/shower/WC; hair-dryer; mini-bar   **Facilities:** Lift; restaurant   **Credit/charge cards accepted:** All

VESTERSØHUS ♦♦♦♦
Vestersøgade 58, DK 1601   *Tel: 33 11 38 70   Fax: 33 11 00 90*

This is a curious hotel, away from the centre by one of the lakes around the older part of the city. It's part of a long, four-storey, red-brick block of flats. The hotel is a warren of 44 rooms, almost all different. Some are big, others are small with a balcony. Some have kitchenettes, some have two lavatories. Check carefully what you are booking. There's no lounge, but there is a spacious breakfast room and a tiny roof garden which is good for sunbathing.

Bedrooms: 44, half with shower/WC, half with bath/WC **Facilities:** Lift; tennis; sauna **Credit/charge cards accepted:** All

Hotel prices Symbols indicate approximate prices per room per night for a double room with bath. Many large hotels run special breaks which work out far cheaper. (See page 14 for further details.)

♦ = under £50; ♦♦ = £50 to £80; ♦♦♦ = £80 to £100;
♦♦♦♦ = £100 to £140; ♦♦♦♦♦ = over £140.

DUBLIN

- Despite being the capital and business centre of the Republic of Ireland, with suburbs stretching for several miles around Dublin Bay, Dublin seems more like a town than a city, with a compact centre
- The city is historically and architecturally interesting – with newly renovated areas like Temple Bar alongside elegant Georgian streets
- With several fine libraries and bookshops, Dublin has a special appeal for the literary-minded
- Nightlife is plentiful – Dublin is particularly well-endowed with theatres, pubs and bars and various music venues
- The charm of Dubliners is part of the city's attraction

DUBLIN and its suburbs spread out from the banks of the River Liffey, with the sweep of Dublin Bay almost visible to the east, and the Wicklow Mountains, almost a background presence, to the south. High ground drops to the Liffey above the Linn Dubh (black pool) where the tributary River Poddle, hardly visible now, runs in. On this ridge, St Patrick's earliest Christian converts built churches, and the Vikings established a town after winning the Battle of Dublin in 919. A century later the Irish, under Brian Boru – whose harp is incorporated in the familiar Guinness motif – defeated the Vikings at the Battle of Clontarf in 1014. Since neither event was convenient for 'millennium' celebrations in the 1980s, the city selected an interim (Irish-won) skirmish and dated itself for the purpose from 988.

The commanding ridge above the Liffey was the obvious site for Dublin Castle, the Anglo-Norman fortress begun on the orders of King John. Medieval, Tudor and Elizabethan Dublin expanded around the castle in a sprawl of alleys, wharves and churches. But when the city emerged from the poverty and civil wars of the seventeenth century to the commercial stability of the eighteenth, a grander Dublin was built for the new age of elegance. East of the ridge, wide streets and squares of handsome terraced houses, magnificent public buildings and palatial private mansions made up Georgian Dublin – the fair city of Molly Malone. Rich and poor areas thus clearly defined have polarised Dublin for longer than most cities. However, renovation programmes during the past few years are slowly erasing the contrasts.

Dublin's hub is the staggered crossroads where the portico of the Bank of Ireland faces the gates of Trinity College. Traffic used to forge straight through on the north-south axis from O'Connell Bridge to Grafton Street; the pedestrianisation of the latter swirls it all instead into the one-way systems round the Georgian grid to the east and the older network to the west. The Georgian layout includes the huge green spaces – Merrion Square, St Stephen's Green – once the privilege of a wealthy suburb and now the relaxed central oases. West of Grafton Street the open spaces tend to be building sites or derelict patches used for car-parks. North across the river, O'Connell Street has the proportions of a boulevard without any of the charm: a broad and practical thoroughfare leading up to the widespread remnants of another Georgian area built to complement the fashionable southern suburb. Flowing west to east, the Liffey itself is a broad sweep of light and salty ventilation, a mile of small-scale commerce between the grand civic setpieces of the Four Courts and the Custom House. Half a dozen central bridges link the Liffey's quays, interesting gap-toothed old rows behind surges of one-way traffic.

The atmosphere of this 'Augustan capital of a Gaelic nation' is exuberant: brisk wafts of coffee and malt in the air, with a skirl of seagulls overhead and elliptical Dublinisms at your ears in the street; terrible jokes on the shopfronts ('Blazing Salads') and violently colour-mixed bunches on display at the flower stalls; hefty brewers' drayhorses shouldering through the backstreets, and spirited old nags pulling tourist traps round St Stephen's Green. Dubliners are a literate, theatrical, voluble lot and are welcoming as hosts. The mere visitor can experience an instant nostalgia – coveting membership, or at least sponsorship, from the secret pub-snug to the perfectly accessible elegance of the Shelbourne's coffee-lounge. Visually, Dublin is a detail-spotter's delight. The long façades of a Georgian street, a blighted alley, a glowing pub front or the crumbling charm of a gateway are all captured by camera. It's no accident that the city's best-selling image, in sizes from postcard to poster, is a multiple of themed detail: pub fronts, shopfronts, doorways.

In spite of an unemployment rate of around 17 per cent, business is booming in Dublin and tourism is big business. Strolling crowds in Grafton Street tread the new brick paving laid for the millennium; floodlights illuminate the grandest buildings; large-scale heritage videos present the city's history; and after preservation by neglect for 150 years – and some piecemeal disfiguration in the 1960s – the largest assembly of Georgian architecture in the world is being well cared for. Some of the loveliest ornate ceilings can be inspected in the upper galleries of the Powerscourt mansion-turned-shopping centre. More shops fill the striking 1980s aviary – dominating St Stephen's Green with glass and arched white ironwork. Wandering west you'll find more ethnic shopping centres such as the Victorian red-brick market arcade of homely stalls, and, up the ridge, in the Liberties, the battered, echoing old hall of the Iveagh Market, Dublin's permanent jumble sale of old clothes and rickety furniture. South of the Green, ducks and fishermen and picnickers enjoy a tree-lined stretch of the Grand Canal, Dublin's industrial highway until the railway took over.

WHEN TO GO

Ireland wouldn't be so strikingly the Emerald Isle but for its weather – although the coastal area around Dublin gets less rain than almost any other part of the country. On the other hand, Dublin doesn't benefit as much from the influence of the warm Gulf Stream along Ireland's western coast. The sunniest months are May and June – the best time to see the city.

MASTERING THE SYSTEM

Information Dublin City Tourist Office is at 14 Upper O'Connell Street (tel: 747733). It stocks plenty of books, booklets and maps covering every aspect of Dublin. Staff will also book you a hotel, theatre or tour.

GETTING THERE

Going independently

By air Dublin is one of the easiest cities to reach for a short break as there's a good choice of flights from several airports around the UK. You can fly there in an hour or less from four London airports and 13 regional ones. The main carrier is Aer Lingus, with flights from most regional airports and 14 to 18 daily flights from Heathrow. British Midland flies eight times daily from Heathrow; Brymon Airways, Gillair, Loganair, Manx Airlines, Ryanair and SAS also operate to Dublin from many UK airports. SuperPEX and APEX fares are generally cheapest and are the same price all year round, but enquire about special deals (Aer Lingus' Super-Saver holiday fare, for example). Lowest price is about £60 return.

Dublin Airport This is about seven miles north of the city. It's busy but efficient, with an exchange counter open daily 6.45am to 10pm (9pm in winter) and a tourist information office. Departing, with some time to spare, you'll find the airport restaurant offers a reasonably priced three-course meal with coffee; wine, here as in most of Dublin, starts at around £10 a bottle, and a Guinness or even a mineral water in the bar will cost you more than down by the Liffey.

Among the shops selling Irish souvenirs, a tempting last-minute extravagance is vacuum-packed, smoked Irish salmon – though it's no cheaper in the duty-free area than downtown. Dublin Bus offers a fast service between the airport, the central bus station and major hotels in the city, running every 20 minutes from early morning until midnight; an ordinary double-decker which stops along the 41A route is a cheap and friendly alternative.

Maps A good colour map is produced by the listings magazine *In Dublin* (15 Lower Baggot Street, tel: 61555): it has room for bus-route numbers, and gives much valuable information in a clear layout on the back.

Sightseeing tours Dublin Bus, opposite the tourist office at 59 Upper O'Connell Street (tel: 734222), operates a twice-daily two and a quarter-hour tour of the city in a double-decker (open topped in fine weather). Grey Line (tel: 74466) organises selective tours, including visits to some of the sights. Information and leaflets on these and other tours are available from the tourist office.

A signposted tourist **walking trail** takes you all over the city centre and the accompanying guidebook is available from book-shops and the tourist office. You can follow the progress of Leopold Bloom through the Dublin of James Joyce's *Ulysses* with a simple map or a hefty literary guidebook. In summer you can also join a literary pub-crawl on weekday evenings. The Irish

---

By ferry Two sailings a day (four in high season) from Holyhead are operated by both Sealink Stena (to Dun Laoghaire – eight miles from Dublin) and B&I Line (to Dublin). The journey takes three and a half hours on either route. Fares vary according to the time of year, with both lines offering a range of promotional faresavers. The off-peak return fare for foot passengers is about half the cost of the return airfare. All-in packages which include the cost of rail or coach travel from your home to Holyhead are available, too, from Sealink Stena, B&I and British Rail. If you're travelling with children, British Rail's family fares are a bargain.

By car If you take a car over to Dublin, the fare will be the same whether one, two, three or four passengers go with it. It is very expensive in high season, but so is car hire in Ireland, so the more passengers the better.

By rail An integrated arrangement called InterCity Ireland gets you from all parts of England and Scotland to a British port, and on from an Irish one, with Saver and Family fares available. From London to Dublin you can also get an Advance Purchase Return. Details are given in the brochure *Ireland by Rail and Sea*, from travel agents and railway travel centres.

Tour operator packages

A number of tour operators have short-break packages using accommodation ranging from small guesthouses to luxury hotels. Travel is usually by scheduled flights from London and other UK airports, but some brochures give you the cheaper option of getting to Dublin by ferry. In 1992, a three-night break in a three-star hotel/B&B, ranged from £180 to £260, so it's worth looking around. For a list of tour operators see page 385.

Tourist Board (Bord Fáilte – headquarters at Baggot Street Bridge, tel: 765871; open March to October) offers a programme of walks with qualified guides, covering historic and literary themes.

Banks Dublin Airport bank is open 7.30am to 11pm every day except Christmas. All other banks are open Monday to Friday, 10am to 12.30pm and 1.30pm to 3pm (5pm on Thursday). Lunchtime opening is being phased in according to local demand.

Opening hours and days Shops open Monday to Saturday, about 9am to 5.30pm, with late-night opening on Thursday (till 8pm or 9pm); some book and gift shops are open on Sunday afternoons, too. It's important to plan your sightseeing, for example, Trinity College Library is closed on Saturday afternoon and Sunday; Dublin Castle has erratic opening times so check first; and the National Museum is closed on Monday and Sunday morning.

GETTING AROUND

CIE, the national public transport company, can provide information on trains and buses (in UK tel: 081-686 0994; in Dublin, at 59 Upper O'Connell Street, tel: 734222).

Buses will, in theory, get you everywhere and save your feet between far-flung sights. The Dublin Bus city tour leaflet gives the relevant bus-route numbers for all the main ones. You can pick up bus timetables from newsagents or tel: 734222. 'An Lar' on the front means 'the centre'.

Taxis can be hailed in the street, but it is often quicker to go to a rank: these include St Stephen's Green (tel: 762847 and 767381), College Green (tel: 777440) and O'Connell Street (tel: 744599 and 786150).

The DART (Dublin Area Rapid Transport) system serves 25 stations from Howth to Bray and takes you right into the centre of the city: Tara Street Station for O'Connell Street Bridge, and Pearse Station, Westland Row, for St Stephen's Green/Grafton Street. The Dublin Explorer ticket costs IR £10 and is valid for four days on all Dublin buses and suburban trains, including the DART. It may not be used before 9.45am, but there is no evening restriction.

Only the most talented and intrepid visiting driver will enjoy getting round central Dublin by **car**. One-way systems and a severe shortage of signposts are the main drawbacks. Secure car-parks are few and the competition for meters cut-throat.

Cycling, on the other hand, should be an effective way of getting around the city. In practice, however, you don't see throngs of cyclists. The streets are not bike-friendly – some barely wide enough for the car and bus traffic – and though parking a bike is a simple matter so is stealing one. Bike-hire addresses, none of them very central, can be obtained from the tourist office.

UNMISSABLES

Trinity College Old Library
Dublin's single-college university was founded by Elizabeth I in 1592 'to civilise Ireland with both learning and the Protestant religion'. Its site, in the city centre, was once monastery land. The magnificent buildings distributed around its lawns and cobbled courtyards range from ornate eighteenth-century classical to streamlined modern. The Long Room, located in the 1712 Old Library, is one of the world's most satisfying interiors. Its proportions date from 1859, when the height was doubled to provide more shelf space. Over 200 feet long, a cathedral-like perspective of mellow book-lined bays rises from floor to gallery and up to the barrel-vaulted roof, side-lit from tall windows. A double file of benefactors' busts surveys a line of showcases, displaying Ireland's literary roots. Two volumes from the Book of Kells lie open, one displaying illuminated text, the other a page of exquisite illustration. Reproductions in the library shop are desirable souvenirs.

Dublin Castle
No longer a castle, this is now an enclave of wide courtyards, offices and ceremonial accommodation set on Dublin's high ground but totally obscured by the surrounding buildings. It has been a fortress, prison and central core of civil and military power. Its major remodelling was in the sixteenth and seventeenth centuries for the English viceroys, who then moved out to a more salubrious residence in Phoenix Park. You can enter from Cork Hill, where Justice, on the gateway arch, turns her back on the city, or up little Palace Street past the appealing house labelled 'Sick and Indigent Roomkeepers Society' (the oldest charity in Dublin), to the Lower Yard. Here is the only Norman remnant, the round Record Tower, and tacked on to it the neo-Gothic Chapel Royal – now a Catholic church. In the imposing Upper Yard the most attractive building is the clock-towered Genea-logical Office with the State Apartments opposite. Unless they

are in use for some ceremonial occasion you can visit (guided tour only) the ornate halls and galleries, throne- and drawing-rooms, corridors and ante-rooms, all having elegant furniture.

The National Gallery of Ireland
The National Gallery (entrance from Merrion Square West) has, on four floors, displays of paintings from Irish, American and all the major European schools. Famous favourites include Pieter Bruegel's *The Peasant Wedding*, and Chardin's delicate *Young Governess*. The red walls circle around a fine spiral staircase and show off the Irish portraits, winding down from Yeats and Joyce to the beautiful Countess Markievicz. If your energy flags, the café is particularly good.

OTHER PLACES TO VISIT

Cathedrals and churches

Christ Church Cathedral (Church of Ireland, diocese of Dublin) It was founded in the early eleventh century, but its magnificent Gothic stonework dates from the thirteenth and was restored and in parts rebuilt in the 1870s. Among its dead is St Lawrence O'Toole, Dublin's patron saint, who is represented by his heart in a heart-shaped iron casket hung on a chapel wall. The dusty expanses of the Norman crypt store crumbling sections of arch and column, a pair of dandy but noseless statues and a homely collection of kitchen chairs and folding tables.

St Patrick's Cathedral (Church of Ireland, national cathedral) This was founded in the late twelfth century, with the intention of being independent of Christ Church's monks. It was built on the marshy side of St Patrick's Celtic church. The Early English stonework has been repeatedly restored (notably in the 1860s) though scarcely altered, and the church is stuffed with monuments and memorials. Jonathan Swift, its dean for three decades, is buried in the nave. There is no statue of him (here or anywhere else in Dublin) but space has been found in a corner for a bust and his chair and pulpit. The Cathedral School dates from 1432, and it is possible to see the choir at practice. Archbishop Marsh's library is around the corner in St Patrick's Close. An almost miniature copy of Trinity's, it was opened to the public in 1707, who read its books in locked cages, which are still intact.

St Mary's Pro-Cathedral (Catholic) This was built in the 1820s, not on the site first envisaged (the General Post Office got there first) but discreetly in Marlborough Street which is, unfortunately, much too narrow for visitors to gain a proper view of its dome and Doric-pillared façade. It has an uncluttered Renaissance interior, all grey and white and steady candle flames. Tourists are tolerated, but its rightful visitors drop in while shopping to pay their devotions.

St Michan's This little church north of the river was rebuilt in 1686 on top of its eleventh-century foundations. The sexton, setting his own pace, will show you its charms – including some beautiful wood carving, and an organ once played by Handel – before leading the way round the outside to the macabre vault. Visitors squeeze down through a door resembling a coalhole hatch to gaze from a dusty rubble-strewn passage into a chamber just large enough to hold three open coffins, displaying corpses naturally mummified by the very dry atmosphere of magnesian limestone.

Dominant buildings

The major city landmarks of Dublin's architectural history are designed for external impact – but you can also go inside all but one. The striking white edifice opposite Trinity College, with the roof statues, 22 great columns, blind windows and protective cannon, is now the **Bank of Ireland**. It was originally the Irish Parliament House, begun in 1729, extended in 1785 and closed when the 1800 Act of Union propelled its occupants to Westminster. Four years later the former House of Commons began dispensing cash and can now be strolled through. The preserved House of Lords can be visited by groups on arrangement or singly on impulse if you pick a quiet time to approach an official.

One of the buildings that conceals Dublin Castle is **City Hall** (designed in the 1770s as the Royal Exchange), which also obscures the view from the Liffey up Parliament Street. The Hall, which is wonderfully floodlit at night, is also beautifully lit by day. The glass-topped dome enables natural light to accentuate the lush frescoes and fluted columns. The motto in mosaic on the floor is straightforward: 'An obedient citizenry creates a happy city.'

Look upstream from a Liffey bridge and the green dome of the **Four Courts** (law courts) dominates. Observe it from an opposite quay to enjoy the splendid frontage – *Moses* flanked by *Justice* and *Mercy* above its Corinthian portico – but if you're passing, slip inside. Not necessarily into a court (originally those of Judicature, Chancery, King's Bench and Exchequer), but into the high-domed circle of the lobby, which hums with the concentrated consultations of wigs and clients, particularly at the beginning of the lunch recess.

Dublin's biggest landmark is the **Custom House**, a building which deserves a detailed inspection. *Hope* stands tall on the green dome, but only from close to can you see the keystone heads along its frontage of Portland stone – riverine gods, and benevolent bulls for the meat trade. The massive building was burned to a shell in 1921 and, in the garden behind, a Mother Ireland statue mourns her dying children. Across the road is the trade unions' new Liberty Hall and the recently completed Docklands scheme.

The Ionic portico of the **General Post Office** has dominated O'Connell Street since 1818 and now serves as a review stand during parades and rallies. It has been enshrined in the nation's heart since the Easter Rising of 1916, when it was the headquarters of Patrick Pearse's Irish Volunteers, whence the Proclamation of the Irish Republic was read. It was gutted by British shellfire after a six-day siege – a plaque outside tells the story. Inside, there is a small but powerful bronze of the legendary Cú Chulainn.

A 135-foot Nelson Column used to stand opposite the GPO in the middle of O'Connell Street, but it was blown up in 1966. A long-haired bronze Anna Livia rests naked and supine in rippling water, and is disapprovingly dubbed the Floozy in the Jacuzzi. (Her sister, the Tart with the Cart, is a busty Molly Malone at the corner of Grafton Street.)

Museums and galleries

The Chester Beatty Library and Gallery of Oriental Art These house the astonishing collections of Alfred Chester Beatty, a millionaire American mining engineer with Irish ancestry and the instincts of a scholarly magpie. They are displayed in discreet buildings (one built in 1953, the other in 1975) among lawns and rosebeds off a suburban avenue. Inside, the lines of showcases look sober but their contents are vividly appealing: paintings, prints and fairy tales, lacquer and jade, snuff bottles and figurines, rare rhinoceros-horn cups.

The Guinness Hop Store Museum A lofty warehouse display area (in Crane Street) occupies a fraction of the brewery's sprawling acreage. Here every stage of producing Ireland's *vin du pays* – yeast and grist, wort and mash – is explained on well-arranged information boards amid splendid old machinery. You can sample a free half-pint in the huge bar.

The Hugh Lane Municipal Gallery of Modern Art This gallery is so named because of the Hugh Lane Bequest, paintings about which Dublin was in prolonged dispute with the Tate Gallery. The benefactor went down with the *Lusitania*, leaving a will of doubtful interpretation. All settled, the gallery's excellent collection covers paintings from the French Impressionists to modern Irish artists, and some sculpture.

The National Museum (Kildare Street entrance and archaeological section closed for restoration until December 1993) The main building has a lovely circular entrance-hall, ornate but friendly. The outstanding display is the Treasury: early Irish artistry in crowns, crosses and croziers, and the famous eighth-century Ardagh chalice and Tara brooch. Other striking collections include Viking artefacts, exquisite glass and a patriotic roomful of presidential-related items.

Dublin Writers Museum The finely restored Georgian building houses an exhibition on Ireland's literary heritage, including letters, photographs, memorabilia and first editions. There's also a varied programme of special exhibitions, lectures, readings and workshops.

Other attractions

The Zoo On a fine day, Dublin's is an unusually enjoyable zoo. It has a fine sweeping layout round a long lake, modest buildings and magnificent animals. They're proudest of their lions, who breed contentedly here – one of them immortalised as the MGM trademark. The zoo enclosure occupies part of the enormous leafy Phoenix Park, seven miles round, the name derived from *fionn uisce*, 'clear water'. The site of the original spring is near the sea lions' pool.

Excursion

Howth Thackeray called Dubliners 'the car-drivingest, tay-drinkingest, say-bathingest people in the world', and indeed they make full use of the beaches Southside and Northside of the Liffey where the city suburbs melt into seaside resorts. The northern promontory of Howth has a couple of beaches. But the focal point of an excursion here is the 'wild-as-Connemara' cliff walking on its rugged green headland and also its fishing village charm, which has survived the modernisation of the thriving harbour. The West Pier is strewn with chandlers and net-makers, the East ends with a lighthouse. There are boat trips across to the tempting little island called Ireland's Eye, and a picturesque row of pubs and shops. Howth Castle is a private residence, but some of the best views are from its accessible grounds, where there are 2,000 varieties of rhododendron.

SHOPPING

Grafton Street is the prime shopping thoroughfare in Dublin, with two elegant department stores, glass, linen and silver specialists and the usual range of upmarket high-street clothes stores, interspersed with fast-food outlets. The original Bewley's Oriental Café is here, a Dublin institution whose interior splendours have been rather diluted by refurbishment, though still serving distinctive coffee and plentiful Irish baking. Nassau Street offers geneaology (1,000 coats of arms in stock) and Irish souvenirs from classy cashmere, tweed and crystal to the tritest shamrockery. Sweaters are the best value – but shop around for an Aran (prices are lower north of the river). The Powerscourt Townhouse Centre, a restored eighteenth-century mansion, is a very attractive assembly for art, antiques and Irish fashion designers; the St Stephen's Green Centre is hi-tech, with escalators and pop music instead of polished stairs and piano.

Side-streets off Grafton Street are crammed with trendy little shops and bars. To the north-west, the lanes round Temple Bar are a concentration of pop, folk, trad, occult and green establishments. North of the river, the commerce of O'Connell Street and nearby thoroughfares is more practical than prestigious, with a range of comprehensive family shopping emporia. West, down Henry Street, is market territory – budget produce stalls in Moore Street, and the wholesale fruit and vegetable market in the chaotically small Mary Street, crammed solid in the morning with vans and patient drayhorses. It's worth exploring for its ornate brick buildings decorated with carved fruit and animals. The huge ILAC shopping centre off Henry Street is ideal for bargain-basement browsing – try Dunnes Stores for Aran and other sweaters.

Bookshops are widespread and plentiful, many of the best combining new and second-hand stock. Opposite Trinity College, on Nassau Street, Fred Hanna's is comprehensive and usually very crowded. Irish writing is the speciality in Trinity's Library Shop and in Hodges Figgis in Dawson Street; Greens at the corner of Merrion Square is a charming Victorian warren of shelves, its stock spilling out into pavement trays along its canopied, green wrought-iron frontage. Over on Ormond Quay, just west of the pretty little Halfpenny Bridge, the Winding Stair occupies two floors of an old warehouse and combines splendid second-hand browsing with coffee and snacks while overlooking the Liffey.

EATING AND DRINKING

Eating out is a delight in Dublin, starting with the chewy Irish bread, good coffee and creamy Irish milk you're likely to encounter at breakfast. Cream, whipped or thickly poured, is a constant temptation. For mid-morning coffee Bewley's in Grafton Street is one standard of excellence and the Shelbourne Hotel's lovely lounge another. Good places for sustaining informal meals, notably in the Temple Bar area, include Fat Freddie's and the Bad Ass Café. Potato pancakes and Irish stew are available at Gallagher's Boxty House, or versatile vegetarian meals at the Well Fed Café (behind Well Red Books, in Crow Street). You can dine out excellently in French style at Le Coq Hardi and Patrick Guilbaud's. Italian cuisine is well represented, Russian and even Czech each have a following, and there's a wide range of places for a juicy steak.

You are never very far from a pub in Dublin. Open from 10.30am to 11.30pm (except on Sundays when they close for the 'holy hours' between 2pm and 4pm), there are dark brown historical pubs, flamboyant theatrical pubs, and pubs which are places of literary pilgrimage. Oldest is the Brazen Head, in a bleak part of Bridge Street near the river – it's rowdy at night but a peaceful daytime refuge with an attractive little courtyard. Cosiest is Doheny & Nesbitt in Lower Baggot Street, divided into snugs and corners by wooden partitions. Toners nearby has the same unmodernised authenticity. Off Grafton Street Neary's is solidly Victorian and the Bailey young and trendy. *In Dublin* magazine keeps in touch with the changing ambiences and clientele of Dublin's pubs, but the well-poured Guinness and the hard core of regulars are constants. You can obtain a filling hot meal in most pubs for less than £5, lasagne/quiche and salad for about £3.50, sandwiches for around £1.50, plus coffee.

NIGHTLIFE

Dublin's theatrical tradition is alive and well. The Abbey, the Gate, the Gaiety and the splendid old Olympia present the classics, Irish drama, mainstream plays and popular commercial shows. Smaller houses offer the experimental and adventurous – the Peacock underneath the Abbey, the Players' Theatre in Trinity College, the Focus and the Project Arts Centre. You can always listen to classical music at the National Concert Hall and often in a church or gallery; rock, jazz and folk venues are widespread. O'Donoghue's in Merrion Row is the most famous venue for traditional Irish music, and many pubs and bars have singers.

HOTELS

Most of the hotels are in the centre of town. The general standard is reasonable, with a handful of luxury hotels. Some of the larger hotels used by tour operators are a bit further out – you will need public transport to get to the centre. Guesthouses and town houses where you can rent private rooms can be found all over Dublin. The Bord Fáilte publishes a list of all registered and approved accommodation. Make sure you book early during the Dublin Horse Show at the beginning of August and around the Rugby Internationals. Many hotels offer good weekend deals. Beware of the 10-15 per cent service charge which is added to your bill.

THE FITZWILLIAM ♦♦
41 Upper Fitzwilliam Street　　　　　　*Tel: 600199　Fax: 767488*

In an attractive Georgian square only minutes from the main shopping area, the Fitzwilliam looks like a private house. The plain, high-ceilinged sitting-room combines period and modern furniture. The bedrooms were renovated in 1992 and, with their long windows, are light and cheerful. The hotel serves breakfast only, but an independent restaurant in the basement has an excellent reputation. A cheap, unassuming hotel in a good position.

Closed: Mid-Dec to early Jan; restaurant closed Sat lunch and Sun
Bedrooms: 12, most with shower/WC, some with bath/WC; hair-dryer
Facilities: Restaurant　**Credit/charge cards accepted:** All

GEORGIAN HOUSE AND ANTE ROOM ◆◆◆
20-21 Lower Baggot Street   *Tel: 618832   Fax: 618834*

The hotel is an attractive house in a busy shopping street with a slightly shabby charm, near St Stephen's Green. The interior is civilised and neat with a sitting-room on the ground floor. The seafood restaurant is open to all, advertising its fare on a street board. The bedrooms at the back are quieter.

Bedrooms: 33, all with bath/WC   **Facilities:** Restaurant; private parking   **Credit/charge cards accepted:** All

GRESHAM ◆◆◆◆
23 Upper O'Connell Street   *Tel: 746881   Fax: 787175*

This is the city's oldest hotel. Now part of the Ryan Hotel chain, it has recently undergone a facelift, and the royal blue carpet gleams with golden 'G's. The main sitting area is a busy thoroughfare to the other rooms, but it is comfortable in a sedate sort of way with unobtrusive piped classical music. The bedrooms are modern and comfortable with bland, high-quality furnishings. If you want to be north of the Liffey in comfort, this is the place for you.

Closed: Chr   **Bedrooms:** 200, all with bath/shower/WC; hair-dryer; trouser press   **Facilities:** Lift; restaurant; bars   **Credit/charge cards accepted:** All

JURYS HOTEL AND TOWERS ◆◆◆◆
Pembroke Road, Ballsbridge   *Tel: 605000   Fax: 605540*

Further out in Ballsbridge, a ride away from the centre, is this huge hotel, popular with tours and conferences. It provides extreme comfort and all the facilities you could want in international style, but lacks atmosphere and personality. It has bars and restaurants and various levels of luxury bedrooms.

Bedrooms: 384, all with bath/shower/WC; hair-dryer; some with mini-bar; trouser press   **Facilities:** Lift; restaurants; bars; heated indoor/outdoor pool; hairdresser; masseuse   **Credit/charge cards accepted:** All

---

◆ = under £50; ◆◆ = £50 to £80; ◆◆◆ = £80 to £100;
◆◆◆◆ = £100 to £140; ◆◆◆◆◆ = over £140.

LEESON COURT HOTEL ♦♦
26/27 Lower Leeson Street   *Tel: 763380   Fax: 618273*

About five minutes' walk from St Stephen's Green is this restored Georgian house. The road is busy in rush hours, but double glazing has been installed. The public rooms are good for a hotel of this size, with a new conservatory restaurant added on to the bar. All staff are friendly and helpful. Bedrooms have recently been refurbished.

Closed: Restaurant closed Sun and one week at Chr   **Bedrooms:** 20, some with bath/WC, all with shower/WC   **Facilities:** Lift; bar; restaurant   **Credit/charge cards accepted:** All

RUSSELL COURT ♦♦
21-25 Harcourt Street   *Tel: 784066   Fax: 781576*

These adjoining Georgian houses have recently been totally refurbished. Only a few minutes' walk from the centre, the hotel is a popular meeting place with a fashionable air. It has a chic bar with nightly pianist, a small, intimate restaurant and a nightclub. You can escape from these into the quiet and comfortable reception room and residents' sitting-room and bar. The bedrooms, decorated in pastel shades, are large and airy with immaculate bathrooms.

Bedrooms: 42, most with shower/WC, some with bath/WC; all with hair-dryer   **Facilities:** Lift; restaurant; nightclub; private parking   **Credit/charge cards accepted:** Access, Amex, Visa

THE SHELBOURNE ♦♦♦♦♦
27 St Stephen's Green   *Tel: 766471   Fax: 616006*

Overlooking the huge, leafy St Stephen's Green is this stately Georgian building. High ceilings, pillars and elaborate cornicing in all public areas emphasise its grandeur. Rooms are divided by stuccoed arches and the furnishings are elegant and comfortable. It is a meeting place for locals and visitors alike, and the new bar serves food until 8pm. Bedrooms are large, decorated with high-quality fabrics, quilted bedspreads and antiques. An extremely civilised place to stay, with friendly staff.

Bedrooms: 164, all with bath/shower/WC; all with mini-bar; some with hair-dryer   **Facilities:** Lift; restaurant; beauty salon; private parking   **Credit/charge cards accepted:** All

FLORENCE

- Primarily a city for art lovers – the extent and quality of its art and architecture are unrivalled. Although you may appreciate aspects of the city other than the contents of the churches and museums, if you don't enjoy the art you won't enjoy Florence
- Central Florence does not charm in the way that other Italian towns and cities do – the streets are narrow and lined by tall, stern grey buildings; there are few spacious, quiet places for taking a break from the sightseeing
- You'll have to be prepared to share the master-pieces with hordes of other tourists
- If, like many people, you find the experience of Florence thoroughly exhausting, you can quickly escape to the quiet Tuscan hills nearby.

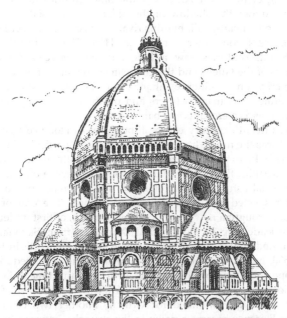

FLORENCE'S fame as the first city of the Renaissance makes an introduction almost superfluous. Unfortunately, if somewhat inevitably, that same fame has turned Florence into a city which seems to be populated entirely by visitors. Slow-moving groups of tourists, jammed streets, queues for art galleries and the inescapable proximity of your fellow sightseers are irritation enough. Add to them the perennial Florentine annoyances of heat, humidity, pollution, macho motorcyclists, bizarre opening hours, and the removal for restoration of the very paintings you had wanted to see, and there's enough to make a saint curse.

Yet Florence makes an ideal city for a short break. It simply requires rather more advance planning and rather more flexibility than you might have to apply to other cities. There is so much to be seen in such a compact area that even the most convinced agoraphobe can usually find a splendid church, cloister, museum or gallery off the beaten track. If you find that crowds make the Uffizi Gallery, the Pitti Palace or the Duomo intolerable, then you can turn your back on them without too much regret. The satisfaction to be got from the relaxed study of a 'minor' sight is likely to be greater than you would get by craning to see Botticelli's *Primavera* between the heads of the crowd.

Florence started as a Roman city, commanding a strategic crossing of the River Arno. For the first centuries of its life it existed under the shadow of the older Etruscan settlement of Fiésole on a nearby hill, but this rivalry was eventually settled in Florence's favour after a battle in 1125. The thirteenth and fourteenth centuries saw a long struggle between the rival factions of the Guelfs and the Ghibellines, but also an increasing prosperity and influence, thanks on the one hand to the Florentine cloth manufacturers and on the other to the skill of Florentines as merchants and bankers.

The fifteenth century can be thought of as Florence's golden age. It was the time when the Medici family, in particular Cosimo *Il Vecchio*, Piero and Lorenzo *Il Magnifico*, virtually ruled the city – their wealth, their love of the arts, and their political and commercial astuteness combining to make Florence one of the most respected and famous cities of Europe. The end of the century brought a new republican government, at first under the heady leadership of the fanatical Dominican friar, Savonarola, who lasted only four years before being burnt as a heretic in 1498. By 1530, however, after Florentine defeat by the combined forces of Pope and Emperor, the Medicis were back, this time as Dukes of Florence, and later as Grand Dukes of Tuscany. Their absolutist reign continued for virtually another two centuries before Florence became a pawn in the struggles between France and Austria. March 1860 saw Florence as part of a unified Italy and it was, for a short time, capital of the Italian Kingdom.

A sad chapter was added to the city's history in 1944, when the retreating German army blew up all the ancient bridges, sparing only the Ponte Vecchio – but at the expense of the destruction of the medieval neighbourhoods at either end of it. In 1966 came the great flood, when the Arno overflowed its banks and put many of the most lovely buildings and works of art under water. The work of restoration which this disaster entailed is now largely complete, but much was irretrievably lost.

For the visitor, Florence is bounded now, much as it was in medieval times, by its great churches. Everything you are likely to want to see lies in, or within the shadow of, one of them. Although the medieval walls are now replaced by a ring road (the Viale), the pattern of the city within them is largely unchanged. The cathedral (Duomo) dominates the centre, although its bulk more or less fills the piazza in which it and the ancient Baptistery stand, and there is little space for contemplative gazing. To the north is San Lorenzo, the parish church of the Medici and site of their huge, gloomy mausoleum. In the surrounding streets, market stalls sell leather, sweaters, T-shirts and food. Further north still lies San Marco, an old monastery, now a tranquil, shady place notable for the frescoes of Fra Angelico. Savonarola was once its prior. Around San Marco lies the university area, full of bicycles and bars, which spills over into the Piazza SS Annunziata with its lovely loggias, its orphanage and its dark church.

The Dominican church of Santa Maria Novella sits at one end of a grassy piazza west of the cathedral – the closest open space to the railway and bus stations, lined by cafés; the streets around are populated by antique shops and wine merchants. South of the River Arno, in the old artisans' district of the Oltrarno, the two churches of Santa Maria del Cármine and Santo Spirito lie close together – the former's piazza filled with ranks of cars, the latter with trees and a market nearby.

To the south-east of the Duomo stands Santa Croce – possibly the loveliest church in Florence. Its colourful façade faces a spacious but somewhat grim piazza surrounded by leather shops and self-service cafés. In the long thin streets nearby, smart galleries rub shoulders with untouristy restaurants and grocery shops. Michelangelo's house isn't far away, nor is the flea market. The area around Santa Croce is endlessly satisfying to explore, especially when the crowded city centre drives you to search for some genuine Florentine life.

On the slope of the steep hillside which rises to the south of the

Arno stands San Miniato al Monte. This is one of Florence's oldest, smallest and most perfect churches, with a beautifully proportioned façade. The view from the doorway is of a landscape of rounded hillsides and distant mountains, while the red-tiled roofs of Florence form a compact mass in the valley below.

Two further, secular, piazzas lie at the heart of Florence. One is the Piazza della Signoria – the administrative heart of the city. The castellated tower of the Palazzo Vecchio rears above it, the Loggia dei Lanzi (still covered in scaffolding) runs along one side and the colossal Neptune fountain stands in one corner. The Uffizi Gallery runs down behind the Palazzo Vecchio towards the Arno.

The Piazza della Repubblica, on the site of the Roman forum, is a nineteenth-century intrusion on the medieval city. The old market area and much of the sixteenth-century ghetto was demolished to make room for it. Despite the architectural unpleasantness, its central position draws people to its cafés – some of the most expensive in Florence.

It is impossible to do justice to the Florentine Renaissance within a single chapter. The results of that curious flowering of genius in architecture, sculpture, painting and science lie all over the city. Although it has some of the greatest galleries in the world, Florence is less a city of art collections than a place where artistic endeavour is part of the fabric of the city. There is scarcely a church without a notable painting, fresco or terracotta, scarcely a square with no fine architecture.

If one person can be said to have put a stamp on Florence, it is probably the fifteenth-century architect Brunelleschi. His buildings range from the engineering miracle of the dome on the Duomo to the miniature perfection of the Pazzi Chapel by the church of Santa Croce. By his use of perspective and mathematical proportion he transformed Florentine, and consequently European, architecture.

Donatello, who studied with Brunelleschi, runs him a close second in architecture, and is probably the greatest Florentine sculptor (Michelangelo fans will disagree). As you wander through Florence, these two names crop up again and again. So too does that of the della Robbia family, whose glazed terracotta reliefs are to be seen all over the city. Often almost ignored in favour of more famous names, these pieces of mere 'pottery' embody a delicacy and sensitivity to rival better-known works in marble and bronze.

It is probably those who want to look closely at the Florentine painters who will be most frustrated by the city's failure to cater to their needs. Many of the great frescoes must be seen in three-minute bursts as the light-meters in churches tick away 500 lire-worth of illumination. Many of the most wonderful paintings of the Renaissance hang in poorly lit corners against shabby and smudged walls. Only in a few quiet corners – San Marco is one – are you likely to find the surroundings and the peace in which the full glory of the paintings can be appreciated.

WHEN TO GO

Choosing the right time of year to visit Florence is probably more important than for many of the other cities in this book. Winter sightseeing, relatively uncrowded, can be very pleasant. Though on average it rains on almost as many days as in London, Italian rain tends to be torrential and soon over (and museum-hopping is an excellent way of taking shelter). Temperatures are often comparable to those of an English spring. However, works of art in churches are even more difficult than usual to appreciate in poor light, and excursions to the countryside are less appealing.

May, September and October are obvious months to choose for a fair chance of good weather with temperatures that are not too sapping – though there will be crowds. In March and April Florence is often overrun with boisterous parties of Italian schoolchildren. The Maggio Musicale, an important classical music festival, takes place in May and June. Another interesting June spectacle, almost worth a journey in itself, is the series of medieval football games known as the Giocio del Calcio.

If you visit Florence in July or August, you are unlikely to enjoy the city. Enclosed in its ring of hills, Florence stays hot and humid all summer, simmering like a cauldron at midday, with little relief at night (though you could briefly escape by going to the summer music and drama festival at Fiésole). Mosquitoes can be an added nuisance: they thrive in the humid heat.

MASTERING THE SYSTEM

Information The UK Italian Tourist Office is at 1 Princes Street, London W1R 8AY, tel: 071-408 1254. The main city tourist office in Florence is at 15 Via C Cavour 1r, tel: 55 27 60 382. It is open Monday to Saturday, from 8.30am to 1.30pm only. Queues can be long, but it is useful for providing up-to-date lists of opening hours, and for giving guidance on which famous works of art are out of circulation. Staff will also advise on hotels, but cannot book them for you. A free hotel booking service is offered by Florence Promotel, 72 A Volta, tel: 55 57 04 81.

Opening hours and days These are the bane of visitors to Florence, making it vital to plan your sightseeing in advance. The rule of thumb is: state museums and galleries open 9am to 2pm (1pm on Sunday) and close on Monday. Most churches open

GETTING THERE

Going independently

By air Florence Airport is tiny, but there are now direct daily flights from London with Air UK (0345 666777) and Meridiana (071-839 2222). Far more flights go to Galileo Galilei Airport at Pisa, nearly 60 miles away and an hour's train journey (there are trains every hour). British Airways (081-759 5511) and Alitalia (071-602 7111) have daily flights to Pisa from Heathrow. APEX fares are cheapest (book seven days in advance) and go up by about £40 during the peak July to September holiday season. You can save money – particularly out of season – by taking a charter flight to Pisa. Specialist tour operators for scheduled and charter flights include Citalia (081-686 5533), Cresta Holidays (061-929 9995), Falcon Flights (071-831 7000), Italy Sky Shuttle (081-748 1333) and Skybus Holidays (071-373 6055).

Galileo Galilei Airport This is small, provincial and informal, but has a bar where you can have an espresso and a sandwich while waiting for the rail connection to Florence. It also has a bureau de change and a rail ticket booth. It's not the place for buying souvenirs, and the duty-free shops in the departure lounge has a limited selection of goods.

Trains run from the station next to the air terminal every hour, but don't always connect with flights and you may have to wait for up to an hour. The timetable is prominently displayed in the terminal. There are more frequent trains from Pisa Central Station to which you can take a taxi from the airport – but you're unlikely to save much time. The train journey from the airport to Florence lasts about an hour.

Tour operator packages

There are lots of operators offering short-break packages to Florence, typically for three to five nights' B&B and travel by charter or scheduled flight to Pisa or Florence. Transport between Pisa Airport and the hotel may or may not be included. Prices depend on which hotel you choose and the season. Prices in 1992 for three-night packages to hotels recommended in this chapter ranged from £351 to £482. By booking independently and searching for a cheap flight you can save around £60. For a list of tour operators that go to Florence, see page 385.

from 7am or 8am to noon and again from 3pm or 4pm for a couple of hours. Shops take a two- or three-hour break from 2pm also. Museums run privately or by the city vary their closing days, so there are some places to visit on Monday, such as the Casa Buonarroti, the Horne Museum and the Santa Croce Museum (all in the Santa Croce area), plus the Cathedral Museum (also open in the afternoons), the Palazzo Medici-Riccardi and the Palazzo Vecchio. The Uffizi and the Palazzo Vecchio are open from 9am until 7pm (but closed on Monday and Saturday respectively). Get the list of latest opening times from the tourist office.

Sightseeing Whether a Florentine sight is 'unmissable' or not depends, more in this city than in others, on where your interests lie. To try to cram the famous galleries, museums and churches into a three-day stay is logistically virtually impossible, and would condemn you to an exhausting and crowded rush-around. Our three-day selection of sights (inevitably governed to some degree by taste) would be as follows: Cathedral and Baptistery, and Cathedral Museum; Bargello Museum; Museum of the Old Florentine House; Museum of the History of Science; San Miniato al Monte and Santa Croce churches; Palazzo Medici-Riccardi.

If you follow this, you will leave Florence without seeing Michaelangelo's *David* (often half invisible behind the crowds anyway) in the Accademia Gallery, and much more. But you will have seen more than just the obvious sights, and in one or two of the (lesser-known) sights you will have had the chance to escape the crowds. You will also be exhausted.

All of the sights we list under *Other places to visit* are in themselves first rate, and there are many more museums and churches which contain fine works of art. Details of **organised sightseeing** tours are available in most hotels and from the tourist office. Typically they include afternoon tours of Pisa, whole-day tours of Siena and San Gimignano and half-day tours of Florence by coach taking in the famous sights and Fiésole. Prices are not cheap, and you often end up being rushed around half a dozen famous sights or works of art.

Guidebooks and maps Of all the guides to Florence, only the *Blue Guide to Florence* (A & C Black) has sufficiently complete listings to prevent you being left in ignorance of what you are looking at. Its disadvantage is its tiny print (hopeless in a dark church). For more colour, try the *Companion Guide to Florence* (Collins). *Florence Explored* by Rupert Scott (Bodley Head) suggests some interesting walks around the city. We recommend the Hallwag map of Florence as being the easiest to use, both for getting around on foot and for using public transport.

Giocio del Calcio Florence has a medieval spectacle as least as exciting but much less well-known than Siena's famous Palio horse race. This is the series of medieval football games, played out on two days in June between teams from rival districts of the city. The Piazza Santa Croce is often the venue. The game, apparently without rules, is played in medieval costume, refereed by gentlemen in plumed hats who break up fights with swords, and is amazingly violent and passionate. It is preceded by a parade, banner-tossing and other medieval pageantry, all of which is used by the hugely partisan crowds as an excuse to cheer on their own side and mock their opponents. The first game is always played on 24 June (St John's Day), the second a few days later. Tickets are available from Chiosco degli Sportivi, a kiosk on Via Anselmi, near Piazza della Repubblica, tel: 55 29 23 63. It's wise to book well in advance.

GETTING AROUND

Although it's not an ideal city to explore on foot (noise, traffic, cobbles and narrow pavements), Florence is really too compact a place for public transport to be useful. The **bus** system is efficient but rather complicated by the one-way system. You can buy a ticket from the bus terminal near the station, or from bars or tobacconists (marked with a 'T'); on the bus, it needs to be fed into an automatic punching machine. Unless you are very fit, a bus is needed for the steep climb to San Miniato al Monte (No 13, a good round trip which ends near the train station). You can also get a bus No 7) up to the old town of Fiésole. **Taxis** wait in ranks on the main squares.

If you have a **car**, you'll be made to park it outside the 'residents-only' zone of the inner city unless you specify to the traffic police which hotel you are staying in. This attempt to reduce Florence's traffic problems has been only partly successful. The streets in the centre are less jammed than they used to be – but the motorcyclists and the remaining cars now have freer rein. The streets round the Duomo, in particular, sometimes resemble a racetrack. If you do bring a car into Florence (and your hotel has no car-park or garage), we advise leaving it in one of the number of 24-hour supervised car-parks. They aren't cheap, but the alternative of leaving it in the streets will almost certainly either get you a ticket or a smashed window.

UNMISSABLES

Uffizi Gallery

The crowds are frustrating, the alarm bells distracting, the rooms seemingly endless . . . nevertheless the Uffizi remains the number one Florentine sight for most visitors because of the fame of the paintings inside: Botticelli's *Birth of Venus* and *Primavera*, one third of Uccello's *Battle of San Romano* (the other two parts are in the Louvre and the National Gallery, London), Filippo Lippi's *Madonna and Child with Two Angels*, Leonardo da Vinci's *Annunciation* and *Adoration of the Magi*, Michelangelo's *Tondo Doni*, Titian's *Urbino Venus*, works by Tintoretto, Rubens and Caravaggio, and much, much more. Most visitors virtually ignore the classical statuary which ranges the corridors, the only piece of sculpture drawing their attention being the Medici *Venus*, a curiously coy piece whose erotic attraction for earlier generations is hard to understand today.

The Uffizi is inevitably plagued by tour groups. In summer you may well have to queue for entrance. It is, however, the only gallery in Florence to stay open until 7pm on weekdays, and visiting it between 5pm and 7pm is probably your best bet (though winter evenings show up the lighting defects). Don't miss the view from the southern end of the gallery.

Palatine Gallery (Pitti Palace)

The collection assembled by the Medici grand-dukes is hung as it would have been in the eighteenth century – crowding the walls in a magnificent display of colour and gilded frame. Rooms in the Palatine are small and it is almost impossible to avoid becoming sandwiched between tour groups. Try tagging on to one with a knowledgeable guide and follow it round. Titian and Raphael are the stars here, but there are many other famous names and pictures.

Bargello Museum

A massive thirteenth-century building which was once the seat of government and later a grim prison, the Bargello now houses a magnificent collection of Renaissance sculpture. Key pieces are three Michelangelo sculptures, including the *Drunken Bacchus*, Giambologna's *Mercury* and Donatello's *David* and *St George*. The trial reliefs by Brunelleschi and Ghiberti were entries for the competition to design the doors of the Baptistery; both repay a detailed look. The Bargello also contains some of the della Robbia family's best glazed terracotta pieces and a lovely collection of bronze birds by Giambologna.

San Marco (Fra Angelico) Museum

The warm stone of the old convent, the shady cedar in the entrance cloister and the sense that this is a place of repose combine to make San Marco one of the more tranquil of Florence's museums. It is also unmissable for the frescoes of Fra Angelico, which adorn the monks' cells on the first floor. Each cell has one, the pastel colours and still figures remarkably delicate and serene. His works in the Old Pilgrims' Hospice are more viciously imaginative – look out for the beastly devils in his *Last Judgement*. Don't miss the *Last Supper* by Ghirlandaio in the Small Refectory.

Accademia Gallery

This is where Michelangelo's *David* is housed – under a specially designed nineteenth-century tribune. The statue's enormous bulk dwarfs the crowds of flash-photographers beneath it. The *Slaves* are less photographed but, for many, much more interesting. Only a small proportion of visitors go on to look at the Accademia's collection of Florentine and Tuscan painting.

Cathedral Museum (Museo dell' Opera del Duomo)

A cool, white-walled museum designed by Brunelleschi in the fifteenth century houses works of art from the cathedral and its treasury. Four exhibits in particular make this unmissable: Michelangelo's unfinished *Pietà*, designed for his own funerary chapel; two organ-lofts (*cantorie*) by Donatello and Luca della Robbia, complete with toe-tapping cherubs; and *St Mary Magdalen* by Donatello, a wooden figure of an old women wracked by age and suffering, one of the most expressive statues in Florence. The original panels from Ghiberti's Baptistery doors are being moved here after restoration, and the original reliefs from Giotto's bell-tower are also on display.

OTHER PLACES TO VISIT

Churches

Duomo and Baptistery The **Baptistery** is one of the oldest buildings in Florence – probably sixth- or seventh-century. Its most famous exterior features are two sets of bronze doors (on the north and east sides) by Ghiberti, a superb craftsman and an inventive storyteller, whose reliefs provided generations of painters and sculptors with motifs and ideas. The reliefs are often hidden behind crowds of admirers, but pollution is more of a threat to them (they are being replaced by copies as they are removed for restoration). Inside, sumptuous mosaics lend light and colour to the octagonal building. The curious shouts you'll hear are tour-guides demonstrating the acoustics.

The dome of the **Duomo**, symbol of Florence, is the crowning centrepiece of the skyscape. From the outside, the building, sheathed in multicoloured marble (much of which is quite modern), is difficult to gain an impression of. Inside it's gloomy and chill, but under the octagon, the scale of Brunelleschi's dome at once becomes apparent. If you want to climb the dome (435 steps, steep and tortuous), get there as early as possible before crowds clog the staircase; on the way, you'll have fascinating close-ups of the cathedral's structure, and the stained-glass windows in the drum. For another bird's-eye view, down over the Baptistery, the long climb up the **campanile** is slightly less unnerving.

Palazzo Medici-Riccardi Administrative offices now occupy much of this huge rusticated building where the Medicis once lived. But the chapel, with its newly restored frescoes of the *Journey of the Magi* by Benozzo Gozzoli, is free and well worth a visit. The paintings, bursting with detail in jewel-like colours, include portraits of the Medici and Gozzoli himself.

Santa Croce From the outside it is long and thin like a crouching lion. Impressions of the inside depend on the weather: light and spacious or gloomy and cold. The Franciscan church is full of tombs and monuments and other important works of art – including a relief of the Annunciation by Donatello. The eastern end is notable for the frescoes by Giotto and his school.

Next to the church is one of the most famous monuments of the Renaissance, Brunelleschi's **Pazzi Chapel**; and in the old refectory, flanking the main cloister, the **Museo dell'Opera di Santa Croce** contains a crucifix by Cimabue – much-damaged in the flood of 1966, but still a very moving image.

San Lorenzo, the Medici chapels and the Laurentian Library San Lorenzo, parish church of the Medicis, is simple and harmonious (another Brunelleschi design). The best-known members of the family are commemorated very simply; it was the later, minor Medicis who really went to town in the Medici chapels (entrance in Piazza degli Aldobrandini). Tour groups are again a menace in the confined spaces in front of Michelangelo's *Day* and *Night*. Go through the cloister to the left of the church's façade and follow the signs to the Laurentian Library. The entrance vestibule and the staircase were designed by Michelangelo, and the result is unlike anything else in Florence. The staircase that is the centrepiece is disturbing, its single flight splitting suddenly into three, like a frozen waterfall, so that you don't know quite how to walk up it. Beyond lies the reading room, and a series of small rooms where treasures from the Medici library are displayed.

Santa Maria del Cármine After nine years of restoration the famous Masaccio frescoes in the Brancacci Chapel can at last be seen in all their glory and Masaccio's skills as a landscape painter be fully appreciated. Look out for a grief-stricken Adam and Eve being expelled from the Garden of Eden.

Santa Maria Novella The colourful marble façade is bright and harmonious; inside, it's Gothic and gloomy. There's much to be seen – including frescoes by Masaccio and Ghirlandaio, and works by Filippino Lippi – though most is barely visible. In the Green Cloister there are recently restored frescoes by Paolo Uccello. The chapter-house, or **Spanish Chapel**, contains a famous series of tapestry-like frescoes by Andrea Bonaiuti.

Santo Spirito The splendidly proportioned interior by Brunelleschi houses paintings by Filippino Lippi and Verrochio.

San Miniato al Monte It's not just the position of this church which attracts, but the remarkable harmony of the Romanesque building. The façade is one of the finest in Florence – simple and yet infinitely pleasing in its design. The interior has a choir raised above a large crypt. Roman capitals crown many of the pillars.

Other attractions

Bóboli Gardens Maps don't show how steep these formal gardens are, but there is plenty of shade if exhaustion threatens. Dusty paths lead up from behind the Pitti Palace towards the Belvedere Fortress at the top, from where there are great views over the city.

Orsanmichele Statues commissioned by the various trade guilds of Florence occupy niches in the walls of this granary-turned-church. The havoc wrought by pollution here is distressingly obvious. Some of the best have been taken away for restoration.

The work of the restorers can best be seen in the **Opificio delle Pietre Dure**, in Via degli Alfani, which also contains an eccentric little museum of inlay work in semi-precious stone. You can trace the gradual degeneration of this Florentine art from elaborate and beautiful tables (one of the best is in the Uffizi Gallery) to nineteenth-century tourist tat.

Palazzo Davanzati (Museum of the Old Florentine House) This museum – a restored fourteenth-century town house, furnished with items from the fifteenth to seventeenth centuries – provides an intimate glimpse of how a wealthy Florentine family might have lived in the Middle Ages. It extends over four floors, from the entrance courtyard at ground level to the kitchen at the top of the house. There are some lovely painted ceilings and some fine pieces of period furniture. Schoolchildren are more of a hazard here than tour groups, but there's room to breathe.

Palazzo Castellani (Museum of the History of Science) A fine museum of mathematical instruments that demonstrates the extraordinary skill of sixteenth- and seventeenth-century tool-makers. There are cases of astrolabes, surveying and navigational instruments and armillary spheres. The collection was assembled by the Medicis, and much was drawn from Germany and England. The star attraction is the lens used by Galileo to discover the moons of Jupiter (the gory-minded can also admire the scientist's middle finger on display). The explanations of what all these instruments were used for are comprehensive, but you really need someone to demonstrate them for you. The museum makes a splendid break from the fine arts.

Palazzo Vecchio The Salone dei Cinquecento at the heart of this old administrative palace is an exercise in grandiose decoration. But don't miss the tiny *studiolo* of Frances I, or the recently restored *Judith and Holofernes* by Donatello in one of the upstairs rooms.

Ponte Vecchio You are almost bound to cross this bridge over the Arno anyway, but you shouldn't leave Florence without doing so. Don't expect to find many bargains among the goldsmiths whose stalls and workshops line it. On the upstream side, the buildings are two storeys high; the top storey is part of the private corridor, built in the sixteenth century by Vasari, which ran all the way from the Uffizi Palace to the Pitti Palace to keep the Medicis dry when moving from one to the other.

Excursions

A popular coach excursion from Florence is the whole-day trip to **Siena** and **San Gimignano**. These towns are worth more time than you are likely to be given on a short tour, but if this is the only way you are likely ever to see them, it's worth considering. A shorter and in some ways more interesting excursion is to take one of the blue country buses (from the bus terminal next to the station) to **Greve in Chianti**. Greve is a pretty town with a seventeenth-century arcaded square and *enoteche* for wine tasting; you'll get a glimpse of the Chianti countryside *en route*.

Bus number 7 will take you up to the small hill town of **Fiésole**, an Etruscan city which until the twelfth century dominated its lower neighbour; it has long been much favoured as a residential area away from the bustle and heat of the city. The town's eleventh-century cathedral has a fine interior.

SHOPPING

Florentine craftsmanship is legendary. Since the Renaissance the Florentines have excelled in the production of gorgeously embroidered fabrics and finely wrought jewellery, and all over the city are little workshops where picture frames are carved, leather tooled or fashioned into bags or belts, books beautifully bound with marbled endpapers. Even down the scruffiest streets you can find beautifully created clothes, and it's a first-class place for furniture – antique, restored or reproduced. But there are also plenty of shoddy goods that are aimed at tourists, and shops in the middle-price bracket are surprisingly hard to find.

The most exclusive street is Via de Tornabuoni, with the big names of Gucci, Ferragamo and Valentino, but busy traffic lessens its appeal. More fun, and virtually as exclusive, are the chic boutiques in Via della Vigno Nuova and Via del Parione, the narrow streets west of Tornabuoni. Borgo San Lorenzo is good for cheap leather shoes; Via Roma and Via dei Calzaioli have expensive ones. The San Lorenzo market often has some good bargains in leather items and sweaters.

A Florentine speciality is marbled paper – some even using gold leaf. You can buy endpapers for bookbinding, desk sets, photograph albums and frames, and pretty boxes, notebooks and pencils. Embroidered linen and lingerie, particularly silk, can be a good buy, and Ognissanti is a good area to try.

Florence is full of jewellers, often with tiny one-room shops, some with workrooms behind. The greatest concentration of jewellers is on the Ponte Vecchio. Costume jewellery can be found at the market stalls at San Lorenzo.

EATING AND DRINKING

You can eat well in Florence – generally better than elsewhere in Italy. The best food is invariably found in small backstreet *trattorie* which are often cramped and inconspicuous. International-style *ristoranti* are best avoided, with the notable exception of Florence's most expensive (and arguably the best) restaurant, the

Enoteca Pinchiorri. A typical Florentine restaurant is the cellar-style *buca*, with a barrel-vaulted ceiling. There are cheap self-service restaurants around the cathedral and San Lorenzo.

Santa Croce and the Oltrarno offer more characteristic local eating places, often good value. Here a simple three-course meal with wine will cost about the same as a pizza and wine in a central square. Particularly enjoyable are La Maremma, with a huge spread of *antipasti*, and Cibreo, with a classy restaurant at the front and a basic *trattoria* at the back, where you share tables and the food is half the price (both in the Via de' Macci, east of Santa Croce); and Angiolino, a large bustling place with no-frills service (in Via Santo Spirito in the Oltrarno).

Most main courses are plain – roast or grilled meats – with the emphasis on high-quality ingredients. Specialities include *bistecca alla Fiorentina* – a vast juicy T-bone steak which can usually be shared by two – and tripe. The Florentine version of *fritto misto* consists of a mix of frittered artichoke hearts, calf's brains, mozzarella and courgettes. Starters are wholesome soups, Tuscan hams, pasta or *crostini* – liver or wild boar pâté on country bread; desserts include fruit, cheese and chocolate cake. Many restaurants offer a fixed-price *menu turistico*, which includes three courses, cover charge and occasionally wine; these meals, however, are likely to be basic and boring.

For variety and quality Florentine ices are outstanding. The reputation of Vivoli at 7 Via Isola delle Stinche (near Santa Croce) is legendary. Florence has plenty of bars, but few open-air-cafés – except in Piazza della Repubblica and Piazza della Signoria. Try the hot chocolate at Rivoire, opposite the Palazzo Vecchio, but be prepared for haughty service and a high bill.

Florence is close to the best-known wine-growing area in Italy – Chianti. The white wines are rarely distinguished, but the reds can be excellent. They can vary from the light, refreshing, inexpensive drink labelled simply 'Chianti' to the fully flavoured, deep-red, estate-bottled, barrel-aged reserve wines. Chianti Classico, Chianti Rufinà and Chianti dei Colli Fiorentini are often better quality than wines from Chianti's other zones. House wine, *vino della casa*, is likely to be a simple Chianti, served in a carafe or traditional raffia-covered *fiasco*. Superior Chiantis are sold in straight claret-shaped bottles. Other Tuscan wines of distinction include Vino Nobile di Montepulciano and Brunello di Montalcino (or the cheaper and lighter Rosso di Montalcino).

NIGHTLIFE

Florence is lively after dark, but mostly with people window-shopping or eating late. The Maggio Musicale music festival from mid-May to the end of June is a big event, with the top names in concert, ballet and opera. It's well worth getting seats for one of the concerts held throughout the summer in cloisters, piazzas or the Bóboli Gardens. Occasional summer concerts are also organised in the Roman amphitheatre in Fiésole (Estate Fiésolana festival). Nightclubs are few and far between, and discos are patronised mainly by locals.

HOTELS

Hotels in Florence don't come cheap and often are not even good value. Look for places on the banks of the Arno or the hotels on the top floors of old *palazzi*, away from traffic noise and with light rooms and roof terraces. The leafy residential area around the Teatro Communale, west of the centre, is also a good base. The station area has the most hotels, but it's not the best region to stay in. In summer, mosquitoes can be a nuisance – check to see if your room has screens and take anti-insect devices. You'll find several of the hotels listed in tour operators' brochures.

APRILE
Via della Scala 6   *Tel: 21 62 37*

The Aprile is situated in the station area, with a fresco of *David and Goliath* on its fifteenth-century façade. Persian rugs are thrown over speckled stone floors, walls are covered in prints and dark oil paintings, the small lounge bar is comfy and the breakfast room particularly lovely: it faces a high-walled small patio, well shaded for cool breakfasts. Bedrooms range from the vast, with vaulted ceilings, to small, very simple rooms. Via della Scala can be quite noisy and only a few of the rooms face the back.

Bedrooms: 29, most with bath/shower/WC, some with none; all with mini-bar; none with TV   **Facilities:** Lift   **Credit/charge cards accepted:** Access, Amex, Visa

---

◆ = under £50; ◆◆ = £50 to £80; ◆◆◆ = £80 to £100;
◆◆◆◆ = £100 to £140; ◆◆◆◆◆ = over £140.

ARIELE
Via Magenta 11   *Tel: 21 15 09   Fax: 26 85 21*

The building is handsome, fifteenth century, and formerly a residence for diplomats. The Bartelloni family has run it as a *pensione* for 20 years. Downstairs, rooms with terracotta floors are connected by rounded archways, and there are fresh wax polish smells. The salon is ornate and pleasantly cluttered. Some bedrooms are enormous, some small and dark. There's a pebbled garden, with trees and cushioned chairs for hot summer days. The hotel is in a quiet residential area near the Arno, a 15-minute stroll from the Ponte Vecchio.

Bedrooms: 40, all with bath/shower/WC; mini-bar   **Facilities:** Lift; bar; private parking   **Credit/charge cards accepted:** Access, Amex, Visa

HERMITAGE
Vicolo Marzio 1   *Tel: 28 72 16   Fax: 21 22 08*

On the upper floors of a large yellow house near the Ponte Vecchio is the Hermitage Hotel. After a cramped lift ride you'll find the breakfast and sitting-rooms: full of light, a cosy fireplace, yellow upholstered sofas and paintings of Florence. There's a beautiful roof-top garden, with a green pergola, where you can view the city over breakfast or a drink. Bedrooms are medium-sized, clean and traditional. The quietest look out on to a small square at the back; others have river views.

Bedrooms: 22, some with bath/WC, some with shower/WC, some with neither; all with air-conditioning; none with TV   **Facilities:** Lift   **Credit/charge cards accepted:** Access, Visa

LOGGIATO DEI SERVITI
Plaza della SS Annunziata 3   *Tel: 21 91 65   Fax: 28 95 95*

The sixteenth-century building – built for the order of the Serviti fathers – is the exact twin of Brunelleschi's Ospedale degli Innocenti across the beautiful but busy Piazza della SS Annunziata. It has a cool and elegant austerity, with twisting narrow stairways and whitewashed vaulted ceilings. There is a small lounge bar and breakfast room. Some bedrooms are vast – terracotta tiles, wrought-iron beds and solid antique chests and wardrobes. The rooms facing the back are monastically peaceful.

Bedrooms: 29, most with shower/WC, some with bath/WC; all with air-conditioning; mini-bar   **Facilities:** Lift   **Credit/charge cards accepted:** All

MONNA LISA
Borgo Pinti 27   ♦♦♦♦
                                        Tel: 24 79 751   Fax: 24 79 755

Not far from the Duomo, you can stay in a Renaissance palace, complete with grand entrance, curving *pietra serena* staircase, panelled ceilings, arched windows, Corinthian columns and polished tile floors. The furniture is antique, and portraits, busts and sculptures are on display in the cool, darkened salons. There is a small inner courtyard and a leafy garden with tortoises. Bedrooms range from grand to cramped and noisy. Despite the elegance, it's the sort of place where you can curl up with a book on the sofa.

Bedrooms: 30, all with bath/shower/WC, some with whirlpool bath; air-conditioning; mini-bar   **Facilities:** Lift; private parking   **Credit/charge cards accepted:** All

PLAZA LUCCHESI
Lungarno della Zecca Vecchia 38   ♦♦♦♦
                                        Tel: 26 41 41   Fax: 24 80 921

This is a nineteenth-century building on the right bank of the Arno, with Santa Croce just behind. Piped jazz plays in the lounge, which has groups of grey and white sofas, glass-topped tables and mirror-panelled walls. In the restaurant, white-jacketed waiters glide among formal tables. Groups of many nationalities come and go. The bedrooms are good-sized, furnished in pastel colours, with views of the Arno or Santa Croce.

Closed: Restaurant closed Aug and Suns   **Bedrooms:** 97, most with bath/WC; all with air-conditioning; mini-bar   **Facilities:** Lift; restaurant   **Credit/charge cards accepted:** All

LA RESIDENZA
Via de Tornabuoni 8   ♦♦♦
                                        Tel: 28 41 97

On a central street, full of smart shops and old *palazzi*, this friendly *pensione* on the top floor of a *palazzo* is reached by a polished wood and glass lift. The small lounge bar has squashy sofas, soft lights and watercolours on the walls. Narrow carpeted steps lead to another chintzy lounge with a roof terrace. Some bedrooms are modern, but the prettiest are the older ones with rustic beds and wardrobes, stone floors, rugs and a small terrace outside, reached via your window.

Bedrooms: 24, half with bath/WC, half with shower/WC; some with air-conditioning; none with TV   **Facilities:** Lift; restaurant   **Credit/charge cards accepted:** Amex, Diners, Visa

SPLENDOR ♦♦
Via San Gallo 30   *Tel: 48 34 27   Fax: 46 12 76*

This is a friendly family hotel in a street of bars and shops; its décor is an incongruous mix of the original features and the 1950s, when the building was restored and had two floors added. The best part of the hotel is a terrace, with roses, creepers and terracotta pots, facing San Marco. Bedrooms are on the small side, impeccably clean; baths are tiny, but tiled and new. Ask for a room facing San Marco.

Bedrooms: 31, most with bath/WC, some with shower/WC, some with neither; some with air-conditioning   **Facilities:** Lift   **Credit/charge cards accepted:** Access, Visa

TORNABUONI BEACCI ♦♦♦♦
Via de Tornabuoni 3   *Tel: 26 83 77*

This hotel is on Florence's busiest shopping street. The entrance to the fourteenth-century Palazzo Minerbetti Strozzi is grand enough, but will not prepare you for what you find – a hotel that's more like a lavish apartment. The salon is particularly elegant, with a floor-to-ceiling tapestry of white wreathed maidens. The bedrooms are well furnished with brass beds and painted furniture. The roof garden with cloth-covered tables is lovely, shaded by a leafy pergola. Booking priority is given to guests opting for half-board.

Bedrooms: 30, all with bath/shower/WC; air-conditioning; mini-bar
Facilities: Lift; restaurant   **Credit/charge cards accepted:** All

Hotel prices Symbols indicate approximate prices per room per night for a double room with bath. Many large hotels run special breaks which work out far cheaper. (See page 14 for further details.)

♦ = under £50; ♦♦ = £50 to £80; ♦♦♦ = £80 to £100;
♦♦♦♦ = £100 to £140; ♦♦♦♦♦ = over £140.

ISTANBUL

- Istanbul is still the exciting, exotic city of legend and travellers' tales. Palaces, churches and mosques jostle for prominence along the city's famous minaretted skyline on the Bosphorus
- Topkapi Palace is an enthralling centrepiece for your visit but other sites – Hagia Sophia, the Blue Mosque, Süleymaniye Mosque – are not far behind in interest. And on no account miss a romantic cruise up the Bosphorus itself
- Shoppers will never tire of Istanbul. The Grand Bazaar is endlessly fascinating
- Don't be put off by the hustle and bustle. The Turks are faultlessly hospitable and Istanbul is basically a 'safe' city. You can wander freely at night and need take no more precaution than usual

EN ROUTE from Istanbul Airport to the centre of town, most visitors could be forgiven for some apprehension at the sight of the drab tenements lining one side of the dual carriageway, or the smell of diesel oil from tankers moored in the Sea of Marmara on the other. Only when they round the curve known as Seraglio Point will the Istanbul they have imagined become apparent – jostling crowds and hooting cars, ferry boats weaving around the cruise liners, a graceful skyline of soaring domes and minarets.

Here, along the waterfront, the city's layout is easily followed. The famous Galata Bridge – once a landmark – has been removed and replaced by a more functional namesake. It crosses the Golden Horn, a narrow inlet opening into the Bosphorus and separating the two European parts of the city. To the north, the district of Beyoğlu is the most modern part of the city; its focal point is Taksim Square, where the city's major international hotels and nightclubs are gathered. The area between Galata and Taksim is where European émigrés lived under an Ottoman Sultan, and it retains a nineteenth-century feel; the main street, Istiklal Caddesi, is now a fashionable shopping area, but you can still see the grand consular buildings of the Great Powers.

South of the Golden Horn lies the Old City, which contains most of the famous sights – Topkapi Palace, the Blue Mosque, the Grand Bazaar – grouped around Sultanahmet Square and stretching down Divan Yolu. The Old City comes closest to the Istanbul of travellers' tales – a honeycomb of noisy, colourful side-streets filled with the lingering smell of spices; courtyards and bazaars crowded with pedlars and traders of every kind.

Across the Bosphorus to the east is Üsküdar, the Asian part of the city, an area of quiet, attractive suburbs connected to Istanbul proper only by the Bosphorus Bridge or local ferries.

On arrival in Istanbul, you are likely to experience culture shock from the number of people, the constant noise of trading, the jostle for space and the overwhelming greyness. Don't be disheartened. Dive straight in by walking alongside the Bosphorus, and try to absorb the scene: the streets choked with traffic and fumes; Turkish music blaring from yellow taxis; crowds spilling from ferries that belch black smoke. Fishermen in boats shout prices at passers-by; pedlars spread blankets displaying T-shirts, watches and camera film; men chatter and smoke as they dangle fishing lines in the water. And suddenly, above the heat and noise, comes the piercing call of the muezzin to afternoon prayers.

The significance of Istanbul's geography and its multi-faceted history is likely to impress the visitor from the start. For centuries the capital of the Western and Near-Eastern worlds, the city was the frontier of different cultures, a meeting point of East and West. As Byzantium, it was chosen by Constantine to become the capital of the Roman Empire, renamed New Rome and later Constantinople. The 'City of Gold' acquired most of Rome's Greek treasures and became the greatest repository of ancient art in the world. After the division of the Empire into Latin west and Byzantine east, the Graeco-Roman city – with its huge system of multiple walls and towers protecting landward and seaward sides – resisted all invasions for almost 1,000 years. Its most glorious period was in the sixth century under Justinian, who brought to the capital the most distinguished architects, mathematicians and craftsmen from the whole Empire. Under him, the cathedral of Hagia Sophia was built – the biggest and most splendid church in Christendom, the visual expression of the greatness of the Emperor and of the Christian church. Most other Byzantine masterpieces live on only by reputation, for almost all were looted or destroyed in 1204, during the cataclysmic period of the Fourth Crusade, when the city was sacked. The greatest and richest imperial city was laid bare: 'So much booty had never been gained in any city since the creation of the world,' wrote the Crusade's chronicler. A short-lived Latin Empire and a weakened Byzantine 'Renaissance' which followed served only as a prelude to the city's conquest by the Ottoman Turks, who made it the Muslim capital of their Empire in 1453.

The ruins of the Byzantine city, many pieces of which now lie among the crumbling alleys of the Old City, were used as quarries of stone or marble for the new rulers, whose mosques, minarets and palaces remain as testimony to the opulent lifestyle of the Ottoman élite.

Building activity was at its most prolific under the 46-year rule of Sultan Süleyman the Magnificent in the sixteenth century, by which time the Empire stretched from the gates of Vienna to the Indian Ocean, and encompassed almost all the lands around the eastern Mediterranean and the Black Sea; the Ottoman armies struck terror into the monarchs of Christian Europe. But little more than a century later the Empire started a slow and painful decline, finally becoming a pawn in the rivalry between the British and Russian Empires.

Istanbul eventually became a secular city in the new Turkish Republic founded by Mustapha Kemal Atatürk in 1923. The capital moved to Ankara, but Istanbul remains the country's largest city, port, commercial and cultural centre.

WHEN TO GO

The best months to visit Istanbul are from May to October. From November to April it may rain; from January to March it can even snow. In the height of summer you may need a sweater in the evenings. If you want to swim, it's best to visit between June and September. July and August can be uncomfortably hot during the day, when temperatures reach 30°C. The Istanbul Festival, an international cultural festival, begins in late June and continues through the first half of July.

GETTING THERE

Going independently

Visas You'll need to buy a visa on arrival – it costs £5.

By air The flight to Istanbul from London takes about four hours. British Airways and Turkish Airlines have two flights each on most days throughout the year from Heathrow. The best fare bookable is the PEX, costing around £250 and going up by nearly £100 during the peak July to September holiday season. You won't have any trouble finding cheaper fares, though, on either scheduled or charter flights to Istanbul. Charters fly all year (more in summer) but don't offer as much flexibility for a short break as the daily scheduled services. Operators offering low fares to Istanbul include Regent Holidays (0983 864212), Cresta Holidays (0345 056511), Data Travel (0424 722394) and Flightfile (071-323 1515).

Atatürk Airport About 15 miles west of the city, this is a modern and well-organised airport, although it lacks decent tourist shops and cannot be relied on for last-minute presents. Taxis are freely available from the rank outside 'Arrivals'; they are usually metered and you should pay around 150,000 Turkish lire (TL) for a trip to the centre of town. If you're not staying somewhere famous, write the hotel name on a piece of paper and show it to the driver. An airport bus goes every half-hour from the domestic terminal to the Turkish Airlines terminal in Sishane Square near the Galata Tower. Free shuttle buses link the international and domestic terminals.

Tour operator packages

In 1992 the cost of a three-night package in a three-star hotel varied enormously, from £199 in low season to £375 in high season.

Most tour operators also include a travel pack which consists of maps and general information on excursions and sights in and around the city. For a list of tour operators see page 385.

Packages are often good value, so check the brochures before you book independently. Istanbul's hotels are fairly pricey.

MASTERING THE SYSTEM

Information The Turkish Information Office in Britain is on the first floor at 170/173 Piccadilly, London W1V 9DD, tel: 071-734 8681. In Istanbul there are several tourist information offices run by the Ministry of Tourism: the main one is at Beyoğlu Meşrutiyet Cad 57/6, tel: 145 6875. Others can be found at Atatürk Airport, in the International Maritime Passenger Terminal at Karaköy Seaport, at the western end of the Hippodrome in Sultanahmet, and in the Hilton Arcade at the entrance to the Hilton Hotel just off Cumhuriyet Caddesi. The sign of the Ministry is the Hittite sun motif.

Tourist offices are good sources of free maps and helpful advice about using public transport. If you arrive without anywhere to stay, they are prepared to ring round and find accommodation for you.

City maps The city is honeycombed with streets and you will need a good map to avoid getting lost. The best is probably the one produced by Hallwag (1:10,500).

Changing money Always have your passport with you. Many tourist shops, travel agencies, expensive restaurants and hotels have licences to accept foreign currency.

Banks open from 8.30am to noon, and 1.30pm to 5pm, Monday to Friday. Changing money can take about 25 minutes, so be patient. Some banks charge a fee for changing travellers' cheques, but most charge nothing. Save your currency receipts; you'll need them to convert Turkish lira back into sterling. Exchange bureaux (Döviz Büroso) are also dotted around the city and are usually quicker than banks. They open from 9am to 6pm.

Opening hours and days Museums (including Hagia Sophia) are generally closed on Monday; the Topkapi Palace is closed on Tuesday and the Dolmabahçe Palace closes on Monday and Thursday. Mosques are open from dawn until dusk; you'll be asked to leave when a service is about to start. Shops are generally open 9.30am to 1pm and 2pm to 7pm Monday to Saturday; the covered bazaar is open 8am to 7pm.

Customs and etiquette The Turks are sticklers for etiquette. In mosques, respectful dress is expected (no shorts), women may be asked to cover their heads (there is normally a scarf seller nearby), shoes are removed (remember to tip the attendant who looks after them). Aside from religion, Turks revere their national flag and Atatürk, whose statue you will see everywhere; there are strong laws against insulting either of these.

Public conveniences These are generally of a reasonable standard, although they aren't widespread throughout the city. If possible, it's best to stick to toilets in good-quality hotels. 'Turkish' toilets are of the squat/'elephant's feet' variety – you'll need to have your own toilet paper and remember to jump when you flush.

GETTING AROUND

The cheapest way of getting round is by **bus** – though they are slow and get very crowded in the rush hours. On the European side the main bus routes start from Taksim Square, Eminönü and Beyazit (near the covered bazaar). On the Asian side there are departures from Üsküdar and Kadiköy. There's a flat-rate fare. Buy your tickets from the little red kiosk at main bus stops before you get on. The destinations are shown on the side and front of the buses. Drop your ticket in the box as you enter and press the button above the exit when you want to get off. Local bus 96 goes to the airport from Yenikapi (near Aksaray) about every hour and takes about 40 minutes. Otherwise you can get the airport bus from the Turkish Airlines Service at Sishane (every half-hour).

The easiest way to get about is by **taxi**. All the cars are metered and its costs only about £2 for a journey from Taksim to Sultanahmet. If the taxi driver doesn't understand the name of a place, try telling him the district – for instance ask for Sultanahmet if you want to go to Topkapi Palace. The only time you're likely to have trouble is around lunchtime, when the roads clog up and taxi drivers like to quote a fixed fare – it could take up to an hour to get from Topkapi Palace to Dolmabahçe Palace.

You can also have a go at catching a **dolmuş** – a shared taxi that operates along specific routes with fixed fares. The system is easier to crack on the Asian side, where the *dolmuş* seem more numerous and their destinations are clearly displayed. The fun is in taking a ride in the amazing old cars used – Buicks, Dodges and stretch Mercedes. A woman is expected to choose a window seat, not a middle seat between two men. If a man and woman get into the front of a car, for example, the man goes first and sits next to the driver.

The most pleasant way of seeing Istanbul and its skyline is from a **ferry boat**. You can take a trip up the Golden Horn to Eyüp, hop over to the Asian side, visit the peaceful residential Princes' Islands or, best of all, cruise up the Bosphorus. The main cluster of ferry terminals is at Galata Bridge. The destinations are painted in huge letters on each terminal, and blackboards give more detailed timetables. Buy a *jeton* from the kiosks or the many lads selling them and press through the turnstiles into the throng. Study the ferry as it comes in to work out how you can get to the best seats, and stand your ground as the crowd surges forward. Once on board, settle down to watch the constant stream of vendors selling nuts and crisps, biros, razor blades, clothes pegs, tea and *ayran* (a yoghurt-like drink) from silvery trays.

Between Karaköy and the south end of Istiklal Caddesi there's a **funicular railway** (Tünel) – built by French engineers over a century ago to allow European merchants to get from their offices by the docks to their homes up the hill. It runs every five to ten minutes until about 10pm. Buy a token and enter through the turnstile.

As usual, **walking** is the best way of getting to know the city, particularly as the traffic is so heavy. Don't expect car drivers to stop for you – drivers always assume they have right of way. Women walking alone attract constant attention (Turkish women keep well covered, and Turkish males seem particularly attracted by any display of legs).

UNMISSABLES

Topkapi Palace

Fortress, palace and ornamental gardens, the residence of the Ottoman Sultans is one of the most romantic palaces in the world. Your trip to Istanbul should start here, for its beauty and the fascination of its history will condition your entire stay. Allow the best part of a day, avoiding the coach parties by arriving promptly at opening time. Passing through the outer courtyards you enter shady and tranquil gardens. Before exploring it's worth buying a ticket for the guided tour, without which it's impossible to visit the famous Harem – the Sultan's private residence. It was here that he could relax with his several hundred select beauties guarded by eunuchs and presided over by the Queen Mother – an immensely powerful woman. Few who entered the harem ever came out again, and life inside was shrouded in mystery for centuries. Now you can enter these extraordinarily rich quarters – each room a masterpiece of Ottoman decoration, of domed ceilings and graceful arches, of chandeliers and canopied thrones, of Iznic tiling inlaid with calligraphy from the Koran, of dazzling mother-of-pearl traceries. Even this tour takes in fewer than 40 of the 400 rooms.

Don't let crowds deter you from visiting the Treasury (in a

separate part of the palace), which contains a priceless collection – jewelled pistols and swords, precious stones as big as your palm, golden thrones, the famous gold and emerald Topkapi Dagger and the 86-carat Spoonmaker's Diamond, which rotates to catch the light. The wealth and artistry of the collection is a breathtaking testimony to the power and prestige of the Ottomans and their capital.

Hagia Sophia

The sixth-century Cathedral of the Divine Wisdom is the supreme monument of Byzantine architecture, and provided the model for countless (smaller) churches all over the Christian world and for many of the great mosques which were built after the Ottoman conquest. Its great dome – 107ft in diameter and 180ft above the ground – rests like a canopy over the centre 'as if suspended by a chain from heaven'; flanking and supporting it are half-domes, arches, galleries and more than 100 marble columns. At a circle in the centre of the church the Byzantine Emperors were crowned. In 1453 Mehmet the Conqueror rode his horse into the church and proclaimed it a mosque; the framing minarets were then added. In the 1930s the building became a museum.

Much of the original mosaic decoration of the nave has been lost, but several later mosaics (post-ninth century) have been restored and now mingle with Ottoman chandeliers and Arab calligraphy. As you enter from Sultanahmet Square there are exquisite gold mosaics over the outer doors; and as you leave by the gallery there's a very fine mosaic of the Virgin and Child – with Constantine offering her the city of Constantinople on the left, and Justinian offering her Hagia Sophia on the right.

Blue Mosque

Built next door to Hagia Sophia in the early seventeenth century, the Mosque of Sultan Ahmet I was intended to outstrip its Byzantine neighbour. The building is distinguished by six minarets which flank its dome and half-domes; the interior is dominated by four massive supporting piers, which somewhat detract from the sense of divinity and space achieved inside Hagia Sophia. No matter – the mosque is still fascinating for its graceful domes, intricate decoration and the blue Iznik tiling from which it takes its name. This is a working mosque, and many visitors come to worship as well as simply to admire.

Süleymaniye Mosque

The richest and most powerful of the Ottoman Sultans, Süleyman I (1520-66), matched military with domestic achievements, commissioning the master-architect Sinan to build a civic complex – hospital, schools, baths, soup kitchens, workshops and living quarters, with a mosque at its heart. The result is a masterpiece built on one of Istanbul's hills dominating the Golden Horn, and providing a landmark for the whole city. Inside, the main features are similar to the Blue Mosque – massive pillars, soaring arches, rich decoration – but the overall effect is both simpler and more elegant.

A trip on the Bosphorus

Istanbul's history and the atmosphere of the city are fascinating enough; a boat excursion along the Bosphorus is a charming bonus. It's more fun to arrange your own trip than to join one of the many chartered tours; the 'standard' cruise leaves Eminönü at 10.30am and 1.30pm daily and lasts two and a half hours (one way, but you can break your journey by stopping at any of nine stops and exploring, returning by taxi or *dolmuş* if you wish). Plan your trip in advance by wandering along the ferry docks to find times and destinations. Don't be put off by the crowds and apparent disorganisation: times and prices are clearly marked, and the ferry system is well organised and easy to use. If in doubt, don't hesitate to ask for help at a ticket window. Some of the highlights include passing the wedding-cake façade of Dolmabahçe Palace (*see below*), the soaring arches of the Bosphorus Bridge, and the ancient fortress of Rumeli Hisarí (where Mehmet the Conqueror laid siege to the Byzantine city). The sleepy fishing villages of Tarabya and Saríyer have excellent lunch restaurants. Those without the time for the full cruise shouldn't despair: you can buy a *jeton* at one of the ticket windows at Dock 1 or 2, and enjoy the famous minaretted skyline by taking a quick hop over to the Asian side. The ferry will be there and back from Kadiköy or Üsküdar in just over an hour!

Galata and Pera

In the rush of trips to mosques and palaces, it would be a mistake to overlook a walking tour of the European quarter – the areas known as Galata and Pera. Start from Taksim Square, walk down Istiklal Caddesi, and stock up on the way with pistachios or Turkish delight from one of the sweet shops. The area around Galatasaray Square was the social and diplomatic centre of Istanbul from the seventeenth century onwards; the maze of streets and alleys with European-style houses formed the émigrés' quarter of town. Highlights include the wonderful little flower-passage called Çiçek Pasaji; the famous Pera Palas Hotel, whose chandeliers and antique lifts evoke the unmistakable aura of Hercule Poirot-style intrigue; and the Galata Tower, built by Genoese merchants in the fourteenth century, which boasts marvellous views from the observatory and restaurant at the top.

OTHER PLACES TO VISIT

Museums

Archaeological Museum Most of the museum is closed, and its charms may be lost on those expecting more than a couple of rooms of sarcophagi; labelling is in Turkish and French only. However, opposite the museum, the **Çinili Kiosk** is a minor masterpiece of Ottoman architecture and houses a collection showing the development of Iznik ceramics from the fifteenth century onwards. And the neighbouring **Museum of the Ancient Orient** houses pre-classical finds from Turkey and the Middle East, including works from Babylon.

Museum of Turkish and Islamic Arts The former palace of Ibrahim Pasha (1524) has been refurbished to house the most intelligent and enjoyable of Istanbul's 'general' museums. Supported by videos and photographs, the exhibits allow you to trace the origins of Islamic culture back to the early Middle Ages. A selection of gold-embossed Imperial Decrees (including those of Süleyman the Lawgiver) shows the growing confidence of style and decoration resulting from the expansion of empire in the sixteenth century. Finally, the downstairs rooms bring you back to the present, with an ethnographic exhibition of the costumes and lifestyles of people throughout modern Turkey.

Other attractions

Kariye Museum The former Church of the Holy Saviour in Chora is slightly out of town but well worth a visit. The eleventh- and twelfth-century church was exquisitively decorated in the fourteenth century with frescoes and dazzling Byzantine mosaics covering ceilings and cupolas. To get there either go by taxi or get a bus from Sultanahmet Square going to Edirnekapi. Get off when you see the old city walls.

Dolmabahçe Palace Built between 1843 and 1856 to mimic the palaces of Europe, the residence of the last Sultans is more impressive for its wedding-cake exterior than for its almost absurdly dedacent contents. The inside can be seen only on an hour-long guided tour – a dash along gloomy corridors with peeps into darkened rooms with heavy drapes and massive chandeliers. On the way the guide points out Atatürk's deathbed, covered in the Turkish flag, in an austere room. Despite the grandeur, the palace provides a rather melancholy commentary on the decline of the nineteenth-century empire.

Eyüp Mosque By the Golden Horn beyond the old city walls, the Mosque of Eyüp has considerable religious significance in Muslim history. It is the shrine of Job (Eyüp), the standard-bearer of the Prophet Mohammed. The late eighteenth-century mosque is notable for an ornate style of building and in particular for its magnificent decorative tiling. A long line of pilgrims files slowly past the tomb: it is still customary to pay a visit to Eyüp on the way to the Holy Pilgrimage in Mecca. (To go there get a taxi, or catch the ferry boat going up the Golden Horn from Galata Bridge to the dock at Eyüp Sultan.)

Hippodrome Site of the chariot races in Byzantine times, the wide 'horse-guards parade' dominated by the Blue Mosque served as a military and political centre for Byzantines and Ottomans alike. The four famous gilded bronze horses which adorned the Hippodrome in Roman times were removed to Venice at the time of the Fourth Crusade. Now a park, it's a place for a rest, a shoe-shine and enjoying the view.

Yerebatan Saray Across the street from Hagia Sophia is the 'Sunken Palace', one of the many vast underground cisterns built by the Roman emperors to store water (brought by aqueducts) for their capital. The roof is supported by 336 columns; floodlights light up the Medusa heads carved on the bases of some. Beethoven's Fifth is piped throughout.

A Turkish bath For something a little different, treat yourself to a *hamam*. A couple of the oldest (and most touristy) are Cağaloğlu Hamami, Caddesi 34, Cağaloğlu Yerabatan, and Tarihi Galatasaray Hamami, Turnacibasi Sokak 24, Galatasaray (near the Greek Consulate), first built as the palace baths in 1481. Neighbourhood *hamams* (just look for a *hamam* sign) are usually just as clean and a lot cheaper.

There are special entrances for men and women, and sometimes special opening days or times for women only. Inside, you undress and are led into a hot room where you pour hot water over yourself and are left to perspire. Your attendant will bring tea and then, just when you've started to relax, will instruct you to lie down to be roughly massaged and scrubbed. You certainly emerge feeling squeaky clean. If you don't think you can resist a hard sell while being massaged naked, book the top level of service at the start. You'll pay about £5 to £10, and your attendant will ask for a tip.

SHOPPING

For the serious shopper, Istanbul offers one of the ultimate challenges. The Grand Bazaar is a crowded mini-city encompassing 4,000 shops, perfect for practising negotiating skills and for bargain-hunting. Entire streets are dedicated to particular crafts – jewellery, clothing, carpets and so on – and the unwary can wander, lost in admiration for hours. To keep control, enter at the Beyazit entrance and work systematically up and down the streets to your left (navigating by returning each time to Jewellers Street) until satiated. At the centre is the Old Bazaar, core of the more expensive and better-quality shops.

The key skills are to do with courtesy rather than haggling. Get to know the market by asking prices in different shops; don't expect the shopkeeper to meet your price without a long courtship; be patient; and don't bargain unless you are seriously interested in buying. Traders will be perfectly happy if you turn them down by saying you 'have one already'.

In the streets outside the Bazaar are shops and traders offering more everyday, but reasonably priced, goods. If you leave from the Beyazit exit, turn sharply right to enter the wonderful Old Book Bazaar, a shady courtyard to delight even the not-so-serious book lover. Finally, after your 'serious shopping' test, you can try the 'junior exam' by wandering down to the Egyptian Bazaar, a smaller version of the Grand Bazaar specialising in the most exotic herbs and spices. Through the Bazaar gates the air is heavy with the aroma of cloves, nutmeg and cinnamon. At the back entrance, you will undoubtedly feel you've earned a pastry and a tiny glass of fresh Turkish tea.

For more relaxed window-shopping, take a stroll up Istiklal Caddesi – once known as the Grand Rue de Pera – where the tourists mingled with the commercial élite. The recently developed Galleria shopping complex at Ataköy also has some elegant shops.

One of the best buys can be a Turkish carpet or *kilim* – you'll find look-outs by the bazaars constantly offering to take you to their cousins' shops. If you know nothing about carpets take some time to examine what's on offer, and get a feel for prices. A good rug will cost hundreds of pounds. To examine a carpet, turn a corner over and look at the closeness of the weave (the more knots per square inch the better the quality); look at the bottom of the pile (if the colours are more vivid; it's probably faded in the sun); take a white handkerchief, lick it and run it over the carpet (you shouldn't get a mark on it from carpet dye). Always get a receipt to say that the carpet isn't an antique (to get you past

Turkish customs) and to record how much you paid for it, so that British customs will be able to calculate the duty payable.

Turkish miniatures, though not regarded as being as fine as Persian, are easy to come by. Prices start from around £10 and rise rapidly. If it's a good old miniature the trader is not likely to be interested in haggling over the price.

Gold jewellery tends to be heavy Arab style rather than European chic. If you're interested in a piece make sure you see it being weighed and ask what part of the price is for the gold, and what for the workmanship. The gold price is fixed. You can bargain on the workmanship part.

Other good buys are leather goods (check the workmanship), copper knick-knacks and ceramics. On every street corner you'll find traders offering fake Lacoste T-shirts for around £2.

Traders like cash (dollars or sterling are very acceptable) or travellers' cheques. If you use your credit card they may well charge you extra.

EATING AND DRINKING

Turkish cooking is said to be one of the three great world cuisines and there are certainly enough restaurants in Istanbul to test this out. Starters are a particular speciality – waiters will parade huge trays laden with little dishes for you to pick your selection: aubergine salads; *cacík* (yoghurt with grated cucumber and garlic); perhaps a sheep's brain as a centrepiece. To eat cheaply try one of the *hazin yemek* (ready-food restaurants). Just point to the food in the display cases and waiters will bring the meal to your table. *Kebapçi* and *koftezi* restaurants specialise in grilled meat, with soups, salads and possibly dessert. Otherwise, try a *pastahane* (pastry shop) for tea and a choice of types of *baklava*. Prices are always prominently marked, according to law.

There are good low-priced restaurants along Istiklal Caddesi. For some 'fast food' a delicious alternative is the 'fish sandwich' served by boatmen themselves – fried turbot steaks in a quarter of fresh bread with onion and salt added to taste from the bags tied to the railings (pull the backbone out first before tucking in!). For authentic Turkish cuisine pride of place goes to Pandeli, inside the Egyptian Bazaar. An alternative choice across the bridge is Liman Lokantasi, in the international passenger terminal; if there is no ship moored alongside, the panorama out over the Golden Horn is one of Istanbul's finest. Finally, at the far end of Topkapi

Palace, there is Konyali's, with superb food and fine views over the Bosphorus (although you must avoid the lunchtime crush between noon and 1pm). These three are lunch-only restaurants.

NIGHTLIFE

Istanbul's nightlife is somewhat tame compared with the images of sailors, belly-dancers, bars and strip-joints conjured up by the city's cosmopolitan past. Most of the floorshows have a strong tourist slant, and the Kervansaray Club (along Cumhuriyet Caddesi) is about the best of these. This elegantly decorated former theatre provides a two-hour show including folk-dancing, a magician, three different belly-dancers and a male/female duo topping the bill singing mid-European songs of the 'oompah' variety. The waiters carefully explain the pricing policy (about £25 for dinner plus show; £15 for show plus one drink only). Standards elsewhere are variable; the appeal of the Galata Tower floorshow is limited by its dingy entrance, gloomy atmosphere and densely packed tables. Turkish *gazinos* are open-air nightclubs, usually with Turkish singers; they are very popular in the summer. The best are along the shores of the Bosphorus.

More 'cultural' entertainment can be found at the Atatürk Centre (in Taksim Square), home of Istanbul's State Symphony Orchestra, State Ballet and State Opera. The Istanbul Festival in June and July offers a programme of international drama, opera, symphony concerts and so on; tickets are available from the side-door of the Centre. The highlight is the production of Mozart's *Abduction from the Seraglio* in the gardens of Topkapi Palace itself. A free *son-et-lumière* takes place at the Hippodrome, featuring a floodlit Blue Mosque. The commentary is in a different language each night (the Tourist Information Office can tell you when it's English).

Most of the international hotels have discos, some with spectacular roof-balcony views of the city. For cinemas, head north along Cumhuriyet Caddesi from Taksim (*Renkli Orijinal* on the poster indicates that the film is in the original language with Turkish subtitles). The usher will expect a small tip for showing you to your seat. You can generally buy your tickets a few hours in advance.

Istanbul does not specialise in pavement cafés, but you come closest to the atmosphere at Çiçek Pasaji, whose arcades and inner courts are crammed with food-and-beer restaurants. Find a table at the corner of the dog-leg-shaped passage and you will usually be entertained by a commotion of some sort: strolling music players, itinerant pedlars or boisterous sing-songs. Arrive between 8pm and 9pm because the passage begins to close down by 11pm. Finally, one of the most romantic evenings can be spent taking a cruise up the Bosphorus (the ferries run until past midnight) and then eating at a shoreside restaurant. The villages of Bebek and Tarabya both specialise in outdoor fish restaurants right by the Bosphorus; the Abdullalı Lokantasi, above the village of Emirgan on the European shore, and Hidiv Kasri at Çubuklu on the Asian, are two excellent restaurants – popular too, so you'll need to book in advance. Set off early enough to catch the ferry both ways or combine the ferry with a 30- to 45-minute return taxi ride.

HOTELS

The most important choice is location. The large international hotels are in the new part of the city around Taksim Square. You're a taxi ride from the major sights, but it is the area to be in in the evening, with a wide choice of restaurants and nightlife. If you stay in Sultanahmet you may find your hotel surrounded by slum clearance programmes (though this isn't the case for our recommendations) and be forced to try further afield for a good restaurant in the evening. Laleli, also in the old town, is the university district, full of small shops and cheaper hotels. The back streets are mostly pleasant and tree-lined.

Hotel prices Symbols indicate approximate prices per room per night for a double room with bath. Many large hotels run special breaks which work out far cheaper. (See page 14 for further details.)

♦ = under £50; ♦♦ = £50 to £80; ♦♦♦ = £80 to £100;
♦♦♦♦ = £100 to £140; ♦♦♦♦♦ = over £140.

AYASOFYA PANSIYONLARI
Sogukcesme, 34400 Sultanahmet   *Tel: 513 36 60*

This hotel comprises an attractive row of historic houses that back on to the walls of Topkapi Palace, with a quiet cobbled street at the front. There are no public lounges and it feels more like sharing a house than staying in a hotel: you get keys for your front door and for your room. Bedrooms are comfortable and fair sized. They are furnished in nineteenth-century Turkish style: rugs, dark wood and brass bedsteads. Front rooms (more expensive) with a view are best; back rooms can be claustrophobic.

Bedrooms: 57, 24 with bath/WC, 33 with shower/WC; none with TV
Facilities: Restaurant   **Credit/charge cards accepted:** Amex, Diners, Visa

ISTANBUL HILTON ♦♦♦♦♦
Cumhuriyet Caddesi, 80200 Harbiye   *Tel: 231 46 46   Fax: 240 41 65*

If you can't afford to stay here, visit to take tea on the terrace with wonderful views of the Bosphorus. It's well back from the main road in beautifully tended gardens, about ten minutes' walk from Taksim. The beige marble reception and lounge area is set round a courtyard thick with greenery. Bedrooms are large, modern and well co-ordinated, with thick carpets, light wooden furniture and large picture windows – try to get a room with a view of the Bosphorus.

Closed: Poolside restaurant closed Sept to May, rooftop restaurant closed Sun   **Bedrooms:** 498, all with bath/WC; air-conditioning; mini-bar
Facilities: Lift; restaurants; indoor and outdoor pools; gym; sauna; squash; tennis   **Credit/charge cards accepted:** All

PERA PALAS
Mesrutiyet Caddesi 98-100, Tepebasi   *Tel: 25 14 560   Fax: 25 14 089*

A place for romantics. Built in 1892 for Orient-Express passengers, this grand old hotel has played host to Agatha Christie, Mata Hari and Edward VIII. It's in the new part of town, half an hour's walk from Taksim Square, down a dusty side-street. There is no grand entrance but the main lounge has pillars and balconies, heavy chandeliers and dark rugs. The main restaurant has ornate ceilings and red velvet curtains. Bedrooms are old-fashioned, with dark wood furniture and satin bedspreads.

Bedrooms: 145, all with bath/shower/WC; air-conditioning; mini-bar; some with fridge; some with TV   **Facilities:** Lift; restaurants; private parking   **Credit/charge cards accepted:** All

RAMADA
Ordu Caddesi 226, 34470 Laleli   Tel: 513 93 00   Fax: 513 93 40

About 15 minutes from the Grand Bazaar, this conversion of four apartment blocks has to be seen to be believed. Domed glass roofs, glass lifts and galleried public rooms now fill the roads that once divided the blocks. The lounge and café feature birds and goldfish, and there's a sophisticated oriental restaurant. Standard bedrooms are small, with views over the shabby rooftops of the old city; if you're lucky you can see the mosque.

Bedrooms: 275, all with bath/WC; air-conditioning; mini-bar   **Facilities:** Lift; restaurant; private parking; indoor heated pool; whirlpool bath; sauna; masseur; casino   **Credit/charge cards accepted:** All

YESIL EV
Kabasakal Caddesi 5, 34400 Sultanahmet   Tel: 517 67 85   Fax: 517 67 80

The Yesil Ev is wonderfully positioned in the gardens between Hagia Sophia and the Blue Mosque – though that does mean you will be woken by the call to prayer. The hotel, painted apple green, is a lovingly restored nineteenth-century wooden mansion. In the garden is an open-air restaurant, and alongside are small craftsmen's workshops. The house is warmly comfortable, with velvet chairs, gilt mirrors and fresh flowers. The beds, with their heavy brass bedsteads, fill the bedrooms.

Bedrooms: 20, all with shower/WC; one with TV; mini-bar; Turkish bath   **Facilities:** Restaurant   **Credit/charge cards accepted:** Access, Amex, Visa

ZURIH
Vidinli Tefvik Pasa Caddesi
Harikzedeler Sokak 37, Laleli   Tel: 512 23 50   Fax: 526 97 31

About ten minutes' walk from the Grand Bazaar in a pleasant, fairly busy tree-lined side-street, the Zurih's concrete lines are softened by plant-filled balconies. There is small airy lounge. Bedrooms are a fair size and uncluttered, with beige carpets and dark wood furniture. The basement restaurant is a bit cramped, but there's a pianist every evening, and a regular oriental floorshow complete with belly-dancers. A good-value package hotel.

Bedrooms: 132, all with bath/shower/WC; air-conditioning; mini-bar   **Facilities:** Lift; restaurant   **Credit/charge cards accepted:** All

LISBON

- Not the most exciting European capital but Lisbon has a charming provincial atmosphere and is conveniently small scale
- Few great buildings in the city itself, although plenty of architectural detail and decoration to admire
- Startlingly beautiful landscape and castles make a day's excursion to the town of Sintra a priority
- Portugal joined the European Community in 1986, but still lags far behind many of its partners in economic terms

VIEWED from one of the seven hills over which it is ranged, or from the River Tagus which divides the historical quarters from the industrial suburbs, Lisbon is one of Europe's most appealing capitals. Crowned by the crenellated walls of a Moorish castle, baroque domes and state-of-the-art skyscrapers peek up from an undulating and softly hued cityscape. Close up, the city is a patchwork of diverse, even conflicting quarters. You can travel in a few minutes – in a stubby Edwardian-looking tram – from the grimy, traffic-congested city centre into hilly neighbourhoods where narrow cobbled streets wind past houses of flaking stucco or cracked *azulejos* (painted tiles), and where old men spend their days sitting outside bars, and old women gossip from balconies.

In the city centre there are scenes redolent of the Third World: stone-breakers chip tesserae of limestone and basalt to repair the distinctive mosaic-patterned pavements; on riverside Praça do Comercio, the children of immigrants from Portugal's ex-colonies guide civil servants to parking spaces; on Largo Intendente prostitutes seek custom from the lorry-drivers playing poker on the pavements; and throughout the centre shoe-shine boys, beggars and lottery ticket sellers vie for your attention.

The skyscraper banks, luxury hotels and shopping complexes testify to the wealth of at least part of the population, but it is nevertheless difficult to believe that the city was once the most important port in Europe.

In the early fifteenth century, Prince Henry the Navigator founded a school, gathering together Europe's top cartographers, navigators and seamen to pass on their expertise to the Portuguese. By the end of the century the Portuguese had discovered Madeira, the Azores, Africa, India and Brazil, and they dominated world trade. But just as today, when little of the business community's wealth seems to filter through to the rest of the population, in the past the income from gold, spices and precious stones remained with the monarchy, nobility and a handful of foreign merchants.

The new-found wealth and confidence was expressed in the flamboyant and architectural style known as Manueline, named after King Manuel I. An extravagant version of late Gothic, it incorporated nautical motifs, with exotic beasts and columns carved into loops and twists to resemble ropes. But the heady days were soon over. Much of the rural population abandoned their farms for the cities, resulting in a shortage of meat and cereals; prices of spices and other imported commodities fell; and the burden of maintaining a vast fleet and extensive empire eventually led to the collapse of the economy.

Other than the doorway of the Conceição Velha Church off Praça do Comercio, and the superb Monastery of Jerónimos and the Torre in the suburb of Belém, few of the buildings of Lisbon's brief Golden Age survive, for in 1755 the city was virtually destroyed. At 9.30am on 1 November, while most of the population was in church celebrating All Saints' Day, a tremendous earthquake struck: the tremors were felt as far away as Scotland and Jamaica. Fires, kindled by thousands of church candles, raged through the city, and people fleeing to the waterfront were swept away by an immense tidal wave. Out of a population of 270,000, 40,000 were killed. The chief minister, Marquês de Pombal, took charge, saying, 'Bury the dead, feed the living and close the port'; he later had the city rebuilt. Pombal's rational grid of neo-classical buildings, Europe's first example of urban planning, still forms Lisbon's core.

The Baixa, as Pombal's city is known, is now elegant only from a distance – a closer look shows peeling paint, and few of the shops and cafés have the sophistication one might expect of a European capital. The streets of Baixa run from the central Rossio Square down to Praça do Comercio. Bordered on three sides by symmetrical coral and cream porticoed buildings, and open on the fourth to the River Tagus, Commerce Square is now used as a car-park and tram terminus.

The Baixa is flanked by hills: to the west, the city's classiest street, Rua Garrett, is approached along temporary wooden walkways through the haunting shells of buildings gutted in a fire in 1988. At its head is Largo do Chiado, best admired from the tables outside the city's most elegant café, A Brasiliera. Above it are the steep, dark, narrow streets of the Bairro Alto, dull and dingy by day but brash and bustling at night with many restaurants, *fado* houses and a scattering of trendy nightclubs.

To the east are the appealingly scruffy, tangled streets of Alfama, Santa Cruz and Mouraria, crowned by the turreted walls of the Moorish Castelo de São Jorge, which largely escaped the ravages of the earthquake. There's a village-like feel to the streets, with fish-wives returning from the early-morning market and canaries fluttering in cages hung outside the houses; but there's a sobering reminder of local poverty in Santa Cruz's public bath-house just below the walls of the *castelo*.

Stretching north from Rossio, the broad Avenida la Liberdade, lined with hotels and airline offices, climaxes on the traffic-congested rotunda of Praça do Marquês de Pombal, dominated by a statue of Pombal on a lofty column. Above it is the gently sloping Parque Eduardo VII, overlooked by some of Lisbon's most luxurious hotels.

WHEN TO GO

Winters in Lisbon are quite mild and summers, though hot, can be disappointingly dull. The most colourful time to go is at Carnaval, which takes place around Shrove Tuesday, and in June, when three major saints' days (St Anthony, St John and St Peter) are celebrated with processions, concerts, fireworks and street parties. The liveliest revelry is for St Anthony on 12 June.

GETTING THERE

Going independently

By air It takes about two and a half hours to fly to Lisbon from London. British Airways and Air Portugal have direct flights daily from Heathrow. Air Portugal also flies several times a week from Manchester. The cheapest fare bookable is the Supersaver; the price varies throughout the year but peaks around Easter and during the July/August holiday season. Cheaper charter flights are also available to Lisbon all year round (more so in summer) from Gatwick, Luton and Manchester airports, but as most are based on one- or two-week holidays it isn't easy to find one that fits around a short break. Operators include Thomson (081-200 8733), Falcon Flights (061-831 7000) and Avro Elite (081-543 5833). Cresta (0345 056511), Data Travel (0424 722394) and Flightfile (071-323 1515) offer discounts on scheduled fares.

Portela Airport Lisbon's airport is modern, clean, well organised and clearly signposted in English. The *turismo* bureau is open 24 hours a day and has a hotel booking service; there's a 24-hour exchange service; and a travel agency where you can book excursions. Facilities in the departure lounge have improved. Seating at peak periods can be limited, and the shops, although selling crystal, porcelain, jewellery and the like, should not be relied on by the last-minute present buyer. There is, however, a reasonable selection of port in the duty-free shop.

The airport is five miles north of the city centre. The cheapest way into the centre is by bus – the express *Linha Verde* runs every 15 minutes between 7.30am and 1.30am. The journey to Rossio Square takes about 20 minutes. Taxis are cheap too but there are often long queues at the taxi rank.

Tour operator packages

Many British tour companies run two-, three- and four-night packages to Lisbon, but you may find going independently slightly cheaper. A three-night package in a three-star hotel would typically range from £189 in low season to £349 in high season. Few of the hotels we recommend are used for package holidays. If you do decide to take a package it's worth shopping around, as high season prices vary from one company to another. For a list of tour operators, see page 385.

MASTERING THE SYSTEM

Information The Portuguese National Tourist Office is at 22-25a Sackville Street, London W1X 1DE, tel: 071-494 1441. In Lisbon the most convenient tourist offices are at the airport (tel: 89 36 89) and in the Palácio da Foz (tel: 36 36 24) on Restauradores Square, adjoining Rossio Square. They have a hotel booking service and up-to-date information on the opening hours of museums, but their free maps are inadequate.

Maps You'll probably need to buy a map, and the best is published by Falk-Verlag, available in the UK as well as in Lisbon. This has a street directory and marks the underground lines as well as all tram and bus routes.

Changing money Most hotels will change money for you, but banks give a better rate. Most are open Monday to Friday from 8.30am to 11.45am and 1pm to 2.45pm; certain city-centre branches are open 6pm to 11pm Monday to Saturday. There are a number of automatic cash dispensing machines around the city – the most convenient is at the Caixa Geral de Depositos opposite Rossio Station.

Sightseeing tours There are several companies running out-of-town excursions, sightseeing tours around the city, and visits to *fado* clubs and the casino at Estoril. Excursions to the palaces at Sintra (*see p.193*) also cram in the less interesting palace at Queluz and a couple of seaside resorts.

You can take a two-hour **boat trip** up the Tagus as far as the Torre de Belém, passing the 25 Abril suspension bridge and modern docks. The commentary is interesting, covering aspects of modern as well as historical Lisbon, and the ticket price includes a free glass of port. Boats leave daily at 3pm between April and October from the terminal just off Praça do Comercio.

Bullfights Portuguese bullfights are more humane than the Spanish version, as the bull is not killed. Bullfights are held at the Campo Pequeno in the north of the city, generally on Thursday and Sunday from Easter to October. The booking office is the green kiosk at Restauradores (open daily from 9am to 10pm).

Opening hours and days Most shops are open Monday to Friday from 9am to 1pm and 3pm to 7pm, and on Saturdays from 9am to 1pm, although a few now remain open at lunchtime. The Amoreiras shopping centre is open daily from 10am to 11pm. All Lisbon's museums are closed on Monday. In Sintra the Palácio Nacional is closed on Wednesday, the Palácio de Peña on Monday.

GETTING AROUND

The city centre, Alfama and the Bairro Alto are best explored on foot, but you'll need transport to get to some of the museums. Negotiating the **bus** and **tram** system without a good map is difficult, as the public transport kiosks (found in the city centre at Elevador and on Praça do Marquês de Pombal) often run out of route maps. Buses have a flat-rate fare; the tram fare depends on the length of journey. Tickets can be bought from the driver, or in advance from one of the public transport kiosks.

Lisbon's snub-nosed trams rattle up and down some alarmingly sheer gradients. Not surprisingly, two of the hills, on routes No 12 (from Largo Martin Moniz) and No 28 (from São Vicente) are the steepest ever to have been scaled by tram. A trip on tram No 28, in particular, is a fine way of seeing the city, as you roller-coaster through Alfama, down across the Baixa, and up through the Bairro Alto to the baroque Basilica de Estrela and its adjacent gardens.

The **underground** (metro) system is of little interest to tourists, as stations are mainly in the residential district of the city. **Taxis** are among Europe's cheapest, though patience is needed to flag them down (they're recognisable by the black livery with green roofs, and are available for hire if the small green light is on).

UNMISSABLES

Calouste Gulbenkian Museum

The outstanding private collection of the Armenian oil baron Calouste Gulbenkian forms Portugal's greatest museum (admission free on Sunday). Gulbenkian settled in Portugal after the government agreed to give him total tax exemption in return for his priceless collection. The Gulbenkian Foundation continues to finance a wide range of cultural events in Portugal – and also in Britain, where he once lived. The museum is just a part of a complex which includes shady peaceful grounds, concert halls, an outdoor amphitheatre, exhibition spaces and the Centro de Arte Moderna, a challenging collection of contemporary art.

The main museum is divided into two sections: the first devoted to ancient and non-European art and the second to European art. Though the collections are relatively small, the sheer quality can be overwhelming, and it's advisable to take a break in the beautifully landscaped grounds or in one of the cafés (the nicest is in the same block as the Centro de Arte Moderna).

The first section is a celebration of decorative arts, spanning centuries and continents: arcane Ancient Egyptian reliefs and sculpture, an exquisite red-figured Greek *krater*, iridescent Roman glassware and perfectly preserved Macedonian coins are effectively illuminated in subdued rooms; these give way to Persian ceramics and gorgeously opulent costumes, brocades and velvets; and the last hall holds Chinese porcelain ranging from the delicate to the gaudily grotesque, and a fine collection of Japanese lacquer boxes inlaid with shimmering mother-of-pearl.

The European section is a rather more conventional collection of paintings. Among the Flemish works, portraits by van der Weyden, Rembrandt and Van Dyck stand out, as does Rubens' disturbingly erotic *Centaurs*. Italian work ranges from the Renaissance formality of Vittore Carpaccio to cheekily exuberant *putti* frolicking in tapestries based on cartoons by Giulio Romano. Most striking of the English works is a powerful shipwreck by Turner, while the French are represented by Corot landscapes and a handful of Impressionists. Finally, there's a room devoted to the weird and fantastic jewellery of René Lalique.

National Museum of Azulejos
In the converted buildings and cloisters of the sixteenth-century convent of Madre de Deus there's an attractive museum charting the development of *azulejos*, or painted tiles. The church itself forms the centrepiece, a sumptuous fantasy of twisted and gilded wood and paintings; elsewhere in the museum is a 36-metre-long panorama of pre-earthquake Lisbon, and examples of contemporary *azulejos*. There's also a traditionally decorated café looking on to a shady courtyard, and a limited selection of tiles on sale.

Castelo de São Jorge
Crowning the old Alfama quarter are the walls and towers of the honey-gold Castelo de São Jorge, built by the Moors. The Portuguese, aided by Crusaders, beseiged the castle for 17 weeks in 1147 before they succeeded in capturing it. Later kings strengthened and embellished it, and in the fourteenth century it was named after England's patron, St George, in celebration of the Treaty of Windsor – an alliance with England which has still not been abrogated.

The *castelo* has now been laid out as a park, with gardens, peacocks strutting among the oleanders, an enclosure of white deer, a café/restaurant (very pricey), terraces and rampart walkways.

Belém: the Jerónimos Monastery, Monument to the Discoveries and Torre de Belém

In the suburb of Belém, west of the centre and close to the mouth of the Tagus, is the magnificent Jerónimos Monastery, one of the few buildings of Lisbon's Golden Age to have survived the 1755 earthquake. It was from Belém that Vasco da Gama set sail in search of India in 1497. Eighteen months later his semi-wrecked ship limped back to Belém, its hold crammed with precious stones and spices, but with half the crew dead. The survivors were welcomed back by King Manuel I, who, a few years later, erected the monastery on the site of the hermitage as a thanks-offering to the Virgin for making Vasco's voyage so successful.

Fittingly, the building was financed by what was known as the 'pepper penny' – five per cent of all gold imported from Guinea, and of the income from Indian spices and precious stones – while the exuberant Manueline style displays the pioneering influences on the imaginations of Portugal's architects.

The south portal is a particularly rich example, with columns carved to resemble twisted rope, and saints standing in attendance on Henry the Navigator among a forest of flowers, fruit and foliage inhabited by monkeys, griffins and birds.

Exotic and nautical themes continue inside, with tombs supported on the backs of elephants and vaulting knotted into a fabulously intricate cat's cradle of stone. The highlight, however, is the cloister, where the rope-like scallops, pretzels and trefoils of the stone arches appear almost supple.

Across the road from the monastery, the formal gardens of the Praça do Imperio, bisected by the railway line, lead down to the **Monuments to the Discoveries**. A concrete prow juts out into the Tagus, surmounted by Henry the Navigator and sundry followers looking out to sea. The lands that Henry and later generations of Portuguese explorers discovered are mapped in mosaic on the pavement below the monument. The tower is open to visitors, and gives good views of the 25 Abril suspension bridge, the modern docks, a distant Lisbon and the **Torre de Belém**.

The Torre, dating from the same period as the Jerónimos Monastery, is a fair walk down river (but there are usually plenty of taxis about). Surrounded by water at high tide, with fancy balconies, lacy balustrades, swirling pinnacles and segmented domes resembling peeled tangerines, it seems tailor-made for a fairy-tale princess. In fact it's a defensive tower: the tangerine domes shelter sentry boxes. Prisoners were incarcerated in the dark dungeons as late as the nineteenth century. Incidentally, with the walls between the turrets barely a foot high, young children will need supervision, especially in strong winds.

Excursion to Sintra

Byron thought the village of Sintra 'perhaps in every respect the most delightful in Europe'; and driving up to its palaces and Moorish castle along steep, tortuous lanes through luxuriant forests mottled by the sun, it's hard to disagree.

Sintra (16 miles west of Lisbon) consists of three distinct villages. Sintra-Vila is the main one, dominated by the bizarre **Palácio Nacional**, the summer retreat of Portuguese kings, with immense chimneys rising above its Gothic/Manueline façade.

The interior too has its curiosities: the Sala dos Arabes, tiled with *azulejos*, the Chinese Room with an ivory pagoda, the Sala dos Cisnes named after the swans on its ceiling, and the Sala das Pegas, whose flock of painted magpies was a comment by King João I on the gossipers at court, after he had been caught by his queen kissing a lady-in-waiting.

The quirks of the Palácio Nacional pale into insignificance beside the eccentricities of the **Palácio de Peña**. Fused to a rocky pinnacle above a fairy-tale forest, it's a crazily built folly: a fantasy of domes and turrets, prickly diamond-pointed towers, oriental horseshoe arches, Italianate loggias and Manueline columns. Converted from a monastery into another royal retreat in the nineteenth century, the rooms remain as they were in 1910, when they were hurriedly abandoned by King Manuel II after he was overthrown by the military.

Among such extravagance it's hard to isolate highlights, but don't miss the toilet decorated with blue vegetables or the *trompe-l'oeil* perspectives of the Arab room.

On the way back from Peña is the entrance to the Moorish castle, restored in the nineteenth century. Paths lead through dense woods up to a walkway along the turreted walls.

Sintra's loveliest gardens are those of the abandoned oriental-style **Quinta de Monserrate**, to the west of Sintra-Vila, partly designed by the head gardener at Kew.

Finally, returning to Sintra-Vila, you pass the Palace of Seteais, now a beautifully converted hotel and a fine place for tea.

Although there are organised excursions to Sintra from Lisbon, these also take in the less interesting Palace of Queluz and the coast, and do not leave enough time to absorb Sintra. It's better to hire a car for a day, or do the 50-minute journey by train from Lisbon's Rossio Station (every 20 minutes). Once you arrive in Sintra, buses leave at 10.45am, 3pm and 4pm for the Palácio de Peña, returning 75 minutes later. Taxis have fixed rates for all the palaces and the Moorish castle and the drivers will pick you up at a designated time. If you have time, there's no better way to conclude the day than to take a taxi to the Cabo de Roca, the westernmost point in Europe, for an unbeatable sunset. There are trains back to Lisbon from Sintra until after 1am.

OTHER PLACES TO VISIT

Cathedral and churches

Cathedral Founded in 1150 to celebrate the seizure of the city from the Moors, Lisbon's cathedral is a plain, weighty building flanked by two turreted towers. Earthquakes, fires and injudicious restoration have left little of note in the interior, save the light, airy Gothic apse. The most appealing feature is the decayed Gothic cloister which shelters architectural fragments.

Carmo This Gothic church, once the largest in Lisbon, was shattered by the 1755 earthquake, and its skeletal vaults now stand open to the sky. Birds nest in the nooks and crannies of statues; grass and wild flowers grow in the nave. Concerts are given here in summer, and beneath the umbrella vaults of the apse is a small haphazard archaeological collection.

São Roque Although from the outside the church of São Roque, at the foot of the Bairro Alto, is one of Lisbon's plainest, its interior is lavishly baroque. The sacristan will take you round the opulent chapels, the most extravagant of which is that dedicated to St John the Baptist. Designed by the Italian architect Vanviteli, it was actually built inside the Vatican so it could be blessed by the Pope before being dismantled and shipped to Lisbon. An elaborate concoction of lapis lazuli, porphyry and agate, encrusted with cute *putti*, and with scenes of St John the Baptist's life in mosaic masquerading as paint, it ranks as one of the world's most expensive chapels.

São Vicente de Fora This rather severe Renaissance church, designed by an Italian architect, is worth a brief visit if you're in the area. Its cloisters, tiled with eighteenth-century blue and white *azulejos*, depict scenes from La Fontaine's fables.

Museums and galleries

Museum of Ancient Art (Museu Nacional de Arte Antiga) Portugal's national collection of art is laid out in a seventeenth-century mansion. The collection of fifteenth- and sixteenth-century Portuguese art, all of it religious, is more interesting than you might expect, as the biblical scenes are transported into contemporary settings, most significantly in the St Vincent altarpiece – the only surviving work of Nuno Gonçalves. St Vincent, Lisbon's patron saint, is welcomed to the city by a group of fifteenth-century citizens, ranging from King Afonso V, Queen Isabel and Henry the Navigator to a Moorish knight, a beggar and a fisherman.

Equally fascinating, although in a very different sense, is the surreal and violent *Temptation of St Anthony* by Hieronymus Bosch.

Museum of Decorative Arts (Fundação Ricardo do Espirito Santo Silva) An exquisitely decorated and opulently furnished seventeenth-century mansion, between the *castelo* and the Alfama, this would be delightful if you could wander through it at your own pace; unfortunately guided tours are obligatory.

Museum of Puppets (Museu de Marioneta) This tiny museum close to the *castelo* has a small theatre, as well as a collection of puppets, model theatres and old posters. If you go in the morning you may be lucky enough to catch a performance.

Museum of Costume (Museu do Trajo) This museum is in a beautifully restored mansion set in a luxuriant park in the northern, and extremely poor, suburb of Lumiar. Though the collection is vast, the costumes are displayed in rotation on particular themes. In an adjoining workshop you can buy traditional rugs made on the eighteenth- and nineteenth-century equipment, while the café and restaurant in the heart of the park make a picturesque lunch-stop. The **Theatre Museum** nearby has exhibitions charting the history of the Portuguese stage.

Museums of Belém Several museums are grouped near each other in the Belém district. Laid out in a wing of the Jerónimos Monastery, the **Naval Museum**'s collection ranges from models of Phoenician and Ancient Greek boats to models of twentieth-century battleships. Elaborately carved and gilded royal barges are displayed in a hall across the courtyard.

A ten-minute walk up the hill behind the Jerónimos Monastery is the **National Museum of Archaeology and Ethnology**. The temporary exhibitions from Portugal and its former colonies are excellent – imaginatively displayed and dramatically lit.

Lisbon's most visited museum is reputedly the **National Coach Museum**, a short walk from the Jerónimos Monastery, with gilded, painted and carved carriages in a frescoed hall.

In the **Folk Art Museum**, between the monastery and the Torre de Belém, are displays of pottery, textiles, clothes and furniture.

Other attractions

Santa Luzia Belvedere The belvedere outside the church of Santa Lucia, close to the Museum of Decorative Arts, gives a superb view over the Alfama's jumbled maze of red roofs to the river. On the wall of the church itself are panels of eighteenth-century blue and white *azulejos*.

Eduardo VII Park and the Estufa Fria On a gentle slope above the Praça do Marquês de Pombal, the broad mosaic-tiled boulevards of the Parque de Eduardo VII were laid out in 1903 to celebrate the visit of Edward VII. Though the park itself is not among Lisbon's most attractive, being rather scruffy and littered, in the top left-hand corner the bamboo-slatted canopy of the Estufa Fria shelters a jungle oasis of sub-tropical trees and cacti punctuated by pools, grottoes, waterfalls and vaguely classical statues.

Elevador One of the more eccentric of Lisbon's sights, this lift, encased in a metal neo-Gothic tower, was designed by Gustav Eiffel. It links the Baixa with the Largo do Carmo.

Botanical Gardens On the slopes above the Avenida da Liberdade a luxuriant oasis of tropical trees forms a deliciously fine spot in which to escape the heat.

SHOPPING

As a whole, Lisbon has few tempting shops, and most of the high-street shops are not on the streets at all but in modern shopping malls. The most convenient of these forms part of the Rossio railway station, but the small exclusive mall on Rua Ivena, off Rua Garrett, is rather more interesting. Although there are clothes, shoes and jewellery shops throughout the Baixa, in particular on Rua Augusta and Rua Aurea, for really serious shopping head for the Amoreiras shopping mall, which has over three hundred shops and boutiques housed in a surreal pink and blue sky-scraping complex on the outskirts of the city.

More inspiring than any of these, however, are the shops selling traditional Portuguese ceramics and *azulejos*, embroidery and rugs. Among the best in ceramics and *azulejos* shops is Viuva-Lamego (open Monday to Friday 9am to 1pm; 3pm to 7pm) incongruously set in the heart of red-light Lisbon on Largo do Intendente. There's a wide range of crockery and tiles. Easier to carry home yourself are the rugs and embroidered tablecloths, blouses, bags and purses from the Azores at the Casa Regional

Ilha Verde on Rua Paiva de Andrada just off Rua Garrett. And worth a look, even if you can't afford the steep prices charged for its sumptuous rugs and traditional tapestries, is Quintão at 30-34 Rua Ivens.

Lisbon's flea market (Feira de Ladra) is held on Tuesday and Saturday mornings, sprawling over the Campo de Santa Clara between the churches of São Vicente and Santa Engracia. Aimed at the Portuguese rather than tourists, most of what's on sale is either new and tacky or old and jumbly, though glazed terracotta pots and bright woven rugs are good buys and are better bargains than you find in the shops.

For great selections of wine, port and madeira at half the price of the trendy off-licences in the Baixa, look around Rua de Arsenal near Cais do Sodré railway station.

EATING AND DRINKING

Portuguese food is simple or boring, depending on your taste. Fish features heavily on menus: fresh sardines, especially when grilled on a barbecue, are delicious; crawfish (*lagosta*) are a traditional, though increasingly rare and expensive, delicacy; while clams (*ameijoas*) are served with pork in *porco alanteijo*. Salt cod (*bacalhau*) is the national dish and can be found everywhere; however, it's an acquired taste. There are also many traditional soups: *caldo verde* is made of shredded cabbage in a potato broth and comes with slices of peppery sausage floating in it, and *açorda* is made of bread, resembles a garlicky porridge, and can come with poached eggs or seafood.

There are several prestigious restaurants in the city, serving a combination of Portuguese and international cuisine – but sitting among the gilt and chandeliers of Tavares on Rua Misericordia, or in the opulent turn-of-the-century dining-room of Antonio y Clara, at Avenida de Repubblica 38, you could be anywhere in the world. For excellent and imaginative food in the heart of the Bairro Alto, Pilau au Face, Rua Barocca 70, is hard to beat – sophisticated yet friendly, with a pleasant bar.

Choosing a more modest restaurant can be a hit and miss affair; restaurants in Bairro Alto are generally good value. Try Rua Atalaia and judge the restaurant by the length of queues of Portuguese. There are fewer restaurants in the Alfama but Mestre Antonio on Rua Remedios is simple, unpretentious and lively, with seats inside and out; it serves meat and fish grilled outside on a barbecue.

The normal time for dinner is around 8pm. The Portuguese tend to go for an afternoon snack in a café – sweet or savoury pastries, meat or cod croquettes or even cold, battered fish. Cafés also sell rather more conventional snacks like buttered toast and toasted sandwiches as well as cakes. Coffee can be an Italian-style espresso (*bica*), a small, milky *garoto*, or a large milky *galao*. The most pleasant of Lisbon's cafés are the nineteenth-century A Brasiliera at the top of Rua Garrett, and the Pastelaria Suica on Rossio.

As well as port and madeira there are also several good table wines. There are good but expensive red wines from the Dão region, and whites include the faintly sparkling *vinho verde*.

NIGHTLIFE

The classic night out in Lisbon is a visit to a *fado* club. *Fado* singing – wailing and passionate – is definitely an acquired taste, and many of the clubs, concentrated on Rua Queimada in the Bairro Alto, are rather seedily glitzy. You can book an organised '*fado* with dinner' excursion, but before committing yourself, stand outside one of the clubs for a free sampler! The most famous *fado* club is A Severa on Rua das Gaveas in the Bairro Alto, but a less touristy option is Timpanas, outside the centre in the Alcantara district, at Rua Gilberto Rola 16.

The Gulbenkian Foundation sponsors ballet and concerts. The main opera season is from November to June.

Lisbon is lively at night, and wandering its streets is a pleasant way of winding down after dinner. The maze-like streets of the Alfama are particularly attractive, with children playing and locals chatting. The Bairro Alto is busier, boisterous, verges on the sleazy and is the focus of Lisbon's contemporary club scene. For a more sedate stroll head down to Avenida da Liberdade.

The best place to sample port is the Port Wine Institute (Solar do Vinho do Porto) at Rua São Pedro de Alcantara 45 (open Monday to Saturday, 10am to midnight). Other bars include Bacchus, Rua de Trinidad 9, small and intimate among the carved columns, statues and oriental jugs; and Metro e Meio, Avenida Cinco de Outobro 174, with a warren of rooms decorated with arty and folksy artefacts.

HOTELS

The most convenient hotels lie just off the main avenue, Avenida da Liberdade, and on Rua Castilho overlooking the Parque Eduardo VII. These are all mainstream city hotels, however, and if you're looking for something more individual, options are thin on the ground. The attractions of York House outweigh the disadvantages of its position, and the simple Senhora do Monte is spectacularly sited on the brink of Graça Hill.

AVENIDA PALACE   ♦♦♦♦♦
Rua 1 de Dezembro 123   *Tel: 346 01 51   Fax: 342 28 84*

This hotel overlooks noisy, traffic-congested Rossio Square. The interior, however, is quiet, stately and civilised; the lobby, lit by a chandelier, has a black-and-white-tiled floor and classical statues. Elaborate chandeliers, brocaded walls and gilt mirrors lend an air of refinement to the lounge and restaurant. Rooms are individually furnished with antiques and decorated in subdued shades. There is some street noise in the front-facing rooms.

Bedrooms: 200, all with bath/WC; air-conditioning; mini-bar   **Facilities:** Lift; restaurant   **Credit/charge cards accepted:** All

---

CAPITOL   ♦♦
Rua Eca de Queiroz 24   *Tel: 53 68 11   Fax: 352 61 65*

A fairly small hotel just off Avenida Duque de Loule, close to Parque Eduardo VII and Plaça do Marquês de Pombal. Old leather chairs add a homely feel to the small lounge/TV room, though the restaurant and bar are functional rather than atmospheric. Refurbished rooms have modern, pale wood furniture and colour co-ordinated furnishings.

Bedrooms: 58, some with bath/shower/WC; all with air-conditioning
Facilities: Lift; restaurant; private parking   **Credit/charge cards accepted:** Diners, Visa

---

Hotel prices Symbols indicate approximate prices per room per night for a double room with bath. Many large hotels run special breaks which work out far cheaper. (See page 14 for further details.)

♦ = under £50; ♦♦ = £50 to £80; ♦♦♦ = £80 to £100;
♦♦♦♦ = £100 to £140; ♦♦♦♦♦ = over £140.

LISBOA PLAZA
Avenida da Liberdade, Travessa do Salitre 7   Tel: 346 37 22   Fax: 347 16 30

This is a stunning, subtly decorated hotel in a quiet street off Avenida da Liberdade. Behind the ugly grey façade the pleasant reception area is paved in cream marble. The lounge is airy and summery, and the cocktail bar tasteful. The restaurant, with wood panelling and imitation marble columns, looks on to a tiled wall behind an ornamental pool. Bedrooms are elegant, decorated in pastels with small, but well-planned, marble bathrooms.

Bedrooms: 106, all with bath/WC; air-conditioning; mini-bar   **Facilities:** Lift; restaurant; private parking   **Credit/charge cards accepted:** All

MERIDIEN LISBOA
Rua Castilho 149   Tel: 69 09 00   Fax: 69 32 31

A hi-tech glass and marble hotel, whose stepped façade overlooks Parque Eduardo VII. Centrepiece in the cool airy reception area is a geometric fountain, surrounded by plants and reflected in the mirrored ceiling. Opening off the reception is a quiet brasserie and a comfortable bar. There's also a light, summery indoor patio. Rooms are serene and tastefully decorated with traditional woven curtains and bedspreads. Bathrooms are fitted out in marble. Suites are vast and stylish.

Bedrooms: 331, all with bath/WC; air-conditioning; mini-bar; hair-dryer
Facilities: Lift; restaurant; sauna; hairdresser   **Credit/charge cards accepted:** All

PRINCIPE REAL
Rua da Alegria 53   Tel: 346 01 16   Fax: 342 21 04

On a quiet, steep street above Avenida da Liberdade sits the Principe Real, convenient for the city centre and the Bairro Alto. Behind the salmon-pink façade, the small quarry-tiled reception area is immediately welcoming, with oriental rugs and a leather chesterfield sofa. The lounge is cosily elegant, with a tasteful mixture of modern and antique furniture. There is a small bar, and the restaurant has panoramic views across to the Alfama and *castelo*. Rooms are simple but welcoming.

Bedrooms: 24, all with bath/WC; air-conditioning; mini-bar   **Facilities:** Lift; bar; restaurant   **Credit/charge cards accepted:** All

REX
Rua Castilho 169 Tel: 388 21 61 Fax: 388 75 81

A short distance from the Meridien, also overlooking Parque Eduardo VII, this hotel is smaller, cheaper and simpler, but nevertheless has some style. The small Restaurante Panoramico has, as its name suggests, superb views of the city, and is decorated in shades of green. Rooms have quality furniture and pastel furnishings. Bedrooms are small but prettily tiled with *azulejos*. Views from the front rooms stretch from the park to the *castelo* and river.

Bedrooms: 68, some with bath/shower/WC; air-conditioning **Facilities:** Lift; restaurant; private parking **Credit/charge cards accepted:** Diners, Visa

ALBERGARIA SENHORA DO MONTE
Calçada do Monte 39 Tel: 886 60 02 Fax: 87 77 83

Perched on the lip of a hill above Lisbon, this small, friendly hotel has panoramic views of the city. The reception area sets the tone, with its shiny marble floor and antique-style furniture, and the bar/breakfast room has an outdoor terrace and hand-painted modern *azulejos* on the wall. Rooms are simple and tasteful, with tiles in the bathrooms. Book in advance if you want a room with a view, as the hotel is extremely popular.

Bedrooms: 28, all with bath/WC; some with air-conditioning; some with balcony/terrace **Facilities:** Lift **Credit/charge cards accepted:** All

SHERATON
Rua Latino Coelho 1 Tel: 57 57 57 Fax: 54 71 64

This is a 30-storey skyscraper, dominating the skyline, a ten-minute drive from the centre and a short walk from the Parque Eduardo VII. It's an international hotel, with many comforts and facilities, and an effort has been made to introduce Portuguese motifs. The basement breakfast room is light and summery, blue and white, with wicker furniture and plants. There are spectacular views from the Panorama Bar/Restaurant. Rooms are spacious and smart, with large marble bathrooms.

Bedrooms: 384, all with bath/shower/WC; air-conditioning; mini-bar **Facilities:** Lift; restaurant; outdoor heated pool; health club **Credit/charge cards accepted:** All

TIVOLI LISBOA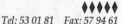
Avenida da Liberdade 185   Tel: 53 01 81   Fax: 57 94 61

A luxury hotel, conveniently rather than pleasantly positioned on busy
Avenida da Liberdade – but the lush walled garden compensates for the
location. The large reception area gleams with marble and has islands of
velvet seats around glass-topped tables. Public rooms are smart but lack
atmosphere. Rooms are decorated with good-quality furniture, but
without the usual trappings to suggest that you are in Portugal; the suites
are furnished in eighteenth-century style. There is a roof-top restaurant.

Bedrooms: 342, all with bath/WC; air-conditioning; mini-bar   **Facilities:**
Lift; restaurant; outdoor heated pool; hairdresser   **Credit/charge cards
accepted:** All

YORK HOUSE
Rua das Janelas Verdes 32   Tel: 396 24 35   Fax: 397 27 93

A beautifully restored sixteenth-century convent in a walled garden close
to the Museu Nacional de Arte Antiga. You enter through a small
gatehouse, up steps through bowers of ivy to the building, with a palm-
shaded courtyard for drinks or meals. The elegant reception area has the
air of a country villa. Rooms have quarry-tiled floors strewn with
traditional rugs.

Bedrooms: 36, all with bath/WC   **Facilities:** Bar; restaurant   **Credit/
charge cards accepted:** All

Hotel prices Symbols indicate approximate prices per room
per night for a double room with bath. Many large hotels run
special breaks which work out far cheaper. (See page 14 for
further details.)

♦ = under £50; ♦♦ = £50 to £80; ♦♦♦ = £80 to £100;
♦♦♦♦ = £100 to £140; ♦♦♦♦♦ = over £140.

MADRID

- Though not the most beautiful, Madrid is one of the most exciting of European capitals: a good-time city, open 24 hours a day
- There's plenty to see and do – including the Prado, one of the world's greatest art galleries, the Thyssen collection and lots of smaller museums and galleries. But leave time to shop, explore the city, and absorb the vibrant and varied life on the streets
- Madrid streets are choked with traffic. Wind down in cafés, stroll in the parks or escape on an out-of-town excursion to medieval Toledo
- It's a city of great vitality, particularly in the evenings, when what seems like the entire population turns out to parade on the streets and meet friends

BILLBOARDS proclaiming the virtues of Christ may be juxtaposed with those singing the praises of Schweppes, but there's little doubt that Madrid is a resolutely contemporary, secular city. Its cathedral is only half-finished, and its most magnificent buildings are banks, hotels and the post office. Madrid's vitality is most evident at night. As Hemingway wrote in *Death in the Afternoon*: 'Nobody in Madrid goes to bed until they have killed the night.' The optimum time for dinner is 10.30pm, cafés stay open till midnight, and in the city's discos Madrid's young hedonists dance the dawn in. Street life is varied and visible: off the Gran Vía, the prostitutes ply their trade under flashing neon lights to an accompaniment of electronic blips from sleazy amusement arcades; and around midnight on Plaza Santa Ana, children play on climbing frames while their parents sit in pavement cafés, unperturbed by down-and-outs getting ready for a night on a bench or the hisses of 'hash, hash' with which dope-dealers greet every passer-by.

The exuberance and variety of Madrid's street life is nothing new: its low life was the inspiration behind many a picaresque novel (Cervantes lived in Madrid); Casanova visited specifically to sample the decadent delights of its pre-Lenten festival; and in the nineteenth century its population was described as 'the most extraordinary vital mass to be found in the entire world'. Today it is still a fun city, upbeat and trendy, open 24 hours a day. It's also extremely smart – you'll need to wear your best clothes even if you're not staying at the Ritz. Above all, Madrid has something to suit all ages, and at any time of day there's always something to see, something to do and somewhere to go.

Madrid was made the capital only in 1561 and has none of the architectural beauty or historical significance of the great old cities of Spain. When the Habsburg King Philip II moved his court there Madrid was just an obscure medieval town occasionally used by the royal family when they were hunting in the surrounding oak woods. Philip's prime reason for selecting Madrid – on a high plateau 300 miles from the coast – was that it stood virtually bang in the centre of the country, which he considered appropriately symbolic of the absolute impartiality of the monarchy in its dealings with all parts of the nation. As the population grew under the Habsburgs, the city expanded haphazardly, and the surrounding woods were cleared to provide timber for houses. The earth dried out, and fertile fields became barren, creating what has been called the 'hideous, grassless, treeless, colourless, calcined desert' on which Madrid sits today. Apart from the elegantly restrained Plaza Mayor and a handful of dull churches, the legacy of two centuries of Habsburg rule is less apparent on the streets than in the superb collection of paintings (by Velázquez, El Greco and great artists of the Italian and Flemish Renaissance) in the Prado art gallery.

The Bourbons, who succeeded the Habsburgs in 1700, made more of an architectural impact on the city, which by then had the reputation of being one of the filthiest in Europe. They built the opulent Royal Palace, opened parks to the public, paved streets and embellished them with grand triumphal arches and elaborate fountains.

On 2 May 1808, the French seized Madrid, an event hauntingly captured by Goya in a pair of paintings (*Dos de Mayo* and *Tres de Mayo*, now in the Prado). Napoleon's brother Joseph found time during his brief reign to improve the city further by laying out new squares, notably starting work on the elegant Plaza Oriente near the Royal Palace. Despite this, the city came into its own only when the building of railways and roads made its central location an advantage. Madrid's real splendours date from the nineteenth and early twentieth centuries: in particular the flamboyant commercial buildings and hotels lining Gran Vía and Calle Alcalá, and on Plaza de la Cibeles.

The centre of the city, and the point from which all distances in Spain are measured, is the Puerta del Sol, a square whose time-honoured role as a meeting place is more interesting than its architecture. Leading out of Sol, Calle Carmen and Calle Preciados are the main shopping streets and focus of the evening stroll, or *paseo*. Apart from the occasional museum, most of what you'll want to see by day is within walking distance of Sol, in the area bounded to the west by the Royal Palace, and to the east by the Prado.

After the *paseo*, many people head for neo-classical Plaza Mayor, once a scene for bullfights and festivals (and, during the years of the Inquisition, for numerous trials, executions and *autos-da-fé*), and nowadays the heart of tourist Madrid. The pompous, uniform façades shelter over-priced *tapas* bars and restaurants; there are buskers and portrait artists, and well-heeled foreigners who step past heroin addicts slumped in forgotten doorways.

South of Sol there are the old working-class quarters of Latina and Lavapiés, with narrow streets enclosed by tall dark tenement buildings. There's a closed, slightly sinister feel to the quarters, and little to attract the visitor apart from the Sunday morning Rastro flea market and the restaurants of the somewhat gentrified Cava Baja.

North of Sol is the Gran Vía, on which grand old façades – confections of cream-washed stucco and fancily wrought iron –

provide a note of splendour among the gaudy cinema hoardings, fast-food outlets and screaming lanes of traffic. Gran Vía stretches from the Manhattan-style skyscrapers of Plaza de España to Plaza de la Cibeles, where the city's cathedral-like post office and almost equally fancy Banco de España overlook an elaborate fountain depicting fertility goddess Cybele on a chariot. The Chueca quarter, north-east of Gran Vía, is an up-and-coming area, with trendy nightspots, restaurants, and the shops of young Spanish designers. Abutting Chueca are the narrow streets of the Malasaña quarter, the territory of prostitutes, punks and junkies.

Running north out of the city towards the airport, the Paseo de la Castellana was developed in the late nineteenth century: nowadays luxury hotels and soaring skyscrapers dwarf the few remaining fancy villas, and under the trees in the centre is a string of outdoor bars, or *terrazzas*, where the wealthier elements of Madrid's youth sip away the evening hours. At its foot, linking it with the parallel Calle de Serrano, are the Descubrimiento Gardens, laid out in the 1970s, dominated by a statue of Columbus. Calle de Serrano and the streets off it form the city's most upmarket shopping area, where designer-dressed *madrileños* cast an eye on Armani and Versace window-displays.

WHEN TO GO

Madrid is unbearably hot in summer, with temperatures reaching 38-39°C; most *madrileños* abandon the city for the entire month of August, and many museums, restaurants and shops are closed. Winters are cold, and can be dull and rainy, so the best times to go are spring and autumn. You could make an exception for the February carnival, when there are parades and street dancing. The main festival, however, is San Isidro on 15 May: the celebrations spill into the week before and the week after. From July to September the city council sponsors the *Veranos de la Villa*, a season of cultural events, including free concerts in the parks.

MASTERING THE SYSTEM

Information The Spanish National Tourist Office is at 57/58 St James's Street, London SW1A 1LD, tel: 071-499 0901. It's not very good at supplying detailed information. Tourist information offices (*Oficinas de Información Turistica*) in Madrid can be found at the airport (Monday to Friday 9am to 7pm, but currently closed for repairs); at Plaza Mayor 3, tel: 266 5477 (Monday to Friday 10am to 8pm, Saturday 10am to 2pm); and on the ground floor of the Torre de Madrid on Plaza de España, tel: 541 2325 (Monday to Friday 9am to 7pm and Saturday 9.30am to 1.30pm).

The tourist office produces a *What's On* brochure with listings of theatre, flamenco and opera performances, and exhibitions; and will provide details of festivals, concerts and bullfights. There's also a leaflet on museums, which gives public transport details but is unreliable on opening times. There are several listings magazines which are useful for up-to-date information on restaurants, bars and clubs.

Maps The free tourist office map *Madrid Plano Monumental* indicates main sights and museums, and includes a plan of the underground (metro) system; the free transport map of Madrid is also quite useful. If you're intending to go off the beaten track, especially at night, it's worth investing in the Firestone map, *Madrid y sus Aldrededores* (available in the UK, £3.50), which has a street directory.

Sightseeing tours There are several companies which operate tours and excursions that can be booked at your hotel. If you don't want to tackle the Prado alone, it could be worth taking a half-day guided tour which also includes the Royal Palace. Night-time excursions include visits to flamenco shows, but these cost about twice as much as going independently. Of the out-of-town excursions, a one-day or half-day trip to Toledo is a must, but El Escorial is of limited interest.

Changing money Most large hotels have bureaux de change, but you will get a better rate from a bank. Banks are generally open Monday to Friday 8.30am to 2pm and 9am to 1pm on Saturday. These times may change in the summer months, when many branches close on Saturday. There is a bureau de change open 24 hours a day at Barajas Airport.

Opening hours and days Most museums close on Monday and public holidays, but some smaller museums close for an additional day. They generally close at lunchtime. Most smaller shops close at 1.30pm or 2pm and re-open from 5pm until around 8pm, but large department stores stay open all day, from 10am to 8pm.

GETTING AROUND

The cheapest and quickest way of getting about is by **underground** (metro). The system, with ten lines, runs from 6am to 1.30am and is reasonably comprehensive – but as there are few maps posted in stations, it's worth carrying the *Plano Monumental* (available free from tourist offices). You can buy single-journey tickets, or a (better value) booklet of ten tickets.

Buses are fairly easy to use, run regularly from 6am till midnight, with a skeleton service till 2am and one bus an hour till 6am. The routes are listed on the bus-stop. Tickets are bought from the driver. Booklets of ten tickets can be bought from information kiosks on Puerta del Sol, Plaza del Callao and Plaza de la Cibeles.

Taxi fares are metered and are reasonably cheap.

UNMISSABLES

The Prado

This is one of the world's oldest, largest and most magnificent collections of paintings. The gallery was opened to the public in 1819, and owes its magnitude and quality to the taste and wealth

GETTING THERE

Going independently

By air It's a two and a half hour flight from London to Madrid. Between them, Iberia (071-437 5622) and British Airways (081-759 5511) have several flights a day from Heathrow and Gatwick. Iberia and BA also fly daily from Manchester. The cheapest fare bookable is the Saver or Seat Sale – but these are quickly taken up. Fares vary according to the time of year and peak at Christmas, Easter and during late July and August; it's also between £5 and £30 more expensive to fly at weekends instead of weekdays. Check on special offers.

There are charter flights to Madrid, too, although being based around one- or two-week holidays they are generally much less flexible than the daily scheduled flights. At the time of writing there were a couple of return fares for £99. Operators to try include Marsans International (071-224 0504), Hamilton (071-287 2425), Holidaymaker (081-664 1234), Comet Travel (071-636 6060), Meridian Tours (071-499 0673), Iberian Services (081-968 9855) and Euro Express (0293 511125).

Barajas Airport Madrid's airport is little more than functional. The arrivals lobby has a tourist office (closed for repairs at time of writing of generations of royal collectors. Although limited space means that only 1,200 of its 8,000 paintings are on show, the gallery can still be overwhelming.

Perhaps the best place to start is with the superb collection of seventeenth-century paintings by Velázquez. The immediately recognised *Las Meninas* is an obvious highlight, showing Velázquez in his studio with the Infanta Margarita and maids of honour, watched by King Philip IV and Queen Mariana shown reflected in a mirror. But don't neglect the rooms of royal portraits – wandering through them is akin to leafing through a family photo album.

There are more royal portraits by Goya – daringly unflattering works that make one wonder how he kept his job at the court. These are just a small part of Goya's output, and the Prado collection does justice to his extraordinarily emotional and stylistic range. Moving from the sensuality of works like *La Marquesa de Santa Cruz*, *La Maja Vestida* and *La Maja Desnuda* to the crazed fanaticism of battle in *Dos de Mayo* and the terror of execution in *Tres de Mayo*, it's hard to believe they are by the same man. There are even more unheroic depictions of war in the series of so-called 'Black Canvases' on the ground floor. These hauntingly introspective works, with nightmarish figures emerging

but normally open Monday to Friday 9am to 7pm) which has maps and information on the city and a hotel reservations bureau. Souvenirs are of the flamenco doll and matador hat type, but for last-minute presents the duty-free shop has a reasonable selection of wines, and Spanish gin is very cheap. The ten-mile journey to the city centre is cheapest by bus (around every 15 minutes) from outside 'Arrivals'. These drop you on Plaza de Colón, a metro ride (for Gran Vía or Sol, change at Alonso Martinez) from the centre. The bus journey takes about 30 minutes. A taxi journey costs around six times as much (to save argument, insist that the meter is switched on).

Tour operator packages

Many British tour operators run two-, three- and four-night packages to Madrid. These can be an extremely good deal if you want to stay in a luxury hotel like the Palace or the Ritz, but, if you prefer a mid- or low-price hotel, going independently can work out cheaper. Because so many sights close on Monday and at lunchtime on Sunday it's better to go for a Thursday departure to make the most of your time. If you do decide to take a package, it's worth shopping around, as the high season periods vary from one company to another. Three nights in a three-star hotel in high season cost around £300 in 1992. A city guidebook is sometimes included in the price, and transfers to and from the airport, too. For a list of tour operators, see page 385.

out of the darkness, seem to foreshadow Expressionism. The most exciting works by the third big-name Spanish artist, El Greco, are the visionary, virtually apocalyptic, religious canvases. However, if you're pushed for time, El Greco is better represented in Toledo (*see opposite*).

The Prado collection is not limited to Spanish works. There's a reasonable cross-section of Italian Renaissance canvases – Titian and his fellow Venetians, Tintoretto and Veronese, are the best represented – but it's the Flemish and Dutch collections which are of really startling quality. Undoubted highlights are the surreal hallucinatory works by Hieronymus Bosch.

Thyssen-Bornemisza Museum
In October 1992 one of the most famous private art collections in the world was opened to the public in the Villahermosa Palace, just across from the Prado. Amassed by Baron Heinrich Thyssen-Bornemisza and his father, the collection includes Old Masters such as Caravaggio, Goya and Holbein as well as twentieth-century works by Matisse, Picasso, Dali, Magritte and Miró.

Guernica
Hanging behind a bullet-proof screen in the Casón del Buen Retiro alongside Retiro Park, Picasso's *Guernica* is one of the most politically controversial paintings of the century. He was commissioned by the Republican government early in 1937 to paint a picture for the Spanish pavilion at the Paris Exposition. Picasso did not settle on a subject until 26 April, when an appalling bombing raid by the Nazis – in support of Franco and the Fascists – on the Basque town of Guernica left over 2,000 civilians dead. The painting came to Spain only in 1981, for Picasso had stipulated that it should remain outside the country until democracy was restored.

Royal Palace (Palacio Real)
Alongside Madrid's still skeletal neo-Gothic cathedral is the graceful Italianate Royal Palace. It was built on the site of an old palace which burnt down on Christmas Eve 1734, and was home to the Spanish royal family until Alfonso XIII was forced to abdicate in 1931. The present royal family lives elsewhere in less luxurious surroundings, but continues to use the Royal Palace for state occasions.

Guided tours take you through rooms of increasing splendour. Cascading chandeliers, ceilings encrusted with gilt and stucco or frescoed with cloudy *trompe-l'oeil* fantasies, and walls hung with tapestries and brocades combine to form a gloriously rococo backdrop for ritzy furniture, collections of crystal, clocks and porcelain, and portraits by Goya.

The entrance ticket gives access to other sections of the palace, although these are inevitably an anticlimax, and you might prefer to wander round the topiaried Jardines Sabatini at the far end of the palace. Even better, enjoy the view of the building from the elegant Café del Oriente on the Plaza Oriente, studded with statues of royals intended to grace the palace's façade but discovered to be too heavy.

For those who wish to see more of the palace, a separate guided tour is necessary to see the library. There's also a carriage museum, a pharmacy and the Royal Armoury.

The Goya Pantheon
The Ermita de San Antonio de la Florida has magnificent frescoes by Goya. It has been undergoing restoration for a considerable period, but visitors are allowed in to see the paintings while the work continues (Monday to Friday 9am to 1.30pm).

Excursion to Toledo
This wonderful medieval city, walled and gated, sits on a craggy hill in a loop of the River Tagus, 43 miles south-west of Madrid. The imperial capital of Spain from Visigothic and Moorish times, Toledo is the seat of the Catholic primate and remains the country's religious capital.

A day-trip will give you time to explore and to see the major sights, while even a half-day excursion will leave you with a powerful impression of the city.

Toledo's Gothic **cathedral** is a visual feast of intricate carvings, wrought-iron, opulent treasures, and (in the sacristy) paintings by Goya, Velázquez and El Greco. It is especially lovely in mid-afternoon, when the sun streams through the Transparente behind the altar, illuminating a baroque fantasy of marble cherubs and gilded rays.

El Greco, who lived and worked in Toledo for almost 40 years, is better represented elsewhere in the city. There's a fine collection of his canvases in his rather phonily restored home, the **Casa del Greco**, including the famous *View of Toledo*, while his undisputed masterpiece, *The Burial of Count Orgaz*, hangs in an annexe to the church of Santo Tomé for which it was painted.

The church of **San Juan de los Reyes** was founded by Ferdinand and Isabella, whose marriage, uniting Castile and Aragon, marks the beginning of modern Spain. Dangling from the façade are the chains of Christian prisoners released after the liberation of Granada. The highlight is the beautiful carved cloister, and there is more good sculptural decoration inside, featuring the interlinked crests of Castile and Aragon.

Until the Inquisition expelled them in the fifteenth century, Toledo had Spain's largest Jewish community. Two of the synagogues survive: **El Tránsito**, with lacy oriental stucco-work, is particularly enchanting; but **Santa Maria la Blanca** (so-called because after the expulsion of the Jews it was converted into a church) also has an eastern feel, with horseshoe arches, snail-like furls on column capitals and complex stucco tracery on the walls.

Wandering through the streets is the most pleasant way of spending any time you have left – although you might like to take a look at the **Alcázar**. Romans, Visigoths, Moors and Christian kings all had fortresses on the site, but the present building was founded by Alfonso VI in the eleventh century, after he seized the town from the Moors. It was almost completely restructured by Charles V, and has since been heavily restored. There are, however, good views of Toledo from its top storey.

Toledo is one and a half hour's drive from Madrid, and can be visited on an excursion tour or independently by bus from the Estación Sur de Autobuses on Calle Canarias.

OTHER PLACES TO VISIT

Museums and galleries

Archaeological Museum A magnificent and wide collection which ranges from Ancient Egyptian mummy-cases to Greek pottery and from inlaid Visigothic jewellery to Ibizan idols. Roman mosaics, Islamic architecture and Romanesque sculpture combine to give a taste of the richness and complexity of the Spanish artistic inheritance. Finally, beneath the courtyard is a reproduction of the Altamira Caves with their prehistoric bison frescoes. The museum's exhibits are not labelled in English.

Ethnological Museum Costumes, crafts, tools, weapons, ceramics and musical instruments from all over the world are housed in this museum. Though beautifully displayed, items are not labelled in English.

Lázaro Galdiano Museum A museum in which to savour detail. Although there are a couple of paintings by Goya and Velázquez, it's the *objets d'art* which are most compelling. These include Limoges enamels, Byzantine *cloisonné* work, exquisite Renaissance bronze statuettes and a superb collection of jewellery.

Museum of the Americas Closed at present, but with a reputedly excellent pre-Columbian section, along with Hispano-American crafts and Inca and Aztec artefacts.

National Museum of Decorative Arts Laid out in an elegant old mansion are period furniture and a collection of *objets d'art* ranging from Chinese figurines to Lalique glassware. Most appealing are the gorgeous collections of fans and toys (including dolls' houses and a miniature Singer sewing-machine), and the top-floor room laid out as a kitchen.

Spanish Museum of Contemporary Arts Out of town, on the university campus, this museum is worth visiting if there's a good temporary exhibition. The fine grounds have sculpture laid out among fountains and trees, and there's an excellent shop.

Other attractions

Parque del Buen Retiro Better known as plain Retiro, this park once formed the gardens of a seventeenth-century palace built for Philip IV as 'a place for pleasure and laziness'. The palace was destroyed by Napoleonic and, later, English troops in the nineteenth century, and only two buildings survive, both of them now outside the boundaries of the park: the Casón del Buen Retiro, today sheltering Picasso's *Guernica*, and the Salón Grande, housing an Army Museum.

The gardens were opened to the public in 1868, and have entertainments ranging from rowing-boats to rock concerts. Formal gardens opposite the Casón del Buen Retiro gave way to shady clumps of trees and an artificial lake, El Estanque, dominated by a grandiose colonnade and statue to King Alfonso XII. Kiosks sell drinks, sandwiches and ice-creams, tarot card readers tell fortunes, and on Sunday mornings what seems like half the population of Madrid turns out for a stroll. Art exhibitions are frequently held in one of the two pavilions, the pretty Palacio de Velázquez and the Palacio de Cristal, based on London's Crystal Palace and standing on the shores of a small pond.

Parque del Oueste This park is home to one of Madrid's weirdest sights – a reconstructed Egyptian temple, given by Egypt to Spain in recognition of the work done on the Aswan Dam (which flooded the temple's original site) by Spanish engineers.

Royal Tapestry Factory (Real Fábrica de Tapices) You can visit this on weekday mornings and watch tapestries and carpets being woven on handlooms to designs by Goya just as they were in the eighteenth century.

Botanical Gardens Right next to the Prado, the botanical gardens are an ideal place in which to unwind after visiting the gallery.

They were opened in 1781 by Carlos III, and *madrileños* still theoretically have the right to take cuttings of any of the numerous medicinal plants.

Bullfights and Bullfighting Museum Bullfighting remains a Madrid institution, though somewhat less popular than football. Fights are held from spring until early October on Sunday afternoons at the Las Ventas bullring at Plaza de Toros. Tickets are available at hotels and at the booking office on Plaza del Carmen. Next to Las Ventas there is a museum of bullfighting.

Las Descalzas Reales Convent In the heart of Madrid, dwarfed by an immense department store, is the Monasterio de las Descalzas Reales. It was founded in the sixteenth century by Philip II's sister Juana who, widowed at 19, decided she wanted a retreat away from the duties of state. Although Juana died before it was completed, many aristocratic women joined the order – the reason why the convent is today packed with treasures. Many are in dubious taste – notably the blood-splattered Christs, and altars featuring 3-D tableaux, artificial flowers and Madonnas with glittery tiaras. For the rest, among dull portraits of nuns and stiffly ruffed aristocrats, there are some reasonably attractive Flemish and Italian works, but nothing really to grab the attention.

Torre de Madrid On the Plaza de España, the city's tallest skyscraper tops the adjacent old New York-style Edificio de España by eight storeys. There are superb, if dizzying, views of the city from the café on the top floor, and a tourist information office on the ground floor.

Excursion

El Escorial There are half-day excursions from Madrid to El Escorial, a combination of monastery, palace and mausoleum, built for the ascetic Felipe II, and from which he claimed to 'rule the world with two inches of paper'. With walls the colour of honey mingled with putty pierced only by tiny windows, it's a severe, prison-like building. This is the architecture of authoritarianism, and seems designed to intimidate. The interior of the basilica is extraordinarily unwelcoming, a grim, soulless place, with the altar, painted by the Italian Tibaldi, providing the only colour.

Downstairs, in the Panteón de los Reyes, the marble tombs of kings and queens are stacked on shelves around the octagonal walls, and in the two palaces flanking the basilica the bleak, sinister atmosphere makes more of an impact than the abundant tapestries and clocks.

SHOPPING

Madrid is a wonderful city for shopping. Good buys include shoes and traditional ceramics. The main shopping streets, Calle Carmen and Calle Preciados, are packed with shoe shops; but their clothes shops are unexciting. At the foot of Calle Preciados are two immense department stores, Corte Inglés and Galerías Preciadas, selling everything from cosmetics to kitchenware. Modern ceramics are good value, as are Italian-style hob-top coffee-makers.

Calle de Serrano, parallel Calle Coello and the streets in between hold most of the big-name designer boutiques, while up-and-coming Spanish designers are based on and around Calle Almirante. The street for more youthful clothes is Calle Argensola.

If you're in the market for exclusive and expensive crafts, branches of Artespaña on Plaza de las Cortes and at Calle Hermosilla 14 off Calle de Serrano sell textiles, ceramics and furniture from all over Spain. Even more upmarket, Najera on Plaza Independencia is worth visiting, even if you can't afford to buy its beautiful tapestries, porcelain and ceramic urns.

For more bargains, try Cava Baja, in the Latina quarter between Plaza Mayor and the Rastro. Antonio Sanchez at No 19 has traditional glazed earthenware and a limited range of painted plates. Other unusual presents to look out for include lovely polished wooden salad bowls and musical instruments – especially guitars.

On Sundays, between 10am and 3pm, the streets around Latina Metro station in downtown Madrid are crammed with a colourful and chaotic flea market, the Rastro. Stalls filled with grubby and crumpled jumble and junk have now been joined by a host of crafts, jewellery, and ethnic and alternative clothes stands. Be prepared to haggle over prices, and watch your bag.

EATING AND DRINKING

Madrid abounds with restaurants, the best of which serve regional specialities from all over the country. Local dishes include *sopa castellana*, a garlicky soup in which an egg is poached at the last minute; *callos a la madrileña*, stewed tripe; *cochinillo asado*, the roast suckling pig beloved of Hemingway; and *cordero asado*, roast lamb. You'll also find classic regional dishes such as Andalucian *gazpacho*, a chilled soup of tomatoes, onion and peppers, and Valencian *paella*; and you can explore less familiar regional specialities – notably Basque dishes of casseroled fish, and red meat or game cooked in wine.

Meals are eaten later in Madrid than in the rest of Spain – 2.30pm or even 3pm for lunch and around 10pm or later for dinner. Most people stave off starvation with *tapas*, snacks served in *tascas* or taverns. These include slices of Spanish omelette, olive, anchovies, peppers, salads, squid and *chorizo* (spicy sausage). Though many people treat lunch as the main meal of the day, you might prefer to have a light lunch of *tapas*. If you want a large portion ask for a *ración*, and if you want your *tapa* sandwiched in French bread, ask for a *bocadillo*: omelette sandwiches are particularly delicious. There are many *tascas* on Plaza Mayor, but if you want somewhere less touristy try the Cercevería Alemana on Plaza Santa Ana, or have a light, sit-down lunch at the Taberna Toscana, Calle Ventura del la Vega. After visiting the Prado, try the upmarket buffet in the Galería del Prado shopping mall beneath the Palace Hotel, which serves a wide range of salads, hot and cold meats and tempting puddings. For coffee and sinfully rich cakes try Café Concierto, Calle Prado 4. Open from morning till after midnight, the Café de Oriente on Plazá Oriente opposite the Royal Palace serves *tapas* upstairs and has a good restaurant downstairs.

Breakfast receives little attention; best are the buffet-style breakfasts in large hotels. Cafés often have freshly squeezed orange juice, and a selection of croissants, heavy pastries and buns on the counter. Be warned that toast is cooked on an oily plate. Most foreigners find the classic Spanish breakfast of *churros* (rings of deep-fried dough) and thick hot chocolate rather too much first thing in the morning, but it can make a deliciously decadent late-night snack – head for the Chocolatería San Ginés off Calle Arenal behind the Joy Esclava disco.

Madrid has many highly rated restaurants. Considered top of the top-notch restaurants by *madrileños* at present are El Cenador del Prado, Calle del Prado 4 (where the choice might range from fried eggs with caviare, bread and tomato to chicken stuffed with shrimps served with couscous); Juan de Alzate, Calle Princesa 18, whose cuisine is a happy fusion of the traditional and sophisticated and the puddings irresistible; and Luculo, Calle Genova 19. Prices in the very top restaurants range from around £30 for a set meal to anywhere up to £100. On average, you can expect to pay about £60 to £70.

Fortunately, there are many good, reasonable restaurants. Those on and around Plaza Mayor are very touristy, though you might like to try Hemingway's favourite restaurant, El Botín, Calle Cuchilleros 17, which specialises in roast suckling pig and baby lamb (*lechal*). A good, traditional and unpretentious place is Casa Ciriaco, Calle Mayor 84, which does a delicious veal dish casseroled with Rioja, tomatoes and peppers and vast salads with fresh tuna and hard-boiled egg. There are more traditional restaurants specialising in roast meats on Cava Baja. Other streets worth exploring are those above Plaza Oriente, such as Calle de la Unión, Calle Amnistía and Calle de Vergara. In some, like El Oboe, on Calle de la Unión, you eat to the accompaniment of classical music. In the medium-priced restaurants you can expect to pay between £10 and £25 per head.

Spain produces some excellent wines, including those from Rioja, and Penedés in Catalonia. The Rioja reds are oaky (although softer than they used to be), the whites crisp and generally for drinking young. Sparkling wines from Catalonia (known as *cava*) are some of Spain's best.

NIGHTLIFE

Madrid's nightlife is among the most exciting in Europe: many bars and cafés stay open until the early hours, and some nightclubs do not close until breakfast time. There's an enormous range of bars. The most dense concentration is in the area around Plaza Santa Ana – notably on Calle de las Huertas. Though most throb with Euro-pop, some have live jazz; and there's taped jazz in the gorgeous old Los Gabrieles (Calle Echegeray 17), which is decorated with vibrant *azulejos*. On Plaza Santa Ana there's the Cervecería Alemana, an old haunt of Hemingway, with wood-panelled walls, carved beams, and old photographs of bullfighters. It is crowded in the evenings, but has a traditional, relaxed feel during the day.

More unusual are bars where you can listen to classical music – such as La Fidula at Calle de las Huertas 57 and the civilised but unpretentious Solesmes at Amnistía 5 (behind Plaza Oriente). Café Concierto on Calle del Prado 4 features jazz as well as classical music, with live music every Thursday.

For sophistication (and an unforgettable gin fizz), head for Chicote at the Calle Alcalá end of Gran Vía, another ex-Hemingway haunt. Behind it on Vía Reina is Cock, a beautiful old cocktail bar retaining its twenties décor. Equally chic is Café de Oriente on Plaza Oriente near the Royal Palace, which serves expensive food in its basement restaurant as well as expensive drinks and snacks upstairs.

By contrast, Madrid's traditional old cafés seem rather staid and spartan. In summer the focus of the pavement café scene is Paseo de la Castellana, which has a string of *terrazas* under the avenue of trees in its centre.

Flamenco is not indigenous to Madrid, and venues such as Café de Chinitas, Calle Torija 7, and Arco de Cuchilleros, just off Plaza Mayor, are extremely expensive and rather touristy. You can see operatic and guitar concerts at a new theatre, the Auditorio Nacionale, at Principe de Vegara 136. In September/October there is an arts festival, the Festival des Otono.

Zarzuela is a traditionally colourful Spanish opera which also sometimes includes dance, and can be seen at the Zarzuela Theatre. Ballets are also performed there.

HOTELS

The most atmospheric locations for hotels are in the old town between Puerta del Sol and the Prado, though there is one tiny *pension* wonderfully sited on Plaza Oriente opposite the Royal Palace. The convenience of staying on the Gran Vía compensates for the brassiness of the surroundings, and the facilities in hotels on Paseo de la Castellana for the inconvenience of being outside the centre.

AROSA ◆◆◆◆
Salud 21, 28013   *Tel: 532 1600   Fax: 531 3127*

A grand old hotel on the corner of Salud and the Gran Vía, the Arosa has many gorgeous, individually decorated and furnished rooms. The tone is set as you enter the lobby, with its red velvet walls, chandelier and fresh flowers. The second-floor reception leads into the elegant lounge, part of which doubles as a breakfast/lunch area. New rooms are contemporary, slick and stylish; others are decorated in a period style. Rooms facing Gran Vía are double glazed.

Bedrooms: 139, all with bath/WC; air-conditioning; mini-bar; safe
Facilities: Lift; coffee-shop   **Credit/charge cards accepted:** All

---

◆ = under £50; ◆◆ = £50 to £80; ◆◆◆ = £80 to £100;
◆◆◆◆ = £100 to £140; ◆◆◆◆◆ = over £140.

VILLA MAGNA
Paseo de la Castellana 22, 28046   *Tel: 576 7500   Fax: 575 9504*

An extremely luxurious contemporary hotel on a busy avenue with trendy pavement cafés. Though a taxi ride from the centre, the hotel is convenient for Madrid's exclusive shopping streets. The ground floor, with marbled lobby, lounge and piano-bar extending to a small courtyard and tree-lined garden, is open-plan. The basement restaurant is smart and stylish. Rooms are spacious but intimate, and are decorated in pastels. Dressing rooms lead into marble bathrooms.

Bedrooms: 182, all with bath/shower/WC; air-conditioning; mini-bar; safe
Facilities: Lift; restaurant; sauna; hairdresser   **Credit/charge cards accepted:** Amex, Diners, Visa

OPERA
Cuesto Santo Domingo 2   *Tel: 541 2800   Fax: 541 6923*

Though the exterior is prison-like and the atmosphere sterile, this 1960s hotel is clean, reasonably priced, and one of the few hotels in the area around the Teatro Real and Royal Palace. Some of Madrid's most civilised cafés and restaurants are close by. The reception area, bar and breakfast cafeteria are merely functional, but the lounge is relaxing. Rooms are plain and institutional with small, but adequate, tiled bathroms.

Bedrooms: 75, all with bath/WC; air-conditioning; none with TV
Facilities: Lift   **Credit/charge cards accepted:** Amex, Visa

PALACE
Plaza de las Cortes 7, 28014   *Tel: 429 7551   Fax: 429 8266*

Directly opposite the Ritz, the Palace is its younger sister. Although more relaxed than the Ritz, past guests include Mata Hari, Hemingway, Rubinstein, Joan Baez and Placído Domingo. The restaurants and bar open off a summery lounge, where a hand-made carpet reflects the colours of the vast stained-glass dome above. Approximately half the rooms have been refurbished, but even those which have not are elegant and comfortable.

Bedrooms: 480, all with bath/WC; air-conditioning; mini-bar; hair-dryer
Facilities: Lift; restaurant; hairdresser   **Credit/charge cards accepted:** All

VILLA REAL

Plaza de las Cortes 10, 28014   *Tel: 420 3767   Fax: 420 2547*

A short walk from the Prado and the sociable Santa Ana area, the Villa Real stands on a small, busy square opposite the parliament building. The hotel is new, but is built in a turn-of-the-century style. The reception area is furnished with reproduction antiques and embroideries, and the large lounge also has a traditional air, with leather sofas. Rooms are split-level with a small sitting area, and are decorated in pastels.

Bedrooms: 115, all with bath/WC; air-conditioning; hair-dryer   **Facilities:** Lift; sauna   **Credit/charge cards accepted:** Amex, Diners, Visa

RITZ

Plaza de la Lealtad 5, 28014   *Tel: 521 2857   Fax: 532 8776*

The Ritz, a sumptuous belle époque hotel next to the Prado, was built so that the guests of King Alfonso XIII could be kept in their accustomed style. It is exquisitely decorated and the rooms are individually furnished with reproduction antiques. Service is excellent and the strict dress code adds to the atmosphere. The dining-room is among the best in Madrid: if you can't afford to stay here, dress up and have brunch or a drink in the terrace garden.

Bedrooms: 56, all with bath/shower/WC   **Facilities:** Lift; restaurant; hairdresser   **Credit/charge cards accepted:** All

SANTANDER
Calle Echegeray 1, 28014   *Tel: 429 9551*

A rambling 1930s mansion with a frescoed façade stands on the corner of Carrera San Jerónimo and Calle Echegeray. The small lobby has traditional character, with ornate carved wood, brass candelabras and a moulded ceiling. Rooms are large, with parquet floors and original furniture. Though the hotel has undoubted style and atmosphere, rooms facing the Carrera can be noisy. Smoking is not allowed in rooms.

Bedrooms: 36, most with bath/shower/WC   **Facilities:** Lift   **Credit/charge cards accepted:** None

TRYP FENIX

Hermosilla 2, 28001

Tel: 431 6700   Fax: 576 0661

A little out of the centre, but convenient for the summer *terrazzas* and designer shops, the Fenix is an elegant, comfortable hotel. The marbled reception area is impressive, dominated by the gilded balustrade of a curving staircase, but the lounge is less formal. Plants flank the entrance to the bar, and the breakfast room has a warm, spring-like feel. Rooms are elegant and restful. The Plaza Colón is busy, but double glazing cuts down the traffic noise to a murmur.

Bedrooms: 228, all with bath/WC; air-conditioning; mini-bar; safe; some with hair-dryer   **Facilities:** Lift; restaurant; hairdresser   **Credit/charge cards accepted:** Amex, Diners, Visa

TRYP VICTORIA

Plaza del Angel 7, 28012

Tel: 531 6000   Fax: 522 0307

This hotel is a striking, metal-framed, cream building, dating from 1925, overlooking Plaza Santa Ana, and a couple of minutes' walk from Calles Huertas and Echegeray. It is ideally located for those who want to be at the heart of Madrid's night scene. The spacious reception area is paved with ivory marble beneath a glass dome. The bar is restful and comfortable, with traditional rugs and furniture, and the restaurant is pretty and spring-like. Rooms are smart and colour co-ordinated, and though some of the bathrooms are small, they are well designed.

Bedrooms: 200, all with bath/WC; mini-bar   **Facilities:** Lift; restaurant   **Credit/charge cards accepted:** All

---

Hotel prices Symbols indicate approximate prices per room per night for a double room with bath. Many large hotels run special breaks which work out far cheaper. (See page 14 for further details.)

♦ = under £50; ♦♦ = £50 to £80; ♦♦♦ = £80 to £100;
♦♦♦♦ = £100 to £140; ♦♦♦♦♦ = over £140.

MOSCOW

- Moscow is a varied city of Stalinesque skyscrapers, Orthodox churches, vast avenues and tiny downtown streets
- The trick to getting the most out of your stay is to divide your time between organised trips to major sights and exploring the city alone
- Since the disintegration of the Soviet Union, no new system has replaced the old – it's a city of change and uncertainty
- The changes that Russia has undergone, and is still undergoing, mean that the future is hard to predict. Market reforms have caused much hardship but have also resulted in more opportunities – for both locals and tourists. Be prepared for the unexpected

CAPITALISM has come to town. The most visible signs are the throngs of street kiosks selling everything from coffee and alcohol to bubble gum and TV sets; the branches of hard-currency shops selling clothes and food (and filled, for the most part, with Muscovites); youths hawking newspapers in subways; and fruit sellers by metro stations.

On the down side, the rate and extent of the changes in the former Soviet Union have caused hardship and insecurity among many local people. Elderly people beg on the streets, and nobody speaks of *glasnost* or *perestroika*. The effects of *glasnost*, however, should not be underestimated: many new newspapers openly discuss and criticise the changes, and pornographic magazines are sold on nearly every street corner.

As a tourist in Moscow, you can make life easy by sticking to the excursions laid on by tourist agencies: a coach tour of the city, a visit to the Kremlin, a shopping trip to Moscow's biggest hard-currency shop, the *beriozka*. But to leave Moscow without walking the narrow streets of the old city, having a look at the bizarre street markets, or getting lost on the underground, would be to leave without even beginning to understand the city and its people. For, as befits the capital of a nation which used to stretch from Finland to China and from the Baltic to the Pacific, Moscow is a vast, overwhelming city. Two million of its eight million inhabitants are non-Russian, restaurants serve Uzbekistani, Azerbaijani and Georgian food, and in the co-operative market, trays of pistachios, tangerines and sachets of saffron are sold alongside pickled garlic, potatoes and cabbages.

Endless suburbs of drab apartment blocks confirm precon-ceptions of life in an absolutist state, and, in the centre, ten-laned roads converge on immense squares criss-crossed by a disorien-tating warren of subways. Any pedestrian foolhardy enough to brave the traffic will be rewarded by a blast of a policeman's whistle (when walking the streets, or filing through subways, bear in mind that pedestrians, like the traffic, keep to the right).

But Moscow is far from being dull and uniform. Stand on the Moskvorestky Bridge below the Kremlin, and the city surrounds you in all its bold complexity. The river embankment is lined with elegant mansions which once belonged to the city's merchants; behind you looms Moscow's largest hotel; the skyline is punctuated by the Gothic megaliths of the Stalin era; and peeking above the scalloped wall of the Kremlin are the gilded domes of cathedrals.

The Kremlin stands at the heart of the series of concentric roads that encircle the city. The innermost, nine kilometre-long Bul'varnoye Koltso (Boulevard Ring) is in fact barely more than a semi-circle, being bounded in the south by the River Moskva. It follows the route of a sixteenth-century defensive wall and within it lies what remains of old Moscow. Although invasions and Stalin's heartless rebuilding scheme succeeded in destroying many historic buildings, and time has dilapidated others, many cathedrals survive – notably the gaudily brilliant St Basil's and those of the Kremlin. With the increasing tolerance of the state towards religion, many churches and newly flourishing monasteries now hold services twice daily.

Grand bourgeois mansions along the river and on Gogol Boulevard, and elaborate buildings such as GUM on Red Square and the stock exchange on Ilyinka Ulitsa, testify to Moscow's experience of capitalism in the late nineteenth century. Along with the palaces of the aristocracy on the Arbat and Myasnitskaya Ulitsa, and the outrageously opulent treasures of church, tsars and aristocrats in the Kremlin's Armoury Museum, they are the ciphers of one half of the social equation that led to revolution

The second ring road, Sadovaya (Garden) Ring, encircling the city north and south of the river, became a symbolic border between the old city of the merchants and aristocrats and the grim new suburbs of factories and workers' slums. The industrial revolution hit Russia in the 1890s; thousands of ex-serfs, liberated only in 1861, provided the workforce, and between 1840 and 1914 the population increased from 340,000 to 1.4 million. Working hours were long, living conditions crowded and insanitary; the suburbs inevitably became a fertile breeding ground for revolutionary ideas. In 1905 the workers attempted to storm into old Moscow at what is now Vostaniye Ploshchad (Uprising Square). They were driven back and set up barricades until they were shelled into submission by the army. Today Vostaniye Ploshchad is overshadowed by a grim Stalinist skyscraper.

Not far from this square the main events of the August 1991 coup took place. The Russian 'White House' – where the Government of the Russian Republic used to sit – is on the bank of the River Moskva. The bricks of the bridge, which was part of a revolutionary monument, were used to build barricades by those who defeated the White House during the coup.

WHEN TO GO

Summer is short and reasonably warm. Temperatures rarely rise much above 23°C (73°F), though there have been some unseasonably hot summers in the past few years. Leaves fall in August, frost sets in in September and snow begins to fall in October; it isn't until April that the ice on the River Moskva begins to break up. Winter is very cold, although crisp and clear rather than damp; as long as you wrap up as well as the locals it is an attractive time to visit, and public buildings are very well heated.

GETTING THERE

Although no longer the state tourist agency, Intourist is still the most experienced tour operator in Russia and has lots of local information. Its office is at Intourist House, Meridian Gate, 219 Marsh Wall, London E14 9FJ (071-538 8600).

Tour operator packages

The major tour operators to Moscow and St Petersburg are Intourist, Sovereign and Thomson. All have seven-day dual-centre packages as well as packages to Moscow only.

Packages work out cheaper (and easier) than going independently, if you don't mind taking half- or full-board. The tour operator will organise your visa for you; dinner and certain excursions are included in the package price; and you can pre-book other sightseeing trips or evening entertainment swiftly and relatively easily through your rep. There's no obligation to stay with your group once you arrive.

In 1992 three nights on half- or full-board in a mid-range hotel cost from £275 in low season to £395 in high. For a list of tour operators see page 385.

Going independently

This works out more expensive than going on a tour operator package, and, although not as easy as group travel, is much easier than it was. Excursions can be booked in hotels, and there are many more restaurants and bars. Russian tourism is still geared to groups, not individuals. There's little available information – you'll need to get to grips with the service bureau at your hotel.

Flights from London to Moscow take nearly four hours. British Airways and Aeroflot have one flight a day from Heathrow; Aeroflot has two flights on Friday, Saturday and Sunday. Aeroflot also flies once a week from Manchester. The APEX fare is still expensive. A few operators, including Flightfile (071-323 1515), Data Travel (0424 722 394), Cresta Holidays (0345 056511) and Regent Holidays (0272 211711), offer considerable discounts on scheduled flights.

Formalities *(see page 313, under St Petersburg)*

MASTERING THE SYSTEM

*For information on language, hotels, changing money, the black market,
shopping, restaurants and etiquette see pages 314-17, under St Petersburg*
Information Intourist, the main tourist organisation, has offices
at the airport and at hotels, and can organise bookings for
restaurants, excursions and cultural events. It's worth going on
some of their excursions, but for restaurants it's cheaper to book
yourself or to ask locals to do it for you. It is also possible to
arrange a car and a private guide for any museum – well worth it
if you have a special interest, as only the major sights have
explanations in English.

Maps The *New Moscow City Map and Guide*, published by
Northern Cartographic, is available in Britain (£4.95). It has most
of the new street names and metro stations.

Public transport is easier. Both trains and stations contain plans
of the metro system using the new names of the stations. You can
also usually buy new metro maps from news kiosks and street
traders.

Opening hours and days Many museums close on Monday but
as times are liable to change it's advisable to check with Intourist
before setting out. Lenin's Mausoleum currently closes on
Monday and Friday, the Kremlin and Armoury on Thursday and
the Pushkin Fine Arts Museum on Monday. Most shops close on
Sunday and for an hour at lunchtime. They stay open until 7pm
or 8pm. They may also close on the first or last day of the month
for stocktaking.

GETTING AROUND

Once mastered, the **underground** (metro) system is the quickest
and most efficient mode of transport. Trains run every minute at
peak periods and you'll rarely wait for longer than three. There
are no tickets: for each journey of whatever length you simply
drop a one-rouble coin in the barrier at the entrance. Wait for the
light to change from red to yellow before crossing the barrier. Buy
your tokens from the ticket office (*kassi*) in the station. Changing
trains can be complicated as it can involve changing stations as
well as lines. If you are changing lines, look for a sign which
includes the word *liniya* and follow it. If you have to change
stations, look for the sign saying *perehod na* . . . and the name of
the station you want. At some point you are bound to panic and
get lost – but as long as you can point on your map to where you

want to go, you should have no trouble finding someone to help. Incidentally, the distances between stations interlinked by subways can seem endless.

For shorter distances, **trams**, **buses** and **trolley buses** are useful, though usually crowded. Buy tickets in advance in strips of ten from news kiosks or metro ticket offices: don't risk being able to buy them from the driver. When you get on the bus or tram you have to punch your ticket to make it valid: watch the locals to see how.

Finding a **taxi** is usually quite easy (and most car-owning Muscovites are willing to moonlight as taxi-drivers). Most drivers will want to be paid in hard currency, so it's a good idea to take a supply of small denomination (dollar) bills, unless you're willing to argue.

UNMISSABLES

City tour

Even if you loathe guided coach tours, it's worth putting up with this one, as it gives a good overview of the city. The first stop is on Red Square (*see below*), after which you cross the river for a fine panoramic view of the city from outside the British Embassy, usefully positioned directly opposite the Great Kremlin Palace. Next stop is the **Novodevichy Convent**, whose lengthy restoration is virtually complete. Built in 1524, it was also used as a fortress to guard the trading route into Poland. Soon, though, its fortified walls served less to keep invaders out than to keep the nuns in: royals and noblewomen were forcibly despatched here when their husbands died. The most notorious royal nun was Peter the Great's half-sister Sophia, who was imprisoned here, not because she was widowed but because she led a coup against him. Today the convent is a peaceful place, its red and white buildings standing among trees and graves within fortified walls, and the rare sixteenth-century frescoes in the main church, the Cathedral of Our Lady of Smolensk, are now open to visitors. The tour gives you just 15 minutes at the convent, and if you want to see the frescoes you could abandon the tour here. This also gives you the opportunity to visit the adjoining cemetery, where you can visit the graves of, among others, Gogol, Chekhov, Krushchev, Eisenstein, Stanislavsky, Scriabin and Prokofiev (cemetery open 10am to 5pm, tickets from a small kiosk opposite the entrance).

If you stick with the tour, it proceeds across the river to the immense Stalinist Gothic university building on Lenin Hill (now Vorobievy Hill). On clear days there is an extensive, if depressing, view of Moscow from the belvedere in front, by the artificial ski slope, with the domes of the Kremlin glinting in a concrete jungle of tower blocks.

Red Square and Lenin's Tomb

If there is one image which summed up the former Soviet Union for Westerners, it was that of the row of grey-overcoated Politburo members standing on the granite dais of Lenin's Mausoleum, addressing the crowd gathered on Red Square to celebrate May Day or the anniversary of the Revolution.

Today there are no military parades on May Day or the anniversary, but for most Russians Red Square remains the heart of their country. It is dominated by the symbols of two very different traditions. Directly opposite the mausoleum is GUM, Russia's largest department store, a neo-Gothic shrine to late nineteenth-century capitalism with a palatial interior which forms an ironic backdrop for the drab and tacky goods; and to the right are the fancy red-brick towers and multicoloured domes of St Basil's Cathedral.

Tourists from all over the world stand huddled round their guides, half-listening to deadpan accounts of the square's history, as they await the hourly changing of the goose-stepping guards. There are no queues outside the mausoleum now (open daily, except Monday and Friday, 10am to 1pm). You do not need a ticket. Once inside, you file slowly past the embalmed body, with the familiar pointed beard still jutting from the waxy yellow chin. After paying your respects to Lenin, you walk out past the graves of prominent Soviets: Dzerzhinsky, founder of the KGB; Yuri Gagarin, first man in space; and Gorbachev's predecessors, Chernenko, Andropov, Brezhnev and Stalin (who until his denunciation in 1961 was on display alongside Lenin). At the beginning of *perestroika* there was much talk of burying Lenin, but some Russians now feel that the mausoleum should be left where it is as a symbol of respect for the country's history.

St Basil's Cathedral

With domes like psychedelic turbans and vibrant swirls of additive-rich ice-cream, St Basil's is Moscow's most exotic building. It was commissioned by Ivan the Terrible, who, according to legend, was so stunned by the achievement of his architects that he had them blinded, so that they could never again create such a splendid church. In fact, at least one of the architects is known subsequently to have designed a church in Kazan. The interior is far less elaborate and not really worth queueing for.

It was on the gentle slope in front of St Basil's that the young German Mathias Rust landed his light aircraft in 1987, earning himself an 18-month spell in prison and precipitating rapid dismissals among the upper echelons and air defence staff.

Pushkin Fine Arts Museum

One of Russia's largest art galleries, the Pushkin's collection of French Impressionists and post-Impressionists also makes it one of the most enjoyable. Rooms 17, 18 and 21, with works by Manet, Monet, Renoir, Pissarro, Degas, Gauguin, van Gogh, Kandinsky, Matisse, Picasso and Dufy are exceptionally fine; and the rich collection of Ancient Egyptian art in room 1 is also worth a visit. Other highlights include Botticelli's *Annunciation* and Bronzino's *Holy Family* in room 5; and works by Poussin, Lorrain and Watteau in room 13.

The Kremlin

Once the centre of Soviet power, the Kremlin is now the home of the Russian Government, led by Boris Yeltsin. Surprisingly, the Kremlin is no grim Stalinist edifice, but a complex of lacily stuccoed primrose palaces and golden-domed cathedrals embraced by the swallow-tailed red-brick walls.

Although Intourist runs tours around the Kremlin, these are not necessary. The ticket office is below the Trinity Gate in the Alexander Gardens, and if you go at lunchtime you should avoid the worst of the crowds. Tickets for the Armoury Museum are sold from an office at New Arbat 1, just opposite the Trinity Gate.

There have been fortifications on this low hill above the River Moskva since Moscow's foundation in 1147. Indeed, the very name *kreml* means fortress. As the city's territory gradually expanded it became the centre of the Orthodox church, and the first stone churches were built within the Kremlin walls. These churches were replaced in the late fifteenth and early sixteenth centuries, the era in which Ivan the Great unified Russia and threw off Tartar rule. Constantinople, capital of the Byzantine Empire, had fallen to the Turks in 1453, and Ivan considered himself the natural successor to the Emperors of Byzantium. He set about making Moscow a worthy capital, importing Italian and Greek craftsmen and architects, in the absence of home-grown talent.

The first buildings you see as you enter the Kremlin by the Trinity Gate date from much later. To the right is the Kremlin's only modern building, the glass and marble **Palace of Congresses**, whose 6,000-seat auditorium – when not being used for congresses of people's deputies – is a second theatre for the

Bolshoi. Opposite, and out of bounds, are the three yellow and white neo-classical palaces in which the Soviet government was based. After the August 1991 coup, Yeltsin moved his office from the 'White House' to the Kremlin, thus symbolising that the Russian Government was in real control. In the central, triangular Senate, Lenin had his offices and an apartment, and, after the suicide of his wife, Stalin moved into cramped quarters on the first floor.

Across from the third building the Cathedral of the Twelve Apostles (Sobor Dvenadtsati Apostolov) and adjoining Patriarch's Palace now house the **Museum of Seventeenth-Century Life**. Misleadingly named, it is largely a museum of seventeenth-century ecclesiastical paraphernalia, with richly embroidered and jewel-encrusted robes, pearl-studded Byzantine icons, and, most interestingly, a large stove used for the preparation of consecrated oil.

In front of the cathedral is the Tsar Cannon. Cast in 1586, it is five metres long, weighs 39,000 kilograms, and has almost certainly never been fired. Beyond is the **Ivan the Great Bell Tower**, at 73 metres the focal point of the Kremlin. At its foot lies the Tsar Bell which, weighing 201,900 kilograms, is the world's largest (Big Ben, by comparison, weighs just 13,700 kilograms). In 1737 a fire raged through the Kremlin; water was poured on the red-hot bell and a massive chunk cracked off.

You now enter Cathedral Square, the heart of Ivan the Great's Kremlin. The kind of square a child might dream up for a fairytale king, it is beautiful at any time, but especially in sunshine, when the light sharpens the facets of the diamond-pointed Granovitaya Palace, bleaches the stone of its cathedrals, and glints on the clusters of golden domes which bubble up on their roofs.

The **Cathedral of the Assumption** or **Dormition** (Uspensky Sabor) was intended by Ivan to be the flagship of the Russian church and state. The Italian architect Aristotle Fioravanti was brought in because its Russian-built predecessor collapsed before it was finished. The interior decoration is cunningly propagandist. The iconostasis trumpets Ivan's annexation of various principalities to form the Russian state: each of the icons on the lower tier was carried off as a trophy from a conquered principality. As a final vindication of Moscow's position as capital of Russia, the country's most venerated icon, the Virgin of Vladimir, was brought to the church. The icon had previously been in the former capitals of Kiev and Vladimir, and the presence of this icon in a particular city was taken as virtual proof of its worthiness to be capital. The original has been kept for safety in the Tret'yakov Gallery since the Revolution, but there are two copies in Uspensky: the finest is the fifteenth-century version, encased in glass, next to the west entrance. Uspensky's status cut no ice with the Napoleonic troops who stormed the Kremlin in 1812, and they stripped over 5,000 kilograms of gold from the church in the process of converting it into a stable. Cossack troops later recovered much of the silver, which they presented to Uspensky in the form of the weighty Christmas tree-shaped candelabra which hangs in the centre of the church.

The tiny **Church of the Deposition of the Virgin's Robe** (Rizpolozheniya), tucked behind Uspensky, has brilliantly coloured domes on its roof, but inside, the seventeenth-century frescoes and icons have been restored and are of minor interest.

With its nine golden domes, the **Cathedral of the Annunciation** (Blagoveshchensky Sabor) is one of the Kremlin's most striking churches. Adjoining the tsar's palace, it was designed as a private family chapel.

Paved with burgundy and toffee-hued jasper and with the subtle shades of its frescoes and icons glimmering in the half-light, the church is at once rich and intimate. The iconostasis is among the world's finest, with icons by the great Greek artist Theophanus and his Russian counterpart Andrey Rublyov. These were painted for the first church, and until the 1920s it was thought that they had perished in a fire, but restorers discovered them beneath layers of oil-paint added by later artists. There is a useful key to the icons in English in front of the iconostasis.

The **Cathedral of the Archangel Michael** (Archangelsky Sabor) is a bizarre fusion of Venetian and Italian architecture: a restrained Renaissance cuboid sprouting onion domes and bulging with apses. The interior is crammed with 46 tombs containing the remains of princes, tsars and military rulers.

Beyond Cathedral Square is the magnificent **Great Kremlin Palace**, marzipan-yellow, piped with white ogee gables, and decked with fancifully carved pilasters and spun-sugar window frames. Built in the nineteenth century, it is now used for official state functions, but its almost obscenely opulent rooms are occasionally open to the public.

The **Armoury** beyond is similarly confected, and houses one of Russia's richest collections of decorative and applied art. Costumes of tsars, tsarinas and ecclesiastics are heavy with jewels or silver and gold embroidery; and thrones are inlaid with ivory, encrusted with precious stones and, in one case, studded with over 800 diamonds. The collection of carriages includes a gilded rococo monstrosity sprouting with caryatids, and the small Fabergé collection scales the heights of frivolity with a jade hippo and an egg in a model of the Kremlin.

Just outside the Kremlin walls, in the Alexandrovsky Garden, is the **Tomb of the Unknown Soldier**, where an eternal flame burns in memory of those who died during the Second World War. You may see a bride and groom bringing flowers on their wedding day to pay homage to the dead.

The Arbat

A pedestrianised street lined with stuccoed mansions in pretty shades of pistachio, pink, ice-blue and peach, this is Moscow at its most relaxed. There are stand-up *shashlik* and coffee-bars and a pretty outdoor ice-cream and milk-shake parlour, well patronised even in winter. Muscovites queue to pose on a static motor-bike for a street photographer, and gaze at a silhouette cutter skilfully snipping profiles. And crowds gather anywhere there is anything new to see or buy, whether it be a stall of novelty key-rings, a souvenir shop selling military watches, a display of photographs from a soft-porn show or a mouse on a wheel in a pet-shop window.

The Tsvetnoi Boulevard Rynok

The quality of produce in the co-operative *rynok* would put many British markets to shame. The geographical immensity of the Soviet Union means that the range of produce is vast: mountains of persimmons, oranges and lemons; heaps of dried apricots, pistachios and walnuts; tiny sachets of saffron, fennel seeds and cumin; and trays of cabbage salad and pungent garlic. Many of these goods are now also available at other *rynoks* or near metro stations.

OTHER PLACES TO VISIT

Museums and galleries

Central Lenin Museum Sited in one of the pair of red-brick pseudo-Russian buildings at the west end of Red Square, this museum will appeal most to those already familiar with Lenin's life and beliefs. Most evocative are the reconstruction of his Kremlin office, his 1914 Silver Shadow (regularly serviced by a Rolls-Royce mechanic) and the bullet-pierced overcoat he was wearing in 1918 when Dora Kaplan attempted to assassinate him. Two new halls contain displays entitled 'Tragedy of Lenin's Last Two Years of Life', supporting the belief that many of his ideas and thoughts during his last two years of illness were 'corrected' and changed by those around him.

Leo Tolstoy House Museum Next door to a shambling old factory and overlooked by apartment blocks is the green and brown painted wooden house of Leo Tolstoy, who moved here with his wife and daughters in 1882, having already written *War and Peace* and *Anna Karenina*. The glimpse you can have into his everyday life is gripping. The dining-table is set ready for a meal, his fur coat hangs on a nail, his bicycle stands by the study, and even his socks are on display. Though the house is fairly large, conditions for the Tolstoys' servants were rather cramped: the nurse slept with the baby, the governess in the boys' schoolroom, and the housekeeper and seamstress together in a tiny bedroom.

Tret'yakov Gallery and Picture Gallery of the USSR A great collection of Russian and Soviet art is housed in the Tret'yakov Gallery and its huge annexe, the Picture Gallery of the USSR, a kilometre or so down the river. The Tret'yakov, now partly open after restoration, holds the world's finest collection of Russian icons, dating from the twelfth to the sixteenth century. Highlights are the *Virgin of Vladimir*, fondly attributed to Saint Luke but in fact the work of a sixteenth-century Byzantine artist; icons by the fourteenth-century Theophanus the Greek; and, above all, the brilliant *Trinity* by Andrey Rublyov.

The Tret'yakov also has Russian paintings from the eighteenth to the twentieth centuries. It is intended that the collection of post-Revolutionary art will be housed in the Picture Gallery of the USSR.

Vasnetsov House From the outside this pretty little house with its fancy wooden garret looks like something out of a fairytale. It's no surprise, then, to find that this was the home that the architect, artist and illustrator of fairytales, Viktor Vasnetsov, designed for himself in the late nineteenth century. It's a delightful place, with carved wooden furniture and frescoes and canvases of kings, queens, princesses and knights on white horses. Open only on Tuesday, Thursday, Saturday and Sunday.

Other attractions

Gorky Park With its frozen network of paths and lakes, Gorky Park is a skaters' paradise in winter, when the lakes become ice-rinks and the paths are flooded and frozen. Skates are available for hire.

During the rest of the year, concerts and even lectures are often held at weekends in its indoor and outdoor theatres, but during the week it can feel rather a dismal place, with rock music filtering weakly over the Tannoys. The park is dominated by an immense Ferris wheel, the most impressive of the permanent funfair's rides, and there are pedalos to hire on the main lake.

It's also worth taking a trip up the river from the boat station for good views of the Kremlin and Vorobievy Hills (boats run mid-April to mid-September, weather permitting).

Riding the metro 'We do not need a dead mausoleum of art where dead works are worshipped but a living factory of the human spirit – in the streets, in the tramways, in the factories, workshops and workers' homes,' declared the Futurist poet and playwright Mayakovsky in 1918. The architectural achievement of Soviet society seems dubious, but the stations of the underground are triumphant examples of the policy of bringing art to the people. Known as the palaces of the working class, the most elaborate stations are the earliest, built under Stalin in the 1930s. The first line to be opened was the red central line, Kirovsko-Frunzenskaya: highlights are Revolyutsii Ploshchad, where idealised bronze figures of youth represent the heroes of the revolution; Komsomolskaya, with its gilded stucco and marble glittering in the light from the immense candelabra; and the art nouveau Arbatskaya. On Kol'tsevaya, Novoslobodskaya's stained glass incorporates motifs from Russian tapestries, while Kievskaya is notable for its mosaics and sculpture. The station named after Mayakovsky is also worth seeing.

A Russian Orthodox Service Since 1988, the thousandth anniversary of the introduction of Christianity to Russia, the church in Russia has enjoyed increasing freedom and respect. Danilovsky Monastery, after being used as an electrical factory and home for delinquent boys, was restored in time for the millennium celebrations (when it was visited by President Reagan) and has become the seat of the Russian Patriarch. This, and other churches around the city, hold services twice daily.

SHOPPING

(See also 'Shopping' under 'Mastering the System', page 316)

To begin to understand what everyday life in Moscow is like, head for the main shopping street, Tverskaya Ulitsa. Beneath the gilded stucco and inlaid wooden ceiling of Duema, there are hunks of dried-out and darkened meat, slabs of cheese and cartons of milk. Further up at No 14 is Gastronom No 1, a *fin-de-siècle* extravaganza of cascading chandeliers, stained glass, mirrors and gilt. Delicacies such as smoked fish, salamis and arabica coffee beans are juxtaposed with packet soups and tinned fish, while the ad hoc selection of fruit and vegetables, though cheaper than in the *rynok*, is of a far poorer quality.

In spite of this, there are signs on Tverskaya of consumerist innovations. Branches of hard-currency shops include Christian Dior, Estée Lauder and Yves Rocher, and the Irish House on Novy Arbat is very popular with Muscovites (the Irish bar is also a useful place to rest after running round Moscow).

Given the current exchange rate, there are incredible bargains to be had. Records cost just a few roubles (but their quality deteriorates rapidly). Melodiya, at Novy Arbat 40, also has CDs of classical and Russian folk music. Hardback translations of classical and modern literature, historical and political works cost a couple of roubles. The best selection is at Progress Books on Zubovsky Boulevard – just after the Park Kultury Metro station, on the way to the Tolstoy House Museum. Dom Knigi, at Novy Arbat 26, has a more limited range of books in English, but a tempting collection of posters. Even better for posters is Isskutsv at Arbat 4. The Arbat is also a good place to buy arts and crafts.

If you have children with you or at home, don't miss Detsky Mir (Children's World) on Teatralny Proyezd. This is the largest children's department store in Russia, occupying the same place in the national consciousness as Mothercare and Hamleys do in Britain. The construction and electronics kits and, above all, the video games arcade, attract as many adults as children.

EATING AND DRINKING

(*See also St Petersburg chapter, pages 327-8*)

Breakfast in a Russian hotel is rarely an inspiring start to the day: thin slices of white and black bread, stodgy sweet buns, with one curl of butter per person, jam if you're lucky, and slices of cheese and a garlicky mortadella-like sausage. Coffee and tea will be served at some point. It's difficult to appreciate, until you see what's on offer in the city's *bufets* and cafés – where the bread is staler, the cheese drier and butter non-existent.

Bufets and cafés also sell some manner of lukewarm carbo-hydrate for lunch, but you'd be better off going to one of the hotels which have Swedish-style buffets where you pay 150 roubles and take as much as you like. The most central is in the modern Hotel Intourist near the beginning of Tverskaya Ulitsa. The Moskva Hotel offers a Russian-style buffet for 100 roubles, which is not as good. If you prefer to eat with Russians, the snacks on sale outside metro stations vary in quality; it might be worth trying *blitzi* – savoury doughnuts filled with spicy cabbage or onion. If the weather's reasonable, bread from a bakery, fresh fruit and salad from the Tsvetnoi Boulevard market (*rynok*) and cheese and salami from Gastronom No 1 (or your hotel breakfast table) will make for a healthy picnic. For a more substantial lunch, the café at Arbat 6 serves good salads and hearty soups and stews.

Ice-cream is sold and eaten in the streets throughout the year, and is well worth trying. The Pinguine shops on Arbat and Tverskaya and in the Hotel Moskva sell the best-quality ice-cream, though it is more expensive.

Most hotel restaurants serve a bland combination of Russian and international fare at dinner; the best food is served in the stylish old dining-room of the National Hotel (closed for restoration in 1992), where the view of the Kremlin almost compensates for the racket of the band.

Noisy entertainment is the norm in most state-run restaurants. The entertainment in Aragyi (Tverskaya Ulitsa 6, tel: 229-3762) is relatively unobstrusive, and the set Georgian menu not too bad. Black marketeers make the rounds while you eat, offering army watches and other cut-price goodies. In Uzbekistan (Neglinnaya Ulitsa 29, tel: 924-6053) the food is also passable, the atmosphere lively, verging on the boisterous, and in summer you can eat in the garden.

Ideal for a last, alcohol-charged night with your tour-group cronies is the Slavyansky Bazaar (Nikolskaya Ulitsa 13, tel: 921-9853). Big, brash and boisterous, the Slavyansky is crammed with long tables of partying locals and parties of tourists. The tackiness of the décor and floorshow is of an extremity that makes it perversely enjoyable, though it can't really be recommended for small groups. Starters (*zakuski*) are generous, though stamped with the hallmark of mass-catering, and the beef and vegetable stew is piping hot, even if chewing the meat is a lengthy process.

In general, however, eating in one of the burgeoning numbers of co-operative-run restaurants is far pleasanter. The Italian food at Lazania (Pyatnitskaya Ulitsa 40, tel: 231-1085) is generally good, though the signature lasagne is disappointing; you will need to book well in advance. For Russian food, Razgulyai (Spartakovskaya Ulitsa 11, tel: 267-7613) is also good, and its Old Russian décor a visual feast; while Moscow's first co-operative restaurant Kropotkinskaya-36 (Prechistenka Ulitsa 36, tel: 203-1738) now takes only hard currency. With a hushed and sedate clientele politely listening to a pianist and violinist playing classical music, it has been so successful that its owner opened a branch in New York. Tren Mos Bistro at Ostozenka 1 (tel: 202-5722), not far from the Pushkin Museum, has a French chef and features the work of Moscow artist Renat Sadekov. On Monday and Tuesday evenings at 10pm his assistant turns up at the restaurant to meet would-be buyers. The bar is open from 5pm to 1am for hard currency only.

NIGHTLIFE

Moscow is a joy for lovers of classical music, ballet or opera. Tickets for the Bolshoi ballet and opera and for concerts are available through Intourist. Tickets can also be bought for hard currency from touts at the entrance, but it's best to avoid these unless you can read Russian and can make out where the seats are. Ballets and opera are not always staged in the opulent Bolshoi Theatre: the modern Palace of Congresses inside the Kremlin is frequently used.

The other great cultural attraction is the Moscow State Circus: again, tickets are available through Intourist. The skill, daring and ingenuity of the performers puts British circuses in the shade.

The one time of year when Moscow goes wild is New Year, when the ban on drinking in the streets is forgotten and Red Square hosts one big party. Music festivals are also held in Red Square during the summer.

Other than restaurants and theatres, nightlife in Moscow is thin on the ground, though nightclubs and cabarets are slowly opening up. For jazz, try the Bluebird Café on Chekhova Ulitsa, but phone first (tel: 299-8702) to make sure it is open.

NICE

- Though no longer the super-fashionable resort of the British beau monde, Nice is still a large prosperous city frequented by the wealthy – from all over the world
- Despite the (high season) crowds and traffic it's a delightful place, mainly because it combines an old Italian port town with parks and flowers and the candy-floss architecture of the Riviera's belle époque
- Nice is particularly good for strolling, window-shopping and for sipping drinks in pavement cafés when it's dismal and cold at home
- There are plenty of excursion opportunities, whether or not you have a car; the mountainous hinterland is particularly beautiful
- Good-value hotels are not that easy to find

THE pleasure of a trip to Nice begins up in the air, as you watch the snow-capped grey peaks of the maritime Alps unfold towards the sparse and hilly coastal hinterland and then trace the thick ribbon of heavily built-up resorts at Cannes and Antibes. Large yachts scar the blue Mediterranean waters with chalky white lines. As the plane descends towards Nice you see the city spreading along the wide Bay of Angels and rising up into the amphitheatre of hills behind. The first scent of the French Riviera's glamour comes on landing: special signs direct those arriving in private jets, in the luggage queues there's talk of yachts and villas and in the ranks of rental cars outside the airport building there are more BMWs than Renault 5s.

A select few wintered in Nice as far back as the late eighteenth century. Asthmatics and consumptives were particularly attracted by the balmy and mild climate and the fresh sea breezes. But the real boom started in the late nineteenth century, after the railway reached the Riviera. Luxury trains brought the cream of the aristocracy – British and Russian – from Calais, St Petersburg and European capitals. An English newspaper announced the new arrivals, and winter became a continuous ball. By the turn of the century, Nice had become the meeting place for the international beau monde. Social life revolved round the salons of sumptuous villas, presided over by noble hostesses. Royalty mixed with writers, artists and the plain wealthy. In the late 1920s the increasing number of Americans started the fashion for summers on the Riviera. Nice is still a wealthy place, but under the onslaught of modern tourism the truly rich and famous have retreated behind the high fences of the villas on the St-Jean-Cap-Ferrat peninsula further along the coast.

You'll speed along the long Promenade des Anglais, Nice's most distinctive landmark, almost as soon as you leave the airport. Last century, the British community liked to stroll and socialise by the sea, but found the foreshore unsuitably swampy. So it funded a footpath in the 1820s which was further widened and surfaced some 30 years later. Now it's a six-lane highway of cars speeding between fat palms.

Along the Promenade were built idiosyncratic villas with fanciful façades and extravagant domes – a few can still be seen peeping out between the square new blocks. The grand hotels are here, too: the neo-baroque pink-domed Negresco is the most splendid, built by a Romanian businessman-violinist for a very select clientele (don't be shy to enter and view its gilded interiors and the Salon Royal, with a crystal chandelier which weighs over a ton). The nearby art deco Casino Méditerranée is now decayed and shuttered after a corruption scandal.

On the seaward side across the lanes of traffic the prom is still a popular place for strollers and a great place from where to watch the world go by. There are joggers and crisply dressed sailors, an inordinate number of poodles that take spiky-heeled ladies for walks, and hundreds of tourists. Beneath the promenade, sun loungers and wooden walkways (even carpets) cover the uncomfortable grey pebbles on the long beach, which is divided into private concessions, each marked by a flag and a list of prices at the entrance. Nice is not a place for a beach holiday, but the beach comes in handy for a cool-off after serious bouts of sightseeing.

But there's far more to Nice than the belle époque and the famous promenade. A good way to get a first taste of the various parts of the city is to take the miniature, toy-like tourist train which starts on the waterfront by the beach of the Beau Rivage. It may be naff, but it's a practical form of travel as it trundles slowly through the most interesting areas of the town and ends up high on the castle hill from where you can walk down again and explore at your leisure. Turning away from the sea, the train takes you past the Jardin Albert I, a large area of grass, flowers, trees and restful benches laid along the bed of the covered-up Paillon river, which marks the boundary between new and old Nice. Further inland, the course of this river has been used as spare ground for the city's modern prestige developments: the incongruously named massive concrete and glass structure of the Acropolis, used mostly for the many trade fairs and business conventions; and the newest hi-tech development of the Musée d'Art Moderne et d'Art Contemporain.

Place Masséna borders the Albert I gardens. It's wide, arcaded and symmetrical, in the neo-classical Italian piazza style, with sandy red façades. Bronze horses struggle out of the waters of the fountain in its southern corner. Only minutes away you come to the old town of Nice which, despite the recent gentrification and the spreading avant-garde boutiques, still has the atmosphere of an Italian harbourside community (from 1388 until 1860, with a few short interruptions, Nice was ruled by the Italian House of Savoy). The cramped sunless streets are named after their old uses: Halle aux Herbes or Rue de la Boucherie. Baroque churches dwarf tiny squares, their ornate gloomy interiors enlivened by flickering candles. The Ste-Réparate Cathedral and the churches of St-Martin and St-Jacques (Gésu) are well worth popping into. Washing is draped over the narrow gaps between pastel-painted, shuttered houses, and old couples sit on rickety chairs outside street cafés in silent communion. The pedestrianised Cours Saleya is the marketplace for flowers, food and bric-à-brac. By the afternoon trestle tables are cleared and pavements hosed down and the café and restaurant life takes over – youths in ripped designer jeans meet for coffee, tourists wander from menu to menu and buskers try to entertain with honky tonk blues and renditions of old rock-and-roll favourites.

Up a steep path lies the rocky outcrop of the castle hill. It's a 92-metre high headland which separates the rectangular port area of Nice from the long beach and promenade. There's no longer a castle at the top (it was destroyed in 1706), only a few ruins – unlabelled and sprouting wild flowers. Now the whole hill is a shady park where a decorative waterfall splashes down the hillside through the warm scents of Mediterranean pine. At the highest point, a terrace packed with souvenir stalls has a lovely panorama of the city. The flat sweep of the Bay of Angels curves into the distance and the old town lies within a triangle at the foot of the hill, its terracotta roofs and maze-like streets hemmed in by the regular rows of modern white buildings which rise into the hills inland.

The most substantial proof of the Roman occupation of Nice is on the hill of Cimiez, now a peaceful and smart suburb of villas and gardens. Queen Victoria favoured this hillside retreat, too; the Grand Hotel, where she stayed, is now divided into hundreds of private apartments.

In the new town, to the west of the railway station, you can see an extraordinary piece of old Russia. The Notre Dame Orthodox church has twisted bulbous domes with gold and icons inside. At the turn of the century the Russian expatriate community was the largest in Nice after the British.

WHEN TO GO

Despite its fame as a winter watering place, Nice has its high season in summer, when along with the rest of the Côte d'Azur it gets impossibly crowded. But you should follow the example of the first tourists and come here in winter, spring or autumn. While it's cold and rainy at home, shorts and sunglasses are *de rigueur* in Nice. The city has about 150 hours of mid-winter sun a month (compared with about 50 hours on France's north coast). The mountainous hinterland shelters it from the cold north *mistral* wind. The season is long: in April, while London can count on only 38 per cent of sunshine hours a day, Nice has 60 per cent (with only a little less in October); even in late October, it's sunny enough to sunbathe. At carnival time (Mardi Gras), in the fortnight before Lent, the whole city goes quite mad: there are parades of floats and flower battles, masked balls and fireworks. Make sure you book a room well in advance at this time of year.

MASTERING THE SYSTEM

Information The French Government Tourist Office is at 178 Piccadilly, London W1V 0AL, tel: 071-493 5174. The Nice Tourist Office (Syndicat d'Initiative) can be found on Avenue Thiers (tel: 93.87.07.07), at the SNCF railway station. It's open July to September, Monday to Saturday 8.45am to 7pm, Sunday 8.45am to 12.30pm and 2pm to 6pm, and October to June, Monday to Saturday, 8.45am to 12.30pm and 2pm to 6pm. You can also find branches at 5 Avenue Gustav V (across from Jardin Albert I in the centre of town) and in the Acropolis Centre on the Esplanade Kennedy (mostly business and trade information). They have a good free map of the city which marks all the main sights, has a street index, and a map of the surrounding region on the reverse side. You can also get a free plan of the town's bus routes, information about trains and coaches that travel along the coast, a useful leaflet in English giving details of all the museums and a free 'what's on' magazine called 7 *Jours* 7 *Nuits* which covers the whole region (there's another one called *La Semaine des Spectacles* which is available from newsagents for 5F). The tourist office will also help with booking accommodation – for a small fee, which is then deducted from your hotel bill.

Sightseeing tours Half- or full-day tours are available to all the Riviera resorts, both east and west of Nice. There are also trips to inland villages and the maritime Alps. Some excursions even go across the border into Italy, to the market at Ventimiglia or to San Remo. There are plenty of excursion bureaux around the town centre (one is inside the railway station) and information is also available in hotels and at the tourist office. Bateaux Gallus, at 24 Quai Lunel by Nice harbour, organises boat trips along the coast to Monaco, Cannes and as far as St Tropez. Special day excursions by train are offered from June to September: information is available from either the 'Chemins de Fer de Provence' stand in the station foyer or from the office at 33 Av. Malausséna (tel: 93.88.28.56).

Changing money There are plenty of banks and exchange offices, which generally open weekdays 8.30am to noon, and 1.30pm to 5pm; a few are also open at weekends (including the exchange offices at the airport and railway station). Credit cards are widely accepted, particularly Visa. You get a better rate of

GETTING THERE

Going independently

By air The flight from London to Nice takes just under two hours and is really the only way to travel for a short break. Air France has two flights daily from Heathrow and three in summer; British Airways has three flights daily throughout the year as well as a daily service from Gatwick. Air Canada also flies from Heathrow on most days of the week during the summer and two or three times a week in winter. APEX fares, bookable 14 days in advance, are cheapest but make sure your travel agent compares the airlines' fares. Fares go up during the July to September holiday season. There are charter flights to Nice as well, but you're restricted to a seven-day minimum stay. Operators whose fares are worth checking include Euro Express (0444 235678), Falcon Flights (061-831 7000), Cresta Holidays (061-929 9995), Data Travel (0424 722394), Avro Elite (081-543 5833) and Flightfile (071-323 1515). A few charters leave from Manchester Airport.

Nice Airport The airport is about four miles from the city centre on the coast to the west. It's a spacious, airy and pleasant place with good facilities – lounge with bar, cafés and restaurant, shops, bureau de change and tourist information. There's a private lounge for private jet travellers.

A taxi journey to the centre of town is a steep £12 to £18, depending on the quantity of luggage. Buses run every 20 minutes (less frequently early morning, on Sundays or holidays) and cost less than a fifth of that; there are stops all along the Promenade des Anglais, and the terminus is at the bus station (Gare Routière) on Boulevard Jean Jaurès.

By rail Rail is probably not a viable option for a weekend break. It will cost you less than flying, but it's a seven-hour journey by high-speed train from Paris and more than double that from London. One option might be the overnight service, leaving London Victoria in the early afternoon and arriving in Nice the following morning.

Tour operator packages

The standard short-break packages to Nice by air consist of stays of two to five nights (your stay must be over a Saturday night) in two- to four-star hotels, and include continental breakfast and (usually) transfers to and from the airport. Once delivered to your hotel you're left to your own devices. In 1992 the price per person in a three-star hotel for three nights B&B ranged from £216 in low season to £375 in high season. Sea or panoramic views cost extra, as do single rooms. For a list of tour operators, see page 385.

Going on a package is convenient and easy, but prices don't necessarily work out cheaper than going independently and sometimes they are considerably more expensive, particularly if you are able to find a cheap flight independently.

exchange for French francs if you buy them in the UK before you go. It's best to take Franch franc, rather than sterling, travellers' cheques, though you'll be charged a commission for changing them. Beware high surcharges if paying restaurant or hotel bills by Eurocheque.

Opening hours and days Sights and museums are usually open from 9am or 10am to noon and 2pm or 2.30pm to 5pm (6pm in high season). The Marc Chagall Museum is open 10am to 7pm from July to the end of September; 10am to 12.30pm, 2pm to 5.30pm October to the end of June; closed Tuesday. Most sites close on either Monday, Tuesday or Thursday (as well as some public holidays). The Roman baths also close on Sunday morning. Shops open from 10am to noon and 3pm to 7pm or 8pm.

GETTING AROUND

The narrow streets of the old town are suitable only for **walking**. Once you have braved the six-lane traffic across the Promenade des Anglais the wide seaside pavement is ideal for strolling along. The shopping streets are pedestrianised to the west of Place Masséna.

You can get up castle hill by taking the mini **tourist train** which starts on the promenade by the Beau Rivage beach. Alternatively, you can go almost to the top by a lift which is built into the rock below the Tour Bellanda on the Quai des États-Unis, the continuation of the Promenade des Anglais.

Buses are efficient and frequent and most useful for getting to and from the airport and up to the museums on the Cimiez hill. On some bus stops there's even an indicator board to tell you where the next bus is and how long you'll have to wait. The leaflet that lists all the Nice museums also gives details of the buses that go to them and the stop to alight at. There's a flat fare on city buses and you can buy a good-value block (*carnet*) of five tickets. There are also the *cartes touristiques*, giving one or five days' unlimited travel (the five-day card is worth it if you are likely to go on more then ten journeys during your stay). *Carnets* and tourist cards are available from *tabac* kiosks or newsagents. From the bus station (Gare Routière) on Boulevard Jean Jaurès there are frequent buses for all the Riviera resorts east of Nice as far as Menton.

Taxis are useful for trips to and from the airport or for getting up to the sights in Cimiez; their white light is lit up when they're free. Main taxi ranks are marked on the tourist map of the city and can be called from the hotels.

There's no particular need for a **car** on a short break unless you want to go on excursions into the hinterland or along the coast. It's more expensive to hire a car on the Riviera than anywhere else in France. Street parking in Nice is not easy and underground car-parks expensive; wheel clamping is popular.

UNMISSABLES

Cimiez

When the Romans conquered Gaul they spurned the little seaside market town of Greek Nikaia and set up headquarters on the nearby inland hill of Cemenelum – present-day Cimiez. It became a prosperous administrative and military centre which protected the Via Julia Augusta – the consular road which led all the way to Spain. Now, just a few scant ruins remain, scattered about a lovely olive grove park where mothers bring toddlers and dogs to play and where fairs and concerts take place in summer. You can get here by bus from the centre of Nice (No 15 from Place Masséna), uphill past twisting avenues lined by trees and wealthy villas. Alight by the Villa des Arènes, a rusty red building in seventeenth-century Genoese style with ornate shuttered windows and twin balustraded terraces. Closed since 1987, it is due to reopen in 1993 as the new and refurbished **Matisse Museum**, with temporary exhibitions alongside the artist's major works painted in Nice, as well as his personal belongings and art collection.

Next door is the **Archaeological Museum** in a low white modern building. It's intended as both an information and research complex, and an exhibition of the archaeological findings – ceramics, tools, jewellery, inscriptions and so on – which trace the history of Cemenelum and the Roman province. The small elliptical amphitheatre has its ground concreted over and its crumbling stone archways and banks covered in unsightly scaffolding. The **Roman Baths** are much better – they rank as the best-preserved in France, and if you solve the puzzle of the foundations, crumbling walls, canals and tunnels, you'll get a good idea of their past splendour. The surviving wall of the Frigidarium (cold water bath) still stands over 30 feet tall.

Last but not least on Cimiez is the **Notre Dame de L'Annon-ciation** church and Franciscan monastery, a pleasant walk through the park from the Roman ruins and the Villa des Arènes. The medieval church was extensively restored in the middle of the last century so its façade is a varied but delightful mixture of portico with rounded archways and sharp soaring lines of Gothic-style windows and turrets – all in honey-pink stone. The inside is dark with a frescoed ceiling and a heavily gilded and carved altar. Most impressive are the three large paintings of the medieval Nice school, which you light up with a two-franc piece. Louis Bréa's *Pietà* is the most beautiful – the wan and pale body of Christ draped over the black-clothed lap of his young mother. You can also visit the cloisters (guided tours only, about five times daily) and the Franciscan Museum.

National Museum Marc Chagall

On the slopes of the Cimiez hill, in a garden shaded by olive trees, a gallery was built in 1972 to house Marc Chagall's *Biblical Message*. In the 1950s the painter dreamt of gathering in one holy place (the Calvary Chapel near his home in Vence) the works that expressed his feelings on the relationship between man and God. The plan came to nothing so he donated the paintings in his biblical series to the nation.

In the central hall, light from recessed windows pours on to twelve huge canvases – a glowing sequence of reds, aquamarines, blues and purples – showing scenes from the Bible as a child might see them. Five smaller paintings in a smaller gallery (sometimes closed because of staff shortages) depict the *Song of Songs*: entwined lovers (she in bridal white), snaky and long, like comets, float in dark red skies above villages that defy perspective. Many other works by the artist are on display, including the stained-glass windows which light the music auditorium in vivid blues.

Masséna Museum

André Masséna, a famous son of Nice, was one of Napoleon's favoured generals. His son, Victor, built this mansion on the Promenade des Anglais (entrance is from a parallel street at the back). It's columned, porticoed and balustraded, befitting a grand social salon of the beau monde at the turn of the century. Now the museum satisfies every taste. Downstairs, visitors stand at the roped-off doors of the grand rooms to admire frescoed ceilings, crystal chandeliers, gleaming parquet floors, carved and lacquered doors, candelabra held by bronze figurines, gilt mirror tables propped up by lion heads, and alcoves with ornately decorated vases. Upstairs galleries are devoted to Masséna and Garibaldi (Nice's other famous son), but there are also collections of regional costumes, jewellery from India and Tibet and even a colourful display of carnival puppets. There are also altarpieces painted by the fifteenth- and sixteenth-century Nice 'primitives', of which Louis Bréa and his descendants were the masters. You might not notice their works in the churches of the old town because they're usually shrouded in gloom.

Jules Chéret Museum of Fine Arts

Another opulent villa of the belle époque – this one belonged to Madame Kotschoubey, a Russian princess – houses a small but diverse fine arts collection. The mood changes from dour portraits of the Dutch school on the ground floor to a treasure trove of Impressionists on the first: works by Monet, Bonnard, Signac and Sisley. The works of Chéret himself are placed, almost as an afterthought, up the grand staircase: frothy portraits of women, bright and full of movement, and theatrical posters.

OTHER PLACES TO VISIT

Lascaris Palace This seventeenth-century grand house in the old town was sliced into apartments at the turn of the century, then restored and turned into a museum by the City of Nice. It has a majestic staircase and a fine reconstructed pharmacy, with pottery jars in panelled niches and strange medicinal names on drawers. The rest is rather disappointing, with parts fallen into disrepair; the many visitors marvel at the proximity of the balcony across the street more than at the exhibits on display.

The Malacology Gallery A good place for children, this has cabinets full of clearly labelled, very beautiful shells from all over the world. The information is in French only, but you can just enjoy the shapes, colours and many patterns – reds or browns, spiky or smooth. In the aquarium are fish brought back from the Nice sea-bed by divers: sea anemones trail tentacles and a lone lobster picks its way over a sandy sea-bed.

The Natural History Museum Another gem for children (and adults!): a fun little educational museum, imaginatively displayed and with a particularly good mycology (fungi) section. There are buttons to press which light up displays and set things in motion and a special table with crayons and pictures of toadstools and mushrooms for colouring in. Good clear explanations throughout the museum are in French only.

The Naval Museum Yet another pleasant little museum providing variety on a rainy day. It's in a circular room of the Bellanda

Tower on the castle hill. Models of boats, old maps and navigational instruments bear witness to Nice's importance as a working port – easy to forget nowadays with all those smart yachts and gin palaces.

Excursions

Nice is an ideal base for touring the area. For a day-trip, head along the coast to the east, towards Menton. The highlights are the steep old fishing harbour at **Villefranche** with the small St Pierre chapel on the seafront decorated by Jean Cocteau; the tiny **Principality of Monaco**, where Jacques Cousteau's Oceanographic Museum has a celebrated aquarium; the neo-baroque villas of the principality's town, **Monte Carlo**, whose sumptuous casino was the setting for so many bank-breaking exploits; and the beautiful old town at **Menton** with more of Jean Cocteau's bold charcoal lines on the walls of the Salle des Mariages in the Town Hall.

It's easy to organise your own excursion by train – which follows the shore, and whose stations are conveniently close to the centre of the resorts. But you'll miss one of the best attractions of this very beautiful stretch of coast – namely, the two high roads which supplement the busy and slow coast road, the Corniche Inférieure. The Grande Corniche is the most exciting: it's the far-from-straight old Roman road from Nice to Genoa, reaching a height of nearly 450 metres above sea-level. It passes behind some coastal peaks and offers a range of views down over the bays of the Riviera and up into the barren Alps, snow-covered for most of the year. The Moyenne Corniche gives the most consistent sea views and access to **Eze**, a truly astonishing perched village and one of the most popular excursions from the coast. At the top, on the site of the old castle, there is an exotic garden with cacti. If you feel hesitant about driving along these winding and sometimes precipitous roads, you can go on a coach excursion (although the confident approach adopted by coach drivers may seem even more hair-raising at times).

From Nice a number of roads lead back into the **maritime Alps**, where the enclosed valleys – with cascades and gorges – and numerous hill-top villages are the main attractions. For the winter (and spring) visitor, ski slopes are only a couple of hours or so from the sea. In summer, snowy peaks are still visible well into the season. If you have a car, a short excursion to the perched villages of Peillon and Peille is well worth undertaking.

The coastline west of Nice is less worthy of note than the villages set some way back from it. **Vence**, **St-Paul-de-Vence** and **Biot** are small inland towns full of interest, especially for art lovers, as is the resort of **Antibes**, whose castle houses a fine Picasso museum.

SHOPPING

In Nice it wouldn't be difficult to spend your whole break window-shopping or market browsing, and you're likely to end up buying far more than you had intended. One of the peculiarities of this city is the inordinately high number of hairdressers and poodle parlours. Off Place Masséna, the pedestrianised Rue Masséna and its continuation Rue de France is a mixture of chain boutiques and all kinds of fashion shops as well as pizza parlours and hamburger joints. The upmarket designer boutiques are on Avenue Verdun. In the new town the Avenue Jean Médecin is where the locals go shopping: it has the Galeries Lafayette, a large department store, and further up the shopping centre of Nice Étoile – with hundreds of shops under one roof. There are also lots of food stores and street market stalls here and on its northern continuation, Avenue Malaussena.

The old town is the most satisfying for browsing and finding unusual things, as well as the place to buy your provençal olive oil and fresh herbs. On the streets of du Marché, de la Boucherie and du Collet cheap wares of all sorts spill out into the street or hang in rows under the awnings. Elsewhere in the maze of streets you'll find the odd nineteenth-century corner *drogueries*, as well as little specialist shops selling things such as avant-garde collages, earrings, fashions or bric-à-brac, and souvenir shops with cluttered interiors. The port area, not surprisingly, has chandlers, and more mundane furniture and hi-fi stores.

The main town market is in Cours Saleya. Food and flowers are at the western end and antiques and crafts at the eastern (food daily in the morning, flowers Tuesday and Saturday and Sunday morning, bric-à-brac Monday, arts Saturday afternoon, and crafts Wednesday afternoon). The flower market is a marvellous sight in itself, with stall after stall of colour, scent and freshness. There are petunias, hibiscus, busy lizzies, jasmine, roses, geraniums, potted herbs and even lemon trees.

EATING AND DRINKING

In Nice you'll find all the classic dishes of provençal cuisine, which use olive oil, plenty of garlic and the wild herbs – thyme, rosemary or basil – that grow in profusion on the hills. Even snacks, like cheese-filled baguettes, are dripping with oil and pungent with herbs. Fish is plentiful: grilled with herbs, in *bourride*, a creamy soup, or in the renowned *bouillabaisse*, a mixed fish stew seasoned with saffron, fennel and orange peel, among other things, and served with *rouille*, a strong garlic paste. The Italian influence is also strong in Nice, with pizzas and pasta (a particular speciality is ravioli) widely available. *Salade niçoise*, with French beans, olives, egg and tuna, and *pain bagnat*, a salad and anchovy roll, are popular snacks.

Long known for its light and refreshing rosé wines, Provence is beginning to offer the adventurous wine-drinker a number of more interesting wines that share the spice-drenched flavours of its cooking. Appellations to look out for include Bandol, Côtes de Provence and Coteaux d'Aix-en-Provence for rich reds (their whites and rosés are less interesting), and Palette, which produces high-quality reds and acceptable whites and rosés.

There are plenty of restaurants and cafés. The shopping area around Rue Masséna is full of pizza and pancake places and cafés serving snacks – but the area is expensive. For a leisurely meal or drink the old town is far more pleasant. Cours Saleya teems with restaurants and cafés (with a good variety of lunchtime salads and fish menus) and more are tucked away in the maze of streets behind, where you'll also find cheap drinking dens and good pasta in tiny restaurants of five tables or so. For good local snacks try Place Rossetti by the cathedral, and for oysters and mussels Place Garibaldi (Café de Turin) or the port area, which has the cheaper fish restaurants, more frequented by locals than tourists. For a blow-out meal, the Hotel Negresco's highly rated Chantecler restaurant offers a fine eating experience in luxury surroundings at a steep price.

NIGHTLIFE

The 'what's on' magazines (*see 'Mastering the system'*, *above*) list all the shows and concerts in Nice. There are regular opera and classical concerts at the Opera House and occasional rock concerts at the Théâtre de Verdure in Jardin Albert I. Otherwise, you can go for a spin at the roulette tables or watch a cabaret show at Casino Ruhl or sip cocktails in one of the impersonal hotel piano bars. Clubs tend to be exclusive, with their way in guarded by eagle-eyed bouncers on the lookout for status or money.

HOTELS

Many hotels in Nice are disappointing and overpriced, but standards vary a lot. The seafront is dominated by multi-storey upmarket hotels, including the old grandees from the turn of the century. The 'designer style' is popular – co-ordinated pastels are current favourites. Better value, more homely hotels are in the back streets, still close to the sea. The best area for cheap hotels is around the station – but beware fleapits. Street-facing rooms are often noisy. It's advisable to book in advance at all times of year, particularly during high season, Christmas and New Year, and the carnival before Lent.

DURANTE ♦
16 Avenue Durante, 06000   *Tel: 93.88.84.40   Fax: 93.87.77.76*

Most of the rooms have cooking facilities – helpful if you're doing Nice on a budget or want to be able to make a cup of tea. It's a small, rather old-fashioned hotel down a side road near the station. The rooms are decorated with bold, flowery paper and the kitchenettes are hidden behind double wooden doors. Below the shuttered windows lies a pebbled courtyard, where you can have breakfast or write postcards.

Closed: Nov   **Bedrooms:** 26, all with shower/WC; most with kitchenette
Facilities: Lift   **Credit/charge cards accepted:** Visa

Hotel prices Symbols indicate approximate prices per room per night for a double room with bath. Many large hotels run special breaks which work out far cheaper. (See page 14 for further details.)

♦ = under £50; ♦♦ = £50 to £80; ♦♦♦ = £80 to £100;
♦♦♦♦ = £100 to £140; ♦♦♦♦♦ = over £140.

L'OASIS ♦♦
23 Rue Gounod, 06000　　　　　*Tel: 93.88.12.29 Fax: 93.16.14.40*

A jolly come-as-you-are hotel set back from the road, with a tall pine in the pebbled front garden. Swings and table tennis are set up among the flower-beds. What the bright bedrooms lack in size they make up for in cosiness, but the greatest asset is peace and quiet. The breakfast room is decorated in cheerful pastels and is dominated by a curved white breakfast bar. Dried-flower arrangements decorate each table.

Bedrooms: 38, most with bath/WC　**Facilities:** Lift; table tennis; private parking　**Credit/charge cards accepted:** All

LA PEROUSE ♦♦♦
11 Quai Rauba Capeu, 06300　　　　*Tel: 93.62.34.63 Fax: 93.62.59.41*

The scruffy reception in no way prepares you for the unique rooms tucked into the rock walls of the ancient 'château' hill. From this position, the rooms and balconies command a staggering view of the Bay of Angels. Less surprisingly, a room with a view comes at a price. But all the guests have access to the panoramic terraces – the lower one with a small swimming-pool shaded by lemon trees.

Closed: Restaurant closed mid-Sept to mid-May　**Bedrooms:** 65, most with bath/WC; all with air-conditioning; hair-dryer; mini-bar　**Facilities:** Lift; restaurant; unheated outdoor pool　**Credit/charge cards accepted:** All

LE PETIT PALAIS ♦♦♦
10 Avenue Emile Bieckert, 06000　　　　*Tel: 93.62.19.11 Fax: 93.62.53.60*

If you have a car and don't want to be central, the Petit Palais offers a quiet retreat away from the crowds. It's on a smart residential avenue lying on the Cimiez hillside near the Chagall Museum, a good 20 minutes' walk from town. The rooms are modern and well equipped and some have long views over the rooftops of Nice. Outside there is a geranium-fringed patio where breakfast is served.

Bedrooms: 25, all with bath/shower/WC　**Facilities:** Lift; private parking **Credit/charge cards accepted:** All

VENDÔME ♦♦
26 Rue Pastorelli, 06000   *Tel: 93.62.00.77   Fax: 93.13.40.78*

Modern design has knocked on the door of this imposing belle époque villa and transformed it into a comfortable hotel. The old mouldings around the ceiling have been highlighted in fresh pinks and blues, contrasting with pale yellow walls. These pastel colours seep into some of the newly renovated rooms. The small green salon is more traditional, with period furniture and a crystal chandelier.

Bedrooms: 56, most with bath/WC, 4 with shower/WC; air-conditioning; hair-dryer; mini-bar   **Facilities:** Lift; private parking   **Credit/charge cards accepted:** All

WESTMINSTER CONCORDE ♦♦♦♦♦
27 Promenade des Anglais, 06000   *Tel: 93.88.29.44   Fax: 93.82.45.35*

A staid, old timer of a hotel with considerable sea-front style – one of the oldest in Nice. But it's still fresh and bright from its ice-cream pink façade to its modern bedroom facilities (though some bedrooms are in need of refurbishment). A warmly decorated restaurant opens out on to the promenade terrace in the summer. The breakfast room is of ballroom proportions, its mouldings picked out in gold. Leading off the reception are two tiny salons, one Victorian-style, one Chinese.

Bedrooms: 105, all with bath/WC; air-conditioning; mini-bar   **Facilities:** Lift; restaurant   **Credit/charge cards accepted:** All

WINDSOR ♦♦♦
11 Rue Dalpozzo, 06000   *Tel: 93.88.59.35   Fax: 93.88.94.57*

Book a room overlooking the garden, as those on the Rue du Mar. Joffre are noisy. The hotel is a few blocks from the sea-front. Relaxing rooms have been decorated by contemporary artists. Breakfast is served in the garden under a jungle of green palms. The elegant marble-floored reception has humorous Tintin prints on the staircase to create a stylish but relaxed atmosphere.

Closed: Restaurant closed Sun   **Bedrooms:** 60, half with bath/WC, half with shower/WC; all with air-conditioning; mini-bar   **Facilities:** Lift; restaurant; unheated outdoor pool; gym; sauna; Turkish bath; tropical garden; private parking   **Credit/charge cards accepted:** All

PARIS

- Wonderful sightseeing to suit all tastes
- A stroller's city: amble along the banks of the Seine, through the Tuileries Gardens and up the Champs Elysées. Whatever you choose to do, comfy shoes are essential
- Pavement café terraces make the ideal gallery for watching urban life at its most colourful, vibrant, elegant and French
- Carbuncles or beauty spots? Catch up with the controversial modern architecture – the Louvre Pyramid, another monumental arch, the opera house at Bastille, and the hi-tech science museum complex
- Paris by night offers something for everyone: opera, jazz, discos, strip shows, traditional high-kicking cabaret, or just a special dinner

IS PARIS the world's most beautiful city? Perhaps not. Too many of its great monuments – the Eiffel Tower, Sacré Coeur, Arc de Triomphe, Pompidou Centre – date from the nineteenth and twentieth centuries and are not taken very seriously by high-minded arbiters of beauty. But few would dispute its claim to be the most fun. For over a hundred years Paris has had a reputation as the world's good time capital, ooh-la-la city. It is not just a matter of uproarious high and low life after dark: Paris is for pleasure, whether your idea of pleasure is licking the panes (as the French call window-shopping) of art galleries and the world's top couturiers, trawling department stores, doing the heavy-weight museums, lazing in pavement cafés, strolling the riverside embankments beneath chestnut blossom, visiting the latest blockbuster art exhibition, or eating in local bistros or the world's finest restaurants. Or watching Parisians, which is the most fun of all.

Paris is a dense and compact city, short of parks but otherwise ideal for tourists, since most places are within walking distance of each other. A walk along the Seine from the Eiffel Tower in the west to Notre Dame takes less than an hour. Of the main tourist attractions, only the Arc de Triomphe and Montmartre are more than ten minutes' walk from the river.

The Seine is the oldest thoroughfare and the best aid to orientation: a walk along its banks (*quais*) is the simplest, most enjoyable and most effective way to get the hang of the layout of the city and sample the idler side of its charm on a first visit. As well as great buildings, the *quais* are full of incidental charm: chestnut groves, '*bouquinistes*' selling old books and prints from stalls, pet shops on the Quai de la Mégisserie, a flower market on the Ile de la Cité, artists selling their work on the pedestrianised Pont des Arts, couples entwined in a Rodin embrace in the niches of the Pont Neuf, apparently designed for lovers. Leisurely visitors may prefer to take a boat trip along the river – picturesque enough, but not nearly so much fun as strolling, partly because views from the boat are restricted by the river walls. Walking is so enjoyable in Paris that there is a serious danger of overdoing it. Take your most comfortable shoes, and an umbrella.

The original settlement, by people called Parisii in the third century BC, was on an island in mid-stream. The Ile de la Cité remained the heart of Paris as it expanded on both sides of the river, and is the site of Notre Dame and the Law Courts. The Roman city of Lutetia expanded on the left bank near the island, an area which later became the university or 'Latin' quarter, still the focus of student life in Paris. Later, in the Middle Ages,

Parisians drained and settled the boggy land to the north of the islands, still known as the Marais (or marsh). This was the fashionable residential centre of the city in the period before the aristocracy decamped to Louis XIV's new home for the French court at Versailles in the late seventeenth century. It escaped Baron Haussmann's large-scale redevelopment effort in the nineteenth century and over the past three decades has been the object of a huge programme of restoration of its palatial old town houses (known in Paris as *hôtels particuliers* or simply *hôtels*). Its central square, the arcaded brick and gold Place des Vosges, formerly Place Royale, is one of the most beautiful corners of Paris, one of the most fashionable and, increasingly, one of the most touristy. Exploring the revitalised Marais, which has good museums and an increasing number of fashionable shops and restaurants, is one of the great pleasures of a visit to Paris.

The city is divided administratively into 20 *arrondissements*, which spiral clockwise from the centre (the Louvre); the inner coil of the spiral consists of *arrondissements* 1 to 4 on the right bank (and islands), 5 to 7 on the left bank and, back on the right bank, the ultra chic 8th. Every *quartier* has its business, commercial and residential aspects, and a villagey core of food shops, cafés, bistros and usually a weekly open-air food market.

The Seine divides the city into unequal right and left bank halves, the larger right bank conjuring up ideas of solid establishment values and classic elegance. The left bank has vaguely alternative avant-garde connotations, the home of radical intellectuals, student rioters and artists. The distinction no longer means much, but the idea persists and the atmosphere on the two sides of the river is undoubtedly different.

At the heart of the capital, the Ile de la Cité is for sightseeing, its neighbour the Ile St-Louis a quiet backwater with several good hotels in a perfectly central location. On the left bank, the student quarter around St-Michel is now a bit anonymous and American-ised with shops full of denim and leather and a succession of fast-food restaurants on Boulevard St-Michel. Ethnic restaurants (Greek and Vietnamese, mainly) and cheap accommodation lie to the east of the 'Boul Mich'. To the west lie St-Germain-des-Prés and the Faubourg St-Germain, a more fashionable and very lively area with excellent shops, restaurants, cafés and hotels. To the west of Les Invalides, Louis XIV's home for ex-soldiers best known as the repository of Napoleon, there is little to attract the tourist except the Eiffel Tower, erected as (in Eiffel's words) a 300-metre flag-pole for the centenary of the Revolution in 1889.

On the right bank, the great artery of visitor's Paris is the Rue de Rivoli, which runs from the Marais past the Hôtel de Ville, the

Louvre and the Tuileries Gardens to the Place de la Concorde, named in optimism after thousands had been guillotined there in the 1790s, and planted with an obelisk from Luxor. Other views from the Rue de Rivoli lead up to the spectacularly brassy nineteenth-century opera house; the eighteenth-century Place Vendôme, the most beautiful square in Paris, at the heart of the area of the smartest shops and hotels; and the Madeleine, a neo-classical church built in the style of a Greek temple.

For shoppers, strollers and museum-goers alike, the Tuileries Gardens provide welcome space and chance for a rest, and the enjoyable spectacle of Parisians at play in time-honoured fashion – red-faced tracksuited men at boules, ever-hopeful Polaroid touts pestering tourists, children sailing remote-control boats in the fishponds and playing hide-and-seek behind the beautiful nude sculptures. Less visited and equally charming are the gardens tucked away behind the colonnaded courtyard of the Palais Royal, which was Cardinal Richelieu's home and only briefly a royal palace. Modern ball-bearing fountains and black and white humbug-striped columns add a contemporary touch. The beautiful eighteenth-century arcades surrounding the gardens shelter all sorts of intriguing shops.

From Concorde the Champs Elysées climbs gradually towards Napoleon's Arc de Triomphe. It is a majestic avenue, especially at night when the arch is lit up and the two carriageways are aflame with red and yellow car lights. The bottom half, favourite strolling and dancing grounds in the nineteenth century, is still garden. West of the Rond Point, the Champs Elysées is more businesslike, a succession of cinemas, airline offices, car showrooms and expensive pavement cafés, by no means the most elegant shopping street in Paris, as many visitors tend to assume.

To the east of the Arc de Triomphe stands the 129-metre hill of Montmartre, crowned by the exotic male and female tower and domes of the basilica of Sacré Coeur, built to commemorate the Prussian siege of Paris in 1870-1 and, after the Eiffel Tower, the most familiar spectacle of the Parisian skyline. It is not just the Sacré Coeur that pulls tourists by the hundreds of coachloads to Montmartre, nor even the views from its terrace, but the village's role as the home of impoverished artists of the late nineteenth century, as portrayed in *La Bohème*, and its reputation for cheap bistros and singing and dancing in the cafés. The hilltop village of Montmartre has lost none of its charming good looks but has become seriously touristy, and restaurants need to be chosen with care. At the centre of it all is the Place du Tertre, surely the most painted square in the world. It is still full of artists, but few of them can be impoverished at the rates they charge for a two-minute charcoal portrait sketch. If visiting Montmartre by day, take the métro to Anvers and go straight up to Sacré Coeur by the staircase or funicular. At the foot of Montmartre is Pigalle, famed worldwide for its cabaret and sex shows. The cancan is still alive and kicking, largely thanks to visiting tourists.

The idea that all is traditional and unchanging on the right bank of the Seine is belied by the startling amount of exciting and unashamedly controversial modern architecture: the Palais des Omnisports at Bercy, the opera house on the Place de la Bastille, President Pompidou's cultural centre at Beaubourg, which attracts more tourists than the Eiffel Tower and the Louvre combined, and the neighbouring redevelopment of the old food market, Les Halles, most of which consists of an underground shopping centre. No less controversial was the erection of a tall glass and steel pyramid in the central courtyard of the Louvre, as a gateway to the great museum.

Other striking new architectural complexes include two high-rise colonies on the fringes of the city: Front de Seine to the west of the Eiffel Tower, and the business centre of La Défense, which boasts a monumental arch twice the size of the Arc de Triomphe to complete (for the moment anyway) the perspective from the Louvre Pyramid. If the restorers of old buildings and the drivers of sanitary poop-scooping motorbikes have done a wonderful job cleaning up the face of Paris in the last generation, the architects and their presidential patrons have transformed it. No European city has so much of interest for the student of modern architecture, nor so much modern architecture that engages the interest of those who claim to have none.

WHEN TO GO

If planning a long weekend, take time off at the beginning of the weekend rather than the end: Monday is a general closing day for local shops; Monday or Tuesday for museums. Paris is at its most beautiful in spring. The busiest periods are when there are fashion shows and other trade gatherings, usually in April, May, June, September and October. One of the biggest celebrations is on 14 July, Bastille Day, with fireworks and general festivity. The city is relatively empty in August and at Easter, when many shops and restaurants in residential *quartiers* close.

Mastering the System

Information The French Government Tourist Office at 178 Piccadilly, London W1V 0AL, tel: 071-493 5174, has a public information service. In Paris, the main Office du Tourisme is at 127 Champs Elysées, near the Arc de Triomphe. It's open 9am to 8pm daily. There is a same-day hotel reservation service (small charge). Other tourist information offices can be found at main stations. The weekly *Pariscope* and *Officiel des Spectacles* have lists of shows and exhibitions.

Sightseeing tours There are several rival boat trip fleets, of which the most celebrated are the Bateaux Mouches, based at the Point de l'Alma. Others go from the Pont Neuf (Ile de la Cité) and the Pont d'Iéna (Eiffel Tower). There are also bus tour agencies for excursions and city tours, but a cheaper alternative is to hop on an ordinary bus. Good routes include 69 (Eiffel Tower, Invalides, Musée d'Orsay, Louvre and Bastille), 67 (Montmartre, Palais Royale, Louvre and across Ile St-Louis), and 73 (Champs Elysées, linking La Défense and Musée d'Orsay). Routes are clearly marked on stops and the sides of buses, and a recorded voice usually announces each stop.

The cost of visiting museums and sights can soon add up. If you plan to see three or more museums in one day, it's worth buying a museum card. There are also three-day and five-day cards – useful for returning to museums if you are overwhelmed by their size on your first visit. Not all sights are included – you'll still have to pay for the Eiffel Tower, for example. Museums are often cheaper at weekends.

Maps and guides The *Michelin Green Guide* to Paris is an excellent sightseeing companion and contains enough maps for sightseeing purposes; the accompanying *Red Guide* lists hotels and restaurants. Michelin also produces a street atlas (blue) in book form.

Changing money Many banks do not change money, so look for a sign (*Change*) before queueing. Banks generally open 9am to 4.30pm, and close on the afternoon before a public holiday. Outside banking hours you can change money at the Gare de Lyon until 11pm and at the Union des Banques on the Champs Elysées near the main tourist office until 8pm. There are bureaux de change at main stations and in the St-Michel/Odéon area; the rates they offer vary significantly and are not always worse than in a bank. There is also a bureau de change open every day at the Science Museum in the Parc de la Villette.

Telephoning Coin-operated call boxes have mostly been replaced by a phonecard system. Phoning from a café is the simplest

GETTING THERE

Going independently

By air There's a good choice of flights to Paris – at least 20 out of Heathrow on each weekday, for example, and direct flights from more than 15 other UK airports. The service is slightly reduced at weekends. The cheapest fare bookable is almost always the APEX or SuperAPEX (book 7 or 14 days in advance), which has no seasonal variation; you can fly to Paris from London for around £100 return. British Airways and Air France are the main carriers but others include British Midland, London City Airways, Brymon European and Air UK. Air Europe's fare from Stansted was the lowest at the time of writing and is well worth checking. The flight to Paris from London takes an hour.

Charles de Gaulle Airport This is the Paris airport, used by international flights, at Roissy-en-France, north of Paris. It's an ultra-modern complex, with reasonable facilities and shops; the exposed moving walkways which link various levels are fun for children and adults alike.

The simplest way to get to or from central Paris is the RER underground directly to Gare du Nord, Châtelet, St-Michel and beyond, with connections to the inner métro network (for which you need a *billet combiné*). On the way out to the airport, do not ask for a ticket to Charles de Gaulle (confused with Étoile) but Roissy-Aéroport. Not all trains on the northbound RER line go to Roissy but display boards on the platforms are fairly unambiguous. There is also an Air France bus service, not reserved for Air France travellers, from CdG Airport to Porte Maillot and Étoile. This is a pleasant way to travel but can be very slow at rush hours; it's also more expensive.

By sea If time isn't critical, you could consider going by sea. There are various ways of getting to Paris other than by air, using a combination of either ferry or hovercraft and coach or train. British Rail (ferry and train via Calais or Dieppe) and Hoverspeed (hovercraft and train via Boulogne) have five-day return fares from London to Paris which cost just over half the airfare price. National Express return fare using ferry and coach via Calais is also good value. The quickest journey is by hovercraft and train, which takes five and a half hours; coach and ferry takes between eight and nine hours.

For car drivers, the quickest sea crossing is Dover/Calais (35 minutes by hovercraft, 75 minutes by ferry), and from Calais it's 180 miles to Paris. The nearest port to Paris is Dieppe (122 miles); but the motorway route from Caen (150 miles) can work out quicker.

alternative – a bit more expensive than from post offices but much cheaper than from hotel bedrooms.

GETTING AROUND

The *Grand Plan de Paris* published by RATP (the transport authority) shows RER, métro and bus routes and is available free of charge from métro stations.

The **underground** (métro) is an efficient and cheap way of getting around the city. Paris has 15 underground lines and four suburban lines (RER) crossing the capital and linking up with the métro. One ticket covers any journey regardless of length, except on the RER outside the central area. Tickets are most cheaply bought in books of ten (*un carnet*), for about £4.50. Bought singly, tickets cost nearly double (about 70p a trip). Special passes for unlimited use on buses and tubes for various durations (from one day) can be bought at most métro stations and are possibly worthwhile if you are forever hopping on and off the métro or buses. More likely, you'll find you use only a couple of tickets a day and do the rest on foot: central Paris is that compact. So a *carnet* of tickets between two may well be enough for a short visit.

There's no need to hang on to your ticket once you're in the system, except on the RER lines where tickets have to be pushed through the machines on the way out as well as in.

Despite the large number of lines you rarely have to change more than once. A few stations have displays where routes light up when you press your destination station's button. When changing trains, follow the sign '*Correspondances*' and then look for the name of the station at the end of the line you need. It can happen that you are offered two lines going to the same terminus (Nation, for example) by different routes. Unless you are bound for Nation itself, you will need to establish whether you want Nation via (*par*) Barbes Rochechouart (the northern route), or Nation via Denfert Rochereau (south). Another trap is Charles de Gaulle, the official name for what tourists and Parisians alike call Étoile. If you want a ticket for the RER to the airport of that name, specify *aéroport* or Roissy-en-France, not just 'Charles de Gaulle'.

Buses are less easy to master and more expensive than the métro unless you buy passes valid for the whole RATP system. Tickets are the same as for the métro, but for all but the shortest journeys you need two. If you have to change buses you pay again. Tickets can also be bought on the bus.

Taxis can be hailed in the street (if both of their two roof lights are on, they are free), or ordered by telephone. Although they are good value for short journeys (except in the rush-hour), calling one to your hotel can work out expensive – it may have clocked up around 35F by the time it arrives. And if a taxi driver carries your luggage, he'll charge 5F per bag.

UNMISSABLES

The Louvre

The world's richest museum, formerly the royal palace, has been reorganised to make it more of a pleasure and less of a slog to visit. Access and infrastructure have been greatly improved by the creation of an underground entrance hall and commercial area beneath the main Cour Napoleon, lit by and entered through the controversial glass pyramid. The new central area, which has shops, a café and a good restaurant, also improves communication between the different sections of the enormous museum, variously devoted to painting, sculpture, antiquities and *objets d'art*.

First-time visitors will want to see the museum's most famous masterpieces – the *Mona Lisa*, the *Winged Victory of Samothrace* and the *Venus de Milo* among others. There are leaflets which explain the layout of the museum and pinpoint the star exhibits. There is no question of seeing everything in one visit, so itineraries must be planned and some selectivity employed.

Apart from the Salle des États, which houses the *Mona Lisa* and many other masterpieces of the Italian Renaissance, the highlights are probably the collection of French works from the Revolutionary and Romantic periods (late eighteenth and early nineteenth centuries: David, Géricault, Delacroix, Ingres), Rubens' series of 21 paintings celebrating the life of Marie de Médicis, and the main long gallery's collection of medieval and early Renaissance Italian paintings. For something completely different try the oriental antiquities section, with its towering relief sculptures from the royal palaces of Nineveh. The walls, well and moat of the original medieval fortress, found during excavations for the controversial pyramid, are also on display.

Musée d'Orsay

This turn-of-the-century station and hotel on the left bank of the Seine opposite the Louvre has been converted into a museum of French art from 1848 (where the Louvre's coverage stops) to 1914, and includes the collection of Impressionist paintings previously housed in the Jeu de Paume Museum in the Tuileries Gardens. There is far more to the museum – Rodin's sculpture, art nouveau glass and furniture, architecture and urban redevelopment in the 1860s, for example – than the Impressionists, and if you follow the orthodox chronological route you risk being footsore and visually saturated before reaching them. The museum restaurant occupies the sumptuous old ballroom and does a good self-service cold buffet and wine. There are splendid views over the Seine, the Tuileries and Paris from the top-floor terrace, and through the glass of the station clock. There's an audio-guide in English.

Pompidou Centre

The main interest inside the building is the Modern Art Museum, which takes up French art where Orsay stops, with fauvism (Matisse) and cubism (Picasso, Braque) at the beginning of the twentieth century. The museum is bright, spacious and uncrowded and has a good system of explanatory notes in each room and outdoor terraces giving good views over the Parisian skyscape and the teeming plaza below.

Notre Dame

One of the first (late twelfth-century) and most beautiful Gothic cathedrals is perfectly sited with its south side and buttresses mirrored in the waters of the Seine and lit by searchlights from passing *bateaux mouches* (though its south wing is currently covered in scaffolding). There are fine sculptures on the west end and transept doorways; and the gardens to the back give good views of the apse. The interior soars in harmonious and typically Gothic fashion. If you're feeling strong, tackle the arduous ascent of the towers (a narrow staircase and an entrance charge) for views of Paris and fascinating close-range inspection of the roof and gargoyles.

The Eiffel Tower

Going up the 300-metre tower is an excellent way to get an overview of the city. You can walk only as far as the second floor (about 700 steps), less than halfway up. Those without a head for heights may find the stairs a disconcertingly airy experience, but they are well caged and there is no danger of falling out. The struts of the Tower are decorated with trivia about events such as people riding up on motor bikes. The top viewing platform is now accessible only by lift. Tickets for the top lift are dispensed from machines – go armed with plenty of 5- and 10-franc coins –

as well as from the ticket office. The stairs are closed before the lifts at the end of the day, which means annoyingly long queues for a compulsory lift ride down to terra firma.

There is food and drink at both intermediate levels, a film show and an expensive gourmet restaurant (the Jules Verne) on level one. Dining inside the fabric of the Tower and surveying Paris by night has great appeal, until you realise this is the one place in central Paris from which the illuminated Eiffel Tower is not visible, and that the night skyline without it is not much to write home about.

OTHER PLACES TO VISIT

Museums

Les Invalides: Musée de l'Armée/Napoleon's tomb One of the world's great military museums, in a palatial old soldiers' home built in the late seventeenth century under Louis XIV and dominated by a magnificent domed church, was spectacularly repainted with gold leaf for the bicentenary of the Revolution. After the Revolution the Eglise du Dome became a military necropolis and the interior was rebuilt to give pride of place beneath the dome to Napoleon's porphyry tomb.

Hurried tourists may be frustrated that there are not separate tickets for tomb and museum, and that the tomb cannot be glimpsed from the door. Those with no interest in war or museums may find the presentation old-fashioned, with minimal labelling on the collections of old armour and weapons, costumes, campaign plans, models, and photographs of recent warfare.

Musée de Cluny (Place Paul Painlevé; Métro St-Michel) Medieval art – tapestries, illuminated books of hours, devotional sculpture and church treasures – are displayed in a late fifteenth-century palace, one of the oldest town houses in Paris.

The house was originally built by the Burgundian abbey of Cluny, on the site of Gallo-Roman baths; extensive ruins of the hot and cold bathrooms form part of the visit. The highlight of the museum is the chamber containing a series of tapestries representing the five senses.

Musée Picasso (Rue de Thorigny; Métro St-Paul or St-Sebastien Froissart) This is one of the oldest and most beautiful palaces in the Marais, restored to house Picasso's collection of his own and other artists' works, presented to the state instead of death duties. The works of art are accompanied and illuminated by biographical details and photographs, making this a fascinating tribute and insight into Picasso's life and work.

Musée Rodin (Rue de Varenne; Métro Varenne) Sculptures and drawings by the Michelangelo of the nineteenth century are made all the more enjoyable for their setting in a beautiful eighteenth-century palace and gardens, between Les Invalides and the Musée d'Orsay.

Cité des Sciences (Métro Porte de la Villette) The national science museum is one of the main ingredients of a grand redevelopment of an area of canals and old abattoirs in run-down north-eastern Paris into a zone of recreation and education, with playgrounds, exhibition halls, concert halls, conservatory and science museum. The project is not complete and worth a visit only if you are interested in urban redevelopment or in the museum itself, which is imaginative in design and presentation and has masses of gadgets for technologically minded visitors to fiddle with. There's an audio-guide in English.

The star attraction of La Villette is an apparently floating orb (La Géode) outside the museum, reflecting its moat and the cityscape in its mirror shell and containing a revolutionary cinematic experience with a screen of 1,000 square metres. You usually have to book several hours in advance for a seat. If the visitors' book is anything to go by, the films shown (throughout the day until 9pm) are as banal as the technique is innovative.

Churches

Paris is not primarily a city for church sightseeing, and most tourists will limit themselves to the two showpieces on the Ile de la Cité: Notre Dame (*see 'Unmissables'*) and the **Sainte Chapelle**. This is Louis IX's two-storey royal chapel, built in the early thirteenth century to house the Crown of Thorns, in the courtyard of the then royal palace and now the Law Courts. The architecture of the upper chapel is a flimsy framework for the oldest and most beautiful stained glass in Paris.

St-Germain-des-Prés (Métro St-Germain-des-Prés) is the impos-ing part-Romanesque church of a powerful Benedictine abbey, its eleventh-century tower the centrepiece of an animated café-flanked crossroads, the hub of arty *rive gauche* Paris. The inside is less beautiful than out, sombrely painted in the nineteenth century and hung with a series of dreary paintings.

Other notable churches include: **St-Paul-St-Louis**, a seventeenth-century Jesuit church on the edge of the Marais, with a statue of the Virgin by Pilon (sixteenth century); **St-Germain l'Auxerrois**, a late Gothic/Renaissance church opposite the eastern façade of the Louvre, with beautiful fifteenth-century porch; **St-Eustache**, a cathedral-sized Gothic/Renaissance church at Les Halles revealed by the demolition of the old food market, with many beautiful tombs and paintings; the **Panthéon** (eighteenth-century), a huge cruciform neo-classical temple on the hill near the top of the Boulevard St-Michel, built to house the reliquary of Paris's patroness Geneviève and later transformed into a heroes' pantheon – a fine dome on the skyline but not a very rewarding visit; **St-Etienne-du-Mont**, Renaissance church near the Panthéon, with carved stone choir screen of wonderful delicacy; **St-Séverin**, a broad Gothic church tucked away in the Greek restaurant area near Boulevard St-Michel, with double ambulatory and a forest of pillars; **St-Sulpice**, vast seventeenth/eighteenth-century church between St-Germain-des-Prés and Luxembourg, with Delacroix murals in the first chapel on the right. (*See also 'St-Denis', under 'Excursions'.*)

Other attractions

La Grande Arche (RER La Défense) Those interested in modern architecture and the changing face of Paris will place La Défense high on the list of priorities – a monumental focus to the already interesting, if to many minds unsuccessful, high-rise business/shopping precinct. The arch, a cube with a hole, has offices in its walls and houses an international foundation of human rights in its roof space. The external lift ride is fun but neither the exhibition on human rights nor the view from the roof terrace is outstanding. The arch itself completes the perspective from the Louvre via the Place de la Concorde and the Arc de Triomphe. Huge though it is (110 metres), the arch is dominated by the even taller office towers of La Défense: the Fiat and Elf buildings reach nearly 180 metres.

Jardin des Plantes Or, more to the point, des Animaux. For this is Paris's most popular zoo, a favourite place for a family outing on a sunny Sunday afternoon. The Menagerie is surrounded by botanical gardens and a small park, first landscaped in the seventeenth century and currently under restoration. The Rue Mouffetard, one of the most animated and picturesque of Parisian shopping streets, is within easy walking distance.

Montparnasse Tower (Métro Montparnasse Bienvenue) You can travel by lift, at ear-popping speed, to the 56th floor where there is a café and photos of the tower under construction (1971-3), and then on foot to the 57th, a roof terrace with a view of Paris.

Père Lachaise (Métro Père Lachaise; open every day dawn to dusk). This is France's most illustrious graveyard, covering a broad hillside in a far from salubrious part of eastern Paris. The celebrity tombs include Alfred de Musset's, with his valedictory verse: 'Plant a willow in the cemetery'. Others include Abelard and Héloise in a big nineteenth-century Gothic tabernacle in the bottom right corner; Edith Piaf in the top right corner, near the wall against which the last 140 rebel Communards were executed in 1871 after an all-night battle among the tombstones; Oscar Wilde; Chopin; and a splendid tomb for the painter Theodore Géricault, with relief sculptures of three of his most famous paintings.

Samaritaine department store (Rue de Rivoli, not far upstream from the Louvre) Combine shopping, eating and sightseeing by visiting the roof terrace (with café) of shop 2, not a high vantage point for surveying the city, but a perfectly central one, with a gorgeous panorama of the Seine, the Ile de la Cité, left-bank riverside façades, Montmartre and the Pompidou Centre.

Sewers (Les Egouts; Métro Alma) This fashionable alternative Parisian excursion has plenty of interesting historical information about the growth of the city and its sanitary problems and the work still under way to clean up the Seine. Closed Thursday and Friday. Take a clothes peg!

Trocadéro The terrace between the wings of the graceless pre-war Palais de Chaillot gives a classic view of the Eiffel Tower with fountains and the Seine in the foreground. The terraces and garden paths by the fountains are a favourite place for acrobatic skateboarders, roller skaters and pickpockets and where, for the centenary of the Eiffel Tower in 1989, someone walked a tightrope, without net or safety rope, from the Trocadéro to one of the middle stages of the Eiffel Tower.

Excursions

Few first-time short-stay visitors to Paris will feel the need to stray far from the city centre, still less venture outside the embrace of the Boulevard Périphérique. But for those that do there are regular excursions: information is available from your hotel or the tourist office at 127 Champs Elysées.

Bois de Boulogne (Métro Porte Dauphine, Porte Maillot, Ave Henri Martin, Porte d'Auteuil) The Bois is predominantly *transpériphérique*, although it is within walking distance of the Trocadéro. As woods go it is not particularly beautiful, but on a hot day it offers a welcome escape from city noise and dust. Avoid it after dark, however, as it is also a gathering place for drug-abusers, transvestites and prostitutes. In the southern corners of the Bois are Paris's two racecourses: Auteuil (steeple-chases) and Longchamp (flat racing). There are train rides and other amusements for children in the *jardin d'acclimatation* near Porte Maillot.

Versailles (Trains from Montparnasse, or RER from left bank stations – St-Michel, Invalides, Orsay, Pont de l'Alma etc.) Louis XIV's enormous palace, *trianons* (out-palaces) and park was home of the French court for the century preceding the Revolution. There's an audio-guide in English for the main visit to the Chapel and Grands Appartements.

Fontainebleau (Trains from Gare de Lyon, and a short bus ride or a long walk – mostly through the park if you take the Avenue des Carosses) The royal palace and hunting base built for François I (sixteenth century) was decorated by Florentine artists. Less daunting in scale than Versailles and more varied in decoration, it has sections from all periods from Renaissance to Empire (Napoleon). Beautiful gardens and spectacularly bloated carp in the water near the château.

St-Denis (Métro St-Denis-Basilique) This unlovely northern suburb of the capital was where Denis – the first bishop of Paris – was beheaded in 250. The great church that marks the place, built in the early twelfth century, is usually identified as the first fully fledged example of Gothic architecture. For all but specialists, the architecture is of secondary interest to the basilica's role as a French royal necropolis. Many of the tombs are exceptionally beautiful, especially the elaborate Renaissance tombs of Louis XII, François I and Henri II and their queens.

SHOPPING

Food and kitchen gadgets make fine souvenirs, and high quality can be found in shops large and small throughout the city. Since the demolition of the old central market at Les Halles, the most interesting food markets are the weekly ones (often on Sunday mornings) set up in many *quartiers* – on the Avenue President Wilson between Alma and Trocadéro, for example. Of the permanent food markets, the most picturesque are in Rue de Buci (St-Germain-des-Prés) and Rue Mouffetard (Métro Censier Daubenton).

The big department stores – including Galeries Lafayette and Au Printemps on Boulevard Haussmann, and Samaritaine at Pont Neuf – have good household departments. There is a concentration of luxury food shops near the Madeleine, in particular Fauchon and Hédiard, which sell almost anything, including foie gras, honey, cakes, chocolates, mustard and wine.

Many of the international couturiers (Nina Ricci, Ungaro, Christian Dior) are based on the Avenue Montaigne, between Alma and the Rond Point des Champs Elysées, and nearby streets. Others are on the Rue du Faubourg St-Honoré/Rue St-Honoré (near Concorde). Newer stars in the Paris fashion firmament tend to set up elsewhere, most recently in the Marais and on or near the very trendy Place des Victoires (near Palais Royal) which has several expensive designer shops (Kenzo, Thierry Mugler).

If you're more interested in buying than window-shopping, try the St-Germain-des-Prés/Rue de Rennes area, or any main shopping street in a prosperous part of town (Rue St-Dominique, Avenue Victor Hugo, Avenue de Villiers, Rue du Commerce, Rue de Passy and hundreds of others); one of the big shopping centres (Forum des Halles, La Défense); or the department stores (including C&A and Marks & Spencer) on Boulevard Haussmann near Opéra.

The big names in china, porcelain and glass (Christofle, Lalique, Baccarat, Limoges-Unic) are in the 8th *arrondissement* (Rue Royale) and the 10th (Rue de Paradis). For art, Avenue Matignon is the Bond Street of Paris. Walk from Alma to the Place Vendôme (Avenue Montaigne, Avenue Matignon and Rue du Faubourg St-Honoré, Rue St-Honoré) for the classic window-shopping experience, combining *haute couture* and paintings. The other main art gallery zone is around Boulevard St-Germain/Place St-Sulpice.

Good areas for antique-hunting include Rue du Cherche Midi (south of Boulevard St-Germain, Métro Sèvres Babylone); Rue du Faubourg St-Honoré; streets between St-Germain-des-Prés and the river; Le Louvre des Antiquaires (Rue de Rivoli); Village Suisse (Avenue de Suffren, near Ecole Militaire). The *haute couture* jewellery shops are concentrated in the Rue de la Paix, between Place Vendôme and Opéra.

Paris is a treasure trove of specialist boutiques; there are shops which sell hand-painted lingerie, '50s *objets d'art*, 250 varieties of tea, or nothing but olive oils. The Marais is a good area for browsing and buying – particularly in and around Rue des Francs Bourgeois – as are the back streets of St-Germain-des-Prés.

The main Paris flea market (Marché aux Puces) is open for business on Saturday, Sunday and Monday. There is a vast range of junk on sale, as well as increasing amounts of unremarkable clothes and souvenirs.

EATING AND DRINKING

In Paris, you can find the finest cooking in the world; you can also suffer bad-value and very disappointing eating experiences. Serious gastronomes will not need to be pointed in the direction of Alain Senderens of Lucas Carton and Joël Robuchon of Jamin. The Red Michelin and Gault Millau guides are the best known; good budget guides are *Paris Pas Cher* and *Le Guide du Routard*, available from most bookshops.

In Paris, the foods of all French regions can be sampled. Wonderfully fresh shellfish arrives from Brittany every morning, and the open-air oyster counter can be seen outside many restaurants and cafés. There are plenty of places which specialise in foie gras, *choucroute* (sauerkraut), pigs' trotters and *bouillabaisse*. Parisian restaurants are also much more cosmopolitan than those in provincial France, and there are good restaurants for Vietnamese, North African, Jewish and Russian cooking. You can eat a full meal at any time of the day or night in some places – traditionally the brasseries (restaurants-cum-cafés), for which Paris is famous; many of these have recently been restored to their full gilt and mirrored beauty, and make a splendidly atmospheric place for a late dinner.

Locals in a rush prop up the bar in cafés and knock back *un bock* (a smaller glass of beer than *un demi*) or a morning *café-calva* (coffee with apple brandy). Tourists and those in less of a hurry sit at tables where drinks prices are higher and also include a service charge. Most cafés serve snacks: sandwiches (long sections of French bread underfilled with ham, cheese or *mixte*); *croque-monsieur* (grilled ham and cheese on bread; *croque-madame* has an egg on top); maybe an omelette or a *plat du jour*. *Un café* is a small black espresso coffee, *un (café) crème* is a white coffee, also small unless you specify *un grand crème*. If you take milk in tea, specify *thé au lait*.

Some cafés offer substantial meals in wonderful settings. Two of the most famous are Les Deux Magots (St-Germain-des-Prés), for hot chocolate and croissants; and La Coupole (Boulevard du Montparnasse, 14e), which doubles as a restaurant, and has dancing (waltzes and tangos) in the basement.

Recommendations for expensive restaurants are relatively easy to come by; good cheaper places are more difficult to find. The following list is recommended with a limited budget in mind: Aquarius (Rue Ste-Croix-de-la-Bretonnerie, 4e), Batifol (Rue Mondétour, le), Les Beaux Arts (Rue Bonaparte, 6e), Brasserie Bofinger (Rue de la Bastille, 4e), Aux Charpentiers (Rue Mabillon, 6e), Chartier (Rue de Faubourg-Montmartre, 9e), Chez Jean l'Aubergnat (Rue Lamartine, 9e), Diapason (Rue des Bernadins, 5e), Au Franc Pinot (Quai de Bourbon, 4e), La Gueuze (Rue Soufflot, 5e), Lescure (Rue de Mondovi, 1e), Au Monde des Chimeres (Rue St-Louis-en-l'Ile, 4e), Michel Courtalhac (Rue de Bourgogne, 7e), Le Temps de Cerises (Rue de la Cerisaie, 4e).

For great ice-cream, Berthillon (Rue St-Louis-en-l'Ile, 4e) is the place to go. Le Flore en l'Ile (Quai d'Orléans, 4e) serves good hot chocolate.

NIGHTLIFE

Cinema-going is the preferred nightlife of Parisians. There are lots of undubbed English/American films (look for the label 'VO', *version originale*), and several cinemas specialise in revived classics.

Paris has an old and a new opera house. The old is a supremely ornate late nineteenth-century palace at the top of the Avenue de l'Opéra (which can be visited on guided tours), the new is a huge complex of auditoria on the Place de la Bastille. The building and staffing of the new opera house was beset with many difficulties, and it opened for business to loud cries that its stages were oversized and its seats overpriced.

There are free classical concerts in churches in summer and live jazz in many places – including several in the Rue des Lombards, and in the Latin Quarter. Discos and nightclubs come and go so it's best to consult one of the weekly 'what's on' publications.

Bars stay open till the early hours; some of the most famous and sophisticated are in hotels, such as the Ritz, Crillon, or the rather eccentric left-bank L'Hotel. One which remains popular with Americans and Britons (as well as Parisians) is Harry's Bar (Rue Daunou, near the Opéra).

Theatre is probably of marginal interest to most tourists; an international musical may be more tempting: the Théâtre des Champs Elysées is the best bet. Serious students of French literature, though, may want to sample the more classic formality of a Racine or a Molière at the Comédie-Française, at the bottom of the Avenue de l'Opéra near the Louvre.

Café-théâtres offer semi-respectable playlets and satirical reviews similar to pub theatres in Britain.

Parisian cabaret shows have long been famous. The classic belle époque high-kicking dance shows are still at the Moulin Rouge (near Place Blanche at the foot of Montmartre), the Lido (on the Champs Elysées) and the Paradis Latin (near the Sorbonne).

All cater predominantly for tourists and business travellers, as does the Crazy Horse Saloon (near the bottom – Alma – end of the Avenue George V), which dispenses with the feathers and the cancan music, relying instead on piped international pop and tall women clothed mainly in coloured light.

In the Place Pigalle/Place Blanche area there are dozens of small theatres with girlie shows as soft or hardcore as you like. Most of those calling themselves cabaret serve expensive drinks rather than charge for entrance and are soft, while the so-called theatres charge an entrance fee, serve no drinks and are hard. Do not assume that going on an organised nightlife bus tour will necessarily be softish. Most agencies feature a so-called 'X tour Forbidden Paris' or words to that effect. For striptease and a traditional Parisian dance show, try the tour described as 'Cabaret plus Moulin Rouge'. At the Lido, Folies Bergères and Moulin Rouge, tops but not bottoms are revealed.

HOTELS

Lively, fashionable, central and the hub of an interesting shopping and sightseeing area, St-Germain-des-Prés is perhaps the best base and has plenty of good small hotels, few of them cheap. The Marais is quieter and cheaper and also has lots of interest, especially in the way of bars and cafés. The Ile St-Louis is much quieter. Many tour operators sell holidays in Paris without confirming a specific hotel reservation at the time of booking. However consistent the quality of their hotels may be, this obviously means taking pot luck with location. Few Parisian hotels below the four-star level have restaurants and many two-star hotels have no public rooms at all, apart from a few breakfast tables squashed into the basement or reception area. Single rooms are not much cheaper than doubles, unless very poky. Economic principles of hotel design result in baths of a length that would cramp Napoleon in many new and recently modernised hotels.

Alternatively, bed and breakfast is on offer from an agency called Tourisme Chez l'Habitant. It's arranged through the UK agency Host and Guest Service, Harwood House, 27 Effie Road, London SW6 1EN, tel: 071-736 5645. You pay an agency fee of £10, and the balance in francs to the French agency. Single rooms start from 175F, doubles from 225F.

ANGLETERRE ♦♦♦♦
44 Rue Jacob, 6ᵉ   *Tel: 42.60.34.72   Fax: 42.60.16.93*

Very near to the heart of St-Germain-des-Prés, in an attractive street of
tiny shops and galleries, this nineteenth-century building was once the
British Embassy. There's an elegant small lounge with a grand piano, a
pretty breakfast room, and a bar area by a tiny central courtyard garden
where you can take a drink. Bedrooms vary in size and style – mostly
traditional and comfortable with old-fashioned elegance and absolute
calm.

Métro: St-Germain-des-Prés **Bedrooms:** 29, all with bath/shower/WC
Facilities: Lift; bar   **Credit/charge cards accepted:** All

DU BOIS ♦♦
11 Rue du Dôme, 16ᵉ   *Tel: 45.00.31.96   Fax: 45.00.90.05*

A welcoming and cheerful small hotel used by several British tour
operators, in a quiet but not inconvenient position on the corner of the
Rue du Dôme and the Avenue Victor Hugo, with its smart clothes shops.
It's only five minutes' walk from the Étoile. The bedrooms are bright and
smartly decorated (a bit noisy on the avenue side); there's a small
breakfast area beside reception. The hotel has no bar and lift, and there's
a staircase up to the entrance.

Métro: Charles de Gaulle Étoile   **Bedrooms:** 41, 23 with bath/shower/WC,
18 with shower/WC; all with mini-bar   **Credit/charge cards accepted:**
Access, Amex, Visa

HOTEL DE LA BRETONNERIE ♦♦
22 Rue Sainte-Croix-de-la-Bretonnerie, 4ᵉ   *Tel: 48.87.77.63   Fax: 42.77.26.78*

A few minutes' walk from the Pompidou Centre and Les Halles in the
relative quiet of the Marais stands this seventeenth-century building, now
a hotel. Bedrooms are mostly a generous size and are decorated with
imagination. The young proprietor takes a real interest, continually
refurbishing and redecorating bedrooms, choosing the colour schemes
herself. As well as the smart beamed reception lounge there is also an
exposed stone breakfast room in the basement with dark wooden
furnishings and smart high-backed padded chairs.

Métro: Hôtel de Ville **Closed:** August **Bedrooms:** 31, most with bath/
shower/WC; all with mini-bar **Facilities:** Lift; bar **Credit/charge cards
accepted:** Access, Visa

CAUMARTIN
27 Rue de Caumartin, 9ᵉ   *Tel: 47.42.95.95   Fax: 47.42.88.19*

Between the Madeleine and the Opéra, a popular hotel with business travellers but friendly and well placed for tourists, especially those with shopping high on the agenda: Au Printemps and the Galeries Lafayette are at the end of the street. Single rooms are very small, but most of the doubles are bright and spacious. Good buffet breakfasts.

Métro: Havre-Caumartin/Aubert   **Bedrooms:** 40, most with bath/WC; hair-dryer; mini-bar   **Facilities:** Lift   **Credit/charge cards accepted:** All

CRILLON
10 Place de la Concorde, 8ᵉ   *Tel: 44.71.15.00   Fax: 44.71.15.02*

The Crillon's eighteenth-century façade is a landmark; it attempts to remain authentically French – all renovations retain or recall the classical elegance of Louis XV. The building itself is beautiful: a stately sequence of salons, a graceful inner courtyard, a grand staircase. However rich the décor, tranquil dignity prevails. Only the famous restaurant (with harpist) is unrestrainedly sumptuous. A jazz pianist plays in the velvety bar. Bedrooms and apartments are vast, peaceful and exquisite.

Métro: Concorde   **Bedrooms:** 163, all with bath/WC; air-conditioning; hair-dryer; mini-bar   **Facilities:** Lift; restaurant; bar   **Credit/charge cards accepted:** All

DEUX ILES ♦♦♦
59 Rue St-Louis-en-l'Ile, 4ᵉ   *Tel: 43.26.13.35   Fax: 43.29.60.25*

In the middle of the island on a narrow street of boutiques and restaurants, this is a seventeenth-century building with balconies, converted into a hotel but retaining the atmosphere of a private house. The combined reception and lounge area is most appealing, and there's a fine sitting-room and bar in the vaulted cellars – particularly cosy in winter when there's a log fire. Bedrooms are not large, but comfortable and charming, decorated with provençal cottons. Garage nearby.

Métro: Pont Marie   **Bedrooms:** 17, 8 with bath/WC, 9 with shower/WC; hair-dryer   **Facilities:** Lift   **Credit/charge cards accepted:** None

> ♦ = under £50; ♦♦ = £50 to £80; ♦♦♦ = £80 to £100;
> ♦♦♦♦ = £100 to £140; ♦♦♦♦♦ = over £140.

L'HÔTEL ♦♦♦♦♦
13 Rue des Beaux Arts, 6ᵉ   *Tel: 43.25.27.22   Fax: 43.25.64.81*

This is an ultra-sophisticated little hotel with unique atmosphere and outrageous prices, in a street once the home of artists and academics. The building's not conspicuous, but bears a plaque commemorating Oscar Wilde – here in 1900 he 'died beyond his means' – and his room has been recreated. Décor is mostly eighteenth and nineteenth century, both reproduction and real – with excursions into cocktail modernity. Bedrooms are plush and padded, in many different styles. The few cheaper (but not cheap) rooms are very cramped.

Métro: St-Germain-des-Prés   **Bedrooms:** 27, 19 with bath/shower/WC, 8 with shower/WC; all with air-conditioning; hair-dryer; mini-bar
Facilities: Lift; restaurant; bar   **Credit/charge cards accepted:** All

LATITUDES ST-GERMAIN ♦♦♦♦
7 Rue St-Benoîst, 6ᵉ   *Tel: 42.61.53.53   Fax: 49.27.09.33*

A bright hotel in an excellent location near St-Germain-des-Prés. There's jazz in the basement bar in the evenings. The bedrooms have cheerful colour-schemes and prints of Paris scenes on the walls, and the breakfast area squeezed in beneath the skylight has a bizarre *trompe-l'oeil* château on the wall. A *grand crème* and a *pain au chocolat* at the Deux Magots café just up the road might be a better bet.

Métro: St-Germain-des-Prés   **Bedrooms:** 117, all with bath/WC; air-conditioning; hair-dryer; mini-bar   **Facilities:** Lift; bar   **Credit/charge cards accepted:** All

MOLIÈRE ♦♦
21 Rue Molière, 1ᵉʳ   *Tel: 42.96.22.01   Fax: 42.60.48.88*

What claims to be the oldest hotel in Paris has been thoroughly smartened up, but the refurbishers have taken care to retain many interesting features of the old building, including a theatre where Voltaire gave unofficial previews of his plays, and the beautiful oval staircase. Bedrooms vary greatly in size. The breakfast room and bar are small and bright. A quiet position in an excellent location for sightseeing, shopping and Molière at the Comédie-Française.

Métro: Palais Royal   **Bedrooms:** 32, 21 with bath/shower/WC, 11 with shower/WC; hair-dryer; mini-bar   **Facilities:** Lift   **Credit/charge cards accepted:** All

PRIMA LEPIC ♦
29 Rue Lepic, 18ᵉ   *Tel: 46.06.44.64   Fax: 46.06.66.11*

If you want a cheap, clean, *bon confort* hotel in Montmartre, the Prima on the Rue Lepic, close to the fleshpots of Pigalle, will do nicely, thank you. It has its drawbacks: it is popular with package tours; demand for breakfast in the make-believe indoor garden (plastic flowers, metal chairs and tables) far exceeds the rate at which it can be supplied; and the operation of the reservations book is not the height of efficiency in our experience. Never mind: good humour prevails. Bed/bathrooms are modernised and cheaply but colourfully decorated. Streetside windows are double glazed.

Métro: Blanche   **Bedrooms:** 38, all with bath/shower/WC; hair-dryer
Facilities: Lift   **Credit/charge cards accepted:** Access, Visa

RÉCAMIER ♦♦
3 bis, Place St-Sulpice, 6ᵉ   *Tel: 43.26.04.89*

Located near the shopping streets of St-Germain-des-Prés, and within walking distance of the student haunts of the Left Bank, the Récamier is a good budget choice of hotel. Bedrooms are quiet and old-fashioned with ubiquitous flowery wallpaper and outmoded, serviceable furniture, and bathrooms are spotless. Some rooms have good views over the square. Breakfast comes included in the price, either served in your room or downstairs in a tiny, plainly decorated breakfast room. As hot drinks are kept warm in individual Thermos flasks, they can taste stewed. You may prefer to forgo the Récamier's offering and breakfast in the local café instead.

Métro: St-Sulpice   **Bedrooms:** 30, 12 with bath/WC, 11 with shower/WC, rest with washbasin/WC   **Facilities:** Lift   **Credit/charge cards accepted:** Access, Visa

Hotel prices Symbols indicate approximate prices per room per night for a double room with bath. Many large hotels run special breaks which work out far cheaper. (See page 14 for further details.)

♦ = under £50; ♦♦ = £50 to £80; ♦♦♦ = £80 to £100;
♦♦♦♦ = £100 to £140; ♦♦♦♦♦ = over £140.

PRAGUE

- Prague is one of the most beautiful cities in Europe, with superb architecture: medieval, Renaissance, baroque and art deco
- It's an ideal place to explore during a long weekend. You can cross the centre on foot in less than an hour
- Magnificent museums include a fine collection of European paintings as well as Bohemian arts and crafts, Jewish museums and a castle
- A new generation of entrepreneurs has seized the commercial opportunities open to it, and new restaurants, bars and beer halls – always an important part of Czech culture – are opening at a dizzying rate. Even the locals find it difficult to keep up

FROM Hradčany Castle on a steep hill above the west bank of the River Vltava the princes and kings of Bohemia could look out over the whole of Prague, a view now enjoyed by anyone working in the presidential office. Far below, the cluttered, red-tiled cityscape is pierced by dark, medieval towers with black angled roofs and pointed turrets. Green baroque spires and domes add colour and their own distinctive shapes to the skyline. Only in the distance does the sun catch the windows of more modern developments on the outskirts of the city.

At the foot of the castle are the long straight streets of Malá Strana, the 'Lesser Quarter', which owes much to the fact that many of its streets and houses were destroyed by fire in the fifteenth and sixteenth centuries, and that in the seventeenth and eighteenth centuries further chunks of the area were knocked down to make room for sumptuous palaces for the church and nobility. Renaissance façades were given baroque face-lifts, formal gardens were laid out on the hillsides. Beautifully restored, many buildings now house embassies, and concerts are held in their gardens. In the main square is the showpiece of that extravagant era – the church of St Nicholas, with its great green dome and towers and its garish interior of pink and green marble.

You cross the river by Charles Bridge. Supported on its span of the Vltava by an irregular series of massive stone piers, the bridge is the oldest link between the two sides of Prague. It was commissioned in 1357 by Charles IV, Holy Roman Emperor and founder of Prague University and St Vitus's Cathedral. Under him Prague prospered as the centre of an empire and the cultural and political capital of Europe. Now the bridge is a concourse for tourists (no cars allowed) studying the parade of blackened statues of agonised saints, one above each pier, or gazing up at the dark medieval towers guarding each end of the bridge. Artists and stallholders add to the bustle, selling paintings and other *objets d'art*. One of the most popular souvenirs with Western tourists is a Yeltsin *matryoska*, which unscrews to reveal a sad Gorbachev, then a grinning Brezhnev and finally a devilish Stalin.

Beyond the bridge is the Old Town, Staré Město. It's a town with a split personality – silent medieval alleyways and brash shopping streets. To the south is Wenceslas Square (Václavské Náměstí) – the now famous scene of the huge public gatherings which were the prelude to the toppling of communist rule. The square is in fact not a square, but a very wide street running up the hill towards the vast nineteenth-century National Museum building.

At the top of the hill is the equestrian statue of King Wenceslas,

Prince of Bohemia until he was murdered by his brother in 929, and now patron saint. With him a Bohemian dynasty with Prague as its capital was founded. The city prospered and wealth from the Bohemian silver lodes boosted Prague's international status. Today the statue of Wenceslas looks out over the commercial heart of Prague. The square is lined with hotels and shops and teems with tourists looking for things to buy. The high-sided buildings are a mixture of old and new – a skyline of alternating domes and pinnacles and advertising hoardings.

In the streets around the heart of the Old Town – Staroměstské Náměstí, or Old Town Square – and towards the river, the feeling is different. There's very little traffic, and the echo of voices, or footsteps on the cobbled pavements, can be heard. The tall buildings are beautiful: the skyline above the streets is shaped by the curves and angles of baroque gables and roofs. Dormer windows, like half-open eyes, peep from under the tiled roofs. Around the windows and balconies are elaborate flurries of decorative plasterwork – curls, ribbons, fruit – usually painted white to contrast with the pastel fronts of the houses. The dominant mood of the architecture is baroque, but there are some interesting art-nouveau buildings – square-shouldered giants 'support' balconies on their backs and topless Egyptians with braided hair are carved in relief on the front of a block of flats.

The Old Town Square has seen troubled times. Many of the buildings which surround the large, irregular space have recently been restored: the rather sugary pastel paint makes them seem slightly too perfect, slightly sanitised. They look out on the large melodramatic memorial to Jan Hus (much influenced by Wycliffe) who was burned at the stake in 1415 for his heretical, reformist views. The movement he inspired spread throughout Bohemia and was suppressed only with great difficulty. The nadir came in 1437, when 57 Hussites were executed in the square. Since then it has seen more executions and more deaths, including those in 1968, when Russian tanks entered the city despite bitter and desperate opposition from the townspeople, an ironic contrast to the warm welcome given to the Soviet troops who liberated Prague in 1945. Dubček, deposed by the Russians in 1968, once more addressed the crowds in Wenceslas Square in 1989.

Prague has produced its fair share of intellectuals and artists. Mozart came to the city frequently (the villa where he stayed is now a museum). He wrote the opera La Clemenza di Tito for the coronation of Emperor Leopold as King of Bohemia, and the première of Don Giovanni was held at the Old Town Theatre (now the Nostitz Theatre). The nineteenth century saw a musical renaissance in Prague. Dvořák and Smetana lived and composed in the city and Janáček studied there. Although he wrote in German, Kafka came from Prague (and is buried there). Almost contemporary with Kafka was Jaroslav Hašek, whose novel *The Good Soldier Švejk* won him an international reputation. Contemporary Prague writers have had mixed fortunes. The novelist Milan Kundera lives in exile, and the once disgraced playwright Václav Havel was Federal President from late 1989 till his resignation in July 1992.

WHEN TO GO

The best time to visit Prague is in spring, when the cherry blossom is out. During the annual music festival from the beginning of May to early June, when concerts are held in historic buildings and Malá Strana Gardens, Prague gets crowded and accommodation has to be booked far in advance. May is sunny and warm – although temperatures can drop below freezing at night between the months of October and April. The summer months are warm and wet, with average daily temperatures of 17°C in June and 18°C in August. Winter can be very cold (February 0.5°C), especially at night.

MASTERING THE SYSTEM

Information The Embassy of the Czech Republic is at 26 Kensington Palace Gardens, London W8 4QY, tel: 071-229 1255. The Prague Information Service has two offices in Prague, at Na Příkopě 20 (tel: 221860) and Staroměstské nám 22 (tel: 224453). Any one of a number of travel agencies in Prague can provide information on guides, city tours, excursions, and tickets for evening entertainment (although much cheaper at box offices) and make bookings for you. Most of these services are also likely to be available from your hotel desk. Pragotur, U Obecního Domu 2, Prague 1, can make last-minute hotel or private-room bookings.

Changing money Money can be changed at banks, hotels and numerous exchange offices all over Prague. You are not allowed to take Czech currency (Kčs/koruna) into or out of the country, but you'll be allowed to change any koruna you don't spend back into hard currency before you leave the country, as long as you can produce exchange receipts.

GETTING THERE

Going independently

By air The choice of flights to Prague is limited compared with many other cities. British Airways and the Czech airline, CSA, provide a once-daily service from Heathrow in winter (BA has two flights on Wednesday, Friday, Saturday and Sunday), and a twice-daily service on most days during the summer. APEX fares (bookable 14 days in advance) are cheapest, but the price varies enormously, depending on the time of year. Several operators offer competitively priced scheduled flights, including Cresta Holidays (061-929 9995), Data Travel (0424-722394), Regent Holidays (0272–211711), Canterbury Travel (081-206 0411) and Flightfile (071-323 1515).

Tour operator packages

A few tour operators offer packages throughout the year; these are generally cheaper than if you make your own arrangements unless you opt for accommodation in a private house. Package prices range from about £300 in low season to £434 in high season for three nights in a three-star hotel. Packages to the Spring Music Festival (you can order tickets, too) cost from £350 for three nights. For a list of tour operators see page 385. Packages which combine Prague with Vienna, Budapest or Moscow are also possible.

Formalities

Visitors who have a full British passport do not need a tourist visa. If one is required, you can obtain it from the Embassy of the Czech Republic at 26 Kensington Palace Gardens, London W8 4QY.

Sightseeing tours Numerous travel agencies, including Čedok, organise city tours by coach or on foot, but do not include museum visits and day excursions to spa towns and Bohemian castles. There are boat trips on the Vltava (the booking office and departure point is near the Palacky Bridge). In summer there are also evening beer-tasting excursions which include a visit to the U Fleků brewery.

Maps For clarity and convenience the Falk Plan, which includes a map of the metro and a useful, large-scale plan of the Old Town, is the best. Sights, hotels and theatres are also marked. We found no map which had up-to-date information on tram lines.

Opening hours and days Shops are generally open from 9am to 8pm (department stores until later), Monday to Friday, and till noon on Saturday, although many shops stay open throughout the weekend. Sights are open from about 10am (some from 8am or 9am) to 5pm, and do not close at lunchtime except in winter. Most close on Monday, except the Jewish Museum, which closes on Saturday, and the Smetana Museum, which closes on Tuesday.

GETTING AROUND

Prague is so compact that you'll probably be able to do most of your sightseeing on foot. Otherwise use the **trams**, or the **metro**, both of which are fast, efficient and very cheap. Tickets are available from your hotel desk, news-stands and tobacconists, or machines in the underground stations. A new tram ticket (costing four koruna) must be clipped each time you board a tram – put the end of the ticket with the numbers on into the black plastic lever on the clipping machines and pull it towards you; once punched it is valid for journeys lasting up to 90 minutes. Tickets are also valid on the metro: buy them from your hotel desk or the machines in the metro station.

There are plenty of **taxis**; you can hire them from ranks or hail them in the street. It's wise to fix a price before you start, or insist that the driver uses his meter. Taxis hired through hotels are much more expensive.

UNMISSABLES

The Old Town – Staré Město

Much of the pleasure of the Old Town is in wandering the streets, discovering quiet squares or watching the street life from a café table. But there are some important sights. Just before the hour you'll see a crowd gathering in front of the clock on the **Old Town Hall**. This complicated astronomical clock, built in 1490, not only tells the time, but the date, feast days, the state of the moon and more. The striking mechanism is famous and amusing. Make sure you watch the clock carefully as the striking begins: Death (a skeleton) pulls the bell rope, across the top of the clock there's a procession of the Apostles, and a cock flaps its wings and crows. Next to the Old Town Hall is a pretty Renaissance house, **U Minuty**, richly decorated with sgraffito work (a form of ornamental plastering, Italian-inspired, which is a recurring motif in Prague). Just off the square is the **Týn Church**. The façade is hidden by buildings but its distinctive, turreted towers stick out incongruously above the roof – an impressive landmark on the Prague horizon. It was begun in 1365 but not completed until the seventeenth century. The interior is mostly in baroque style.

Josefov (Jewstown) is the former ghetto area. Much of the housing was demolished in the nineteenth century, and now the five remaining synagogues are surrounded by rather soulless streets. The synagogues which remain form a Jewish museum. Hitler had intended making it a memorial to a vanished race; instead it's a testament to Jewish resilience. In the old ceremonial hall is a collection of children's paintings recovered from the Terezin concentration camp. Some show the harrowing life of the camp; some are remembered scenes of happier days in the fields, by the river. Few of the children survived the camp. Next to the hall is the Jewish cemetery. Hundreds of pink gravestones with eroding Hebrew inscriptions stack and lean against each other, tilting on the mounds of earth piled up over the years to accommodate more burials. Almost 12,000 Jews lie buried here, in perhaps 12 layers – for the Jews of the Prague ghetto were not allowed to bury their dead outside their part of town. The synagogues display different aspects of the Jewish tradition – textiles, manuscripts, religious vessels and objects amassed after the destruction of countless country synagogues and homes.

Hradčany (Castle)

Hradčany doesn't look or feel like a castle any more. The Habsburgs, who controlled the city from 1526 until the First World War, replaced most of the defensive walls with the high-sided, many-windowed buildings which now surround the top of the hill. As you wander through the series of paved courtyards you discover an extraordinary architectural mix. At the heart is the spiky bulk of **St Vitus's Cathedral**, founded in 1344 but added to and decorated by baroque architects and finally finished in neo-Gothic style in 1929. The most beautiful part is the St Wenceslas Chapel, containing the saint's tomb; the walls are encrusted with hundreds of pieces of jasper and amethyst. In the crypt are the sarcophagi of Czech rulers, including Charles IV.

Further on is the **Royal Palace** with its showpiece, the fifteenth-century Vladislav Hall. The long ceiling has five vaulted sections of curving stonework. The hall was built big enough to hold not only coronations but tournaments – there's even a specially built stairway to allow horsemen to enter.

Beyond the Palace is the **Convent of St George** with its Romanesque (a rarity in Prague) basilica; in the former cloisters is the **National Collection of Old Bohemian Art**. Among the delicate icons and haggard crucifixions there is some powerful sculpture. An excellent bronze of St George dates from 1373 – the oldest free-standing sculpture north of the Alps. He frowns as he spears a rather small and unintimidating dragon. Look out too for the stocky sculptures of Charles IV by Peter Parler Hut.

In the north-east corner of Hradčany, under the castle walls, is **Golden Lane**, Zlatá ulička. Its tiny coloured cottages look like models for a fairytale, but they were originally built for the castle guard.

It's worth spending most of a day exploring Hradčany. Outside the immediate precincts of the castle, you can stroll along Castle Square, a medieval marketplace now surrounded by the splendid palaces of the former nobility. The most striking building is perhaps the ornate Renaissance-style Schwarrenberg Palace, with black and white rectangular sgraffito work; it's now the Military History Museum (*see 'Other places to visit'*). Many of the other buildings are baroque, including the Sternberk Palace – which houses the National Gallery (*see 'Other places to visit'*). In spring and summer you can wander through the castle gardens down to the river. At night Hradčany is quiet and peaceful, as the pale and mellow light from the old and ornate street lamps casts long shadows.

Malá Strana

Not the most peaceful area to explore – the streets are rather cramped and busy with trams and traffic, and some of the buildings are buttressed out across the roads and over the pavements. But the area is well worth visiting to see its sumptuous baroque palaces, even though most are now embassies or government departments and out of bounds to tourists (it's a shame – the delight of the buildings lies in their inner courtyards and formal and terraced gardens). You can stick your head into the gateway of the Schönborn Palace (now the American Embassy) and catch a glimpse of the terraces behind; and the huge Wallenstein Palace (now the Ministry of Culture) has fine baroque gardens which are open all day.

OTHER PLACES TO VISIT

Composers' museums The villa where Mozart stayed, the **Bertramka**, is now a museum devoted to the composer. It's some way out of central Prague at Mozartova 2/169 Smichov, Prague 5. Opening hours can be erratic so check with the tourist office before setting out. The **Smetana Museum** is housed in the splendid nineteenth-century former waterworks building on the embankment next to Charles Bridge. There's also a **Dvořák Museum** in the Villa Amerika at Ke Karlovu 20, Nové Město.

Military Museum, Schwarrenburg Palace Grey and white sgraffito covers the exterior walls and gables of this elegant palace with a mixture of abstract rectangular patterns and elaborate floral designs. Inside, the Museum of Military History has exhibitions and models of weaponry, defence works, castles and battle techniques in Czech history from the third century to the Second World War. All the information is in Czech.

National Gallery, Collection of European Paintings This is an outstanding collection of paintings hung in the elegant rooms of the Sternbeck Palace in Hradčany Square. It's strong on Dürer and Cranach, with a good selection of Italian and Dutch works from the fifteenth to the seventeenth centuries. There's a fine view of London by Canaletto – with Lambeth Palace in the foreground, Westminster Bridge still under construction and, in the distance, St Paul's under a gloomy English sky. But the highlight is the superb and representative collection of French painting and sculpture from Corot to Braque plus a late van Gogh and a roomful of Picassos. The **Castle Gallery** nearby has the touching *Young Woman at Her Toilet* by Titian as well as paintings by Tintoretto, Veronese and Rubens.

Museum of Applied Arts In the first exhibition room there's a large display of brilliantly coloured glass vases blown into fantastic shapes. Upstairs there's beautifully carved and inlaid furniture, including a faintly ridiculous 1736 grandfather clock surmounted by a gilded chandelier. Other collections include porcelain and pottery.

Strahov Abbey The main attractions of the abbey on the hill next to the castle are the richly decorated halls of the Philosophical and Theological Libraries, which have recently undergone a major restoration. It's worth looking into the peaceful courtyard with its motley collection of convent buildings shaded by lime trees.

Shopping

Prague is not the prime shopping spot in Europe, but there's much more variety and choice than there used to be. The main shopping areas are Wenceslas Square, Na Příkopě (Kotva, the largest department store, is around the corner in Náměstí Republiky) and the streets running off the Old Town Square, especially Karlova (which has some good craft shops), Železná and Celetná. You'll find furs, leather, linen, china and glass – but you will probably not be overwhelmed by the design or quality, or find the prices particularly low. Bohemian crystal is expensive, but cheaper than at home. Folk art items, such as paintings on wood or glass, are fairly popular. There are lots of bookshops and other outlets selling arts and crafts, crystal, furs, and so on (including the Tuzex chain, formerly the hard-currency shops).

EATING AND DRINKING

Food in Prague is a good deal better than in much of Eastern Europe. It's not refined, and certainly won't do much for your waistline, but you can eat heartily and well (although vegetarians will have a hard time). Main courses are based heavily on meat – beef stews, goulash, pork, roast chicken – mostly served with potatoes or special dumplings (*knedlíky*) made either from dough (*houskové knedlíky*) or potato (*bramborové knedlíky*), sometimes with herbs and tiny pieces of pork. The national dish is roast pork (*vepřová pečeně*) with caraway seeds, served with dumplings and sauerkraut. Duck (*kachna*) and, more rarely, goose (*husa*) come with the same accompaniments. Sausages and salamis, and the delicious Prague ham (*šunka*) feature on cold plates, together with cheese, gherkins and other pickles. In some restaurants hors d'oeuvre such as smoked salmon, caviare or ham are served on garnished bread – two or three may cost more than the main course. Fish is mainly carp (*kapr*) or sometimes trout (*pstruh*). Vegetables are plentiful in season, but there isn't a huge choice. Pancakes or strudels are a good option for dessert and there are also waffle stalls on the streets. Menus are nearly always in Czech and few waiters speak much English, so it's a good idea to have a phrase book with you.

Prague is famous for beer, boasting old breweries dating from the Middle Ages and historic beer taverns and halls. The local Pilsner Urquell (Plzenský Prazdroj) beer is excellent, and there's also Budweiser (Budvar), Bránik and Smíchov; most is strong draught. You'll also find a dark beer brewed by the most famous brewery, U Fleků, at Kremencova 11.

Czech wine is very drinkable: usually white, and drunk quite young. There are Slovak, Moravian and Bohemian wines; the nearby vineyards of Melnik produce the most commonly found white. Bohemian *sekt* is the local champagne.

An expensive meal in Prague including drink would cost around £15 a head but you can eat a full meal with a glass of beer for under £2 if you go for simpler fare. Czechs usually eat their main meal at lunchtime; smaller restaurants may serve only lighter food at night. There are several types of places where you can eat: restaurants, wine bars (*vinárna*), which serve mainly cold dishes, beer taverns, coffee houses and stand-up snack bars. Hotel restaurants are usually reliable but often booked up, so it's worth making a reservation. The restaurant in the Paříž Hotel has a lively atmosphere and musicians, and offers a wide choice of fish. The Ambassador Hotel's downstairs restaurant is practical rather than smart, and suitable for lunch (though Bohemian dumplings with pickled beef in cream sauce followed by plum dumplings with sweet cheese might curtail your afternoon's sightseeing!). In Malá Strana, U Mecenáše on Malostranské Náměstí is a famous restaurant in a medieval building by the Church of St Nicholas; tourists are ushered into the smartest of several sections. Obecní Dům, on Náměstí Republicky, is an original place to try: food is served in a huge art-deco room with a dance band playing traditional Czech numbers on Saturday nights.

NIGHTLIFE

Prague is famous for music. At the Nostitz Theatre, the first performance of Mozart's *Don Giovanni* was staged, after he had finished writing the overture only hours before; the opera is still a popular item in the theatre's repertoire. During Prague's annual music festival at the end of May/beginning of June, concerts are held in historic buildings and the Malá Strana Gardens; and opera, ballets and concerts are performed at the Nostitz and National Theatres and the State Opera House (all year except July and August).

Prague Guide, published monthly, is available from tourist offices and hotels. It is full of information on hotels, shops, restaurants and museums as well as cultural events. *Prognosis*, the English-language newspaper, has lots of information on the arts, entertainments listings of English-language films, and a comprehensive visitors' guide, including restaurant reviews, walking tours and a map of the city. The paper is obtainable from news-stands. You can usually get tickets to something, although seats are often in heavy demand; it's best to go direct to the box office to buy them, as hotels can charge a hefty commission. The best seats at the beautiful State Opera House cost about £10.

There are many theatres. Peculiar to Prague are productions of mime – with light and sound effects at the Black Theatre; or with special effects at the very recommendable Laterna Magika, where the delightful performances appeal to all nationalities and age groups. The Central Puppet Theatre has performances all year (except July and August).

Some beer taverns have entertainments, including nightly 'cabaret' shows for which a knowledge of Czech is necessary to understand the satirical jokes. The more expensive hotels boast Western-style nightclubs; usually late-night bars with a dance floor and some entertainment, depending on the demand. The Alhambra Review also provides late-night shows and dancing girls, and is aimed at tourists.

Cinemas show a surprising variety of foreign-language films, usually sub-titled in Czech.

HOTELS

The simplest way of booking a hotel in Prague is to arrange it through a tour operator in the UK, but it is possible to travel independently and find accommodation when you arrive. Most hotels accept credit cards. Pragotur at U Obecního Domu 2 in the Old Town (tel: 2 317281) can always find you a hotel on the day if you turn up without a reservation. It will also arrange for you to board with local families: the cost is about £15 per person in a double room (minimum three nights). Licensed private agencies throughout the city can also provide a wide choice of accommodation.

ESPLANADE ◆◆◆◆◆
Washingtonova 19, 11001   *Tel: 22 25 52   Fax: 26 58 97*

The Esplanade is located slightly off Wenceslas Square in a pleasant tree-lined boulevard set back a little from the road. The hotel dates from the early twentieth century, and is smart and traditional inside, in parts quite unusual. The large bar/lounge has patterned rugs on marble floors, huge chandeliers and a green marble fireplace. Beyond is a strange, dark and rather theatrical restaurant with an art nouveau stained-glass dome. The bedrooms have less period character but are in good order with decent bathrooms and solid dark wood furnishings. The hotel is undergoing renovation during 1993.

Bedrooms: 63, all with bath/WC; mini-bar; hair-dryer   **Facilities:** Lift; restaurant   **Credit/charge cards accepted:** All

FORUM
Kongresova 1, 14069   *Tel: 41 90 111   Fax: 49 94 80*

A tall plate-glass skyscraper, a short metro ride from central Prague. The immediate surroundings are fairly sterile but it's not an unpleasant view towards the New Town. The emphasis is on the business trade, with efficiency and a wide range of prominent facilities. The décor is bland and conventional, with dark, squashy, leather-look chairs in the foyer beneath 'sixties-style light fittings arranged like batteries of old milk bottles. They serve decent coffee here, and the staff are well trained.

Bedrooms: 531, all with bath/WC; air-conditioning; hair-dryer; mini-bar
Facilities: Lifts; restaurant; indoor heated pool; gym; squash; sauna; solarium; masseur   **Credit/charge cards accepted:** All

INTER-CONTINENTAL
Nam Curieovych 43-5, 11001   *Tel: 28 00 111   Fax: 23 10 500*

The position makes this place what it is. It's right on the river commanding a view of the castle. The Jewish quarter is behind, and it's only a minute or two into the heart of the Old Town. Inside, it's as comfortable and spacious as you might expect of a hotel with this name. It is in the middle of total refurbishment and some reconstruction, which should be complete by the end of 1993. Bedrooms have good views. Staff are efficient and pleasant, speaking excellent English.

Bedrooms: 388, all with bath/shower/WC; air-conditioning; mini-bar; satellite TV   **Facilities:** Lift; restaurants; gym; sauna; swimming-pool (end '93); nightclub   **Credit/charge cards accepted:** All

PAŘÍŽ
U Obecního Domu 1   *Tel: 236 08 20   Fax: 236 74 48*

Next to the marvellous art nouveau Municipal Hall near Wenceslas Square, this apparently modest hotel has far more character than most. The bedrooms are surprisingly comfortable, solidly furnished, spacious and well equipped. Most of the rooms overlook a quiet side-street on the edge of the Old Town. Like its surroundings, the Paříž Hotel is art nouveau. In the restaurant huge mirrors reflect elegant Bohemian crystal chandeliers and turquoise mosaic pilasters. Vivacious musicians play in the evenings.

Bedrooms: 98, most with shower/WC; some with bath/WC; most with mini-bar; air-conditioning   **Facilities:** Lift; restaurant   **Credit/charge cards accepted:** All

U TŘÍ PŠTROSŮ (THREE OSTRICHES) ♦♦♦♦
Drazickeho Náměstí 12, 11800   Tel: 53 61 51   Fax: 53 61 55

You won't find this in any tourist literature, but it's easy to find, on the castle side of the Charles Bridge. It's a charming old building at the heart of some of Prague's most interesting old streets, on the edge of Malá Strana. The entrance is vaulted in the shallow curves typical of Prague, with displays of antiques placed with understated style and grace. The restaurant is an intimate and inviting room with an appealing and very Czech menu.

Bedrooms: 18, all with bath/shower/WC **Facilities:** Restaurant **Credit/charge cards accepted:** None

Hotel prices Symbols indicate approximate prices per room per night for a double room with bath. Many large hotels run special breaks which work out far cheaper. (See page 14 for further details.)

♦ = under £50; ♦♦ = £50 to £80; ♦♦♦ = £80 to £100;
♦♦♦♦ = £100 to £140; ♦♦♦♦♦ = over £140.

ROME

- A starting point of Western civilisation and still the focal point of the Roman Catholic faith, the Eternal City has an enormous amount for the visitor to see

- There is incomparable sightseeing for those fascinated by archaeology and ancient history or by Renaissance and baroque art and architecture. But museums and galleries have maddening opening hours so you'll need to plan your time carefully

- Although traffic and transport are chaotic, much of the unspoilt historic centre is a pedestrian area

- The most appealing smaller hotels, the smartest shops and some of Rome's most popular restaurants are in this area too. Those on tour operator packages will probably find themselves less conveniently, and more noisily, placed

BUILT on the River Tiber, on seven hills, Rome consists of several very distinct areas – which makes life easier for the tourist. Taken chronologically, they consist roughly of Ancient Rome, medieval and Renaissance Rome, plus the Vatican – technically a separate state – and modern Rome.

The heart of the ancient city was slightly to the south of the area now considered central, between the Capitol – from where the city is still governed – and the Via Appia Antica. With the notable exception of the Pantheon, the Castel Sant' Angelo and the ancient city walls (begun by Aurelian in AD 271), most of the really important remains are concentrated in this area. These include the extensive ruins of the Roman forum and of the Imperial forums (with Trajan's Column), the mighty Colosseum and, close to the Tiber, the Theatre of Marcellus and the Temples of Hercules and Fortuna Virile. The approach to the Aventine Hill, a peaceful residential district with two lovely early Christian churches, offers a splendid view over the Circus Maximus, the ancient Roman racing stadium, with the impressive backdrop of the ruined imperial palaces of the Palatine Hill. To the south-east of the Aventine, beyond the Baths of Caracalla, starts the famous Via Appia Antica, lined with early Christian catacombs and churches. Nowadays, the classic entry into Rome from the south is from the Via Ostiense, entering at the Porta di San Paolo with its monumental pyramid, built in 12-11 BC as a tomb.

In the Middle Ages Rome expanded northwards, filling the kink in the Tiber now neatly containing much of the medieval, Renaissance and baroque city. At the heart of this area (often known as Old rather than Ancient Rome) is the venerable Pantheon, a prototype for the Renaissance architect and very much part of the scene today – it is one of the few ancient sights which can be admired from a café table. The charm of this area lies in its narrow streets with their dilapidated old mansions and thriving artisans' shops and especially in its superb piazzas. Of these, Piazza Navona, built on the site of an ancient stadium (which explains its elongated shape), is perhaps the finest: a dramatic stage-set for Bernini's flamboyant baroque fountains. There is also the Piazza Farnese, with one of Rome's most beautiful Renaissance palaces (*palazzi*) and, nearby, the picturesque market square of Campo dei Fiori. Countless churches (and several private *palazzi*) repay diligent inspection of their Renaissance architecture, baroque ceilings and works of art.

On the right bank of the Tiber, a short walk from the old part of Rome, is the Vatican, an independent sovereign state of about 100 acres which attracts thousands of pilgrims each year. Every tourist needs at least a day to visit St Peter's and marvel at

Michelangelo's Sistine ceiling and the treasures accumulated by the Papacy over the centuries. Otherwise, the immediate area is uninteresting. Also across the Tiber is the district of Trastevere, which is sometimes compared to the Latin Quarter in Paris. There are one or two authentic *trattorie* and a Sunday flea market; but there are also rip-offs in the form of touristy restaurants, and petty crime is a problem, especially after dark. The main features of interest are the churches. Nearby, at the foot of the Janiculum Hill, are the Farnesina and Corsini palaces, housing important works of art; higher up is Bramante's Tempietto (in the courtyard of San Pietro di Montorio), one of the most exquisite buildings of the Renaissance. The most picturesque approach to Trastevere is across the Isola Tiberina, an island in the middle of the river, linked to the banks by the oldest bridge in Rome, the Ponte Fabricio (62 BC), and the partly rebuilt Ponte Cestio.

A useful point of orientation in central Rome is the Corso, a mile-long street bisecting central Rome between the fine Piazza del Popolo, designed as a triumphal entrance to the city, and Piazza Venezia, with its ungainly monument to Victor Emanuel II. Beyond the Corso (once a race-track) is another wedge of 'Old Rome', although now the emphasis shifts to the eighteenth century. A narrow grid of smart shopping streets leads to the focal point of the area: the Scalinata di Spagna, or Spanish Steps, leading up to the church of Trinità dei Monti. The lively Piazza di Spagna, with its colourful flower stalls, palm-trees, fountain and waiting horse-drawn carriages, is a popular meeting-place. Nearby, tucked away in a maze of narrow streets, is a baroque favourite – the famous Trevi Fountain. A coin thrown in is said to ensure your return to Rome. To the north of the Spanish Steps, just outside the ancient walls, is the heart-shaped park of Villa Borghese, which has several museums. From one of the main arteries of the park a curving thoroughfare leads back to downtown Rome. This is the Via Veneto, whose pavement cafés and hotels were once patronised by film stars and glamorous exponents of the *dolce vita*, but which now seems rather sedate.

After Rome was declared the capital of Italy in 1870 the city expanded rapidly. In the centre most of the nineteenth-century development is around and to the east of the Via Veneto and the Quirinal Hill – site of the presidential palace. Busy roads like Via Nazionale and Via Cavour recall this era and have some grand old hotels, but the area is generally dull and the immediate vicinity of the station notorious for petty crime and drug-peddling. The saving graces are a few interesting churches and the remains of the Baths of Diocletian, which overlook the Piazza della Repubblica. Rome, has of course, extended far beyond the original city walls. Symbolic of the twentieth century is the suburb planned by Mussolini, known as EUR (Espozione Universale di Roma): a Lego-like block and neo-classical dome can be glimpsed on the journey into Rome from Fiumicino Airport.

WHEN TO GO

If there's a 'right' time to visit Rome, then it is at Easter, when the faithful gather for the Pope's 'Urbi e Orbi' benediction and spring weather is usually at its best. However, unless you have come specifically for the Holy Week celebrations, this is the very time to avoid, as the city is always crowded and many sights are closed. Spring, early summer and autumn are good times to choose; high summer is very hot. If you must take a holiday at this time of year there is a selection of entertainment on offer: from June to September the *Estate Romana* provides extra cultural events, including concerts, ballet and various open-air events, and in July there is a folklore celebration called *La Festa di Noiantri* in the Trastevere district. The month to avoid at all costs is August, when Romans themselves escape on vacation. *Ferragosto* (15 August) is a national holiday, when practically everything closes.

Winter days are often sunny, and the smartest Roman women sit out at café tables in their fur coats. But beware chilly temperatures in the evening and early morning. Cheaper hotels are often not centrally heated. There are fewer guided tours available between November and March but the compensation is that there are fewer fellow tourists around also.

MASTERING THE SYSTEM

Information The UK office of the Italian State Tourist Office is at 1 Princes Street, London W1R 8AY, tel: 071-408 1254. The local Roman tourist information office, Ente Provinciale per il Turismo (EPT), is at Via Parigi 5, tel: 48 83 748. The inconvenient location and lack of essential literature mean that it is not really worth a visit. However, for a free map and basic printed information, it's worth trying a branch of the EPT in the arrivals hall at Fiumicino Airport, tel: 60 11 255. The listings of sights are often out of date and should be used only as a rough guide. The only way to be sure that a museum or gallery is open is to contact it direct (*see 'Opening days', below*).

GETTING THERE

Going independently

By air British Airways (081-897 7400) and Alitalia (071-602 7111) have several flights a day from Heathrow to Rome. The cheapest scheduled fare is the Saver or Sunsaver – bookable within seven days of departure for stays including a Saturday night. Fares increase during the July to September holiday season. Charter flights are available all year round and can work out cheaper than the lowest scheduled fare. Operators worth contacting for fare quotes are Citalia (081-686 5533), Lupus Travel (071-287 1292), Italy Sky Shuttle (081-748 1333), Cityjet (071-387 1017), Ciao Travel (071-629 2677), Volare (071-439 6633), Italian Options (071-436 3246), Italflights (071-405 6771), Ausonia (0293 820020) and Euro Express (0293 511125).

Scheduled flights land at Leonardo da Vinci (Fiumicino) Airport, about 20 miles south-west of Rome. Charter flights fly into Ciampino Airport, 10 miles south-east of the city.

Leonardo da Vinci (Fiumicino) Airport There is an excellent range of shops and cafés; also banks and a currency exchange office. A regular rail service runs to the central Stazione Termini; the journey takes around 45 minutes. A taxi from the airport to a central hotel costs more than L50,000.

By car Rome is encircled by the Grande Raccordo Anulare (ring road) to which all roads lead. Those arriving by car should choose a hotel with a garage – or garage service – if possible. Note that the historic centre, around the Corso and Piazza di Spagna, is closed to traffic, although you should be allowed to unload cases if you give the name of the hotel to the police on duty. Driving in Rome is particularly stressful and should be avoided by first-time visitors (*see also 'Getting around'*).

Tour operator packages

Rome is a popular short-break city and many tour operators include it in their brochures. Typical packages are for stays of two, three or four nights, with either scheduled or charter flights. Where there's a choice, the charter option will be the cheaper. How much you pay depends on where you stay and when you go. July to September is usually the most expensive. A three-night stay in a three-star hotel would cost around £365 in high season. Breakfast is included and sometimes transfers to the hotel from the airport. For a list of tour operators see page 385.

Sightseeing tours These tours are arranged by American Express at Piazza di Spagna 38, tel: 67641; and Green Line Tours at Via Farini 5a, tel: 48 27 480. Both offer basic three-hour city tours by bus, with some short walks and visits to churches or ancient sites. You can choose a general orientation tour or a tour with the emphasis on either Ancient Rome or Rome as the centre of Christianity. The catacombs of the Via Appia Antica can be visited only on a guided tour. There are also guided visits of the Vatican museums, 'Rome by Night' (with dinner or a show), and excursions to Tivoli. The tour companies can also arrange papal audiences and blessings for groups.

Changing money Banks are open from Monday to Friday, 8.30am to 1.30pm and 2.45pm to 3.45pm. Outside normal hours you can exchange money on the Piazza di Spagna, at the offices of American Express (Monday to Friday 9am to 5.30pm, Saturday 9am to 12.30pm). The bureau de change at Fiumicino Airport is open 24 hours a day.

Opening hours and days Opening hours vary greatly and are very confusing, but generally they are as follows. State museums and galleries are open from 9am to 2pm (1pm on Sunday) only, and are closed on Monday. On Monday you can see the Forum till 1pm (also Sunday 9am to 1pm), the Vatican museums (closed Sunday except the last in the month, when admission is free) or private galleries (irregular opening hours and days) instead. Many churches are open every day but not in the afternoons. Early evening is a good time to visit. As mornings are usually taken up with sightseeing you can also save any shopping for the early evening; after a long lunch-break shops re-open in the late afternoon – until 7.30pm or 8pm. They are closed on Sunday and on one afternoon a week. All restaurants close one day a week, often on Sunday or Monday, and it is advisable to book at weekends. Many shut down in August.

Sightseeing in churches It is essential to take a stock of L100 and L200 coins to illuminate paintings – many are barely visible in natural light.

GETTING AROUND

Buses tend to be very crowded. However, if you have your bearings they can be useful for some longer journeys, especially those involving hills or noisy thoroughfares. The best idea is to find the nearest *capolinea*, or terminal (they're in major squares), where there will be a selection of buses and a green ATAC booth for tickets and information. It is worth buying a half-day ticket (valid until 2pm) or a 'BIG' ticket (valid all day, also on the underground). Transport maps, which can be bought at news-stands, are almost indecipherable; it's easier to look at the signs at the bus stops. Useful bus routes include No 49, which stops right outside the Vatican museums, and No 62 for St Peter's. (Another 20 lines also stop in St Peter's Square.)

The No 110 from Piazza dei Cinquecento in front of Stazione Termini follows a route which takes in all the main sights of interest in three hours. This costs more than an ordinary bus ride but much less than a guided tour. In summer this route is run every afternoon at 3.30pm; in winter – weekends and holidays only – at 2.30pm.

There are only a few **tram** routes left. They are unlikely to be useful on a short break. There are two **underground** (Metropolitana) lines, A and B, with a junction at Termini (the railway station). The system is very limited, with the most useful stops for tourists being the Ottaviano (five minutes' walk from the Vatican museums), Spagna (at the Piazza di Spagna) and Colosseo (the Colosseum). Remember to buy tickets, from newsstands or bars, before descending to the station (unless you have change for the ticket machine).

If you must have a **car** in Rome, park it as soon, and as safely, as possible. Make sure the car-park is *custodito* (guarded), and take out the radio if it is detachable. The best long-term car-park is the underground one at Parco Borghese. Some hotels have private ones or will provide a garage service.

Rome's bright yellow **taxis** are best picked up at ranks. Check the meter (there is a standing charge) and be prepared for supplements, which are listed in all licensed cabs. (Drivers can charge double fare for journeys to the airport from the city.)

UNMISSABLES

The Colosseum
The Colosseum, more than any other building in Rome, symbolises the Eternal City. Elliptical in shape, with arcaded tiers, it has 76 entrances and was designed to accommodate 50,000 spectators. The vast arena was the scene of gladiatorial combat and other 'entertainments' from the year AD 80. It was later abandoned and parts of its massive marble walls taken down to provide building materials for other projects in the city. Its restoration dates from the early nineteenth century. Near the Colosseum is the Arch of Constantine, erected to commemorate the victory of the Emperor Constantine at Ponte Milvio in AD 315.

The Forum
The most extensive and, with the nearby Colosseum, the most evocative site of Ancient Rome is the Forum. There is a splendid

panorama from the Campidoglio, and with the help of a good plan you can distinguish the various buildings and piece together what was once the commercial and political centre of the city and the Empire. This, however, is no substitute for the moving experience of wandering among the romantic ruins against the backdrop of the Palatine Hill. Important buildings include the Curia, where the Senate met for hundreds of years; the Temple of Castor and Pollux (consisting of three lovely columns); the Temple of Vesta, with the House of the Vestal Virgins; and the Temple of Saturn. The superb Arch of Titus (AD 81) and the Arch of Septimus Severus (AD 203) were prototypes of the triumphal arch in Renaissance and later architecture.

St Peter's

The centre of the Roman Catholic faith and destination of millions of pilgrims, the church of St Peter is appropriately awe-inspiring in scale. Replacing an ancient basilica, it dates, in its present form, from the fifteenth to the seventeenth centuries and is the work of a number of architects, including Michelangelo, Bramante and Bernini – who designed the sweeping double colonnades which symbolise the embracing arms of the Church. The ancient Egyptian obelisk was erected in 1586. On Sundays, when in residence, the Pope blesses the crowds from the balcony.

The most impressive feature of the huge interior is Bernini's baroque *baldacchino*, or canopy, which covers the revered tomb of St Peter. But amid all the pomp, there is also Michelangelo's exquisite *Pietà*, which outshines all the other statuary for sheer beauty. There are splendid views of Rome from the roof (entrance and lift to the right of the church); the extra steps to the lantern of Michelangelo's dome are recommended only for the fit.

The Sistine ceiling, Raphael's Stanze and the Vatican museums

A comprehensive tour of the Vatican museums is exhausting and not recommended for the short-term visitor. Purists (or the lazy) may proceed direct to the Sistine Chapel, where Michelangelo's visionary genius achieved its fullest expression in the painting of the vault, completed between 1508 and 1512 and illustrating the history of mankind from the Creation to the Flood. This masterpiece of the High Renaissance (and triumph of human endurance) dwarfs the fine wall-paintings by earlier Tuscan and Umbrian artists which depict the lives of Moses and Christ. On the end wall is Michelangelo's apocalyptic *Last Judgement* (1536-41), currently under restoration. The famous rooms (*Stanze*) decorated by Raphael are well worth a close study: the Stanza della Segnatura with *The School of Athens* is generally considered the finest. A short visit should also include the Borgia apartments, decorated by Pinturicchio, and the Pinacoteca, or Picture Gallery. This contains a representative selection of Italian paintings from the eleventh century onwards, including works by Giotto, Fra Angelico, Gentile de Fabriano, Raphael (notably *The Transfiguration*), Caravaggio, Guido Reni and Titian. As the collection is particularly strong on early works, it makes sense to visit the gallery before the Stanze and Sistine ceiling.

OTHER PLACES TO VISIT

Ancient monuments

The **Ara Pacis Augustae**, the beautiful Altar of Augustan Peace dating from 13 BC, is protected from the elements and pollution by glass housing. Nearby is the Mausoleum of Augustus. The **Pantheon**, a temple founded by Agrippa in 27 BC, was rebuilt by Hadrian and later consecrated as a Christian church. Remarkable for its state of preservation and its near-perfect proportions, the Pantheon contains the tombs of Raphael and the kings of Italy. The **Theatre of Marcellus** is the impressive remains of a theatre begun by Julius Caesar and completed by Augustus in 13-11 BC. In the sixteenth century housing was added to the top storey. Nearby is the church of San Nicola, which incorporates the columns of three earlier temples in its structure.
Trajan's Forum is the most interesting of the Imperial forums, and also the latest (AD 113). The splendid Trajan's Column, commemorating the Emperor's military victories over the Dacians, is a masterpiece of classical art. The **Baths of Caracalla** were begun by Septimius Severus in AD 206. They were in use until they were destroyed by the Goths in the sixth century and originally comprised a gym, library and gardens. The *caldarium* is now used for open-air opera (see page 303).

Churches

Gesù An influential building in the history of architecture, the Jesuits' principal church has an early baroque façade and, inside, an amazingly ornate ceiling painting illustrating *The Triumph of the Name of Jesus*.
Sant' Andrea al Quirinale Designed by Bernini, this small, elegant, seventeenth-century church has an unusual elliptical

interior. It is often compared to Borromini's tiny San Carlo alle Quattro Fontane, just up the road.

San Giovanni in Laterano The cathedral church of Rome – and therefore the world – was founded in AD 311 but rebuilt several times, most recently in the seventeenth century. It has a majestic interior and a very beautiful cloister.

San Luigi dei Francesi The French national church in Rome is visited chiefly for the remarkable early works by Caravaggio illustrating scenes from the life of St Matthew.

Santa Maria del Pópolo This Renaissance church contains further masterpieces by Caravaggio (the *Martyrdom of St Peter* and the *Conversion of St Paul*), plus frescoes by Pinturicchio and Raphael's Chigi Chapel.

Santa Maria Maggiore Crowning the Esquiline Hill, this was one of the four great patriarchal basilicas founded in the fifth century. Inside it has precious early Christian mosaics and baroque chapels.

Santa Maria sopra Minerva The restored interior of this Gothic church contains lovely frescoes by Filippino Lippi and a statue of *Christ Carrying the Cross* by Michelangelo.

San Pietro in Vincoli Named after the chains of St Peter, preserved under the High Altar, this church contains Michelangelo's statue of *Moses*, designed to grace the mausoleum of Pope Julius II.

Santa Prassede This early Christian church has important Byzantine mosaics in the chapel of San Zeno.

Museums and galleries

Borghese Gallery and Museum Aficionados of Bernini's sculpture should not miss the chance to see some of his masterpieces in this now dilapidated palace, built in 1613 to house the collections of Cardinal Scipione Borghese. Also here is Canova's *Pauline Bonaparte*. Protracted restoration work at the Casino Borghese means that the number of visitors is limited to 25 at a time and the Gallery (upstairs) is closed indefinitely.

Capitoline Museums Twin buildings on Capitol Hill house important collections of antique sculpture and paintings. Famous statues include the *Dying Gaul* and the *Capitoline Venus*. The picture gallery (in the Palazzo dei Conservatori) contains works by Pietro da Cortona, Caravaggio and Titian, among others. The piazza and palaces were designed by Michelangelo.

Castel Sant' Angelo The Emperor Hadrian's family mausoleum, built from AD 135 to 139, became a fortress during the Middle Ages, and it was here that Pope Clement VII took refuge during the Sack of Rome in 1527. The richly decorated papal apartments contain Renaissance pictures and furniture. There is also an important collection of arms and armour.

Colonna Gallery Open only on Saturday mornings, this is the princely collection of the Colonna family, established in 1703 and displayed in a series of opulent rooms. There are paintings by Veronese, Tintoretto, Rubens and Van Dyck.

Corsini Gallery Once a private collection, but now belonging to the state, this gallery is still housed in the family *palazzo* of the Corsini. Most of the paintings are from the late sixteenth and seventeenth centuries – mainly, but not exclusively, Italian.

Doria Pamphili Gallery An exceptionally fine private collection of European works of art of the Renaissance has masterpieces by Bernini, Velázquez, Titian, Rubens and Caravaggio. There are guided tours (in Italian) of the furnished apartments.

Keats and Shelley Memorial House The house where Keats lived and died is now a small museum with mementoes of Keats, Byron, Shelley and Leigh Hunt. It's one of the few museums to open in the afternoons.

National Gallery (Galleria Nazionale d'Arte Antica) These works are housed in the seventeenth-century Palazzo Barberini. The earliest paintings are from the thirteenth century, with Raphael's portrait of *La Fornarina* the star exhibit. The masterpiece of Pietro da Cortona is his illusionistic ceiling decoration (1633-9), an allegory glorifying the Barberini family.

National Museum (Villa Giulia) One of the great Etruscan collections is housed in a papal villa of the sixteenth century in the Parco Borghese.

National Museum of Rome Important archaeological collections are displayed in part of the Baths of Diocletian and a former sixteenth-century convent. There are some beautiful Roman mosaics and the famous Farnesina murals.

Spada Gallery A small private collection of baroque paintings, including works by Titian, Rubens and Guido Reni, is displayed in four rooms of a sixteenth-century *palazzo*. Borromini's *trompe-l'oeil* colonnade can be glimpsed from the courtyard.

Vatican museums The Pio-Clementino Museum contains the important ancient sculptures of the Belvedere Torso and, in the Octagonal Courtyard, the Laocoon, both very influential on the Renaissance artist. There are also museums of Egyptian and Etruscan art.

SHOPPING

The smartest shops in Rome are concentrated in a small pedestrianised area between the Corso and the Piazza di Spagna. Here Via Condotti and the neighbouring streets are lined by international designer boutiques – fun for window-shopping but extremely expensive. Nearby, Via del Babuino is known for its art dealers and Via Margutta for contemporary galleries. Via dei Coronari, near Piazza Navona, is famous for its antique shops. A flea market is held on Sunday mornings at Porta Portese; real bargains are rare, however. Those wanting to buy presents should think in terms of linen, lingerie or leather – especially gloves.

EATING AND DRINKING

The most appealing area for restaurants is the part of Old Rome between the Pantheon and the Tiber. Traditional favourites include Piperno, in the former Jewish ghetto area (near the Theatre of Marcellus), and some good local *trattorie* near the Campo dei Fiori. The seafood at Ristorante Monserrato, Via Monserrato, has been recommended. The lively Piazza Navona has several cafés and restaurants with tables on the pavement, notably Tre Scalini, which is popular for its chocolate truffle ice-creams. The nearby Caffé della Pace in Via della Pace is a favourite hang-out. And try Focaccetta in Via del Governo Vecchio for customised sandwiches made using warm *focaccia* bread. Other famous cafés are the Caffé Greco on Via Condotti and the quaint Babington's Tea Rooms at the foot of the Spanish Steps; here, and at numerous bars, you can always get a light snack. Up near Piazza del Pópolo, La Penna d'Oca has good food, wine and atmosphere. The area around the Vatican is a gastronomic desert, but Trastevere has some popular *trattorie*. Romans tend to eat out in unpretentious family-run places and to favour straightforward cooking.

Rome has its own favourite pastas: *spaghetti alla carbonara* (with cream, egg and pieces of bacon) originated here, as did *fettuccine all' amatriciana* (Roman tagliatelle with tomato and bacon sauce). Potato gnocchi is also a traditional dish. The best-known main course is *saltimbocca alla Romana* (escalopes of veal with ham and sage). *Carciofi* (artichokes) can be found deep-fried (*alla Giudea*) in Jewish quarter restaurants, and *alla Romana* elsewhere. The local wine is Frascati, from the Alban Hills south of the city. For good reds choose a wine from Umbria or further north.

Nightlife

While young Romans buzz frenetically around on their motor bikes and mopeds or make for the nearest cinema, most tourists prefer to meander around the streets of Old Rome admiring floodlit fountains and façades, or to sit at café tables over an *aperitivo* or an ice-cream. Eating out often means eating outside, and in summer Romans tend to dine quite late – so balmy evenings can be enjoyed to the full. From June to September there are outdoor opera performances in the Baths of Caracalla, tel: 57 58 626. From May to October the tour companies organise evening excursions to Tivoli (about 20 miles east of Rome), where the famous fountains of the Villa d'Este are illuminated.

The main opera season is during the winter at the Teatro dell'Opera di Roma, Piazza Beniamino Gigli 1, tel: 67 59 57 21 for information and bookings, but this is not Italy's best. Music lovers should try to attend a concert given by the Accademia Nazionale de Santa Cecilia, which plays at the Auditorio Pio, Via della Conciliazione 4, tel: 65 41 044, and on the Campidoglio (Capitol Hill) in June. English-language films are shown with the original soundtrack at the Pasquino Cinema, Vicolo del Piede 19 in Trastevere – elsewhere they are dubbed.

An idiosyncratic establishment popular with foreign visitors is Arciliuto, Piazza Montevecchio 5, where the Neapolitan owner entertains guests with spontaneous songs in several languages. There are some smart nightclubs and discos in the Via Veneto area but they are mostly closed in July and August.

Hotels

There are two main areas for hotels. Tour operators tend to use the grand old hotels of the Via Veneto area, now mostly faded and reliant on business and group custom. They can be noisy, particularly on the Via Cavour and Via Nazionale. The smaller and generally cheaper hotels are found in the central area of Rome between the Piazza del Pópolo, the Spanish Steps and the Corso Vittorio Emanuele – a much more attractive part of the city, and usually quieter. However, Rome does not have a tradition of *pensioni* like Florence or Venice, and smaller hotels have minimal public rooms and service. There is hardly any appealing accommodation on the far bank of the Tiber or in the area of Ancient Rome; the station area is to be avoided altogether.

CESARI ♦♦
Via di Pietra 89a, 00186   *Tel: 67 92 386   Fax: 67 90 882*

The Cesari is tucked away in the back streets of Rome, near Piazzi di
Pietra. The hotel dates from the eighteenth century and boasts a host of
famous former guests, including Garibaldi. An original licence for the
hotel, dated 1787, hangs in the reception area. The bedrooms have a
cottagey feel, with plain wood furniture, rugs on a tiled floor and flowery
bedspreads. Breakfast is served in the bedrooms, but as an alternative
there are many cafés nearby. The Cesari is an unpretentious hotel with a
friendly atmosphere.

Bedrooms: 50, most with bath/shower/WC; air-conditioning; mini-bar
Facilities: Lift   **Credit/charge cards accepted:** All

COLUMBUS ♦♦♦♦
Via della Conciliazione 33, 00193   *Tel: 68 65 435   Fax: 68 64 874*

In terms of accommodation the Columbus is about as close as you can get
to St Peter's Square. The hotel has a long history, having been built as a
palazzo in the fifteenth century by a cardinal who was the nephew of Pope
Sisto IV of the della Rovere family. It was converted into a hotel in 1950.
The hotel retains many antique features, such as the frescoes on the walls
and a sixteenth-century salon decorated in gold. The bedrooms have a
more austere, monastic feel and are sparsely furnished. Not very central
for shops and sights.

Bedrooms: 107, most with shower/WC, some with bath/WC; all with
mini-bar   **Facilities:** Lift; restaurant   **Credit/charge cards accepted:** All

EXCELSIOR ♦♦♦♦♦
Via V. Veneto 125, 00187   *Tel: 47 08   Fax: 48 26 205*

One of the grandest of the grand hotels, the Excelsior is on the corner of
the once very popular Via Veneto. Bell-boys in brass-buttoned uniforms
and receptionists in formal black suits bustle around. The reception area
is cavernous, with glittering chandeliers and Persian carpets. The dining-
rooms are on the scale of banqueting halls and are elaborately decorated.
The bedrooms are spacious and complement the hotel's overstated
grandeur.

Bedrooms: 327, all with bath/shower/WC; air-conditioning   **Facilities:**
Lift; restaurant; hairdresser   **Credit/charge cards accepted:** All

FORUM
Via Tor de' Conti 25, 00184 Tel: 67 92 446 Fax: 67 86 479

As its name suggests, the Forum Hotel overlooks the ruins of the ancient Forum. It is on the corner of a narrow, winding, cobbled street which attracts a surprising amount of traffic. The reception has wood panelling on the walls and a pale grey marble floor covered with red Persian-style carpets. The bedrooms are roomy and smart. On the top floor, the restaurant leads out on to a patio with the hotel's best view of the ruins. Although it is well away from the main restaurant and shopping area, it is convenient for the Ancient Roman sights.

Bedrooms: 76, half with bath/WC, half with shower/WC; all with air-conditioning **Facilities:** Lift; restaurant **Credit/charge cards accepted:** All

D'INGHILTERRA
Via Bocca di Leone 14, 00187 Tel: 67 21 61 Fax: 68 40 828

In a prime shopping area, the Inghilterra is an elegant hotel decorated in the style of an English country house. The garden-style restaurant is approached down a spiral staircase into the cellars, where the walls have frescoes of classical Roman garden scenes. Upstairs, a cosy bar with wood panelling and leather upholstered benches has paintings of English hunting scenes on the wall. The bedrooms vary in standard and comfort; the more luxurious rooms have aquamarine and apricot colour schemes and large marble bathrooms. A good choice for a special occasion.

Bedrooms: 102, all with bath/WC; air-conditioning; mini-bar **Facilities:** Lift; restaurant **Credit/charge cards accepted:** All

KING
Via Sistina 131, 00187 Tel: 47 41 515 Fax: 48 71 813

Hotel King is down a busy road leading from Piazza Trinità dei Monti. It has been decorated in a modern style: the bar is in steely grey and pale pink colours, with cube-shaped sofas and potted rubber plants. The bedrooms are similar in design, with modern fitted furnishings. Upstairs is a rooftop garden for sun-worshippers, as well as a small breakfast room. The busy street is not attractive but the hotel is central.

Bedrooms: 74, most with bath/WC; all with air-conditioning; mini-bar **Facilities:** Lift **Credit/charge cards accepted:** All

LOCARNO
Via della Penna 22, 00186   *Tel: 36 10 841*

The Hotel Locarno is close to the Piazza del Pópolo at the northern end of the Via del Corso, the main shopping street in the area. Inside, the Locarno is reminiscent of the 1920s. Tiffany lamps and an ornate antique till adorn the bar by the lobby. In summer you can sit outside on a narrow walled-in terrace. Arched alcoves in the lounge are lit by soft domed lights which reflect in the mirrors on the walls. The bedrooms vary in size. An inexpensive choice in a good location. The hotel also lends bicycles free of charge.

Bedrooms: 38, most with shower/WC, some with bath/shower/WC; all with air-conditioning; mini-bar; safe **Facilities:** Lift **Credit/charge cards accepted:** Amex, Diners, Visa

---

MADRID
Via Mario de Fiori 93-95, 00186   *Tel: 69 91 510*   *Fax: 67 91 653*

On the corner of a busy pedestrianised street packed with boutiques, restaurants, ice-cream stalls and cafés lies the Hotel Madrid. The lobby, with its black and red colour scheme, looks like the entrance to a nightclub, but the bedrooms are less exotic – with muted yellow wallpaper and wooden floors. The breakfast room, with cheerful, flowery tablecloths and garden furniture, is on the top floor. Lower-level bedrooms are noisy, especially in the summer when the streets of Rome come alive. But for those who like to be in the centre of things, this hotel is a good option.

Bedrooms: 26, most with bath/shower/WC; all with air-conditioning; mini-bar **Facilities:** Lift **Credit/charge cards accepted:** All

---

MARGUTTA
Via Laurina 34, 00187   *Tel: 67 98 440*

The Margutta is a small, family-run hotel situated on a narrow cobbled street in the centre of the main shopping area. The rooms are simple and clean and the hotel is remarkably inexpensive for this location. The décor is not very inspired but the friendly management and close proximity to shops and sights compensate for the lack of sumptuous surroundings.

Bedrooms: 21, most with shower/WC, some with bath/WC; none with TV
Facilities: Lift **Credit/charge cards accepted:** All

PORTOGHESI ♦♦
Via dei Portoghesi 1, 00186   *Tel: 68 64 231   Fax: 68 76 976*

The Portoghesi was converted into a hotel 150 years ago. It is next door to the Portuguese national church dedicated to St Anthony. The bedrooms are simply furnished and comfortable, but traffic rumbling by can make street-facing bedrooms noisy. The breakfast terrace on the top floor catches the early-morning light which filters down through the rooftops. On a street with flower vendors and antique restorers and close to the Piazza Navona, the hotel is central and good value for money.

Bedrooms: 27, all with shower/WC; air-conditioning   **Facilities:** Lift
Credit/charge cards accepted: Access, Visa

REGINA BAGLIONI ♦♦♦♦♦
Via Veneto 72, 00187   *Tel: 47 68 51   Fax: 48 54 83*

One of a chain of 'Palace Hotels' in Italy, the hotel has a reception area with high ceilings decorated in soft cameo colours. The bedrooms are spacious with modern-style furnishings; some are decorated with mother-of-pearl ingrained in the bedsteads. The hotel has a grand atmosphere without being intimidating and is less expensive than some of the hotels in the Via Veneto area. It is only five minutes' walk from the Borghese Gardens and the street cafés.

Bedrooms: 130, most with bath/shower/WC; all with air-conditioning;
mini-bar   **Facilities:** Lift; restaurant   **Credit/charge cards accepted:** All

SCALINATA DI SPAGNA ♦♦♦♦
Piazza Trinità dei Monti 17, 00187   *Tel: 67 93 006   Fax: 68 40 598*

This is a small hotel facing a taxi rank at the top of the Spanish Steps. It has a homely atmosphere. Well-thumbed paperbacks, in English and Italian, pack a glass-fronted cabinet. Some of the bedrooms are dowdy, particularly the family rooms. The hotel is relatively expensive for its standard of comfort, but there are good views across the rooftops of Rome from some of the bedrooms, and it has a good central location. There's also a small rooftop garden where you can sit out.

Bedrooms: 15, most with shower/WC, some with bath/WC; all with air-conditioning; fridge; safe   **Credit/charge cards accepted:** Amex, Visa

---

♦ = under £50; ♦♦ = £50 to £80; ♦♦♦ = £80 to £100;
♦♦♦♦ = £100 to £140; ♦♦♦♦♦ = over £140.

SOLE AL PANTHEON   ♦♦♦♦♦
Piazza della Rotonda 63, 00186
                                  Tel: 67 80 441   Fax: 68 40 689

Overlooking the piazza in front of the Pantheon, this hotel claims to be one of the oldest in the world. The room prices reflect the luxurious décor. The bedrooms are high-ceilinged, whitewashed and airy, filled with a mixture of modern and antique furniture. The rooms on the front of the hotel can be very noisy in the summer with the milling café crowds. The small breakfast room leads out into the integral courtyard, which is filled with potted plants.

Bedrooms: 29, most with bath/shower/WC, some with shower/WC; all with air-conditioning; mini-bar **Facilities:** Lift **Credit/charge cards accepted:** All

Hotel prices Symbols indicate approximate prices per room per night for a double room with bath. Many large hotels run special breaks which work out far cheaper. (See page 14 for further details.)

♦ = under £50; ♦♦ = £50 to £80; ♦♦♦ = £80 to £100;
♦♦♦♦ = £100 to £140; ♦♦♦♦♦ = over £140.

ST PETERSBURG

- Usually visited together with Moscow as a two-centre holiday, St Petersburg is the more beautiful of the two cities, though its grand European architecture clashes with the reality of the life on its streets. The historic centre is wanderable and reasonably compact
- As well as the world-famous Mariinsky ballet and opera companies, St Petersburg has tremendous circus troupes. The cultural events and all-night street life during St Petersburg's White Nights festival at the summer solstice in June are a memorable experience
- It's best to go on a package and book guided excursions. But do allow some time to wander off and explore on your own: you're free to do so

ST PETERSBURG has come full circle. Founded as St Petersburg, it has been known as Petrograd and Leningrad before reverting to its original title.

One of the world's most northerly cities, it is on the same latitude as Alaska and Greenland, but its climate is milder than that of Moscow. During the summer, night is reduced to a brief twilight, and for up to six months of the year the River Neva and its many tributaries and canals are usually frozen.

Though St Petersburg's outskirts are clogged with grim apartment blocks and grimy factories, a legacy of the Soviet state, the city's centre is astonishingly beautiful. Baroque, rococo and neo-classical façades painted the delicate shades of Italian ice-cream flank the river, canals and avenues, creating an extraordinary stage-set for the drab scenes of contemporary life.

Elaborate mansions house poky apartments (often shared by two or three families) or dingy shops with half-empty shelves. The streets are a hive of commercial activity: kiosks selling Western goods compete with ordinary citizens flogging everything from clothes and cigarettes to cats and caviare. Not all of them are black marketeers – some are just Russian *babuska*, trying to get along in the emerging market economy. The legalisation of street trading is one of the most visible changes in Russia.

It is on Nevsky Prospekt, now the main shopping street, that the gulf between the Russian lifestyle and that of Westerners is only too apparent. It was once one of the most fashionable streets in Europe, where aristocratic ladies could step out of their palaces to take tea in art-nouveau Yeliseyev's, or indulge in some wildly expensive trinket at Fabergé. Today, Fabergé has closed, Yeliseyev's has become a state-run food shop, and Nevsky Prospekt has become the trading ground of the city's black marketeers.

The parks, palaces and squares belonging to the old city of the tsars lie along the river bank and in the triangle of land bounded by the Neva, the Fontanka Canal and Nevsky Prospekt. Cutting across the Prospekt are three canals built to drain the flood-prone Neva: flowing between pastel-painted façades, they rank in beauty with those of Amsterdam and Venice. Walking (in winter) or taking a boat-trip along them (in summer) should not be missed; neither should the walk along the Neva's banks at night, when the *Aurora* cruiser, Peter and Paul Fortress and Hermitage buildings are floodlit.

The key to getting the most out of a short break in St Petersburg is to divide your time between going on organised excursions and exploring the city on your own. It's worth going on organised excursions to the Hermitage Art Gallery and the summer palaces

310

of the tsars outside the city to learn more about the history, and if you don't speak Russian it's worth booking a private guide to take you round any smaller museum that captures your interest, as few are labelled in English. But to get close to the city you need to see it alone.

Founded by Peter the Great, the city has always been Russia's window on the West. When Peter came to the throne in 1682 Russia was a country frozen in the Middle Ages. He recognised that the key to the future lay in trade with the West, and that this would be possible only when Russia had control of the River Neva, her sole outlet to the Baltic, which had been lost to the Swedes earlier in the century. The Neva was recaptured, and in 1703 work began on the Peter and Paul Fortress. In 1704 Peter was already referring to his new town, St Petersburg, as the 'capital', although it was not until 1712 that the court, nobles and merchants moved, somewhat reluctantly, up from Moscow.

Vast sums of money, and tens of thousands of labourers' lives, were spent on draining the marshy land and building St Petersburg. Russian architects were sent to study abroad, and foreign architects, most of them Italians, were drafted in. The most notable of these was Trezzini, responsible for the Peter and Paul Fortress's ritzy cathedral and the restrained Summer Palace.

Peter's successors continued to glorify the capital and build themselves extravagant country retreats. Elizabeth Petrovna, Peter's younger daughter, had the Italian architect Rastrelli build her the Winter Palace and country palaces at Pushkin (now being renamed Tsarlese Selo again) and Petrodvorets where she could indulge in her favourite pursuit – partying. The Winter Palace is now one of the three buildings that constitute the world-famous Hermitage Art Gallery; the other two were added by Catherine the Great to house her ever-expanding art collection.

The nineteenth century also saw embellishments to the city. Banks and shops competed in magnificence with the palaces of the aristocracy on Nevsky Prospekt; grand warehouses and a stock exchange were built at the port on Vasilyevsky Island; the army's main staff building and the navy's golden-spired Admiralty joined the Winter Palace on Dvortsovaya Ploshchad; and cathedrals added their mighty gilded domes to the city's skyline. This was also the Golden Age of Russian music, ballet and opera. Tchaikovsky and the 'Mighty Handful' (Borodin, Cui, Balakirev, Mussorgsky and Rimsky-Korsakov) were all working in the city; theatres and concert halls were built; and the St Petersburg Conservatory was founded under Anton Rubinstein.

But nineteenth-century St Petersburg was also the poverty-stricken city of Dostoevsky's novels, and it was here that the

Revolution was born. Dostoevsky was only a child when in December 1825 radical young officers and troops attempted to prevent the accession of the reactionary Grand Duke Nicholas. The Decembrists' uprising failed, but nothing was ever to be the same again. Nicholas's successor Alexander II was assassinated, and although his son Alexander III kept the revolutionaries in check for a couple of decades, the growth of the exploited working class gave the intelligentsia the impetus it required for radical change, which ultimately precipitated the 1905 and 1917

GETTING THERE

The specialist tour operator Intourist organises both group packages and tailor-made holidays for individuals. The Intourist office is at Intourist House, 219 Marsh Wall, London E14 9FJ, tel: 071-538 8600.

Tour operator packages

The major tour operators to Moscow and St Petersburg are Intourist, Sovereign and Thomson. All have seven-day dual-centre packages. There are only a few packages offered exclusively to St Petersburg. Packages work out cheaper (and easier) than going independently. The tour operator will organise your visa for you; dinner and certain excursions are included in the package price; and you can pre-book other sightseeing trips or evening entertainment swiftly and relatively easily through your rep. There's no obligation to stay with your group once you arrive.

The St Petersburg Hotel is modern and one of the pleasantest and most convenient. In 1992 three nights full- or half-board stay in a mid-range hotel cost between £299 and £425, depending on the season. See page 385 for a list of tour operators.

Going independently

This works out more expensive than going on a tour operator package, and, although not as easy as group travel, is much easier than it was. Excursions can be booked in hotels, and there are many more restaurants and bars. Russian tourism, however, is still geared to groups, not individuals. There's little available information – you'll need to get to grips with the service bureau at your hotel.

The advantage of travelling independently is that you have some choice over which hotel you stay in. It's worth requesting the art nouveau Yevropaiska, which has recently reopened after restoration as the Grand Hotel Europe.

The flight from London to St Petersburg takes about three and a half hours. British Airways flies direct to St Petersburg three times a week (Monday, Thursday, Sunday). Aeroflot has one flight in and out of Heathrow on Saturday. APEX is the cheapest fare, but several tour operators offer discounted scheduled flights, including Flightfile (071-

revolutions. The city was renamed Petrograd in 1917 instead of the too Germanic-sounding St Petersburg.

On 24 October 1917 the Red Guard occupied key buildings in Petrograd, and the following evening, cued by the firing of a blank shot from the cruiser *Aurora*, stormed the Winter Palace and arrested the members of the Provisional Government. The Bolsheviks took control, moved the capital to Moscow and proved their fitness to rule by surviving three years of bitter civil war – a survival secured only by the establishment of a loyalty-

---

323 1515), Data Travel (0424 722394) and Regent Holidays (0272 211 711).

Formalities

You will need a **visa**. Since the break-up of the former Soviet Union the Russian Consulate at 5 Kensington Palace Gardens, London W8 4QX (071-229 8027) has been issuing visas on behalf of countries that make up the Commonwealth of Independent States, except the Ukraine. You must possess a current 10-year passport valid for at least three months after your return. A British visitor's passport is not acceptable. The tourist visa is a separate document; no stamps or entries are made in your passport. The consulate fee is £5 for those travelling independently, and you need three passport-sized photos and clear photocopies of the information pages of your passport: pages one to five of the old-style British passport or pages 32-3 of the European-style passport. Allow at least two weeks. If you are going on a package the tour operator will usually obtain the visa for you, charging an additional fee for the service.

On the plane, you must fill in a **Customs Declaration Form**. On it you must list all your currency and travellers' cheques, and any valuables. Once there, you should keep all receipts of currency transactions, as these have to be handed in when you leave, along with a second declaration form, listing how much money you have remaining. The import and export of roubles is forbidden, and you'll need to change any left over into sterling before you leave. (*See also* 'Changing money' and 'The black market', page 315-16).

Customs is approached via a metal detector and your luggage will be X-rayed. Things get chaotic at this point, so the fewer bags you have, the better.

What to take with you

It's useful to take camera film, a bath plug, a two-pin adaptor for electrical items (the current is 220V), tissues (toilet paper is scarce in public lavatories), and all toiletries including soap, toothpaste, cotton wool, sanitary towels and tampons (which are virtually impossible to get hold of). Water sterilisation tablets can serve as an alternative to buying mineral water in St Petersburg (*see* 'Water' in 'Mastering the system', page 318).

enforcing secret police force, which was to set the tone for the future and a precedent for Stalin.

But it was not in the Civil War, nor even in the purges of Stalin that St Petersburg (then Leningrad) suffered most. During the Second World War it was blockaded for 900 days by the Nazis, during which time over half a million people died, mostly of starvation. The city was bombed and shelled, but the greatest problem was the lack of food and fuel. In desperation flour dust accumulated over the years was scraped from the walls of mills; 2,000 tons of sheep guts brought to the harbour for export before the war were collected and processed; bread was made largely of wood pulp; and the survival diet included liquid paraffin, glue and soups made from boiled leather. The mass graves of Piskaryovka Cemetery are an unforgettable monument to the courage of the Leningraders.

In 1992 Leningrad became St Petersburg again, in a revolution less bloody but no less painful. Nobody speaks about *glasnost* or *perestroika*. Economic reforms are under way but few ordinary people seem happy with the results.

WHEN TO GO

Summers are pleasantly warm during the months June to August and part of September, with maximum temperatures averaging 21°C (70°F) in the warmest month, July. The cold sets in rapidly in October, when temperatures rarely rise above 9°C (48°F), and spring doesn't really arrive before May. Leningrad has over five months of ground frost and winter is very cold (though slightly warmer than Moscow) but public buildings are well heated and snow makes the city especially beautiful. The White Nights Festival takes place in June.

MASTERING THE SYSTEM

Information Intourist has offices at the airport and at hotels, and can organise bookings for excursions and cultural events. It's worth going on some of the excursions – particularly to museums and royal palaces outside St Petersburg: an experienced guide can tell you a lot about the history. Intourist can also arrange a car and a private guide for any museum – worth it if you have a special interest, as only the major sights have explanations in English.

Language Russian uses the Cyrillic alphabet, which looks like a mixture of the Latin and Greek plus a few letters of its own. Mastering it will make life infinitely easier if you want to explore.

Hotels Most hotels are vast, and getting lost in them is only too easy. On arrival at some hotels you surrender your passport and accommodation voucher for a pass with your room number scribbled on. Once you've managed to find the correct floor, the pass is given to the lady responsible for your stretch of corridor, who will give you your room key. Every time you go out, swap the key for the pass – it will have to be shown to the doorman when you return and gives access to any other hotel in the city. It's not unusual to find your lady missing from her desk when you want her, sometimes leaving the drawer where she files the keys and passes unlocked – do not hesitate to help yourself to your key. It's worth keeping on good terms with your lady – a bar of soap, pair of tights, or packet of Marlboro should do the trick – so you can ask her to book you a table in a restaurant.

The situation is slowly changing – some hotels now hold all the keys on a board on the ground floor.

Changing money and credit cards There are currency exchange desks in your hotel, open longer hours than banks. You will need roubles to pay in cafés or restaurants, to buy souvenirs, and maybe to pay an entrance fee if you go to a museum on your own. Otherwise, you will be paying in hard currency.

The rates of exchange offered by the exchange desks in different hotels vary slightly, but if you're changing only small amounts of money it's not worth the effort of shopping around. When you exchange money you will be given a certificate, which you must produce if you want to change roubles back to hard currency. You will also have to return to the office where you made the original exchange. If you are not sure how many roubles you will need, it's best to change only small amounts of money.

Take cash rather than credit cards or travellers' cheques, and US dollars rather than pounds. Some exchange desks and Intourist offices will accept credit cards and travellers' cheques as well as cash, but some will take only cash.

Most rouble restaurants will also accept hard currency (negotiate with the waiter). Hard-currency restaurants accept cash, credit cards and cheques.

Most street traders will accept hard currency (US dollars or German marks) and will usually offer better rates than banks or hotels (though you will not be able to change money back).

The black market You don't need to look for the black market – it comes to you. The state and the black market have one common desire: hard currency. The state needs reserves of hard currency which can be used on the international market, while for a Russian without hard currency, buying some Western goods and luxuries is virtually impossible. Many Western goods are available in foreign-run currency shops or hotels (but for enormous numbers of roubles).

Black-market transactions are illegal (and you need to show exchange-receipts when changing roubles back into sterling); but many tourists engage in them without repercussion. In fact, totally boycotting the black market is difficult. Black marketeers pester foreigners near hotels and restaurants and on the streets, offering souvenirs, caviare and prostitutes. Hard-currency-hungry taxi-drivers are the hardest to avoid: if you don't speak Russian, forcing a driver to switch on the meter is virtually impossible, and many, particularly those waiting outside hotels, will drive you only for dollars or sterling (even if they let you pay in roubles, you will often be charged more than twice as much as a local). If you have only sterling, this means a minimum of £5 as coins are inexchangeable; you can save time and money with small-denomination dollar bills.

Shopping The first shop you are likely to visit is the hard-currency shop in your hotel. And if you're on an organised 'shopping trip', the excursion will consist not of a tour of the city's regular shops but a visit to a hard-currency shop, though you can ask your guide to show you other shops. There are now plenty of other hard-currency shops besides *beriozkas*. Western beers, fizzy drinks, chocolate bars and cigarettes, previously only for sale in *beriozkas*, are now available from street kiosks, at lower prices than in the hard-currency shops.

As far as a tourist is concerned, hard-currency shops are useful for stocking your bedroom fridge, if you have one, but the souvenirs are vastly overpriced.

In an ordinary shop, buying anything is often a lengthy procedure: you point out what you want to buy to the assistant, who will give you a handwritten slip of paper with the price on it. Having queued to pay, you then return to the counter with your receipt, and queue to collect the goods. It's no surprise that the average Russian woman spends two hours a day shopping (although some food shops have recently switched to a Western supermarket system).

Eating out in restaurants If you are on an organised package, you could eat every night in your hotel or go on organised excursions to restaurants (payable in hard currency). It is, however, more fun to go independently. You can book a table through Intourist (though if you do it officially it can be quite expensive – try asking the Intourist staff unofficially, as a 'favour'). You can also book yourself, by phone (fine, as long as they can find someone who speaks English), or make friends with the lady in charge of your floor in the hotel and ask her to phone for you. If you call in during the day, most restaurants will have plenty of tables available. Tourist agencies will also book you a privately owned, co-operative restaurant for no charge, although you will usually have to pay in hard currency. If you pay in roubles the bill will be two or three times higher. It's best to ask when booking about what sort of currency is preferred.

Etiquette At the theatre, museum or restaurant, you must leave your coats and bags in the cloakroom. In many museums you put on felt slippers (don't wear high-heeled shoes). Smoking is taboo in most public places (including many restaurants). On streets or in subways pedestrians keep to the right.

Maps As we went to press there were still no maps with the new street names. Do not hesitate to ask locals if you get lost – a surprisingly high number speak English.

Sightseeing tours If you're on a package holiday, certain excursions will be included in the price: generally a city tour, a trip to one of the summer palaces and a visit to a museum (not the Hermitage). You will also be able to book optional excursions from your tour operator. Going to museums and the royal palaces outside the city independently is not particularly convenient: it's a long trip by bus or suburban train. It's worth taking organised excursions to the palaces (you can always abandon them and make your own way back), and considering hiring a private guide to take you to some of the smaller museums.

In summer there are trips along the Neva and canals by river-bus, organised by tourist agencies. But there are regular (and much cheaper) public trips, which start earlier and last between one and a half and five hours. Trips up the Neva leave every 15 minutes from the Winter Palace. The canal trip depends on the tides – if the water level is too high the boats won't fit under the bridges. Water levels permitting, they leave every half-hour from Anichkov Bridge by Nevsky Prospekt. A more exciting alternative is to hire a smaller private boat near Anichkov Bridge or near the bridge over the River Moika opposite Kazan Cathedral. A boatload of five people will pay about $25 altogether, and you will see the canals where the larger boats cannot go. Some drivers have English-speaking guides.

Opening hours and days The city's museums and palaces all close on different days, though they are usually open on Sundays. They also close for an additional day in the last week of the month. Times are liable to change – so check with the service bureau in your hotel before setting out.

Most shops close on Sunday, and for an hour at lunchtime. They stay open until 7pm or 8pm. Street kiosks often stay open until 10pm or 11pm.

Water St Petersburg's water should not be drunk: the city is built on marshes and has a low water table liable to contamination. It is suspected that the current source of contamination is the half a million corpses of those who died during the Second World War blockade and who were buried in Piskaryovka Cemetery. Some say it's due to the presence of a particular microbe. Whatever the source of the problem, be prepared to drink mineral water.

GETTING AROUND

St Petersburg's **underground** (metro) system is fairly straight-forward as there are only four lines. The main problem is knowing where to change lines or get off if you can't read Cyrillic. If you have a map, write down the names of relevant stations in Cyrillic; otherwise note down the number of stops between stations. All journeys cost one rouble – you buy a token from the *kacca* (ticket office) and drop it in the barrier as you enter. There are no change machines.

For simple journeys, like going up and down Nevsky Prospekt, **trams, buses** and **trolley buses** can be useful. But for more complex journeys you may find getting off at the right stop a problem. The charge per journey is also one rouble: tickets can be bought from drivers, news kiosks or, failing that, from other passengers. The easiest way of getting about is by **taxi**. This, though, can work out expensive as most drivers will want paying in hard currency as soon as they realise you are a foreigner (*see also 'The black market'*). You'll also find that many car-owning St Petersburgers moonlight as taxi-drivers – just stand in the street, put your hand out and eventually someone will stop.

UNMISSABLES

Dvortsovaya Ploshchad

The main square of St Petersburg, at the head of Nevsky Prospekt, is an immense, theatrical space whose splendid buildings reduce the people crossing it to Lowry-like proportions. It was across here that the Red Guard charged as they stormed the ornately stuccoed Winter Palace in the October Revolution of

1917, an event celebrated the following year by avant-garde artists who swathed the buildings with 15,000 metres of Cubist and Futurist paintings.

In the centre of the square is the gigantic angel-crowned Alexander Column: 47.5 metres high and weighing 704 tons, it took 2,000 soliders and 400 workers to erect it, and it is supported only by its weight.

But the building that really sets the square's tone is the Main Staff, former headquarters of the Russian Army. A sweeping golden yellow crescent featuring a rhythmic white colonnade, designed by the Italian architect Carlo Rossi, it has a mighty triumphal arch as centrepiece, surmounted by an imposing statue group of *Victory* on her chariot. It was here, on 19 July 1914, that the German ambassador delivered the declaration which began the First World War.

Nevsky Prospekt

'There is nothing finer than Nevsky Prospekt . . . in St Petersburg it is everything.' Gogol is right to an extent. Seen from the comfort of a tourist coach, St Petersburg's main street, crossed with canals and flanked by classical, baroque and art-nouveau façades, is indeed fine. But walk down the Prospekt from the golden-spired Admiralty building to Vostaniya Ploshchad, and you probably won't even notice the architecture. For the Prospekt is crowded with street traders offering all kinds of goods, many of doubtful quality.

Nevsky is also the territory of St Petersburg's black marketeers, and you can expect to be offered fur hats, postcards, books on art, souvenirs, and roubles for your dollars or pounds. It will perhaps be only on your second walk down Nevsky, when you have become accustomed to the reality of a Russian high street, that you will be able to appreciate the buildings. To walk the whole length of Nevsky would take half a day; the most interesting stretch is between the Admiralty and Vostaniya Ploshchad, which is dominated by the palatial Moscow railway station. Confine yourself to this section and you will have time to wander along the canals that cross the Prospekt, and to take a break in the quiet refinement of Iskusstv Ploshchad.

Almost every building repays close scrutiny: façades are embellished with delicate moulding, classical motifs, boisterous caryatids and grimacing masks. The Aeroflot headquarters at No 7/9 was built in a style reminiscent of the Doges' Palace in Venice to house the St Petersburg Commercial Bank; Kazan Cathedral, now a museum of atheism, is fronted by a colonnade based on St Peter's in Rome; and beyond, the double-loggiaed Gostinny Dvor department store was designed by Rastrelli, architect of the Winter Palace, and would not look out of place on an Italian piazza. Across the road from Kazan, Dom Knigi, the city's largest bookshop, occupies the art-nouveau headquarters of the Singer Sewing Machine Company, and is still crowned by the Singer trademark of a glass dome; and on the corner with Malaya Sadovaya Ulitsa is a state food shop, Gastronom, whose scant offerings are mocked by the mirrored, gilded and stained-glass interior.

City tour

Try to see something of St Petersburg for yourself before taking the coach tour around the city. The view from the coach window and through the camera lens is of a beautiful stage-set, and can leave you feeling sealed off from the people who live there. However, it is an effortless way of getting an overview of the city.

The first stop is on the Strelka, the eastern tip of Vasilyevsky Island. Until the 1880s this was the city's main merchant dockyard, and it is still dominated by two warehouses – the neo-classical ex-stock exchange and the ugly Rostral Columns, whose protruding ship prows symbolise the port, and whose gas-fired torches (still lit on special occasions) were designed to guide ships safely into harbour. The views from the Strelka are tremendous – across the river are the ornate buildings of the Hermitage, upstream is the golden needle spire of the Peter and Paul Fortress, and downstream is the Admiralty spire and the dome of St Isaac's.

After a brief photo-stop outside St Isaac's, you are driven past the Field of Mars, a marsh drained by Peter the Great and used as a parade ground. It was then a vast, dusty, desolate place, known as the St Petersburg Sahara, and, though it remains bleak in winter, it is cheered up with lilac bushes in summer. The victims of the 1917 revolution are buried here, and, on May Day 1920, 16,000 volunteers laid out paths, lawns and flower beds.

The next stop is outside the gaudily exotic Temple of the Spilled Blood, built on the spot where Tsar Alexander II was killed. A confection of scrolled windows, fancy moulding and vibrant, diamond-pointed onion domes, it is currently undergoing restoration, and when it is re-opened should be well worth a visit, as there are 300 metres of mosaics inside.

You next head east to Smolny Convent, another work by Rastrelli. The name means tar, for it was erected on the site of the old tar and pitch stores. The cathedral (now used as a concert hall) is a blue and white baroque fantasy topped with silvery baubles.

Hermitage Museum

It's an extraordinary feeling, walking through the flamboyantly opulent rooms of the three palaces that comprise the Hermitage. The contrast with what's outside couldn't be greater: rooms caked in gold, malachite and marble, and crammed with priceless *objets d'art* and works by Western great masters. The Winter Palace, a lavish baroque confection of jade, white and ochre-painted stucco, was designed for Empress Elizabeth by Rastrelli. She died before it was completed and the first occupant was her nephew Peter III. He had just three months in the palace before being assassinated in a coup led by his wife Catherine's lover, Grigory Orlov. Catherine (the Great) became sole ruler, took over her late husband's quarters, and installed Orlov in the rooms directly beneath. It was to house her extensive and ever-expanding collection of art that the Small and Great Hermitage Palaces were built. Later tsars continued to gather works of art, and after the Revolution these were joined by private collections requisitioned by the state. The result is one of the world's greatest art galleries. But with over two million exhibits, in 20 kilometres of galleries and corridors, you are bound to get lost – unless you have a plan or take a guided tour. Once inside, there's nothing to stop you abandoning your group, as long as you inform your guide. If you stick with the tour, expect to be herded swiftly through rooms and to have to stand listening to involved commentaries on paintings you may not like.

The highlight for most people is the glorious collection of French Impressionists and post-Impressionists, including familiar works by Matisse, Picasso and Gauguin. They were collected by two Moscow industrialists, one of whom, Shchukin, was an early patron of Matisse and Picasso. The paintings are on the second floor of the Winter Palace.

On the first floor of the Large Hermitage there are collections of Italian Renaissance works, and of Spanish and Flemish art. Familiar names include Botticelli, Titian, Leonardo da Vinci, Velázquez, Rembrandt and Rubens.

On the first floor of the Winter Palace are the Hermitage's most stunningly decorated rooms: the vibrant Malachite Hall, the Nicholas Hall, in which balls for up to 5,000 were held, and the sumptuous suite of rooms used by Empress Maria Alexandrova, wife of Alexander II, which include the Blue Bedroom, and Gold and Raspberry Drawing Rooms.

Finally, if you're interested in jewellery, don't miss the Hermitage's 'special collection' of mostly Scythian and ancient Greek jewellery. To see it you must book in advance through a tourist agency and pay an extra fee.

River Neva

St Petersburg is at its most beautiful at night, when the splendid buildings that flank the River Neva are floodlit. In autumn, their reflections shimmer in the inky waters; in winter, the snow intensifies their delicate pastels. If you start at the St Petersburg Hotel, the walk will take you past the cruiser *Aurora*, resplendent with fairy lights, through the grounds of the Peter and Paul Fortress, and over a little wooden bridge to a houseboat restaurant where you could stop for a meal or drink. After this, you can cross a bridge over the tributary Malaha Neva to Pushkinskaya Ploshchad, on Vasilyevsky Island, giving a superb view of the Winter Palace and Admiralty building. From here, the Dvortsovyy Bridge takes you across the river to Palace Square and, if you have any energy left, Nevsky Prospekt.

In summer, a lazier way of seeing the beauties of the Neva embankment is to take a boat or hydrofoil.

The Royal Palaces

'The wounds inflicted by the invader on our land, our cities and our villages will be healed. Our palaces, museums, picture galleries, fountains and parks will be resurrected.' So said *Pravda* in September 1944 in the wake of damage inflicted on the Soviet Union during the German occupation. The three royal palace complexes outside Leningrad suffered more than most: photographs show them as little more than blackened shells. Now they have been, and are being, painstakingly restored, at a cost of millions of roubles. And though, given the state of the economy, this may seem an extravagance on a par with that of the tsar who originally had them built, the achievement of the restorers is unquestionable.

In summer a visit to **Petrodvorets** is a must. It's worth taking an organised excursion (they run from May to September) to see the ornate interior of the Great Palace, with its hand-painted silk wallpapers, exotic Chinese rooms and glitzy gilt halls and staircases. Tours, however, leave little time to take in the glorious excesses of the grounds: Petrodvoret's fountains, cascading around gilded statues, are among the world's finest; and there are other palaces and follies to see. A good plan is to abandon the tour after visiting the Great Palace and return to St Petersburg by the public service hydrofoil (also May to September).

Many of the places at **Pushkin** are still awaiting restoration, but the splendid turquoise and white Catherine Palace has been returned to its former glory. It was built by Tsarina Elizabeth and named after her mother Catherine, wife of Peter the Great. The interior was later ripped out on the orders of the other Catherine (the Great), and remodelled in a rather flamboyantly neo-classical style by the Scottish architect Charles Cameron. Highlights are the white stuccoed main staircase, the gilt-encrusted Great Hall, and the Green Dining-Room, with delicate pink and white classical bas-reliefs on the walls. The Catherine Park has a lakeside Turkish bath based on the design of a mosque, a Palladian bridge, mock ruins and a cemetery for tsarist dogs.

Charles Cameron was also responsible for the palace of **Pavlosk**, three kilometres beyond. It was a gift from Catherine the Great to her son Paul I (Pavel in Russian, hence the name) and it was here that he was trained by his mother and tutor for the tsarship – a reign that lasted only five years before he was assassinated. After his death his widow Mariya Feodorovna lived at Pavlosk for 40 years. The most appealing rooms are hers: the porphyry columns and Raphaelesque frescoes in her boudoir, and her bedroom, decorated on a garden theme, with a chandelier that resembles a fountain, and hand-painted flowers, fruit and birds on the silk walls. Links with the French royal family are also in evidence – the twin rooms dedicated to War and Peace, and Pavlosk's gardens, with fake ruins and phoney cottages, were inspired by Versailles.

OTHER PLACES TO VISIT

Museums and galleries

Dostoevsky House Museum From 1878 until his death in 1881, Dostoevsky rented a flat on Kuznechnyy Pereulok. It has been furnished as it was when he lived there: bills lie on his wife's desk, a samovar sits on a table in the cosy dining-room, and his children's toys and books remain in the nursery. Best of all is the study, with inkpot, penholder, wallet, books and doctors' prescriptions. On the ground floor are manuscripts of his most famous works (complete with doodles) and disturbing charcoal sketches of madmen. There is an English guidebook.

Pushkin Flat Museum Pushkin lived only for a brief time in this lovely canalside flat, and it was here that he died, after being wounded in a duel over his wife. It's worth hiring a guide to take you round, otherwise the restored rooms will strike you only as displays of nineteenth-century furniture and furnishings.

Russian Museum If you feel, walking through the Hermitage's rooms of Rembrandts and Titians, that you didn't come to St Petersburg to look at Western paintings, the Russian Museum comes as a refreshing antidote. Housed in an elaborate neo-classical palace on fine Iskusstv Ploshchad, it holds a collection of icons, handicrafts, and Russian and Soviet paintings.

Repin is probably the nineteenth-century Russian artist best known outside his country: his portraits of craggy, bearded men in black suits contrast with works like *The Volga Boatmen*, in which men with their feet bound in sackcloth struggle to pull a barge along the river. Another powerful portrait is that of Diaghilev with his nanny, by Leon Bakst. Finally, there are paintings by Kandinsky, and a collection of post-Revolutionary art.

Other attractions

Alexander Nevsky Monastery Founded by Peter the Great, the Alexander Nevsky is the larger of the two functioning senior monasteries (*lavras*) in St Petersburg. Services are held daily at 10am and 6pm. If you're in St Petersburg when the nights are dark, try to make the evening service. Under a winter moon, with its red and white baroque church visible through a skeletal screen of trees, the Alexander Nevsky Monastery is suffused with mystery and enchantment. Inside, gilded icons flicker in the candlelight and the air is heavy with the smell of melted wax. The service begins with the rhythmic, hypnotic incantations of a priest, answered by the eerie harmonies of the small choir.

By day, you can visit the monastery's two cemeteries. Tikhvin is the more interesting, a peaceful garden with spacious alleys in which Tchaikovsky, Dostoevsky and Mussorgsky are buried.

Aurora Cruiser In 1917 the *Aurora* was sitting in the Petrograd docks undergoing a refit. The Bolsheviks won the crew over to their cause and on the night of 25/26 October the *Aurora* fired a blank shot to intimidate the members of Kerensky's government in the Winter Palace. The Red Guard took it as their cue, stormed the palace and arrested the government. The kitchen and sleeping areas of the ship can now be visited.

Peter and Paul Fortress Walking along the far bank of the Neva, one of the nicest places at which to pause is the Peter and Paul Fortress. Soaring above its star-shaped fortifications is a splendid baroque tower – tiers of white marble surmounted by a 58-metre-high golden spire – belonging to a lavish church which holds the tombs of Romanov tsars, including Peter the Great, under whose rule the fortress was built.

Designed as a bastion against the Swedes, this was the first building to be constructed in St Petersburg. The Russian slaves and Swedish prisoners forced to work on the fortress took only seven years to complete it, but by this time Peter's successes against the Swedes had made it redundant, and it was used instead as a political prison. In the nineteenth century many of the major figures of the revolution were imprisoned there – the Decembrists, the anarchist Bakunin, and Lenin's older brother – while others, including Dostoevsky, were tried in the ex-Commandant's house. This now houses the Museum of the History of St Petersburg, with fascinating models, plans and diagrams charting the architectural development of the city. Sadly it is labelled only in Russian – if you're really interested, book a guide through a tourist agency.

In midwinter, when the River Neva is frozen over, hardy St Petersburgers ('walruses') can be seen breaking the ice below the Peter and Paul Fortress and plunging into the waters for a sub-zero swim.

Later in the year, at the first sign of sun, the scant stony beach is packed with semi-naked bodies. There is so little space that most people sunbathe standing up.

Peter the Great's Cabin Peter the Great spent six years living in this log cabin while he awaited the construction of the Summer Palace. In 1784 it was protected with a sturdier stone structure. Inside is a small museum charting the development of St Petersburg, and rooms furnished as they might have been when Peter sat here with his architects planning the city.

St Isaac's Cathedral This nineteenth-century cathedral impresses by statistics rather than beauty. The interior has room for 14,000 worshippers; 100kg of gold was used to cover the dome, and 1,000 people died gilding it; each of the dull red granite columns weighs 116 tons; and special ships and a railway had to be built to transport them from a Finnish quarry.

The interior, with mosaic icons, lazurite and malachite columns and multicoloured marble walls, is splendid. There's also a 93-metre-long Foucault pendulum (which demonstrates the rotation of the earth) suspended from the dome. You can climb to the top gallery for a fine view (although you can't take photos), and visit a museum charting the construction of the cathedral.

Summer Palace and Gardens This modest, two-storey building was the first palace in St Petersburg. It is now one of the city's most appealing museums, with rooms laid out as they were in Peter the Great's time. In contrast with the extravagance of St Petersburg's other royal palaces, this is a remarkably simple place. Peter lived downstairs, his wife upstairs. The most interesting rooms are the kitchen, with eighteenth-century utensils, and the workshop complete with Peter's tools. The gardens around the Summer Palace form St Petersburg's loveliest park. Pushkin was a daily visitor, and would get straight out of bed and walk there in his dressing-gown and slippers. It's still a lovely place in which to relax or picnic in summer.

SHOPPING

(See also 'Shopping' under 'Mastering the system', page 316)

It is not until you have explored St Petersburg's main shopping street, Nevsky Prospekt, that you can begin to appreciate the everyday reality of life in the city. Russian women do not do a weekly shop, but drop in on shops daily to see if something that they might need is available.

One of the most pleasant places in which to queue for food is Gastronom on the corner with Malaya Sadovaya Ulitsa. Though much of the food is canned, packeted or bottled, Gastronom does tend to be better stocked than most other food shops (two kinds of salami, ham, overpriced Western sweets), and the building itself is an art-nouveau extravaganza of stained glass, wrought-iron and elaborate lamps.

A feast for the stomach as well as the eyes is the 'free market', or *rynok*, next to Vladimirskaya Metro station. In contrast with the miserable offerings of the state stores, the quality is superb – shiny apples and tangerines, glistening grapes and berries, piles of fluffy thick cream, and honey sold straight off the comb – but the prices are very high in local terms.

On the ground floor of Gostinny Dvor, St Petersburg's main department store, are counters selling gimcrackery ranging from Russian dolls and artificial flowers to fake pewter and plastic jewellery. More interesting are the clothes departments upstairs, where you can buy a Gorbachev trilby or traditional fur hat, a fake fur coat or heavy overcoat at a fraction of the price charged in the West. There's also a branch of Littlewoods – a joint Russian-British venture – selling goods priced in dollars and roubles; the dollar goods are of better quality. Next door, a Babylon shop sells suits at prices ten times the salary of an ordinary Russian worker.

Across the road is Dom Knigi, St Petersburg's largest bookshop. Upstairs is a wide selection of posters and a few art books with English texts. Melodiya, next to the Yevropaiska Hotels, sells records which range from classical and folk to Soviet jazz and rock, and are very cheap (the sound quality deteriorates rapidly, however). There is little Western pop and rock available in the official shops – but with a blank cassette and five roubles you can have a tape made up (in around three days) at the kiosk at the beginning of Gogolu Ulitsa: there are at least 70 albums to choose from.

The best source of good-quality souvenirs is the arts and crafts market. Prices tend to be high and many of the artists will accept only hard currency. But there are beautifully made rag-dolls and exquisitely decorated sets of Russian dolls.

It's also worth popping in to some of the co-operative shops that have sprung up to compare prices and goods with those of state-run shops.

EATING AND DRINKING

(*See also 'Eating out' under 'Mastering the system', page 316*)
Your first taste of Russian food is likely to be the hotel breakfast: piles of thinly sliced black and white bread, with meagre curls of butter, garlic sausage or cheese; tomato juice or fruit syrup (it's unwise to drink this as it's diluted with the local water) and eventually tea or coffee. Hotel lunches are rather more appetising, with Scandinavian-style buffets where you eat as much meat, salad and soup as you want for a very reasonable flat rate. One of the best is in the St Petersburg Hotel.

Dinners in hotels are rarely good. Starters – *zakuski* – are often the best part of the meal, so don't bother saving room for the main courses. There might be *blini* – buckwheat pancakes served with caviare (*ikra*) and sour cream (*smetana*) – or smoked fish and a selection of salads and pickles. The soup course follows: the famous Russian vegetable soups *bortsch* (beetroot) and *shchi* (cabbage) are not vegetarian (*bortsch* is based on a meat stock and *shchi* usually has cubes of ham or salami floating in it). Main courses usually consist of a limited selection of fish, standards like beef Stroganoff or chicken Kiev, kebabs (*shashlik*), or roast meat. They are often a bit tough. Desserts tend to be ice-cream, or even a bowl of whipped cream (*slivki*).

There are lots of cafés on Nevsky Prospekt, some of them dismal places where you queue for a fake coffee and stale sandwich which is eaten standing up at chest-high tables. For lunch try the café at Gogolu 7 or Café Drushba round the corner on Nevsky Prospekt. The Grand Hotel Europe on Nevsky has a roubles restaurant overlooking the Prospekt and an Italian restaurant, La Trattoria, which takes hard currency. Two other hard-currency restaurants are Chaika baz at Griboedova channel 14 (lots of wines, starters, fish and meat) and Gino-Ginelli next door (ice-creams, burgers, pasta and pizza). If you don't mind eating on the move, there are lots of vendors selling snacks – on Nevsky, in its side streets, and in the forecourt of Moscow Station: *piroshki* are meat pies, and there are savoury doughnuts, hamburger-like meat patties served with rye bread, and ice-cream, biscuits and cakes for dessert. There are also usually a number of fruit vendors near metro stations. Don't be tempted by the machines vending mineral water – most locals won't touch them. To buy in food for a picnic, get bread from one of Nevsky's bakeries, spit-roast chicken from the butchers on the corner with Pushkinskaya, and fruit from one of the Nevsky bazaars or the *rynok*.

Although it's some way out of the centre, next to the Moskovsky metro station, Café Allegro, a joint Soviet-Finnish pizzeria and coffee bar, is well worth the effort of getting there. It's easy to miss as there is no sign outside – it's in a dull concrete block on your right as you leave the metro station. There's no need to book at lunchtime, but for the evenings it's obligatory (there's often a disco).

Entertainment in restaurants is the norm, as there is little else in the way of nightlife. Most refined is the Café Literaturnoye by the Moika Canal on Nevsky Prospekt: you sip your Russian (sweet but pleasant) champagne and eat *blinis* and steak to an accompaniment of opera or classical music. You will need to book in advance, best done in person by dropping in.

You can pay in roubles, but the waiters will be more than pleased if you offer to pay in hard currency. The entertainment in a state-run restaurant like the Neva, Nevsky Prospekt 46, is tackier, but can be fun – expect scantily clad dancers and dated UK top ten hits. Dinner will cost 800 to 1,000 roubles; book in advance (tel: 110 59 80).

The classic drinks to have with a meal are vodka (swigged neat) and sweet Russian champagne. The best wines tend to be Georgian. Mineral water is usually available and varies a lot – some are very salty, others unpleasantly sweet.

NIGHTLIFE

Come to St Petersburg if you can for the White Nights Festival at the summer solstice in June. Street life continues throughout the light evenings and there are plenty of cultural events laid on. The city's world-famous Mariinsky ballet and opera company (former stars include Nureyev and Nijinsky) has plans to introduce modern works by Western choreographers into the repertoire.

The main venue is the Mariinsky (formerly Kirov) Theatre on Teatral'naya Ploshchad, which has a beautiful blue and gold-tiered auditorium. St Petersburg's second venue for opera and ballet is the Maly Theatre on Iskusstv Ploshchad, a delightful baroque theatre where Shostakovich's *Lady Macbeth of Mtsenzk* was premièred. Tickets are available at your hotel through a tourist agency.

Classical music also flourishes. The most atmospheric venue is the Shostakovich Philharmonia on Iskusstv Ploshchad: there is a second, smaller hall at Nevsky Prospekt 30. Tickets are available from the *kassa* round the corner from Iskusstv Ploshchad at Mihajilovskaya Ulitsa 2.

For a more light-hearted evening out, you could go to see the dazzlingly daring and hilarious circus (on the Reki Fontanka Embankment) or to the Bolshoi Puppet Theatre (Nekrasova Ulitsa 10).

SALZBURG

- A beautiful baroque city, in a dramatic mountain setting, Salzburg is chock-full of charm, with a romantic atmosphere comparable to Venice
- A paradise for music-lovers: the birthplace of Mozart and home of the internationally renowned Salzburg Festival
- Summer is crowded: avoid August unless you have tickets for the Festival and pre-booked accommodation. Hotels increase their prices from July to September
- Just right for a long weekend time-wise, but it may be difficult to find convenient cheap flights if you are travelling independently
- Lovely scenery, both within the city and in the Salzkammergut area

SALZBURG is a stately city on a small scale, picturesquely sited in the shadow of the Mönchsberg, which is crowned by a vast defensive fortress. The River Salzach divides the city in two: the right bank, dominated by the Kapuzinerberg, is a more modern mirror image of the left. The old city is remarkable for displaying the harmony which exists between man and nature. In many ways it has scarcely changed since the time of Mozart when the early Romantic poets and artists first admired it.

The old city, or Altstadt, on the left bank, is generally closed to traffic, which contributes to the time-warp effect. Yet, for the visitor at least, this is the centre of activity. All the action appears to be concentrated in Getreidegasse, the main street where Mozart was born (at No 9) in 1756. It is lined with handsome houses and appealing shops proclaimed by elegantly scrolled wrought-iron signs – and is often packed with tourists and shoppers. Most of the main sights are a few minutes' walk from here. The oldest part of the town is the complex of St Peter's, the Benedictine abbey founded in the eighth century by St Rupert, generally considered to be the father of modern Salzburg. He also founded the convent of Nonnberg at Nonntal, now a peaceful suburb at the far end of the old town. But most of the old city is the creation of Wolf-Dietrich, the most famous of a line of powerful Prince-Archbishops who ruled Salzburg until the early nineteenth century. He brought in Italian architects to redesign it, earning the city the inevitable nickname of 'the Rome of the North'. The Romanesque cathedral was conveniently damaged by fire and so was completely rebuilt; squares were opened up, elaborate fountains designed, the medieval Residenz remodelled. In the eighteenth century Wolf-Dietrich's successors employed home-grown baroque architects, including Fischer von Erlach and Lukas von Hildebrandt, to complete the transformation. Yet for all the grandeur, old Salzburg is still predominantly a cosy, provincial town. Much of its charm lies in the fine old mansions and shops, the crooked alleys, the busy market squares and the unexpected peaceful corners. Horse-drawn traps clop around the streets, people go shopping in their *Dirndl* dresses or *Lederhosen*, and guitarists strum irreverently under the statue of Mozart in the square named after him. It can all seem rather unreal.

This effect is rather rudely dispelled when you cross to the newer part of town on the right bank, which expanded in the mid-nineteenth century when Salzburg became part of the international railway network. Beyond the noisy embankments there are some attractive houses and streets, but the area was badly bombed and has little of the charm of the old town. The more mundane services and shops are concentrated here, as well as the larger hotels, including most of those used by tour operators. The main attraction of this side of the city is the Mirabell Palace, originally built by Wolf-Dietrich as his summer residence, and the baroque gardens designed by Fischer von Erlach. These offer arguably the most photogenic view of the city, framed by manicured lawns and formal flowerbeds in the foreground and the rugged backdrop of the Mönchsberg behind the old town. On nearby Makartplatz is Fischer von Erlach's grandiose baroque church of the Holy Trinity. The new town has its own shopping street, the Linzergasse, and two cultural venues: the Mozarteum (concerts) and the Marionettentheater (puppet theatre). All these are close together, and within a few minutes' walk of the old town.

WHEN TO GO

The Salzburg Music Festival is a prestigious international event lasting from late July to the end of August. The city is crowded, hotels put up their prices and if you are not coming to Salzburg specifically for the festival, avoid it at all costs. This applies, to a lesser degree, to the Easter Festival. There are plenty of fine concerts all year round, so music lovers need never be disappointed. On balance, May, June and September are the most appealing months to choose.

However, a winter break is well worth considering. Salzburg is particularly beautiful and romantic in snow (but it can be foggy too, and the lovely fountains are boarded up). Hotels are always kept snug and some of the cellar-like restaurants are cosy too. There is a Mozart Festival in January, but you will miss out on the delights of Hellbrunn (open April to October) and outdoor eating at pavement cafés or in beer-gardens. At any time of year, bring an umbrella: Salzburg is notoriously rainy.

MASTERING THE SYSTEM

Information Salzburg Tourist Office (Fremdenverkehrsbetriebe der Stadt Salzburg) main office is at Auerspergstrasse 7, A-5020 Salzburg (tel: 88987). There are tourist information centres at Mozartplatz 5, in the old town (tel: 847568) and at the station (tel: 871712) and airport (tel: 852451).

The centres can provide much of the information you might need, including a list of sights with current opening hours and prices and a *Salzburg* leaflet with a description of sights and practical information as well as a map of the city centre. The restaurant list (*Gaststattenplan Stadt Salzburg*) is in German, but with some explanation of symbols in English. It is also useful for opening hours.

It is advisable to visit the tourist office first thing in the morning or in the evening to avoid queues. If you arrive without pre-booked accommodation, the tourist office can help you find somewhere to stay.

In the same building as the main tourist information centre in Mozartplatz is the Information der Salzburger Land (tel: 843264) which deals with the province of Salzburg and gives information about excursions outside the city.

It's worth contacting the Austrian National Tourist Office at 30 St George Street, London W1R 0AL (tel: 071-629 0461) for leaflets and information before you go. *Salzburg Events* is a booklet listing the whole year's cultural programme.

Sightseeing tours These start from Residenzplatz or the Mirabell-platz (there are also tours that can be booked through your hotel, which will pick you up from there). There are two classic excursions, offered by several companies: the *Sound of Music* trip (places associated with the von Trapp family and locations of the film) and the lakes and mountains of the Salzkammergut (including picturesque Wolfgangsee). Half-day trips over the border to Berchtesgaden with visits to the salt-mines or Hitler's mountain eyrie are also widely offered – it is embarrassing to leave your passport behind. We recommend the *Sound of Music* nostalgia trip for a good overall view of the city and surroundings, but be prepared for piped 'Doh-a-Deer' and sing-along fellow tourists – bring your sense of humour and leave your English reserve behind. Bob's Special Tours main office in Dreifaltigs-keitsgasse (tel: 872484) offers personalised tours for small groups of English-speakers, including a picnic on the Bavarian (Berchtes-gaden) trip. The two main excursion companies (Salzburg Sightseeing Tours and Salzburg Panorama Tours) and Bob's all have comfortable minibuses. For walking tours of Salzburg, contact City Guides (tel: 88987).

Buying tickets for cultural events It's worth reserving tickets direct from the box office for all musical events (ticket agencies charge around 20 per cent extra). The snag is that you will normally have to pay for and collect the tickets on the day, half an hour before the performance (8pm or 8.30pm), which may disrupt dinner plans. You can buy tickets in advance from the agencies.

For the Salzburg Festival some seats may be available at short notice from the box office. However, it is wise to book tickets (in addition to accommodation) well in advance. The programme is published in November (the National Tourist Office in London should have copies) and applications – to the Ticket Office of the Salzburg Festival, A-5010 Salzburg, Postfach 140 (tel: 844501) – should be received by the first week of January, at least for the best concerts. The programme for the Mozart Week in late January is published a year in advance; for tickets write to the Mozarteum, Schwarzstrasse 26, Salzburg.

Changing money Banks are open on weekdays from 8.30am to 12.30pm and 2pm to 4.30pm, and closed at weekends. Some small local banks are open (hours vary) on Saturday and Sunday, especially during July and August. Open daily are the exchange offices in the railway station ticket hall (7am to 10pm in summer, 7.30am to 9pm in winter) and at the airport (8am to 4pm). For full details look at the 'Money-changing' section in the *Salzburg* brochure.

GETTING THERE

Going independently

By air There are daily scheduled flights from the UK to Salzburg via Vienna or Zurich with Austrian Airlines from Heathrow. The cheapest bookable fare is the APEX (book 14 days in advance), and fares increase in the summer months. Tour operators offering scheduled fares include GTF Tours (071-792 1260), Canterbury Travel (081-206 0411) and Austria On-Line (071-287 0406).

There are many more charter flights into Salzburg from the UK, all year round and from several UK airports; but these are almost always for 7- or 14-day holidays. All the companies listed above have charter flights to Salzburg, as does Thomson (021-632 6282).

If you need more flexibility, consider flying to or from Munich: there are more flights available from more British airports. Several flights a day are offered from Heathrow with Lufthansa and British Airways; BA also flies direct daily from Birmingham, Manchester and Glasgow. Charter flights are offered by GTF Tours (*see above*); DER Travel Service (071-408 0111) and German Travel Centre (071-379 5212) offer scheduled flights.

Munich's new airport, north of the city off the A9 motorway, is connected to the main railway station by underground (maps still show the old airport to the east, so follow the roadsigns round the ring road if you're driving). Frequent trains to Salzburg take about two hours. For the return journey to Munich, see the timetables at the Mozartplatz tourist office or the station.

Salzburg Airport Maxglan Airport, three miles from town, is small, simple and no place for last-minute souvenir hunting; but there's a

Opening hours and days Shops are normally open from Monday to Friday, 9am to 6pm, and on Saturday until lunchtime. During the Festival, city-centre shops stay open on Saturday afternoon. Most sights are open at weekends (a few museums close on Monday).

GETTING AROUND

The old centre of Salzburg is compact and easily covered on foot and you may not need to use public transport at all. If you are staying in the old town, you will need only a ticket for the funicular (*Festungsbahn*) and/or the lift up the Mönchsberg and perhaps a bus to Hellbrunn and back. If you are staying on the right bank you are more likely to need transport.

---

helpful tourist office. It is most crowded during the winter skiing season.

From the airport, bus No 77 departs every 15 to 30 minutes for the station and takes 20 minutes. But unless your hotel is within easy walking distance of the station it is probably more sensible to take a taxi (if there are none outside, use the special telephone just inside the arrivals exit: Salzburger Funktaxi-Vereinigung tel: 81-11 and City Funk tel: 8166). The journey will still be only fractionally quicker, but the cab will be able to take you and your luggage direct to your hotel, even if it is in the old town pedestrian zone.

The taxi ride from the airport to the old town takes you through the Siegmundstor (built in 1767) into a short tunnel bored through the Mönchsberg, to emerge in the Herbert-von-Karajan-Platz with the Archbishops' Horse-Trough of Pferdeschwemme on the left, and then along the river which bisects the city. The bus takes a more roundabout, and duller, route.

By rail The daily train service from London Victoria (via Dover, Ostend and Munich) takes 20 hours and costs slightly less than an APEX flight for a return ticket.

Tour operator packages

Tour operators offer package holidays lasting from two to seven nights. Some fly direct to Salzburg, others go to Munich and transfer from there. Many offer a seven-night 'twin city' package with Vienna. Despite high accommodation charges during festival time, it's generally cheaper to travel independently. Another factor to consider is that many of the hotels used by tour operators are rather dull and in the newer part of the town; the more convenient and intimate *pensions* in the old town generally take individual bookings. For a list of tour operators, see page 385.

A three-day tourist ticket covers buses, trolley buses (most of Salzburg's buses run on electricity), the funicular and lift, and the Salzburg-Bergheim tramway, and is convenient and reasonable value (remember to keep it for the airport bus at the end of your trip). Alternatively, single tickets can be bought from the driver, but this is very expensive. They're cheaper bought in blocks of five from the Salzburger Stadtwerke ticket offices at Griesgasse 21 or Südtiroler Platz 42 or a tobacconist. There is also a 24-hour tourist ticket which includes the funicular, lift and tramway. Children up to 15 years pay half price.

When boarding a **bus** the ticket must be time-stamped in the special machine (this applies only the first time a special tourist ticket is used). For such a small city, the bus map is surprisingly complex; useful numbers to know are the 55 to Hellbrunn and the 77 to the airport – otherwise ask at your hotel or consult the *Stadtplan*. If you are staying in Nonntal (and/or are footsore or rain-soaked), you might use the **minibuses** which circulate in the traffic-restricted old town on weekdays and Saturday mornings. The tourist ticket does not cover these buses.

Radio taxis can be summoned by telephone (tel: 8111 or 8166). There are also several taxi ranks – on the Alter Markt, Makartplatz and Residenzplatz, for instance.

A day's **car rental** is an option worth considering. Most firms charge only a small extra to deliver to your hotel, and you can leave the car at the airport. Beware, however, high tariffs for unlimited mileage deals, or extra mileage rates. It's worth shopping around for the best value.

Bicycle hire is available from Hager Albert, Fürstenallee 39 (tel: 823723); the main station, Schalter Nr 3 (tel: 88875427); Zweirad Frey, Willibald-Hauthalerstrasse 4 (tel: 431682); or Velorent, Josef-Preis-Allee 18 (tel: 8426700).

UNMISSABLES

The Cathedral and Dommuseum

The first Italianate baroque church north of the Alps is rather more beautiful outside than in. But art lovers should visit the Dommuseum, which has rare treasures, ranging from an eighth-century Northumbrian cross to Gothic altarpieces. The Art and Rarity Room (Kunst-und-Wunderkammer) contains natural curiosities and beautiful or strange man-made objects, all in the original showcases. There is Sung Mass in the cathedral at 10am on Sunday.

Mozart's Birthplace and Home

The *Geburtshaus*, the house where Mozart was born in 1756, is a place of pilgrimage. The small rooms contain a museum with original music instruments of the period – including the violin Mozart used as a child and his clavichord – and portraits and memorabilia of the family. The third floor, where the family lived, has been set out as a typical middle-class home of the time. The second floor is devoted to an exhibition on Mozart in the theatre.

Over the river is the house where the family lived from 1773 to 1780 (the *Wohnhaus*). The exhibition here occupies only one room, and is generally less popular than the *Geburtshaus*. Manuscripts and portraits are displayed and there is an exhibition on Mozart and his times.

Mönchsberg and the Hohensalzburg Fortress

It would be a pity to miss the bird's-eye view of Salzburg and its unforgettable domes and spires. One of the most pleasant ways of spending the day, in fine weather, is to take the funicular up (and see the fortress) and then walk along the top where there is a path to the lift back down (follow signs to Schloss Mönchstein). Don't miss the fine view over the other side to the mountains, with Schloss Leopoldskron (used as the Von Trapp mansion in *The Sound of Music*) overlooking the lake. Arguably the best aerial view of the city is from the Café Winkler at the top of the lift.

The largest completely preserved fortress in Central Europe is accessible by funicular (or on foot). For a standard entrance fee you can wander around the ramparts and see the courtyard and exterior of the various parts of the complex, begun in 1077 but extended over the years by various Prince-Archbishops. To see the interior – a series of fine Gothic state rooms – you will have to join a guided tour lasting about 40 minutes and usually in German only (though typed information is supplied in English), or you could attend a concert there instead. The Fortress Museum displays weapons and instruments of torture.

Residenz

The Residenzgalerie, the remains of the art collection of the Prince-Archbishops, contains some big names in European art from the sixteenth to nineteenth centuries. There are works by Rembrandt, Ruisdael, Rubens, Poussin, Bruegel and Titian, although the collection is disappointingly short of really great masterpieces (some of which are now in the Kunsthistorisches-museum in Vienna). The section devoted to nineteenth-century Austrian art includes some early views of Salzburg, easily recognisable today. The display rooms themselves are worth seeing for the period details like stuccoed and frescoed ceilings and ornate stoves.

The 40-minute guided tours of the state rooms are monotonous unless you have a good grasp of German (a fact-sheet in English is supplied, however). Come to a concert here instead: you will see the Carabinierisaal and Rittersaal, both with frescoes by J-M Rottmayr, which give a flavour of the other art exhibits.

St Peter's

This Abbey and Benedictine monastery were founded by St Rupert in 696. The interior of tiny Peterskirche, 'face-lifted' in over-ornate rococo style, is interesting for its Romanesque structure and some fine details, notably the rock tomb of St Rupert and intricate wrought-iron gate, made by the court locksmith. The church is usually overlooked in favour of the romantic old churchyard behind, with its Early Christian catacombs (guided tours last about 20 minutes). This is where the Von Trapps hid from the Nazis before their escape to Switzerland. Also here is the Stiftskeller St Peter, which claims to be Europe's oldest tavern, mentioned in a document of 803 and still surviving.

Hellbrunn

Just within the city limits (bus 55 takes about 15 minutes) is the country mansion of Prince-Archbishop Marcus Sittikus, who ruled Salzburg from 1612 to 1619. Although worth a visit in its own right for the fine Italianate interior, Hellbrunn's main claim to fame is the baroque garden with its trick fountains. Be careful not to catch the eye of the guide, as he might select you for a surprise shower. Conducted tours take 30 to 40 minutes. There is also a zoo and folklore museum. Allow half a day for a visit.

The most appealing way to approach Hellbrunn is from the arrow-straight Hellbrunner Allee, which leads almost from the centre of Salzburg through unspoilt meadows to the Lustschloss, or pleasure palace, itself.

OTHER PLACES TO VISIT

Museums and churches

Carolino-Augusteum Museum If this sounds heavy going, do not be put off. It is a relatively small museum with some very interesting and varied exhibits of high quality: not just archaeology (the Celtic beak-jug of Dürrnberg, dating from around 400 BC, is the star exhibit), but also art (especially Gothic altarpieces), decoration (whole period rooms) and old musical instruments. The toy collection is separately housed in the old hospital (Bürgerspital) nearby.

The Franciscan Church The Franziskanerkirche is stylistically the most intriguing church in the city. It has a Romanesque nave and vault of great simplicity spoilt by dubious baroque chapels, each one even more over the top than the last. The baroque High Altar (1709) by Fischer von Erlach contains a Gothic *Madonna* by Michael Pacher (about 1495), another curious juxtaposition. Sung Mass is at 9am on Sunday.

The Glockenspiel The Mozartplatz clocktower carillon plays tunes (mostly Mozart) at 7am, 11am and 6pm. You can visit the tower daily at 10.45am and 5.45pm (weather permitting) to see the bells in action. If you are staying in a nearby hotel, Mozart may be responsible for your early-morning call.

Haus der Natur This is really a rainy-day place, unless you want a natural history lesson in German and are particularly partial to dioramas. There is a rather gruesome room full of malformed foetuses and other 'natural' curiosities in jars.

Mirabell Palace Most of this fine palace contains offices and is closed to the public. However, those who attend concerts here will see the fine marble staircase and hall. Part of the former Orangery houses a small baroque museum: mainly old sketches and designs for frescoes and altarpieces. The splendid formal gardens are the setting for concerts in summer.

Nonnberg A peaceful backwater just 15 minutes' walk from Mozartplatz, Nonnberg is known as the convent where the Singing Nun was a novice, both in real life and on celluloid. The convent itself, founded by St Rupert *c*.AD 700, cannot be visited but the Gothic church with its ancient crypt, Romanesque frescoes and wooden altarpiece is a place of simple and peaceful beauty.

Rupertinum Tired of all the predictable picture-postcard prettiness? A closer look at the exterior of this house reveals some slightly zany decorative motifs, just a hint that this is Salzburg's modern art museum. The entrance fee is high (higher for the summer exhibition), but the Rupertinum is an attractive showcase for some arresting contemporary art.

Other attractions

Kapuzinerberg Walk up the marked paths, past the Capucin monastery to the Franziskischlossl, looking out for splendid viewpoints.

Grünmarkt The Grünmarkt, or vegetable market, on Universitätsplatz is a lively daily affair. This is where Gretl dropped the big
tomato in *The Sound of Music*. The church on the square is the
Collegiate or University Church, a masterpiece by Fischer von
Erlach.

SHOPPING

Salzburg may be a provincial city, but the shops are chic, and
buying can easily be combined with sightseeing. Most of the best
shops are in the old centre, some in town houses with old
shopfronts. Traditional Austrian clothing is one of the more
attractive purchases. Some shops sell folksy *Dirndls* and *Lederhosen*
which may look idiotic when you get home, but others sell
traditional clothes with some modern styling – *Loden* coats and
capes, thick jersey jackets and accessories (try Trachten Forsten-
lechner on Mozartplatz). These shops are very expensive, but
quality is high. For purchases of over £50 you can apply for a tax
refund; the shop will help you. For cheaper souvenirs you can
buy *Mozartkugeln* – round chocolates wrapped in Mozart's
portrait – in boxes of any shape or size. An older tradition is
hand-made candles: buy them from Nagy's on Getreidegasse.
Other local and Tyrolean crafts include wooden toys (especially
'jumping jacks', quite expensive even at market stalls), baskets,
dried-flower arrangements, dolls in traditional costume and
Christmas decorations. Salzburger Heimatwerk on Residenzplatz
specialises in local crafts.

EATING AND DRINKING

The traditional, typical Salzburg restaurant is the beer garden or
cellar, serving hearty local cooking in rustic surroundings. Any
name with *Brau* ('brew') or *Keller* ('cellar') is of this type; the most
famous are the Sternbrau (at Griesgasse 23) and the ancient
Stiftskeller St Peter (opposite the church), both with a huge
capacity.

For many people the ubiquitous *Gulaschsuppe* is a meal in itself,
ideal for a winter lunch. Specialities of Salzburg include
Frittatensuppe (broth with pancake snippets), *Leberknödelsuppe*

(liver dumpling soup), fish from the lakes, *Bauernschmaus* (a pork stew) and *Salzburger Nockerln*, a sweet soufflé with three peaks representing the mountains which surround the city.

Those with lighter appetites should head for the café-restaurants in Kaigasse, several with tables on the pavement in summer. Many places offer two- or three-course fixed-price menus for lunch, usually displayed on blackboards, along with the day's special. These are normally good value.

If you visit the eighteenth-century cafés (Zum Glockenspiel on Mozartplatz or the smarter and more atmospheric Café Tomaselli overlooking the Alter Markt) you can perch on a balcony or an outside terrace and enjoy the view with a drink or snack.

Note that dinner is usually served early in Salzburg, but several restaurants, particularly around the theatres, stay open late enough for after-concert meals.

NIGHTLIFE

The main place to visit for folk music, dancing and beer is the Gambrinussaal in the Augustinerbräu (in the Klessheim Palace). For those bent on 'real' nightlife there is the Winkler Casino at the top of the Mönchsberg lift, offering French and American roulette, poker, blackjack and baccarat as well as slot machines; spectacular night views are an additional plus.

The most rewarding thing to do in Salzburg is to go to at least one concert. The Salzburger Schlosskonzerte, or Palace Concerts, are performed either in the Marble Hall of the Mirabell Palace, where Leopold Mozart used to give concerts with his prodigy son, or in the Residenz of the Prince-Archbishops in the very room where Mozart conducted his early symphonies. Aspiring and established musicians love to play in these atmospheric surroundings. Candlelight and chandeliers contribute to the romantic atmosphere.

There are regular concerts in the Fortress from May to December (look out for the leaflet *Salzburger Festungskonzerte*) and, for pure Mozart, in the Gothic Hall and the Mozarteum or – in period costume – at Hellbrunn (in the *Mozart-Serenaden* series; another separate leaflet). For all these concerts tickets cost between £15 and £26.

Another typical feature of Salzburg is the Marionette theatre, performed in a charming rococo theatre near the Mirabell Palace in January, at Easter, from May to the end of September, and in

December. For the opera connoisseur or purist this may not be a very satisfactory artistic combination. It is only recommended if you enjoy opera and appreciate puppetry skill. Choose a light-hearted Mozart such as *The Marriage of Figaro* or Strauss's *Die Fledermaus*. Tickets at the back are a false economy here.

HOTELS

The ideal place to be is in the old town, for both location and the character of the hotels, which tend to be smaller and more charming. Hotels are priced by category, so you will not save money by being less central if you are booking a holiday independently. However, most of the hotels used by tour operators for package holidays are on the far side of the river (roughly speaking, the nearer the river, the better the hotel, and the nearer the station, the less desirable). Hotels should be booked in advance, and that means a year ahead during the August Festival. Information on accommodation can be obtained from the main tourist office, Auerspergstrasse 7 (tel: 88987). Prices are 10 to 30 per cent higher from July to September in most hotels.

AUSTROTEL   ♦♦♦♦
Mirabellplatz 8   *Tel: 88 16 88   Fax: 88 16 87*

On a main road close to the Mirabell Palace, a five-minute walk to the old town, is the Austrotel. A thoroughly converted, light blue, Regency-style building, it has pristine modern rooms, a cavernous but cosy cellar restaurant and a popular coffee-shop with revolving cakes. Everything is well maintained and run by young, helpful and efficient staff.

Bedrooms: 74, all with bath/shower/WC; mini-bar **Facilities:** Lift; restaurant **Credit/charge cards accepted:** All

---

Hotel prices Symbols indicate approximate prices per room per night for a double room with bath. Many large hotels run special breaks which work out far cheaper. (See page 14 for further details.)

♦ = under £50; ♦♦ = £50 to £80; ♦♦♦ = £80 to £100;
♦♦♦♦ = £100 to £140; ♦♦♦♦♦ = over £140.

AM DOM   ♦♦
Goldgasse 17   *Tel: 84 27 65   Fax: 84 27 65 55*

Am Dom is an unprepossessing, narrow, six-floored, 750-year-old town building, down a side-street off Residenzplatz. The ground floor is occupied by a Chinese restaurant. Look at the document on the wall of the heavy-beamed breakfast room authenticating the age of the building. The bedrooms are beamed too. They're simple and clean, some with rustic-painted furniture.

Closed: Restaurant closed Jan and Feb   **Bedrooms:** 13, most with bath/WC; none with TV   **Facilities:** Lift; restaurant   **Credit/charge cards accepted:** Access, Amex, Visa

ELEFANT   ♦♦
Sigmund-Haffner-Gasse 4   *Tel: 84 33 97   Fax: 84 01 09 28*

The hotel is perfectly situated down a quiet street in the heart of the old town; the building has been there for over 700 years. The bedrooms are well equipped and have been completely modernised, as has the main restaurant. It's deceptively bigger than it appears and gives the impression of a smart *pension*. Good value.

Closed: Restaurant closed Tue   **Bedrooms:** 36, most with shower/WC, some with bath/WC; all with mini-bar, hair-dryer   **Facilities:** Lift; restaurant   **Credit/charge cards accepted:** All

ZUR GOLDENEN ENTE   ♦♦
Goldgasse 10   *Tel: 84 56 22   Fax: 84 56 22-99*

An eponymous golden duck hangs from a wrought-iron sign outside this medieval building. It's in a side-street joining Residenzplatz and Alter Markt. The rustic restaurant is the focal point: heavy-beamed, with cheerful red-patterned seats and an old map of the city. Most of the rooms are decorated in smart new pine.

Closed: Restaurant closed mid-Nov; Sat night, all day Sun   **Bedrooms:** 17, most with bath/WC; all with mini-bar   **Facilities:** Lift; restaurant   **Credit/charge cards accepted:** All

GOLDENER HIRSCH
Getreidegasse 37

Tel: 84 85 11   Fax: 84 33 49

Wedged between the main shopping street and Universitätsplatz in the centre of the old town – a convenient if not peaceful location – the hotel spans two adjacent fifteenth-century town buildings. *Hirsch* means stag, and antlers protrude from the walls of the bar, a sealed-off courtyard in the heart of the building. Low-ceilinged corridors with creaky floorboards lead to well-furbished rooms. An old-fashioned atmosphere with excellent service are the hallmarks of this hotel.

Bedrooms: 71, all with bath/WC; mini-bar   **Facilities:** Lift; restaurant
Credit/charge cards accepted: All

KASERERBRÄU
Kaigasse 33

Tel: 84 24 06   Fax: 84 24 45-51

This fourteenth-century building once housed a brewery. It's on the main street of the eastern end of the old town and has been a hotel since 1949, run by the same family. You enter up steps with wrought-iron banisters surrounded by murals of classical columns and cherubs. Some public rooms have been modernised, such as the new, luxurious sauna; others, like the sitting-room with stuccoed ceiling, quality antiques and a large Persian carpet, haven't. Likewise the bedrooms – half are in farmhouse style, with old, floral-painted wooden beds, chests, chairs and cupboards.

Closed: Restaurant closed Jan to mid-Apr   **Bedrooms:** 40, half with shower/WC; half with bath/WC; some with mini-bar   **Facilities:** Lift; restaurant; sauna   **Credit/charge cards accepted:** All

ROSENVILLA
Höfelgasse 4

Tel: 62 17 65

A large orange chalet with colourful window boxes – this hotel is in a quiet spot off a main road, on the eastern side of the new town. The rooms are inviting, some in farmhouse style with old, flower-patterned furniture. A large old boiler, decorated with brightly coloured figures, dominates the sitting-room. In good weather you can have breakfast on the terrace overlooking the small garden.

Bedrooms: 17, half with shower/WC, half with bath/WC; all with hair-dryer; some with balcony and safe   **Credit/charge cards accepted:** All

344

SCHLOSS MÖNCHSTEIN
Mönchsberg Park 26   *Tel: 84 85 55   Fax: 84 85 59*

Promoting itself as 'the urban sanctuary of the world', the hotel's position
and style indeed capture Salzburg's rural aspect. Isolated on the
Mönchsberg, it is a ten-minute walk through the woods from the lift
down to the town. The hotel is a fourteenth-century residential castle
with seventeenth-century additions covered with creepers. In summer
there are tables outside by the lush and well-tended garden. It's rather
formal inside, but the restaurant has fabulous views across the city and
the spacious bedrooms are comfortable, with antiques and all mod cons.
It even has its own chapel.

Bedrooms: 17, most with bath/WC; all with mini-bar; hair-dryer; safe
Facilities: Lift; restaurant; tennis   **Credit/charge cards accepted:** All

THEATER
Schallmooser Hauptstrasse 13   *Tel: 88 16 81   Fax: 88 16 86 92*

The Theater is a peachy cream-coloured building in a salubrious but
uninteresting area of the new town, facing a main road. Fortunately, most
of the bedrooms are at the back and are quiet. It's formal but different: a
red carpet lines the entrance steps, and you pass a display of dummies
dressed in period theatre costume into a glitzy, white-pillared reception.
Bedrooms (called apartments) are all named after famous artists, are
comfortable and roomy and have cooking facilities.

Bedrooms: 58, most with shower/WC, some with bath/WC; all with mini-
bar; hair-dryer; kitchenette   **Facilities:** Lift; restaurant; sauna; solarium;
masseur   **Credit/charge cards accepted:** All

WEISSES KREUZ ♦♦
Bierjodlgasse 6   *Tel: 84 56 41   Fax: 84 5 64 19*

Creepers cover the walls and spill over the roofed patio of this Balkan
restaurant-with-rooms. It's set at the back of Kapitelplatz right under the
granite peak of the Mönchsberg and 100 yards from the lift up to the
fortress. The restaurant is low-ceilinged and cosy – a popular winter
escape. The *pension* has a separate entrance but the smell of cooking still
wafts upstairs. The rooms are plain, but light, and some have views over
the town.

Closed: Restaurant closed Jan and Feb; all day Tue   **Bedrooms:** 4, all with
bath/WC; none with TV or phone   **Facilities:** Restaurant   **Credit/charge
cards accepted:** All

WOLF ♦♦
Kaigasse 7   *Tel: 84 3 45 30   Fax: 84 2 42 34*

This is a small *pension* above a restaurant on a main street of the old town, just along from Mozartplatz. The breakfast room is decorated with pictures of cheerful Austrian children and floral-painted furniture; classical music accompanies breakfast. The room converts into a sitting-room in the evening. The wooden-floored pine bedrooms are simple and attractive, some modern, some traditional in style. The place is spotless and efficiently run.

Closed: Feb   **Bedrooms:** 12, most with shower/WC, some with bath/WC; TV available on request   **Facilities:** Restaurant   **Credit/charge cards accepted:** Amex

---

Hotel prices Symbols indicate approximate prices per room per night for a double room with bath. Many large hotels run special breaks which work out far cheaper. (See page 14 for further details.)

♦ = under £50; ♦♦ = £50 to £80; ♦♦♦ = £80 to £100; ♦♦♦♦ = £100 to £140; ♦♦♦♦♦ = over £140.

VENICE

- Venice is crumbling slowly back into its lagoon and everywhere you see decay and neglect. But the cracked stone, bulging walls and crumbling façades only add a tinge of melancholy to a uniquely beautiful city
- Don't be overwhelmed by the endless lists of museums, churches and palaces in guidebooks to Venice. The best of the sights don't compare to the pleasure of simply exploring the unique canals and backstreets
- For a break from sightseeing and the sometimes claustrophobic atmosphere of the narrow alleys and busy canals take a day-trip to one of the nearby islands of Murano, Burano and Torcello – all, in different ways, a contrast to Venice

FOURTEEN hundred years ago there was nothing there but a malaria-infested swamp, a daunting prospect for the Venetians fleeing from the Huns and Lombards who invaded the mainland. The Venetians built and developed their refuge on a foundation of millions of larch poles driven deep into a patchwork of mudflats. Today, scores of canals crossed by hundreds of bridges divide the city, and the Grand Canal – a huge S-shape in the course of an ancient river bed – splits it in two. On this shallow and improbable base rest millions of tons of brick, stone and marble: palaces and churches commissioned and embellished by the great Venetian mariners and traders as they built a unique and beautiful city.

As the Venetians prospered, they plundered. In AD 828 Venetian traders stole the body of St Mark from Alexandria and the building of the great Basilica to house the body was begun. Today St Mark's is weighed down by statues and columns – looted from Constantinople, Acre and Alexandria.

The Fourth Crusade and the Sack of Constantinople in 1204 brought Venice vast amounts of wealth and left the Republic as the dominant military and trading power in the Mediterranean. The rich merchants beautified their city. Plaques and roundels of stone and marble still enliven the walls of buildings, corners are softened by barley-sugar-shaped twirls of grooved stone, and fragments of sculpture embellish doorways. Gothic windows with elaborate pointed arches cluster together on the fronts of palaces, and here and there are balconies with exquisite pierced stonework.

The arts flourished under such extravagant patrons. Codussi and Lombardo built compact, delicately embellished churches such as San Zaccaria and Santa Maria dei Miracoli. They were followed by the great sixteenth-century neo-classical architects: Sansovino, who built the Marciana Library in St Mark's Square, and Palladio, whose San Giorgio Maggiore is just across the lagoon. The last great architect of Venice was Longhena, whose masterpiece is the church of Santa Maria della Salute. His great baroque palaces, the Ca' Rezzonico and the Ca' Pesaro, are two of the most distinctive buildings on the Grand Canal. The father of Venetian painting was Giovanni Bellini, the first Venetian artist to paint successfully in oils and a master of subtly delicate altarpieces. He heralded a golden age of Venetian art at the end of the fifteenth century. It was to become one of the great schools of the Renaissance, dominated by the prodigious Titian, the enigmatic Giorgione and the dramatic canvases of Veronese and Tintoretto. Many of their paintings are still in the churches for which they were originally commissioned.

By the eighteenth century Venice was more a pleasure ground for dilettanti than a great trading state. The city was a compulsory stop on the Grand Tour of Europe. Canaletto and Guardi painted famous views for the tourists to take home with them and Tiepolo decorated churches with sensual, sugary nudes. Vivaldi and Albinoni composed and Goldoni's comedies packed the theatres.

In 1797 Napoleon's army took the city. St Mark's Square was redesigned, as were the lions of St Mark – the symbol of the Republic which decorated many of the buildings. The craftsman who was assigned the job took all the money and left most of the lions. And finally Venice succumbed to the Austro-Hungarian Empire. Its great buildings fell into disrepair. Today, wherever you go, you see evidence of neglect: woodworm in statues, crumbling brickwork, paintings with sticky tape across them to keep the paint from falling off, columns crazily aligned, church towers leaning, cracks in stone and brickwork, peeling frescoes, flaking plaster, iron bars holding back bulging walls, sinking and undulating floors. The good news is that, especially since the floodings of 1966 and 1967, Venetians and others have rescued and restored many buildings and works of art. The bad news is that the work is not even nearly half-way through. The aim, by the year 2000, is to have dredged the canals and incorporated a system of barriers at the entrances to the lagoon to protect the city from *acqua alte* – high tide.

The fragility of Venice, its melancholy, its decay and its beauty, make it like nowhere else on earth. To walk around the city is to experience a perpetual series of visual delights: the green water in the canals, the warm red of brickwork, the icing-sugar white of Istrian stone, the peeling pastel-coloured or ivy-covered stucco and the curious Venetian funnel-shaped chimneys. You plunge out of sunlight into dark, narrow, stone-flagged alleys, and then into daylight again as you cross bridges and stray into open squares. On your way you see black, graceful gondolas with their plush velvet seats; elaborately decorated well-heads in the squares; secret gardens through iron-grilled gateways; and flower-filled window-boxes by green-shuttered windows.

Venice is divided into six *sestieri*, or districts. The boundaries follow the lines of canals and the Grand Canal snakes through the middle. *Cannaregio* divides the original Jewish ghetto and long quay (*Fondamenta Nuove*) in the north, and the hotel and souvenir ghetto around the station to the south. Day-trippers stream out of the station and clog the famous sights, shops and narrow alleys of *San Marco*. Here you'll find the Piazza, as the Piazza San Marco is known, the Fenice Theatre, many of the smartest shops and the most expensive hotels.

Across the Grand Canal *Dorsoduro* has few major sights apart from the Accademia Gallery. But there are fine views, quiet backwaters, students, and large houses with hidden gardens. *San Polo* and *Santa Croce* have large open squares but it's easy to get lost among the dense back streets where the alleys get narrower and the *sottoportegi* (passages under buildings) longer and lower. Finally, *Castello* runs from the Piazza down to the easternmost tip of Venice and includes the Arsenale.

A ten-minute boat ride from St Mark's Square is Venice Lido, a seven-mile strip of land separating the Venetian lagoon from the Adriatic. The Lido was once a fashionable seaside resort, and there are still some expensive hotels and plentiful sports facilities. But the water is polluted and for a beach holiday there are better and cheaper places in the Mediterranean.

WHEN TO GO

The peak tourist season is from May to September. July and August are the worst months for heat, crowds, mosquitoes and smells, but there is plenty going on – several major international cultural festivals and some traditional ones. Venice is also very crowded on Italian national holidays, and on all summer weekends. Autumn is a good season for music-lovers, with concerts in many churches; the opera season starts in November. Winter is relatively uncrowded and a few hotels offer cheaper rates; but although mists can be romantic, it is often just foggy, damp and cold. Before May it can be cool, too. The Carnival is held every year in February and is a lively, picturesque occasion when people wear extravagant costumes to masked balls. It's very popular and very crowded.

MASTERING THE SYSTEM

Information The Italian State Office in the UK is at 1 Princes Street, London W1R 8AY, tel: 071-408 1254. It is not much use if you want detailed information on the city. Local tourist offices (EPT – Ente Provinciale per il Turismo) are at 71c Piazza San Marco (south-west corner of the piazza), tel: 5226356; at Santa Lucia railway station, tel: 719078; and at the airport, tel: 611111. All except the Piazza San Marco office will try to book you a hotel on the spot; and they can provide a free map, a map of water-bus

GETTING THERE

Going independently

By air British Airways (081-759 5511) and Alitalia (071-602 7111) both fly to Venice every day from Heathrow. Both offer a Sunsaver fare – considerably cheaper than APEX. You have to book within seven days of travelling and stay a Saturday night. Fares are seasonal and go up between July and September.

You can also take a charter flight to either Venice or Treviso, about 20 miles to the north. These are best value for travel outside the summer months when they can work out cheaper than the APEX fare; but there are fewer flights to choose from, and you won't find the same flexibility that you get with scheduled flights, as they are generally for 7- or 14-day holidays. Specialists worth contacting for scheduled and charter flights include Citalia (081-686 5533), Ciao Travel (071-629 2677), Volare (071-439 6633), Italy Sky Shuttle (081-748 1333), Cityjet (071-387 1017), Italian Options (071-436 3246), Lupus (071-287 1292), Skybus (071-373 6055) and Italflights (071-405 6771).

Marco Polo Airport The airport is eight miles from Venice on the edge of a lagoon. It includes modern bars, restaurant and a bureau de change. The cheapest way into the city from the airport is by bus, which skirts the mainland and delivers you over the road bridge to the city terminal at Piazzale Roma, near the railway station. Land taxis also serve the terminal. A more romantic entry is to arrive at St Mark's Square by water: the hourly public launch (*motoscafo San Marco*) is well worth the (reasonable) cost; beware of touting water-taxi drivers who may charge about seven times as much. Unless your hotel is very close to your arrival point, you'll need to take some further transport (such as a water-bus – see *'Mastering the system'*) to the stop nearest your hotel and carry your case from there. Porters are rarely available and are very expensive; they may need to take your luggage by water and will charge for the boat fare as well as each item. If you want to guarantee a porter, there's a kiosk at the airport which can book one for you.

By rail Travelling to Venice by rail has little to recommend it for a short break, as the journey takes 24 hours. The most luxurious way to travel is undoubtedly by the Venice-Simplon Orient-Express, which makes the journey twice a week between February and November; the return fare costs well over £1,000 for two nights at the most sumptuous hotels in Venice.

Tour operator packages

Over 20 tour operators offer short breaks to Venice using all standards of accommodation from the very grandest hotels to simple *pensione*. Three nights in a three-star hotel in high season costs around £385. You may find it cheaper to take a charter flight and book your own accommodation. For a list of tour operators to Venice, see page 385.

stops and a list of the tourist sights in Venice.

Maps and guides We strongly recommend buying a detailed map which will help you to choose between following the crowds down the main thoroughfares (distinctive yellow signs point the way to Piazza San Marco, Ferrovia railway station and Piazzale Roma) and taking short-cuts down narrow alleys to avoid them. However, even the best maps don't show every little street and dead end, so it's easy to get lost. Choose between the yellow FMB map or the Hallwag map. The free tourist office map is accurate but not sufficiently detailed.

Tracking down an **address** can be extremely confusing. Addresses usually consist of no more than the name of the *sestiere* and its number (for example, Dorsoduro 4789). It's a good idea to ask for the nearest landmark. **Street signs** are frequent and clear – though the spelling on the wall probably won't match the spelling on your map.

Sightseeing tours These are offered by several companies and prices vary little. The morning sightseeing tour on foot covers the Doges' Palace, San Marco (some tours don't even take you inside the Basilica) and a visit to a nearby glass-making factory. Guides often speak poor English and are barely audible above the crowds, even with megaphones. Better value is a launch trip down the Grand Canal and around Giudecca.

The most popular excursions are to the three main islands in the lagoon (Murano, Burano, Torcello), with visits to glass-making centres; but independent visits using public transport cost about half the price and allow more freedom to explore. Trips further afield include boat and bus excursions down the Brenta Canal, which include visits to Palladian villas.

Changing money Banks are open Monday to Friday, 8.30am to 1.20pm, and 3pm to 4pm. They are closed on Saturday.

Opening hours and days Some shops close on Monday morning and many food shops and supermarkets close on Wednesday afternoon. Churches have erratic opening hours – most close at lunch (sometimes until 4pm) and some are closed in the afternoon. Visitors are requested not to wander around during Mass. Opening hours for museums and galleries vary greatly. Many are open daily, either mornings or afternoons only. Others are open all day, yet close for lunch. If you are keen to see certain sights and are in Venice for only a short time, plan ahead and check opening times locally.

Visiting churches Paintings and frescoes in Venetian churches are frequently hard to see, either because of poor or non-existent lighting or because they're hidden away in some obscure corner. Take 100- and 200-lire coins (and the occasional 500-lire!) for possible slot-machine lighting, and for ceiling paintings ask for a mirror (*specchio*) which will magnify the frescoes and relieve neckache.

GETTING AROUND

Water-buses are an excellent and an entertaining form of public transport. The *motoscafi* are the fastest, but *vaporetti* are more comfortable and provide better views. No 1 (maddeningly called *accelerato*) stops at virtually every landing stage along the Grand Canal, taking about 35 minutes to complete the journey – highly recommended for the first-time visitor. No 2 (marked *diretto*) takes the short cut along the Rio Nuovo, and is more crowded than No 1. In summer only, No 4 is a faster version of No 1. The circle line, No 5, travels right round Venice and to San Michele and Murano; it's well worth a trip in itself. Boats for the Lido (Nos 6 and 11) leave from the Riva degli Schiavoni; the No 12 from the Fondamenta Nuove goes to Murano, Burano and Torcello.

Tickets are bought at landing stages or at some bars and tobacconists. Paying on board costs extra. Books of 10 or 20 tickets are available at no saving. A 24-hour pass allows unlimited travel and is worth buying if you intend to do more than about six journeys. A three-day pass is even better value. Neither pass is valid on Nos 2 or 28 but they can be used on No 12 for a trip to the islands. A suitcase costs the same as a passenger; children under a metre tall go free.

Water-taxis are small, fast and comfortable, but exorbitantly priced. Fares are regulated, and published in the booklet *Un Ospite di Venezia*; it's wise to establish the price before setting off.

Gondola prices are also regulated, but overcharging is common and fares are high. It's well worth bargaining – you might be able to negotiate a much better rate at slack times of the day. At night the cost goes up even more. *Traghetti* are regular-service gondolas which take you straight across various points of the Grand Canal and are good value.

UNMISSABLES

St Mark's Square (Piazza San Marco)

The great piazza, once prized by Napoleon as the 'finest drawing-room in Europe', is now the heart of tourist Venice. The Basilica of St Mark, which squats like some outlandish gaudy insect, is its focus. Thousands mill in and out of the Basilica, feed the pigeons, click their cameras, window-shop for jewellery in the glossy arcade shops and glance nervously at the imperious waiters in the famous (and expensive) cafés.

The great buildings surrounding the piazza are an odd combination – built between the ninth and the nineteenth centuries. At one end of the square is the pink-patterned Gothic Doges' Palace. Opposite, the sixteenth-century Marciana Library is embellished with sculpted cherubs twisting and turning between the arches, loaded with fruit and garlands.

Around the corner the square opens out slightly askew along the repetitive, arcaded façades of the Procurati, built in the sixteenth century to house the Procurators of Venice, who were second in importance only to the Doge. In one corner, the huge red-brick campanile casts a slanting shadow across the piazza. There's a lift to the top – worth taking for the excellent views.

The Basilica of St Mark

The Basilica of St Mark was built to house the body of the evangelist, stolen from Alexandria by two Venetian merchants in 828. The church was also the Doges' chapel, and the wealth and power of the Venetian Republic was invested in beautifying the building. What we see today is an accumulation of different styles of building and decoration. The original plan and structure of the church is Byzantine and it dates essentially from the eleventh century. Much has changed since then: even the great, bulbous cupolas are simply false shells extended above somewhat flatter domes in the thirteenth century to make a great visual impact. In the entrance porticos, shored up by clusters of marble pillars, are some fine thirteenth-century carvings, but only one of the exterior lunettes retains its original mosaics.

As you walk into the church from the light and space of the piazza, you enter a new, gloomy world. The floors are formed from many coloured marbles, and the domes of the atrium, the insides of the cupolas and the walls and ceilings of the interior are covered with gold Byzantine and Renaissance biblical mosaics. Angels, evangelists and saints hover among glittering, glowing patterns, acting out scenes from the Creation to the life of St Mark.

Among the finest of the treasures housed in St Mark's is the jewel-encrusted, solid gold altarpiece, the Pala d'Oro. You have to pay extra to gain access to the high altar to see it, and another entry fee to admit you to the treasury and its collection of silver, gold and precious jewels looted from Byzantium. Don't miss the four bronze Greek horses which used to stand above the main door of the church (they have been replaced with copies) and are now in the Museo Marciano, which has a separate entrance (and entrance fee) in the central porch outside the Basilica. Climb the very steep stairs for a wonderful view of the piazza from the balcony outside the museum.

The Grand Canal

The wide, snaking curves of the Grand Canal – the high street of Venice – are out-of-bounds to large sightseeing vessels, but they remain busy with traffic. Sleek, varnished and incredibly expensive water-taxis purr in midstream; flat, low delivery barges chug in and out of the smaller canals; water-buses crunch clumsily against their grey boarding stations; and shiny black gondolas weave among them all.

The backdrop to the Canal is splendid: flat, high, faded pastel-coloured or white marble fronts of palaces, built to be seen from the canal. The main entrances are always on the waterside, the steps awash with swirling green seaweed. Some palaces gleam from recent restoration, others seem on the point of crumbling into the water.

The best and cheapest way to see the Canal is from one of the front seats of the No 1 water-bus – only in a few places, notably around the Rialto Bridge, can you actually walk along part of the Canal. Sights to look out for on the journey from St Mark's Square to the station include the baroque church of Santa Maria della Salute, with heavy stone scrolls around the base of the elegant white dome; the rickety Palazzo Dario; the elegant Gothic Palazzo Franchetti by the Accademia Bridge; the Ca' Rezzonico (see 'Other places to visit'); the Rialto Bridge – always crowded with tourists leaning over the parapets; the elaborate Ca' d'Oro (currently boarded over during restoration) and the solid façade of the Ca' Pesaro (see 'Other places to visit').

The Accademia Gallery

The rooms of the Accademia have an unrivalled collection and provide a historical overview of Venetian art. The paintings are hung in a rough chronological order. Rooms four and five house works by Giovanni Bellini (c1435-1516), who revolutionised Venetian art with his adoption of oil as a base for his subtly lit and coloured altarpieces. Bellini's pupil, Giorgione, few of whose paintings have survived and whose mysterious subjects still confound historians, is represented by the heavily atmospheric *Tempest* and his portrait of an old lady.

Out of contemporary sequence in a later room is the *St Ursula Cycle* by Vittore Carpaccio (c1470-1523): Ursula agrees to marry the son of a pagan English king on condition that they go on a long pilgrimage with 11,000 virgins. Carpaccio uses clear colours, dramatic architecture and a rather severe perspective in his crowded narratives. In the background of one painting is his imagined depiction of England – he'd never actually been there.

Titian (c1485-1576), the greatest of the Venetian colourists, worked with Giorgione for ten years. As well as his last work, a *Pietà*, painted for his own tomb, the gallery owns a touching *Madonna and Child*. Tintoretto (1518-94) and Veronese (1528-88) are represented by some striking paintings. Most impressive is Veronese's *Feast of the House of Levi*. This huge canvas is really a Last Supper retitled by Veronese after complaints by the Inquisition. You can see its point. The painting is a giant stage-set and the distractions and activity around the table are so absorbing that only one of the disciples appears to be paying any attention to Christ.

OTHER PLACES TO VISIT

Museums and galleries

Ca' d'Oro Although much altered and damaged since it was begun in 1424, the ornate Gothic Ca' d'Oro is one of the most beautiful and unusual of the palaces on the Grand Canal. In 1894 it was bought and restored by Baron Franchetti, a wealthy collector of Gothic and Renaissance art. Highlights include some fine fourteenth-century sculptures of the *Slaughter of the Innocents*; Mantegna's *St Sebastian*; frescoes by Titian and Giorgione; and sculpture by Bernini. The façade was being restored in 1992.

Ca'Rezzonico (Museum of the Eighteenth Century) This impressive white marble baroque palace on the Grand Canal was built in 1667 by Longhena for the Rezzonico family and finished by Masari in 1752. Robert Browning died here in 1889. Today it's preserved as a museum of the eighteenth century with period paintings, furniture and everyday artefacts. Most impressive is the ballroom with effective *trompe-l'oeil* paintings.

Throughout the rest of the palace the eighteenth century comes to life principally through the paintings. There are large canvases by Guardi and some entertaining works by Longhi, including the famous *Rhinoceros*. On the second floor are some frescoes of clowns and carnivals by Tiepolo.

Ca' Pesaro Like the Ca' Rezzonico, this flamboyant seventeenth-century palace on the Grand Canal was built by Longhena. It houses the Museum of Modern Art (now open after a very long closure) and the Museum of Oriental Art. The latter has a varied and well-presented collection which includes Indonesian puppets, Chinese vases and Japanese screens.

Correr Museum The Civic Museum of Venice in St Mark's Square has a fine collection of Venetian painting and a selection of Gothic works. There are several paintings by Bellini and his school and Carpaccio's famous *Courtesans*.

The Doges' Palace The fourteenth-century Doges' Palace was the seat of Ducal power in Venice from the birth of the republic until 1797. Much of the palace interior is closed to the public (there are guided 'secret tours' – in Italian only – which take you round the private apartments: enquire at the booking office for details of times). But you can visit many of the state rooms. They're impressive in size and in the extent of the decoration, particularly the ceiling frescoes with their heavy gold embellishments.

Among the decorative highlights are Sansovino's Scala d'Oro, a staircase studded with white and gilt stuccoes and painted frescoes, and the heavily ornate ceiling of the Sala della Senato with frescoes by Tintoretto. The largest room is the Sala del Maggior Consiglio. The ceiling is so massively ornate that it seems to weigh down on the huge hall. The world's largest oil painting – Tintoretto's *Paradise* – fills one of the walls. When you've tired of the grandeur you can slip into dark, dank passages, cross the Bridge of Sighs (named after the prisoners who sighed as they snatched a last glimpse of Venice through the stone lattices before their incarceration) and visit the dungeons.

Guggenheim Museum The late American millionaire Peggy Guggenheim bought the unfinished eighteenth-century Palazzo Venier dei Leoni in 1949 and established her collection of modern art there. It includes works by Picasso, Braque, Klee, Duchamp, Ernst, Miró, Giacometti, Magritte, Rothko and Bacon. There's also a shady, peaceful sculpture garden.

Mocenigo Palace This small, dark palace has changed little since the late eighteenth century. It is the only Venetian palace open to the public which leaves you with the impression that people actually lived there. You can wander through reception- and dining-rooms, a library and a bedroom. Open Saturday mornings only.

Naval Museum In this museum near the Arsenale there is a wealth of detail covering the life of Venice as a maritime power. Look out for a superb replica of the gilded *Bucintoro* built in 1837 (after Napoleon destroyed the original in 1798) and a sixteenth-century 'galleass' for which would have needed a crew of 700. Your ticket will allow you to visit the sixteenth-century boat pavilions too.

The Scuole The Scuole were charitable institutions set up under the patronage of a saint. Each is richly decorated with paintings. Choose the one you want to visit according to your artistic taste.

The halls of the **Scuola Grande di San Rocco** mark the zenith of Tintoretto's artistic achievement. The ground-floor hall is hung with his huge paintings depicting the life of the Virgin, beginning with a dynamic and ravishing *Annunciation*. The Chapter House on the second floor, lined with low, heavy lanterns, has scenes from the Old and New Testaments. In the Albergo on the same floor is Tintoretto's tumultuous *Crucifixion* and two disputed paintings by Giorgione.

You walk directly off the street into the **Scuola di San Giorgio degli Schiavoni**, a small, dark, wood-panelled room lined with the brilliant narrative paintings by Carpaccio from the lives of SS George, Jerome and Tryphone. Carpaccio's range is striking. St George charges headlong at the dragon, who roars, bloodied among his dismembered victims. St Augustine sits alert and expectant in his study. Carpaccio's figures float in the foreground, but they have poise and character. His backgrounds range from powerful landscapes to cities and interiors.

After the monochrome paintings by Bambini on the ground floor of the **Scuola Grande dei Carmini,** Tiepolo's sugary ceiling paintings in the main hall on the first floor are all the more sensual. His pink and tempting nudes seem to undermine the scuola's emphasis on the virtues!

Churches

San Giorgio Maggiore Andrea Palladio designed this church, separated from the city on its own island, to be seen from afar. Along with Santa Maria delle Salute and St Mark's campanile it dominates the entrance to the city from the lagoon. The interior is clear and light, with a galleried dome. You can walk round the high altar to see the superb carved monks' choir and inspect Tintoretto's *Last Supper*: the table skews across the painting. Climb the bell tower or get a monk to take you up in the lift and you'll get one of the best views of red-tiled roofs in Venice. If Palladio inspires you, visit the Redentore church on the Giudecca.

It's far less crowded than St Mark's campanile, yet the views are just as wonderful.

Santi Giovanni e Paolo Known locally as Zanipolo, this is a huge brick Dominican church in a beautiful square in the north of the Castello *sestiere*. Inside, the brickwork is plastered and painted with a pattern of bricks! Among the many treasures tucked into the side chapels are the tombs of Doges, and Bellini's fine *St Vincent Ferrer*. In the right transept is a fifteenth-century stained-glass window made in Murano. Adjoining the western end of the church is the intricate Renaissance façade of the Scuola Grande di San Marco, and opposite the fine equestrian monument to Bartolomeo Colleoni.

Santa Maria Gloriosa dei Frari The Frari – in San Polo *sestiere* – is the other great red-brick Gothic church in Venice. It's as substantial as Zanipolo and worth visiting for its paintings – including Titian's *Assumption* above the altar and his *Pesaro Madonna*. There is also Bellini's *Madonna and Child with Saints* – and the superb, carved monks' choir. There's a wooden *John the Baptist* by Donatello in the side chapel next to the altar.

Santa Maria della Salute Designed by Longhena and completed in 1681, this beautiful building houses some marvellous works by Titian. It's a short walk from the Accademia.

Santa Maria dei Miracoli Built between 1481 and 1489 by Pietro Lombardo, this tiny, rectangular church is squeezed along a narrow canal opposite a small, scruffy square. The sides are faced with pink, grey and white marble forming broad patterns, crosses and arches. Inside, the barrel ceiling is encrusted with 50 painted square panels showing heads of prophets and saints. The miraculous and richly coloured icon of the Virgin, for whom the church was built, hangs above the altar but access is limited and you'll probably have to be content with examining the glossy reproduction near the main door.

Other interesting churches include the remote **Madonna dell' Orto**, a graceful building with a fine brick front (and good stone carving on it), beautiful marble columns, and fine, though badly lit paintings (a robust Bellini *Madonna and Child* and a tumultuous *Last Judgement* by Tintoretto, who is buried here). The dome and campaniles of the seventeenth-century Dominican church of **Santa Maria del Rosario** (Gesuati) echo the design of Palladio's Redentore across the Giudecca Canal. Inside are ceiling frescoes and an altarpiece by Tiepolo. In **San Pantalon**, an astonishing canvas by Fumiani covers the entire ceiling. **San Sebastiano** was decorated by Veronese. He was buried there in 1588. **San Stefano** is notable for its nine superb marble side-altars and a fine roof like an inverted keel. The unusual, curving, Istrian stone façade of

San Zaccaria is decorated with coloured marble. Inside there is a beautiful *Madonna and Child with Saints* by Bellini.

Excursions

Murano, Burano and Torcello It's worth visiting at least one of these three islands in the lagoon. They're all, in different ways, a contrast to Venice. If you take the usual guided excursion to all three islands you'll probably see nothing of Murano except a glass-blowing factory (you're given a rapid demonstration, then ushered into the sales rooms). If you want to explore the little island, take water-bus No 5 from the Fondamenta Nuove in the north-east of the city.

Much further out into the lagoon than Murano, Burano is famous for its lace. It's well worth visiting the museum of lace and wandering around beside the tiny canals. If you follow your tour guide, you'll end up in the sales rooms again; instead, take water-bus No 12 from the Fondamenta Nuove (there's a bus every hour or so).

Torcello was a powerful island while Venice was still un-developed, but it was destroyed by malaria and is now almost uninhabited. Little is left apart from the cathedral with its beautiful Byzantine mosaics and a few surrounding buildings – including the small circular church of Santa Fosca.

EATING AND DRINKING

Venice is not renowned for good food. Most restaurants cater specifically for tourists, and prices are high. In the famous and reliably good restaurants, such as the Locanda Cipriani on the island of Torcello, the Antico Martini near the Fenice Theatre, or the Corte Sconta in Castello (appreciated by locals and the visiting French), they are very high indeed.

Cost-conscious tourists should avoid the San Marco area. Simple places such as Da Remigio (Salizzada dei Greci, Castello) are more likely to be frequented by locals than tourists and can offer good value for money. If you want only pasta, avoid restaurants where cover charges are high and where you won't be welcome as a one-course customer, and go instead to a pizzeria or wine bar (*bacaro*): a good central one is Vino Vino (near the Fenice Theatre, and under the same management as the Antico Martini). Nearby, in Al Teatro, you can eat an excellent pizza made in a real pizza oven (other dishes here tend to be pricey).

Reliable *trattorie* include Montin (Fondamenta di Borgo, Dorsoduro), Trattoria San Toma (Campo San Toma, San Polo), and Antica Mola (Fondamenta degli Ormesini, Cannaregio), all with gardens; and Ai Cugnai (San Vio, Dorsoduro).

Open-air cafés are a major Venetian attraction. Florians and Quadri's in Piazza San Marco are justifiably the most popular, with their intimate and ornate salons and black-tied waiters; a *cappuccino* here will cost what you might pay for lunch elsewhere! Other cafés are substantially cheaper (and if you are prepared to stand rather than sit, you could save up to half the cost of a drink).

Venetian specialities are limited. *Fegato alla veneziana* (liver and onions) is a safe bet but be prepared for the accompanying slab of *polenta* (often a rather rubbery piece of mushed-up maize). Risottos (especially *risotto di pesce*) and *gnocchi* (a Venetian speciality) are worth trying as a starter or main course. Fish is invariably a better choice than meat, although it's often frozen and portions can be rather mean for the high prices. Specialities are *seppie* (cuttlefish), *San Pietro* (John Dory) and *anguilla* (eel). The fish restaurants on the island of Burano are generally good value (one of the best is Da Romano). The local sandwich (*tramezzino*), sumptuously filled, makes an excellent snack. The favourite Venetian dessert is *tiramisu* – a rich chocolate/coffee gâteau soaked in liqueur.

Local wines include the familiar names of Soave, Valpolicella and Bardolino. The whites range from fairly good to awful. It's worth trying the medium-priced wine from the Colli Orientali de Friuli (both light red and white) and the white Verduzzo di Piave. The local sparkler, Prosecco, is sometimes served as a house wine, or with peach juice, then called a Bellini.

SHOPPING

Window-shopping is one of Venice's greatest pleasures – shops stay open until 7.30pm or 8pm. You'll find carnival-style masks everywhere, but Ca'Macara at Calle della Botteghe 3172 has perhaps the best and most unusual selection. Balocoloc at Calle del Scaleter 2234 sells a good collection of masks and home-made hats. San Marco is the best (and most expensive) area in which to buy clothes, leather, shoes, lace and Murano glass (*see above*) – especially in the galleries of the Piazza and in the streets just to the north and west. Try L'Isola, Salizzada San Moise 1468, for some very good modern glass; and Delphos, Calle Larga XXII Marco 2403, for Fortuny-style ribbed silk bags and scarves. Also in San Marco, further west, towards Campo Francesco Morosini, you'll find specialist shops selling prints (try Piazzesi, Campiello della Feltrina 2511c), marbled paper (Alberto Valese-Ebru, Salizzada San Samuele 3135 and San Stefano 3471) and some intriguing wooden sculpture at Livio di Marche, Salizzada San Samuele 3157a. There's also an excellent cake shop, Marchini Pasticceria, in Calle del Spezier.

Costume jewellery is sold on stalls throughout the city; Toti Campisi, Calle Borgolocco 6106, sells unusual painted leather earrings, and from nearby Al Campanil, Calle Lunga Santa Maria Formosa 5184, you can buy your own mosaic. For books in English or on Venetian art try the area round Campo San Barnaba.

NIGHTLIFE

Venetians eat at around 8.30pm. By 10.30pm, sometimes much earlier, many restaurants are closing. With only two discos, two piano bars and one jazz club, evening entertainment centres around a meal and a stroll. Harry's Bar in Calle Vallaresso is still (after 50 years) a fashionable and expensive place to try a Bellini cocktail and, if you're feeling flush, you could hire a singing gondolier to serenade you along the Grand Canal afterwards.

Opera, ballet, concerts and occasional drama performances (fairly formal and glittering occasions) take place in the enchanting Fenice Theatre (tel: 5210161/5210336 to book tickets in advance from the UK). The main opera season is from November to June. Other theatres include the beautiful small Ridotto and the Teatro Goldoni.

Many churches have evening or lunchtime concerts. There are several cinemas and open-air film shows in summer; foreign films are usually dubbed. It's virtually impossible for tourists to get tickets to the late summer International Film Festival at the Lido.

Un Ospite di Venezia – a free booklet from tourist offices – gives details of what's on.

HOTELS

The quietest and most attractive area to stay in is Dorsoduro. Most of the expensive, established hotels are grouped around St Mark's Square and along the Riva degli Schiavoni – a convenient but very touristy area. If you choose a waterfront hotel ask for a room with a view (this will be very expensive), or you may get put in an annexe or at the back of the building. Avoid the rash of cheap hotels in the station area – standards are low and you'll have a long trek to the sights every day. Space is at a premium in Venice and many hotel rooms are small and cramped. For a larger room try one of the hotels converted from a former palace – planning rules ensure that the rooms are not divided up into smaller ones.

ACCADEMIA ♦♦♦
Fondamenta Maravegie,
Dorsoduro 1058, 30123   *Tel: 52 10 188   Fax: 52 39 152*

This sixteenth-century villa was the Russian consulate before the Second World War. In 1955 it became a cheap *pensione* for the students of the Accademia. Now it's more upmarket and has been extended into what was the servants' quarters, offering very modern and comfortable rooms in a rambling setting. The first-floor salon looks over the front courtyard – with its flagstones and pigeons – and the back garden, leafy with apricot, apple, pear and fig trees. The rooms running off this part have parquet floors and heavy antique furniture.

Bedrooms: 28, most with bath/WC, some with shower/WC; some with air-conditioning; none with TV   **Credit/charge cards accepted:** All

---

Hotel prices Symbols indicate approximate prices per room per night for a double room with bath. Many large hotels run special breaks which work out far cheaper. (See page 14 for further details.)

♦ = under £50; ♦♦ = £50 to £80; ♦♦♦ = £80 to £100; ♦♦♦♦ = £100 to £140; ♦♦♦♦♦ = over £140.

BUCINTORO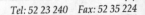
Riva San Biagio, Castello 2135, 30122   Tel: 52 23 240   Fax: 52 35 224

If you want views of the lagoon at an affordable price, this *pensione*, near the naval museum, looks out along the line of the Riva degli Schiavoni and across to San Giorgio Maggiore. The reception is small and a little shabby, but the bedrooms are mostly large, with *terrazzo* flooring and adequate bathrooms. There is a public *salotto* with easy chairs and a large Venetian glass lamp, and a ground-floor breakfast room with delicate ceiling mouldings.

Closed: Dec and Jan   **Bedrooms:** 28, half with bath/WC, half with shower/WC; none with TV   **Facilities:** Restaurant   **Credit/charge cards accepted:** None

---

DANIELI
Riva degli Schiavoni, Castello 4196, 30122   Tel: 52 26 480   Fax: 52 00 208

This sumptuous Gothic palace has been a hotel for over 150 years. Enter via a central courtyard framed by a staircase. The oldest part of the building is decorated with huge mirrors, gilt furniture and marble. The walls are hung with pictures of austere doges. Other rooms are in blue imperial style and there is a 1950s annexe with more modern furniture. The rooftop restaurant has some of Venice's best views over the lagoon.

Bedrooms: 231, all with bath/WC; air-conditioning; mini-bar   **Facilities:** Lift; restaurant   **Credit/charge cards accepted:** All

---

FLORA
San Marco 2283/4, 30124   Tel: 52 05 844   Fax: 52 28 217

The chink of a green entrance beckons invitingly down the long narrow passage that approaches this aptly named hotel. Creeper-clad walls are set around an idyllic gravelled garden, and a three-layered fountain in the centre is topped by a cherub. Chairs are set out for guests. The shuttered windows hide rooms with floral wallpaper, Venetian- or Regency-style furniture and modern bathrooms. Look out for the pen-and-ink drawings of will-o'-the-wisp carnival figures in the breakfast room.

Closed: Late Nov to end Jan   **Bedrooms:** 44, half with bath/WC, half with shower/WC; all with air-conditioning; none with TV   **Facilities:** Lift **Credit/charge cards accepted:** All

GRITTI PALACE
Campo Santa Maria del Giglio,
San Marco 2467, 30124   *Tel: 79 46 11   Fax: 52 00 942*

The Gritti has a fine frontage facing the Grand Canal but the main
entrance is tucked down a side-street in San Marco. The ground-floor
public rooms have been decorated in pastel colours. A huge portrait of
Doge Andrea Gritti hangs in the sitting-room. In contrast the bedrooms
have pictures of voluptuous nudes, large mirrors and brocaded velvet
drapes. The terrace has glorious views of the Santa Maria della Salute.

Bedrooms: 96, all with bath/shower/WC; air-conditioning; mini-bar
Facilities: Lift; restaurant   **Credit/charge cards accepted:** All

METROPOLE
Riva degli Schiavoni, Castello 4149, 30122   *Tel: 52 05 044   Fax: 52 23 679*

A collector's hotel: there are large glass cabinets displaying corkscrews,
nutcrackers and mother-of-pearl calling-card boxes. In the stairwell
there's a large black *felze* (a gondola hood), plus religious artefacts and
antiques everywhere. Some of the bedrooms have regal bedheads and
beautiful views of the lagoon. There's also a small garden.

Bedrooms: 74, all with bath/shower/WC; air-conditioning; mini-bar; safe
Facilities: Lift; restaurant   **Credit/charge cards accepted:** All

DO POZZI
Via XXII Marzo, San Marco 2373, 30124   *Tel: 52 07 855   Fax: 52 29 413*

A narrow alley leads into a *campiello*, with an ivy-covered well and
seating outside the hotel's iron-grilled façade. The rooms can be noisy
and some have rather shabby modern décor. The walk-through lounge is
small, with displays of oriental guns and Venetian glass. Guests are given
a ten per cent discount in the next-door restaurant, Da Raffaele (closed
Thursday).

Closed: End Dec and Jan   **Bedrooms:** 35, most with shower/WC, some
with bath/WC; all with mini-bar   **Facilities:** Lift   **Credit/charge cards
accepted:** All

♦ = under £50; ♦♦ = £50 to £80; ♦♦♦ = £80 to £100;
♦♦♦♦ = £100 to £140; ♦♦♦♦♦ = over £140.

LA RESIDENZA
Campo Bandiera e Moro, Castello 3608, 30122   Tel: 52 85 315   Fax: 52 38 859

Guests enter through thick wooden doors leading off the Campo Bandiera e Moro and into a cool flagstoned courtyard with a moulded well-head, tall ferns and a Venetian lion mounted against a red background. The reception and lounge area is palatial, with two ornate Venetian chandeliers and mouldings in faded reds, pinks, blues and greens. Hanging baskets of trailing plants and ferns surround a grand piano, and a large window with a Byzantine balcony looks from the Gothic façade on to the square below, filling the room with light. The bedrooms have a faded character and modern bathrooms.

Closed: Nov and Jan **Bedrooms:** 15, 3 with bath/WC, rest with shower/WC; mini-bar **Credit/charge cards accepted:** All

SANTO STEFANO
Campo Santo Stefano, San Marco 2957, 30124   Tel: 52 00 166   Fax: 52 24 466

The three green-shuttered Gothic windows on the first floor of this narrow faded pink building overlook the bustling cafés of Campo Santo Stefano. The reception has tarnished mirrors, and pastoral scenes decorate the desk. The breakfast room is dark and functional, but you can sit in the square if you prefer. Traditional Venetian furnishings in pastel colours and wispy flowers decorate the rooms, which overlook either the square or a tiny trellised garden behind.

Closed: 11 Jan to 11 Feb **Bedrooms:** 11, all with bath/shower/WC; mini-bar **Facilities:** Lift **Credit/charge cards accepted:** None

TORINO
Calle delle Ostreghe, San Marco 2356, 30124   Tel: 52 05 222   Fax: 52 28 227

Look for its red neon sign in an understated doorway squeezed in next to a butcher's shop on the twist of an alley. Inside this former fifteenth-century *palazzo* you can see painted beams, and the original staircase is overlooked by an interior window. Behind this there is a tiny lounge furnished with an antique desk and sofas. The bedrooms are quiet and spacious with elegant Italian flower prints and modern shower-rooms.

Bedrooms: 20, all with shower/WC; air-conditioning; mini-bar **Credit/charge cards accepted:** All

VIENNA

- One of Europe's finest capital cities, Vienna has plenty to offer those interested in history, art and architecture – including the treasures of the Habsburg dynasty
- It's the city of 'The Blue Danube' and the Vienna Boys' Choir; and there are always musical events
- Getting tickets for major attractions – especially the Spanish Riding School – is a complicated exercise, requiring pre-trip planning
- The compact area defined by the Ringstrasse (about one square mile) makes Vienna ideal for a short break; orientation is easy and public transport good
- Vienna's coffee-houses and the wine taverns of the Vienna Woods are part of the city's charm

THE capital of the Habsburg Empire, Vienna was once at the heart of civilised Europe, its court a flourishing centre of culture. For the visitor today, it is still a magnificent showcase of imperial grandeur with its baroque palaces and fabulous collections of art and treasures. Its reputation as a city of music was established in the eighteenth century: Schubert was born here, and Mozart, Haydn, Brahms and Beethoven all composed their great symphonies and died in Vienna. The nineteenth century was the era of the waltz and of the operetta, invented by the Strauss family and ever-popular today. Throughout the year there is a perpetual round of musical events, often attracting international stars.

The grand old capital is steeped in the past, rivalling London for ceremony and tradition. An unfortunate fire in the Hofburg at the end of 1992 means that performances of the Vienna Boys' Choir in the Imperial Chapel, and the Lipizzaner stallions in the Spanish Riding School, have temporarily been cancelled. But the Viennese still dress up to go to the opera and some enrol at dance classes to practise their steps for the frantic season of balls around New Year. Despite the grandeur, the centre of Vienna seems more provincial than cosmopolitan. Life proceeds at an old-fashioned pace: trams still trundle round the Ring, and bowler-hatted cabbies drive their *fiacres* around town, or await custom with their blinkered and blanketed horses. The Viennese visit their favourite coffee-houses to meet friends, read newspapers or even while away the hours playing chess, backgammon or cards. Vienna is not the place for a racy time.

Even the twentieth-century side to the city seems rather romantic: the demise of the Habsburg dynasty in 1918, the flowering of *Jugenstil* (art nouveau) architecture, Vienna as a centre of political intrigue and the setting for *The Third Man* – are all elements which continue to exert their fascination. In the old centre of Vienna there is still very little to break that spell.

The city can be seen as a plan of concentric circles, with St Stephen's Cathedral (Stephansdom) at its heart. The centre is defined by the famous Ringstrasse boulevard – known as the 'Ring' – which exactly follows the line of the old moated city walls, demolished to make way for it in the mid-nineteenth century. The area within the Ring is now the first district (of 23); beyond it lie residential districts and suburbs and an outer ring or 'girdle'. Beyond this, clockwise from the north-west, lie the Vienna Woods and the so-called UN City, the Danube (disappointingly grey), the airport and, to the south-west, in the thirteenth district, Schönbrunn, summer palace of the Habsburgs.

Most of the major attractions, with the notable exception of

Schönbrunn Palace, are on or within the Ring, so this is the ideal area in which to stay. Conceived as a grand imperial project, the horseshoe-shaped Ring is lined with imposing buildings including the grandiose neo-classical Parliament building, the Gothic style Votivkirche and Rathaus (town hall), and the Opera, Burgtheater and museums, inspired by the Italian Renaissance.

Within the Ring are several characteristic areas. Bustling, modernised Kärntnerstrasse runs from the Opera to Stephansdom. Off Stephansplatz lies Graben, the smartest shopping street, with the swirling baroque Pestsäule, a monument commemorating deliverance from the plague. Beyond is the former Jewish ghetto area around Judenplatz and the rather dull business district further west. Towards the Danube Canal are fine Gothic churches and the so-called 'Bermuda Triangle' (in the area around the Ruprechtskirche), with some of the city's trendier bars. To the east of the cathedral is the historic university area, a maze of picturesque streets where you can visit Mozart's house or eat in a medieval restaurant. The Hofburg, imperial palace of the Habsburgs, lies between Herrengasse – a street of baroque mansions – and the Ring and is a vast complex of buildings, much extended in the nineteenth century, notably during the long reign of Franz Josef I (1848-1916).

Just beyond the Ring are such notable landmarks as the grandiose Karlskirche, a masterpiece of baroque architecture, and the Secession Building, with its gilded orb of leaves, which symbolises the *Jugendstil* period. Just over the Danube Canal, in the Prater (Vienna's amusement park since 1766), is the Great Wheel, or Riesenrad, symbol of the city since *The Third Man*.

WHEN TO GO

May, June and September are good months to visit Vienna, with average temperatures a few degrees higher than in London. Early spring and late autumn are also worth considering. In July and August you will miss the Spanish Riding School, the Vienna Boys' Choir and the Opera. In winter it is easier to get tickets for the opera and other attractions, but be prepared for very cold weather. Some hotels reduce their rates during winter – but they charge high-season prices over Christmas and New Year. However, if you want to spend the festive break away from home, Vienna is a good choice.

GETTING THERE

Going independently

By air Austrian Airlines and British Airways both fly from Heathrow to Vienna three times a day; BA flies from Gatwick on weekdays. Lauda Air also flies from Gatwick every day except Tuesday and Saturday. APEX fares (book 14 days in advance) are cheapest. Several tour operators offer reductions on these scheduled fares and also have bargains on charter flights to Vienna. These include GTF Tours (071-792 1260), Canterbury Travel (081-206 0411), Euro Express (0444 235678), Data Travel (0424 722394) and Flightfile (071-323 1515). Charter fares are seasonal, but even in the summer months they still usually work out considerably cheaper than the APEX fare, though not as flexible.

Schwechat Airport The airport is easy to use and there are some good, if expensive, shops. It is 12 miles from the centre of Vienna. There is a bus service (every 20 minutes) to the City Air Terminal at the Hilton Hotel, from where you can pick up a taxi to your own hotel. The bus journey takes 20 minutes.

For those arriving on the late-evening flight the journey to the centre creates a memorable first impression. The industrial plants of Schwechat take on an eerie beauty, with their twinkling white lights and chimneys with plumes of white smoke. The daylight view is more mundane. From industrial landscape you are transported very suddenly to the city itself, which appears with its imposing mansions overlooking the Danube Canal. Again, if you arrive at night, the empty, lamp-lit streets can seem eerily romantic.

By rail There are daily departures from London Victoria via Dover and Ostend. The 'Oostende-Wien' overnight train journey takes about 24 hours and the return fare costs more than the APEX airfare. The luxury Venice-Simplon Orient-Express takes one and a half days and costs over £1,000 return.

Tour operator packages

A good range of tour operators offers packages to Vienna, lasting from two to seven nights. There are many 'twin centre' holidays with Salzburg, and also Budapest (the transfer is sometimes by hydrofoil down the Danube). Opera weekends are another option.

Independent travel costs about the same as an equivalent package. Prices for three nights B&B in a three-star hotel vary considerably, starting at £219 in low season, increasing to £343 in high season.

Tour operators use a wide range of hotels including most of the recommended ones – from the grandest down to the larger *pensions*. For a list of tour operators see page 385.

MASTERING THE SYSTEM

Information The UK office of the Austrian National Tourist Office is at 30 St George Street, London W1R 0AL, tel: 071-629 0461. In Vienna, the main information office of the Vienna Tourist Board at Kärntnerstrasse 38 is open daily 9am to 7pm, tel: 5872000, and is often very crowded. There is also an information desk in the arrivals hall at the airport. The Austrian Travel Agency in the Opernpassage sells theatre tickets, books sight-seeing tours and hotel rooms, and changes money. It is open Monday to Saturday 9am to 6pm, Sunday 9am to 2pm. The Vienna Transport Authority (Wiener Verkehrsbetriebe) has information offices at Karlsplatz and Stephansplatz underground stations, with explanatory leaflets in English.

City maps supplied by the tourist office are excellent and include a plan of the city centre (main sights marked in 3D) and a detailed public transport map. Other leaflets to ask for are the list of museums (for opening hours) and hotels (for special deals). The tourist office also publishes a *Monatsprogramm* (available in the middle of the preceding month) and a list of coming events in four languages.

Sightseeing tours Cityrama and Vienna Sightseeing Tours run three-hour bus tours. These may occasionally include tickets for Mass with the Vienna Boys' Choir or a morning performance of the Spanish Riding School. Others include guided interior visits of Stephansdom or Schönbrunn Palace. There is a guided tram sightseeing tour on Saturday and Sunday (May to October) from Karlsplatz (tickets from the Wiener Verkehrsbetriebe office in Karlsplatz underground station). Vienna Guides (tel: 4430940) offers walking tours on specific themes.

Changing money Banks are open on weekdays from 8am to 3pm; on Thursday until 5.30pm. Some are closed for lunch from 12.30pm to 1.30pm. Money can also be exchanged at travel agencies and seven days a week at the Westbahnhof and Sudbahnhof (both until 10pm), the City Air Terminal (Monday to Saturday 9am to noon, 1pm to 6.30pm; Sunday 9am to 1pm) and the airport (8.30am to 11.30pm).

Opening hours and days Shops are normally open from Monday to Friday, 9am to 6pm, and on Saturday until lunchtime. Most shops are closed on Saturday afternoons – except on the first Saturday in the month – as well as all day Sunday. Some major sights (Belvedere Palace and Kunsthistorisches Museum) are closed on Monday.

Buying tickets for special attractions Getting tickets for major musical events and the Spanish Riding School performances (when they start again) takes some organisation. A few tour operators, including Austro Travel, will get tickets for you but they charge agency rates (up to 25 per cent) and an administration fee. If you apply in advance by letter do not enclose payment in any form.

For the **State Opera** or **Volksoper**, write to Österreichischer Bundestheaterverband, Hanuschgasse 3, A-1010 Vienna. Information tel: 51444 ext 2960; credit card bookings are available only six days before the performance, tel: 513513. Programmes are available from the 15th of the preceding month: the National Tourist Office in London should have copies. Applications must be received three weeks before the performance. The season runs from September to May.

Tickets for the opera – both the State Opera and the more informal Volksoper where operettas are performed – can sometimes be obtained at short notice from the central box office at Hanuschgasse 3. Failing that, a ticket agent or your hotel may be worth trying, although they'll charge a commission of up to 25 per cent. Standing-room tickets are sold only at the evening box office on the night of the performance. You will have to queue.

The **Spanish Riding School** normally would give dressage performances on Sunday morning (10.45am) and occasionally on Wednesday evening (7pm) except from December to February and in July and August. Write to Spanische Reitschule, Hofburg, A-1010 Vienna, at least two months in advance; six months in advance for Sunday morning performances. Application details, including prices of seats and the programme of the Spanish Riding School, are clearly set out in a special leaflet obtainable from the Austrian National Tourist Office in London.

There are also short morning performances on Saturdays from March to June, September and October, but tickets are available only from agencies and cannot usually be obtained at short notice. Cityrama (tel: 534130) and Vienna Sightseeing (tel: 71246830) include morning performances and training sessions in some of their sightseeing programmes – again these are often fully booked well in advance.

If you have not booked tickets in advance you can queue at the entrance to see a morning training session (10am, most weekdays except Monday).

Tickets for **Mass with the Vienna Boys' Choir** (most Sundays, 9.15am) at the Imperial Chapel of the Hofburg (when it is reopened, planned for March 1993) can be obtained by writing to Hofmusikkapelle, Hofburg, A-1010 Vienna, two months in advance. But tickets (a maximum of two per applicant) are also available directly from the Chapel from about 5pm on the preceding Friday. Standing room is free, but not recommended. Austria On-line, a ticket agency in London (tel: 0345-581126), also sells tickets for most events.

GETTING AROUND

Getting around Vienna is very simple. Most visitors will want to walk, exploring the streets of the old town as they go. It takes about half an hour to cross the diameter of the Ring. However, public transport can be very useful if spirits flag, and we recommend that all visitors acquire a three-day travel pass. You can buy this '72-hour Vienna' pass (*Netzkarte*) from tobacconists. It saves money on six or more journeys on bus, tram or underground.

The quickest way of getting around is usually by **underground** or U-Bahn (a white U on a blue background indicates stations). The U-Bahn is simple to use, consisting of five lines. The most useful are the U1 (red), which crosses the centre of the city from north to south, the U2 (purple), which runs from Karlsplatz to Schottenring, and the U4 (green), which completes the circle, continuing to the suburbs, including Schönbrunn. The U3 (orange), from Erdberg (east) to Stephansplatz and the Volks-theater, has been extended to the west (Westbahnhof) and is scheduled to open in October 1993. There is also U6, which replaces the former Stadtbahn on the Gurtel.

For journeys around the Ring it is more fun to ride on the old-fashioned **trams** which circle it (via the Danube Canal embank-ment) continuously. They are numbered 1 or 2 and have Ring-Kai-Ring on the front. For short journeys within the Ring you can use the red **buses** (mostly minibuses) which run various circular, or figure-of-eight, routes in the centre. Routes are indicated at stops (marked *Haltestelle*). **Taxis** can be picked up in the main squares, **horse-drawn fiacres** at Stephansplatz, by the Albertina and at the Hofburg (negotiate the fare in advance).

UNMISSABLES

The Belvedere Palace and the Austrian Gallery
The baroque palace built for the dashing Prince Eugène of Savoy, a famous general and diplomat, was designed by Lukas von Hildebrandt, one of the greatest architects of his time. The Lower

Belvedere, the summer residence of Prince Eugène, contains the works of Austrian painters and sculptors of the baroque period and has a magnificent Gold Room. Nearby, medieval religious works are displayed in the Orangery. The Upper Belvedere, from which there are magnificent views of the city, contains an important gallery of Austrian painting of the nineteenth and twentieth centuries. Here the cheerful landscapes of Waldmüller contrast with the stylish, sophisticated portraits of Gustav Klimt and the more neurotic nudes of his contemporary, Egon Schiele. The State Treaty of Vienna, recognising Austria as an independent state, was signed in the Belvedere Palace in 1955.

The Hofburg: highlights include the Vienna Boys' Choir and the Spanish Riding School

The fire at the end of 1992 that caused so much damage means that most of the Hofburg is closed to the public until at least March 1993. The only parts still open are the Imperial Apartments (*see page 377*).

The oldest part of the Palace was the Alte Burg, entered by the sixteenth-century Swiss Gateway. It contained the Chapel Royal, where the Vienna Boys' Choir sang Mass on Sunday mornings. Also here was the Imperial Treasury, or Schatzkammer, where you could see the crown of Rudolph II, Napoleon's cradle, the crown of the Holy Roman Emperor and a fabulous collection of jewellery.

The Winter Riding School, designed by Fischer von Erlach, was the venue for the ever-popular dressage performances by the Spanish Riding School. Here, under glittering chandeliers, the prancing Lipizzaners were put through their paces to the strains of Strauss.

Kunsthistorisches Museum

One of the great art museums of Europe, this is largely the collection of the Habsburg rulers, who were knowledgeable and keen patrons of the arts. The paintings, on the first floor, are arranged by country and include superb Flemish primitives and Italian baroque works. Among the highlights are the huge Bruegels, the sumptuous allegories of Titian and Rubens (three rooms) and superb portraits by Holbein, Rembrandt, Van Dyck and Velázquez. The picture gallery is divided into two parts – Italian and Spanish, and Netherlands and German – which open late (7am to 9pm) on Tuesday and Friday of alternate weeks.

Ideally allow a separate visit for the collection of sculpture and the decorative arts on the ground floor. This includes many beautiful and precious treasures accumulated by Archduke

Ferdinand and Emperor Rudolph II for their Kunst-und-Wunder-kammern (art and treasure rooms) and is of considerable historical and artistic interest.

Schönbrunn Palace

The summer palace of the Habsburgs is set in a fine formal park. It is best reached by underground from Karlsplatz (about ten minutes, plus a short walk).

The chief glory of this rather severe ochre palace is the interior, which can be visited only on a guided tour that takes 45 minutes. During the winter, these may be only in German (though there are excellent notes in English) so you may prefer to take a city coach tour with an independent English-speaking guide.

Most impressive are the rococo rooms of Maria Theresia, Schönbrunn's most famous inhabitant, who reigned from 1740 to 1780. They include the Mirror Room where, at the age of six, Mozart gave a concert to the Empress and her children; the splendid Great Gallery, scene of sumptuous balls; and the so-called Millions Room, panelled with rare rosewood and hung with intricate gilt mirrors. The Carousel Room and Ceremonial Hall contain superb paintings showing imperial pomp and ceremony.

Those wanting to explore the park can return via Hietzing underground station on the far side of the grounds. Hietzing is a typical residential district, with a village atmosphere and a famous cafe, Dommayer's.

Stephansdom

The gaunt Gothic spire of St Stephan's Cathedral is the centre and symbol of the old city of Vienna, not least because much of the city has been reconstructed since the last war. The blackened stone contrasts strangely with the colourful tiles of the steeply angled roof. Only two doors are now used: the great West Door, with its Romanesque portal and sculptures, and the South, from where there is a good view of the spire.

The inside is lofty and rather gloomy, with some interesting features. You will need a detailed guidebook or, better still, a live guide. Failing that, at least glance at the pulpit – to the carved frogs climbing up the balustrade and a cheeky self-portrait of the sculptor (one of the earliest such 'signatures'). Guides will show you the carved Wiener Neustadt altarpiece and the fine tomb of Emperor Friedrich II. Near the entrance is the simple tomb of Eugène of Savoy. Take the lift up the North Tower for a 360-degree view of the city, and to see the famous Pummerin Bell, the second largest in Western Europe and cast from the metal of

Turkish cannon after the siege of 1683. Or you can climb the main tower (nearly 350 steps). Some of the treasures of Stephansdom are in the small **Museum of the Cathedral and Diocese** nearby, which is, by contrast to the cathedral itself, well lit. It contains medieval and baroque paintings and sculpture.

OTHER PLACES TO VISIT

Museums and galleries

Academy of Fine Arts For the keen gallery-goer the Academy offers, most notably, a nightmarish Bosch, several Cranachs, some Rubens sketches, landscapes by van Goyen and Guardi and a regal portrait of Maria Theresia by Meytens.

Albertina This is a vast and priceless collection of drawings, the nucleus being the combined acquisitions of its founder, Prince Albert von Sachsen-Teschen, and of Prince Eugène of Savoy. The half-dozen main rooms, with creaking parquet floors, silk walls and chandeliers, are devoted to regular special exhibitions when some of the most precious works, by artists such as Altdorfer, Dürer, Rembrandt and Rubens may be on show. Otherwise, facsimiles are displayed, and only scholars may see the originals.

Clock Museum A representative collection of timepieces and their history occupies three floors of a picturesque Viennese house. Exhibits range from exquisite, including the smallest pendulum clock in the world, which fits into a thimble, to the grotesque.

Habsburg Burial Vaults/Kaisergruft Nothing in Vienna symbolises the glory and the tragedy of the Habsburg dynasty more potently than the cavernous imperial crypt of the Kapuzinerkirche. Most impressive are the great lead tombs of Elizabeth-Christine (1691-1750) and of Maria Theresia and her consort, François of Lorraine. These are festooned with trophies and skulls, crowns and cupids, trumpeting angels and imperial eagles and are guarded at each corner by veiled female figures symbolising Grief. In poignant contrast is the simple wooden casket of Empress Zita, who died in 1989 after some 70 years of exile and widowhood.

Historical Museum of the City of Vienna On the ground floor there are archaeological remains, armour, early panel paintings and original sandstone statuary from the outside of the Stephansdom. Models, maps, Vienna porcelain and more portraits by Meytens are housed upstairs.

The Hofburg: the rest Much of the Hofburg is now used as government offices. The only parts open to the public since the fire are the **Imperial Apartments**, a rather monotonous series of nineteenth-century rooms. The main features of interest are the apartments of the Empress Elizabeth, complete with gym equipment and poignant mementoes of her death (at the hands of a fanatic in Geneva in 1898), and of her son, the tragic Crown Prince Rudolph, who died at Mayerling in 1889. Winterhalter's famous portrait of the legendary Empress (who was known as 'Sissy') hangs in the Large Drawing Room. Also part of the Hofburg complex is the beautifully Gothic **Augustinerkirche**, one of several churches in Vienna with a Sung Mass on Sundays. The hearts of the Habsburgs are preserved in urns in the Herzgruft.

Composers' homes Mozart's House, the most popular of the many composers' homes in Vienna, is also a small museum. Mozart lived here from 1784 to 1787 and it was during this time that he composed *The Marriage of Figaro*.

A whole weekend could be spent visiting the various houses of Beethoven, the birthplace and last residence of Schubert, the homes of Haydn and Strauss, and the cemetery (Zentralfriedhof) where they lie buried. Mozart aficionados may like to pay a pilgrimage to his simple grave at the Cemetery of St Marx (tram 71 from Schwarzenberg Platz).

Museum of Modern Art Twentieth-century paintings and sculpture are incongruously displayed in the lovely eighteenth-century Liechtenstein Palace.

The Secession Building and **Jugendstil in Vienna** A good starting point for the study of *Jugendstil* (the equivalent of art nouveau) is the area around Karlsplatz. Visit the restored turn-of-the-century Secession Building with the *Beethoven* frieze by Klimt, and Otto Wagner's Majolikahaus overlooking the Naschmarkt, Vienna's Saturday morning flea-market. Wagner also designed the entrance to Karlsplatz underground station, a charming period piece.

Sigmund Freud Museum This is the house where the great psychoanalyst lived from 1891 to 1938. Ring the bell, hang up your hat in the hall, even wait in the waiting room in order to get into the often-crowded consulting rooms to peer at photographs and paraphernalia, with multi-lingual explanations.

Hundertwasser House and Kunsthaus Wien Artist Friedensreich Hundertwasser believes that buildings grow like plants: living and changing continuously. His block of flats is painted in Mediterranean blues, yellows and oranges, splattered with blocks of Byzantine gold, and planted with young trees bending out of small balconies. The nearby Kunsthaus Wien, with its undulating floors and black and white façade, holds a permanent exhibition of Hundertwasser's works, created according to his ecological principles.

Excursions

The Vienna Woods The Vienna Woods are not as romantic as they sound, and some of the wine villages are not particularly pretty – with the notable exception of Grinzing. There are still some unspoilt parts and a few memorable panoramic views. The main excursion companies offer two guided coach tours to the Vienna Woods. Visit either Kahlenberg and the monastery at Klosterneuberg (altar by Nicolas of Verdun, 1181) or take a tour to Mayerling, scene of the tragic death of Crown Prince Rudolph and his mistress, Marie Vetsera, in 1889. A visit to the Cistercian abbey of Heiligenkreuz is included. Boat trips up the Danube in summer can be booked through tour companies or the Danube Steamship Company (tel: 21750 ext 451). There are also numerous day-trips.

SHOPPING

The main shopping streets in the centre, Kärntnerstrasse and nearby Graben, which is more exclusive, are pedestrianised. Fine gifts can be purchased at Lobmeyr, famous for glass, and at Augarten, known for its hand-painted porcelain. Several shops in the centre specialise in traditional Austrian clothing – *Trachtenmoden*. If you buy anything over AS1,000 (around £50), VAT can be reclaimed, but you will need your passport. Cheaper local souvenirs include petit point embroidery, enamelled jewellery, jolly aprons and ceramic models of the ubiquitous prancing Lipizzaners. Candles, calendars, Piatnik playing-cards and chocolates make good presents. The classier coffee-houses, notably Demel's in Kohlmarkt, sell beautifully packaged confectionery, and you can buy *Sachertorte* from the Sacher Hotel (or Demel's, which also claims the original recipe). The streets between Graben and the Hofburg contain many antique shops, art galleries, coin and stamp dealers and the auction house Dorotheum.

EATING AND DRINKING

The coffee-houses are a Viennese institution and range from grand establishments such as the Café Landtmann (on the Ring) and Demel's to the bohemian (Bräunerhof or Hawelka), the spartan (Prückel) or the merely cosy. The simple Aida chain is often considered to provide the best coffee. Most offer full meals as well as coffee and cakes, and the day's specials may be chalked up on a blackboard outside. There are numerous coffee-houses all over Vienna, but notably in the area between the Hofburg, the cathedral and the east side of the Ring. Here, too, are various restaurants. If in doubt, head for the streets around Fleischmarkt. Many restaurants are pleasantly old-fashioned and surprisingly inexpensive. Typical, if touristy, is the quaint Griechenbeisl at Fleischmarkt 11; another good one is Zum Weissen Rauchfang-kehrer at Weihburggasse 4. Bars, *beisl* (pubs) and restaurants in the 'Bermuda Triangle' around Ruprechtskirche are frequented by the young.

Another particularly Viennese experience is to eat at one of the *Heuriger* villages on the edge of the Vienna Woods. The authentic *Heuriger* is the home of a wine-grower who is licensed to sell his wines on certain days of the year (the new wine is proclaimed by fir-branch wreaths hung outside). Nowadays many *Heuriger* offer not only a simple, rustic-style cold buffet but full-blown restaurant meals, often accompanied by the traditional *Schrammelmusik* (a violin and accordion serenade). The most picturesque and popular village, Grinzing, is easily reached by tram 38 from Schottentor – it takes about half an hour. In summer the rural atmosphere is spoilt by fleets of tourist coaches.

Vienna has several of its own gastronomic specialities, the most famous being the ubiquitous *Wiener Schnitzel* (sample giant ones at Figlmüller in Wollzeile). *Tafelspitz*, boiled beef, is best at lunchtime, and filling puddings include apricot dumplings, called *Marillenknödel*, and various pancakes. There is a bewildering choice of types of coffee: a *Melange* is a white coffee, an *Einspanner* a small black coffee with whipped cream. While Viennese food is traditionally hearty, some restaurants offer *neue Wiener küche*: Viennese recipes adapted for today's palate. These are usually the more elegant and pricey establishments, often in hotels.

NIGHTLIFE

Nightlife in Vienna ranges from the sedate to the seamy, with little in between. Piano bars are more popular than discos or nightclubs. Most visitors will be more than content with a night at the opera, a concert and an evening at one of the *Heuriger*.

Classical music remains a major part of the cultural and social life of the city. The opera season lasts from September to June (*see* '*Mastering the system*'). The biggest concert halls are the Musik-verein, home of the Vienna Philharmonic Orchestra (on Karlsplatz, tel: 5058190), and the Konzerthaus (Lothringerstrasse 20, tel: 7121211). There are many other venues, including churches, palaces and cafés (some of which specialise in waltz or jazz music). Evenings of Viennese music and operetta, with dinner and a show, are organised for tourists at places such as the Rathauskeller. These are widely advertised. Grand formal balls are held on New Year's Eve (the Kaiserball) and during January and February. Tour operator packages are available for a four-night stay including accommodation and tickets (ask the National Tourist Office for the *Winter Scene* brochure for details of tickets).

The 'Bermuda Triangle' area is quite lively in the evenings, and the Casino Wien on Kärntnerstrasse is a smart gambling den.

HOTELS

For a short stay, the ideal location is on, or within, the Ringstrasse, although public transport is so good that this is not essential. Tour operators use a wide range of hotels, including the finest traditional city hotels.

Those booking independently should obtain the list of hotels from the tourist office. A separate brochure is published for summer and winter, and another for disabled visitors. Prices must be confirmed when booking, as hotels are apt to put up their prices after the hotel booklet is published.

Hotel prices Symbols indicate approximate prices per room per night for a double room with bath. Many large hotels run special breaks which work out far cheaper. (See page 14 for further details.)

◆ = under £50; ◆◆ = £50 to £80; ◆◆◆ = £80 to £100;
◆◆◆◆ = £100 to £140; ◆◆◆◆◆ = over £140.

BRISTOL   ◆◆◆◆◆
Kärntnerring 1, 1015   *Tel: 51 5 16   Fax: 51 5 16-550*

Facing the opera house, furnished in ostentatious *fin-de-siècle* style with an abundance of marble, gold, velvet, silk, old masters and chandeliers, it's slightly more luxurious, slightly less intimate than the nearby Sacher. A battalion of staff adds the final touches to perhaps Vienna's poshest restaurant. It has a famous speciality cake – the Imperial Torte. The bedrooms are special: soft fabric on the walls, and antique pieces with carefully co-ordinated upholstery.

Closed: Restaurant closed Sat lunch   **Bedrooms:** 144, all with bath/WC; air-conditioning; mini-bar; safe   **Facilities:** Lift; restaurant   **Credit/ charge cards accepted:** All

JOSEFSHOF   ◆◆◆◆
Josefsgasse 4-6, 1080   *Tel: 43 89 01   Fax: 43 89 01-150*

Josefshof is five minutes from the western side of the Ring, down a quiet, cobbled side-street and off a lively main street where there are good coffee shops. Small and friendly, despite its striking, late Biedermeier façade and wide, grand, white-arched entrance hall. Behind the fresh breakfast room at the rear of the hotel is a yellow-walled courtyard. The bedrooms are good: very clean, with rugs on wooden floors, and some attractive antiques. The hotel claims to be the only one in Vienna with its own art gallery.

Bedrooms: 48, most with bath/WC; all with mini-bar   **Facilities:** Lift; bar; sauna; solarium; conference room   **Credit/charge cards accepted:** All

KÄRNTNERHOF   ◆◆◆
Grashofgasse 4, 1011   *Tel: 51 2 19 23   Fax: 51 32 2 2833*

Kärntnerhof is in a quiet location, set through a gate at the far end of a cul-de-sac and in a large, attractive square. A colourful mural depicting the city's sanctity can be seen next to the large nineteenth-century yellow-painted building. A glass lift with leather upholstered sides, like an ancient cable-car, runs up its centre, surrounded by spiral stairs with white lattice railings. The bedrooms are spacious with high ceilings, but a little faded and spartan. The breakfast room is cosier, with flower-patterned seats. An unpretentious place, with helpful friendly staff.

Bedrooms: 43, about half with shower/WC, half with bath/WC; TV available on request   **Facilities:** Lift; private parking   **Credit/charge cards accepted:** All

KÖNIG VON UNGARN
Schulerstrasse 10, 1010

Tel: 51 58 40   Fax: 51 58 48

This sixteenth-century town house just off Stephansplatz, on a narrow but quite busy road, caters largely for the business trade. The focal point is its attractive bar set in an enclosed, glass-roofed courtyard, overlooked by shuttered windows and with a tree in the centre. The bedrooms are modern and well furnished. The arched restaurant, with light-ruby-coloured walls, is a bit stuffy.

Closed: Restaurant closed Sat   **Bedrooms:** 33, most with bath/WC; some with air-conditioning   **Facilities:** Lift; restaurant; bar   **Credit/charge cards accepted:** Diners, Visa

K+K MARIA THERESIA
Kirchberggasse 6-8, 1070

Tel: 52 123   Fax: 52 123-70

Just beyond the Ring, down a cobbled side-street opposite a cosy old candle-lit bar, is the bright yellow, flag-flying façade of a recently converted hotel. Yellow walls predominate in all the public rooms; the corridors have abstract paintings, the reception multicoloured sofas and a circular pine bar in the centre. The bedroom have white walls and interesting polychromatic modern furniture – certainly not the place to nurse a hangover. Some rooms have excellent views.

Bedrooms: 123, all with bath/WC; mini-bar; safe   **Facilities:** Lift; restaurant; snack-bar   **Credit/charge cards accepted:** All

MUSEUM
Museumstrasse 3, 1070

Tel: 93 44 26   Fax: 93 44 26-30

As its name suggests, this hotel is near the museums and also near narrow streets full of curiosity shops with long, high windows. Close by is a cinema showing old black and white films, sometimes subtitled in English. The Museum is also a short walk to the Ring. The upper floors have a good view of the city and some of the rooms have balconies. The bedrooms are enormous and simply furnished – they can seem a bit bleak. The sitting-room is cosy and convivial, the breakfast room a little more formal with high-backed upholstered chairs.

Bedrooms: 15, all with bath/WC   **Facilities:** Lift   **Credit/charge cards accepted:** Amex, Visa

K+K PALAIS ♦♦♦♦
Rudolfsplatz 11, 1010   Tel: 53 3 13 53   Fax: 53 3 13 53-70

Set in the salubrious but rather dull business district of the northern area of the Ring, this hotel faces a leafy square that is used as a playground by children. Formerly the residence of a famous mistress of Franz Joseph I, it's been thoroughly modernised. The ground floor is glass-fronted in pseudo art-deco style, the public rooms are painted yellow. The large, echoey reception leads to a smart, functional bar. Upstairs, the bedrooms are spacious and have wicker chairs.

Bedrooms: 66, most with bath/WC; all with mini-bar   **Facilities:** Lift; restaurant   **Credit/charge cards accepted:** All

IM PALAIS SCHWARZENBERG ♦♦♦♦♦
Schwarzenbergplatz 9, 1030   Tel: 0222-78 45 15   Fax: 0222-78 47 14

Despite palatial surroundings this hotel is small enough to be intimate, occupying just one of the wings of the 300-year-old palace. Guests enter through an enormous courtyard. Out the back is a 15-acre park with tennis courts; all this is just ten minutes' walk from the southern edge of the Ring. A canopied restaurant backs on to the park, as do the pricier bedrooms; all have thick wooden doors and are furnished with antiques. Staff dress in suits, not uniforms.

Bedrooms: 38, all with bath/WC   **Facilities:** Lift; restaurant; tennis; private parking   **Credit/charge cards accepted:** Amex, Visa

PERTSCHY ♦♦
Habsburgergasse 5, 1010   Tel: 53 449   Fax: 53 449-49

In the centre of the Ring, just off the Graben (a pedestrianised shopping area), stands the Pension Pertschy. Horses' hooves punctuate the quiet of the street as the *fiacres* make their tourist rounds. You enter through gates and go up wide stone steps to a first-floor reception. The bedrooms surround an open courtyard; each floor has an exterior walkway carpeted with fake grass, dark green railings draped with multicoloured canvas and an array of flower boxes. The bedrooms are fresh-smelling and decorated with modern furnishings in a traditional and individual style. The public areas are modern and a bit functional.

Bedrooms: 43, about half with shower/WC, half with bath/WC; all with mini-bar   **Facilities:** Lift; garage parking   **Credit/charge cards accepted:** Visa

SACHER
Philharmonikerstrasse 4, 1010   *Tel: 51 4 56   Fax: 51 5 57 810*

Sacher is renowned for its 150-year-old secret chocolate cake recipe and the famous guests who've stayed there since 1876. In the corridors, photographs document this century's visitors – including Queen Elizabeth II – and a tablecloth with copied, sewn signatures reveals less-familiar celebrities. Red velvet, crystal chandeliers, high ceilings and beautiful antiques; a variety of period bars, restaurants and cafés – all make for an evocative atmosphere. The bedrooms are traditionally styled, with brand-new bathrooms. The hotel is opposite the Opera.

Bedrooms: 118, all but one with bath/WC; all with air-conditioning; mini-bar **Facilities:** Lift; restaurant **Credit/charge cards accepted:** All

SUZANNE
Walfischgasse 4, 1010   *Tel: 51 3 25 07*

With a good location in the Ring, near the Opera, the main shopping area and tourist information and right next door to a sex shop, the Suzanne occupies two floors of an unattractive, grey concrete 1950s building – but don't be put off. The bedrooms are welcoming, with old-fashioned striped wallpaper, pictures and comfortable, high-backed armchairs. It's relaxed and informal.

Bedrooms: 24, all with bath or shower/WC; hair-dryer **Facilities:** Lift
Credit/charge cards accepted: Amex, Visa

Hotel prices Symbols indicate approximate prices per room per night for a double room with bath. Many large hotels run special breaks which work out far cheaper. (See page 14 for further details.)

♦ = under £50; ♦♦ = £50 to £80; ♦♦♦ = £80 to £100;
♦♦♦♦ = £100 to £140; ♦♦♦♦♦ = over £140.

TOUR OPERATORS

The tour operators listed below offer a three/four-night break in the cities featured in this book.

Amsterdam   American Express Travel, Amsterdam Travel Service, AT Mays, British Airways Holidays, Caprice Holidays, Cotsworld Travel, Cresta Holidays, Crystal Holidays, Eurobreak, Holland Travel Service, Hoverland European Holidays, JMB Travel Consultants, Kirker Travel, Leisure Breaks, Olau Line, Osprey Holidays, P&O European Ferries, Peltours, Rainbow Holidays, Regent Travel Services, Sally Holidays, Scandinavian Seaways, Sovereign Cities, Stena Sealink Travel, Thomson City Breaks, Time Off, Travelscene, Ultimate Holidays

Athens   Amathus Holidays, American Express Travel, Best of Greece, British Airways Holidays, Cresta Holidays, Eurobreak, Greece and Cyprus Travel Centre, Greek Sun Holidays, Greek Tourist Agency, Osprey Holidays, Peltours, Thomson City Breaks, Travelscene

Barcelona   American Express Travel, AT Mays, British Airways Holidays, Caprice Holidays, Cresta Holidays, Eurobreak, JMB Travel Consultants, Kirker Travel, Magic of Spain, Mundi Color Holidays, Peltours, Rainbow Holidays, Regent Travel Services, Sovereign Cities, Thomson City Breaks, Time Off, Travelscene, Unicorn Holidays

Berlin   American Express Travel, AT Mays, British Airways Holidays, Caprice Holidays, Cresta Holidays, DER Travel Service, Eurobreak, GTF Tours, JMB Travel Consultants, Moswin Tours, Osprey Holidays, Peltours, Scandinavian Seaways, Sovereign Cities, Taber Holidays, Thomson City Breaks, Travelscene

Bruges   American Express Travel, AT Mays, Belgian Travel Service, British Airways Holidays, Caprice Holidays, Cotsworld Travel, Cresta Holidays, Crystal Holidays, Eurobreak, Golden Gateways, Olau Line, Osprey Holidays, P&O European Ferries, Peltours, Regent Travel Services, Rainbow Holidays, Sally Holidays, Sovereign Cities, Stena Sealink Travel, Thomson City Breaks, Time Off, Travelscene, Ultimate Holidays, VFB Holidays, Wallace Arnold Tours

Budapest American Express Travel, Austrian Holidays, British Airways Holidays, Canterbury Travel, Caprice Holidays, Cresta Holidays, Crystal Holidays, Danube Travel, Eurobreak, Hungarian Air Tours, Intourist Travel, Intra Travel, JMB Travel Consultants, Osprey Holidays, Page & Moy, Peltours, Rainbow Holidays, Regent Holidays, Regent Travel Services, Sovereign Cities, Thomson City Breaks, Time Off, Travelscene

Copenhagen Aer Lingus Holidays, American Express Travel, AT Mays, British Airways Holidays, Cresta Holidays, Crystal Holidays, Eurobreak, Holiday Scandinavia, Osprey Holidays, Peltours, Rainbow Holidays, Scandinavian Seaways, Thomson City Breaks, Travelscene

Dublin Aer Lingus Holidays, American Express Travel, AT Mays, B&I Line Holidays, Caprice Holidays, CIE Tours International, Cresta Holidays, Crystal Holidays, Leisure Breaks, Osprey Holidays, Rainbow Holidays, Regent Travel Services, Ryanair Holidays, Thomson City Breaks, Time Off, Travelscene, Ultimate Holidays

Florence Abercrombie & Kent Travel, American Express Travel, AT Mays, British Airways Holidays, Caprice Holidays, Citalia, Cityjet Travel, Cresta Holidays, Crystal Holidays, Eurobreak, Italian Escapades, Italian Options, Italiatour, JMB Travel Consultants, Kirker Travel, Magic of Italy, Osprey Holidays, Page & Moy, Peltours, Prospect, Rainbow Holidays, Regent Travel Services, Skybus Holidays, Sovereign Cities, Sunvil Holidays, Thomson City Breaks, Time Off, Travelscene, Ultimate Holidays

Istanbul American Express Travel, Anatolian Sky Holidays, Authentic Turkey, Bosphorous Holidays, British Airways Holidays, Celebrity Holidays & Travel, Cresta Holidays, Crystal Holidays, Eurobreak, Galaxy Holidays, Intra Travel, Metak Holidays, Osprey Holidays, Peltours, President Holidays, Prospect, Regent Holidays, Simply Turkey, Sovereign Cities, Steepwest Holidays, Sunquest Holidays, Thomson City Breaks, Time Off, Travelscene, Voyages Jules Verne

Lisbon American Express Travel, AT Mays, British Airways Holidays, Caprice Holidays, Caravela, Cresta Holidays, Crystal Holidays, Eurobreak, Kirker Travel, Mundi Color Holidays, Osprey Holidays, Peltours, Portuguese Options, Rainbow Holidays, Regent Travel Services, Sovereign Cities, Sunvil Holidays, Thomson City Breaks, Time Off, Travelscene, Ultimate Holidays, Unicorn Holidays

Madrid American Express Travel, AT Mays, British Airways Holidays, Caprice Holidays, Cresta Holidays, Crystal Holidays, Eurobreak, Galaxy Holidays, JMB Travel Consultants, Kirker Travel, Magic of Spain, Mundi Color Holidays, Osprey Holidays, Page & Moy, Peltours, Prospect, Rainbow Holidays, Regent Travel Services, Sovereign Cities, Thomson City Breaks, Time Off, Travelscene, Ultimate Holidays, Unicorn Holidays

Moscow British Airways Holidays, Intourist Travel, Page & Moy, Peltours, Thomson City Breaks, Voyages Jules Verne

Nice Abercrombie & Kent Travel, Air France Holidays, Allez France, American Express Travel, AT Mays, British Airways Holidays, Caprice Holidays, Cresta Holidays, Eurobreak, France Voyages, French Life Holidays, Osprey Holidays, Peltours, Rainbow Holidays, Sovereign Cities, Thomson City Breaks, Travelscene, VFB Holidays

Paris Abercrombie & Kent Travel, Air France Holidays, Airtours, Allez France, American Express Travel, AT Mays, British Airways Holidays, Caprice Holidays, Cotsworld Travel, Cresta Holidays, Crystal Holidays, Eurobreak, France Voyages, French Life Holidays, Galaxy Holidays, Hoverland European Holidays, JMB Travel Consultants, Just France, Kirker Holidays, Osprey Holidays, Page & Moy, P&O European Ferries, Paris Travel Service, Peltours, Prospect, Rainbow Holidays, Regent Travel Services, Sally Holidays, Sovereign Cities, Stena Sealink Travel, Thomson City Breaks, Time Off, Travelscene, Ultimate Holidays, Venice Simplon Orient Express, VFB Holidays

Prague   Austrian Holidays, British Airways Holidays, Canterbury Travel, Caprice Holidays, Čedok Tours, Cresta Holidays, Crystal Holidays, Eurobreak, Hungarian Air Tours, Intourist Travel, Intra Travel, JMB Travel Consultants, Osprey Holidays, Page & Moy, Peltours, Prospect, Regent Holidays, Regent Travel Services, Sovereign Cities, Thomson City Breaks, Time Off, Travelscene

Rome   Abercrombie & Kent Travel, American Express Travel, AT Mays, British Airways Holidays, Caprice Holidays, Citalia, Cityjet Travel, Cresta Holidays, Crystal Holidays, Eurobreak, Galaxy Holidays, Italian Escapades, Italian Options, Italiatour, JMB Travel Consultants, Kirker Travel, Magic of Italy, Osprey Holidays, Page & Moy, Peltours, Rainbow Holidays, Regent Travel Services, Skybus Holidays, Sovereign Cities, Sunvil Holidays, Thomson City Breaks, Time Off, Travelscene, Ultimate Holidays

St Petersburg   British Airways Holidays, Intourist Travel, JMB Travel Consultants, Page & Moy, Peltours, Thomson City Breaks (with Moscow)

Salzburg   American Express Travel, AT Mays, Austrian Holidays, British Airways Holidays, Canterbury Travel, Cresta Holidays, Crystal Holidays, DER Travel Service, Eurobreak, JMB Travel Consultants, Moswin Tours, Osprey Holidays, Peltours, Rainbow Holidays, Sovereign Cities, Thomson City Breaks, Travelscene

Venice   Abercrombie & Kent Travel, American Express Holidays, AT Mays, British Airways Holidays, Caprice Holidays, Citalia, Cityjet Travel, Cresta Holidays, Crystal Holidays, Eurobreak, Italian Escapades, Italian Options, Italiatour, JMB Travel Consultants, Kirker Travel, Magic of Italy, Osprey Holidays, Page & Moy, Peltours, Rainbow Holidays, Regent Travel Services, Skybus Holidays, Sovereign Cities, Sunvil Holidays, Thomson City Breaks, Time Off, Travelscene, Ultimate Holidays, Venice Simplon Orient Express

Vienna American Express Holidays, AT Mays, Austrian
Holidays, British Airways Holidays, Canterbury
Travel, Caprice Holidays, Cotworld Holidays, Cresta
Holidays, Crystal Holidays, Danube Travel, DER
Travel Service, Eurobreak, Galaxy Holidays, GTF
Tours, Hungarian Air Tours, Intra Travel, JMB Travel
Consultants, Moswin Tours, Osprey Holidays, Page &
Moy, Peltours, Rainbow Holidays, Sovereign Cities,
Thomson City Breaks, Time Off, Travelscene, Venice
Simplon Orient Express

ADDRESSES

Abercrombie & Kent Travel
Sloane Square House
Holbein Place
London SW1W 8NS
Tel: 071-730 9600

Aer Lingus Holidays
83 Staines Road
Hounslow
Middlesex TW3 3JB
Tel: 081-569 4001

Air France Holidays
Galde House
18-24 Turnham Green Terrace
London W4 1RF
Tel: 081-742 3377

Airtours
Wavell House
Holcombe Road
Helmshore
Rossendale
Lancs BB4 4NB
Tel: (0706) 240033

Allez France
27-29 West Street
Storrington
West Sussex RH20 4DZ
Tel: (0903) 742345

Amathus Holidays
51 Tottenham Court Road
London W1P 0HS
Tel: 071-636 9873

American Express Travel
(Amex card-holders only)
PO Box 109
Horley
Surrey RH6 7FD
Tel: (0293) 822000

Amsterdam Travel Service
Bridge House
Ware
Herts SG12 9DF
Tel: (0920) 467444

Anatolian Sky Holidays
Imex House
52 Blucher Street
Birmingham B1 1QU
Tel: 021-633 4018

AT Mays
21 Royal Crescent
Glasgow G3 7SZ
Tel: 041-331 1121

Austrian Holidays
50-51 Conduit Street
London W1R 0NP
Tel: 071-439 7108

Authentic Turkey
20 Notting Hill Gate
London W11 3JE
Tel: 071-221 3878

B&I Line Holidays
Ground Floor
Reliance House
Water Street
Liverpool L2 8TP
Tel: 051-236 8325

Belgian Travel Service
Bridge House
Ware
Herts SG12 9DG
Tel: (0920) 467345

Best of Greece
23-24 Margaret Street
London W1N 8LE
Tel: 071-255 2320

Bosphorous Holidays
28 Maddox Street
London W1R 9PF
Tel: 071-408 0094

British Airways Holidays
Speedbird House
Heathrow Airport
Hounslow
Middlesex TW6 2JA
Tel: (0293) 615353

Canterbury Travel
248 Streatfield Road
Kenton
Harrow
Middlesex HA3 9BY
Tel: 081-206 0411

Caprice Holidays
32a Queensway
Stevenage
Herts SG1 1BS
Tel: (0438) 316622

Caravela's Short Breaks
38-44 Gillingham Street
London SW1V 1HU
Tel: 071-630 9223

Čedok Tours & Holidays
49 Southwark Street
London SE1 1RU
Tel: 071-378 6009

Celebrity Holidays & Travel
18 Frith Street
London W1V 5TS
Tel: 071-734 4386

CIE Tours International
185 London Road
Croydon
Surrey CR0 2RJ
Tel: 081-667 0011

Citalia
Marco Polo House
3-5 Lansdowne Road
Croydon
Surrey CR9 1LL
Tel: 081-686 5533

Cityjet Travel
Cityjet House
65 Judd Street
London WC1H 9QT
Tel: 071-387 1017

Cotsworld Travel
Bearland House
Longsmith Street
Gloucester GL1 2HL
Tel: (0452) 524151

Cresta Holidays
Cresta House
32 Victoria Street
Altrincham
Cheshire WA14 1ET
Tel: 061-927 7000

Crystal Holidays
Crystal House
The Courtyard
Arlington Road
Surbiton
Surrey KT6 6BW
Tel: 081-390 9900

Danube Travel
6 Conduit Street
London W1R 9TG
Tel: 071-493 0263

DER Travel Service
18 Conduit Street
London W1R 9TD
Tel: 071-408 0111

Eurobreak
10-18 Putney Hill
London SW15 7AX
Tel: 081-780 0909

France Voyages
Castle Yard
22a Hill Street
Richmond
Middlesex TW9 1TW
Tel: 081-332 0909

French Life Holidays
26 Church Road
Horsforth
Leeds LS18 5LG
Tel: (0532) 390077

Galaxy Holidays
Pillar and Lucy House
Merchants Road
Gloucester GL1 5RG
Tel: (0452) 308798

Golden Gateways
Hill Place
London Road
Southborough
Kent BN4 0PX
Tel: (0892) 511388

Greece and Cyprus Travel Centre
44 Birmingham Road
Sutton Coldfield
West Midlands B72 1QQ
Tel: 021-355 6955

Greek Sun Holidays
1 Bank Street
Sevenoaks
Kent TN13 1UW
Tel: (0732) 740317

Greek Tourist Agency
Office No 30
Morley House
320 Regent Street
London W1R 5AF
Tel: 071-580 3152

GTF Tours
182-186 Kensington Church Street
London W8 4DP
Tel: 071-792 1260

Holiday Scandinavia
28 Hillcrest Road
Orpington
Kent BR6 9AW
Tel: (0689) 824958

Holland Travel Service
Holland House
24-28 The Broadway
Old Amersham
Bucks HP7 0HP
Tel: (0494) 729333

Hoverland European Holidays
61 Bradford Street
Walsall
West Midlands WS1 3QD
Tel: (0922) 37884

Hungarian Air Tours
Kent House
87 Regent Street
London W1R 7HF
Tel: 071-437 9405

Intourist Travel
219 Marsh Wall
Isle of Dogs
London E14 9FJ
Tel: 071-538 8600

Intra Travel
44 Maple Street
London W1P 5GD
Tel: 071-323 3305

Italian Escapades
227 Shepherd's Bush Road
London W6 7AS
Tel: 081-748 2661

Italian Options
26 Tottenham Street
London W1P 9PP
Tel: 071-436 3246

Italiatour
241 Euston Road
London NW1 2BU
Tel: 071-383 3886

JMB Travel Consultants
(specialist opera agents)
'Rushwick'
Worcester WR2 5SN
Tel: (0905) 425628

Just France
Westbury Travel
1 Belmont
Lansdown Road
Bath
Avon BA1 5DZ
Tel: (0225) 446328

Kirker Travel
3 New Concordia Wharf
Mill Street
London SE1 2BB
Tel: 071-231 3333

Leisure Breaks
33 Dovedale Road
Liverpool L18 5EP
Tel: 051-734 2344

Magic of Italy
227 Shepherd's Bush Road
London W6 7AS
Tel: 081-748 7575

Magic of Spain
227 Shepherd's Bush Road
London W6 7AS
Tel: 081-748 7575

Metak Holidays
70 Welbeck Street
London W1M 7HA
Tel: 071-935 6961

Moswin Tours
Moswin House
21 Church Street
Oadby
Leicester LE2 5DB
Tel: (0533) 719922

Mundi Color Holidays
276 Vauxhall Bridge Road
London SW1V 1BE
Tel: 071-828 6021

Olau Line
Sheerness
Kent ME12 1SN
Tel: (0795) 662233

Osprey Holidays
Broughton Market
Edinburgh EH3 6NU
Tel: 031-557 1555

Page & Moy
136/140 London Road
Leicester LE2 1EN
Tel: (0533) 524433

P&O European Ferries
Channel House
Channel View Road
Dover
Kent CT17 9TJ
Tel: (0304) 214422

Paris Travel Service
Bridge House
Ware
Herts SG12 9DF
Tel: (0920) 461221

Peltours
Sovereign House
11-19 Ballards Lane
Finchley
London N3 1UX
Tel: 081-346 9144

Portuguese Options
26 Tottenham Street
London W1P 9PP
Tel: 071-436 3246

President Holidays
542 Kingsland Road
Dalston
London E8 4AH
Tel: 071-249 4002

Prospect Music & Art Tours
454-458 Chiswick High Road
London W4 5TT
Tel: 081-995 2151

Rainbow Holidays
Ryedale Building
Piccadilly
York YO1 1PN
Tel: (0904) 450400

Regent Holidays
(Budapest, Istanbul)
Regent House
31a High Street
Shanklin
Isle of Wight PO37 6JW
Tel: (0983) 864212

Regent Holidays
(Prague)
15 John Street
Bristol BS1 1DE
Tel: (0272) 211711

Regent Travel Services
4 Exmoor Street
London W10 6BD
Tel: 081-960 9066

Ryanair Holidays
311 Tower Building
Water Street
Liverpool L3 1BA
Tel: 051-227 1399

Sally Holidays
Basted Lane
Borough Green
Kent TN15 8BA
Tel: (0732) 780440

Scandinavian Seaways
Scandinavia House
Parkeston Quay
Harwich
Essex CO12 4QG
Tel: (0255) 241234

Simply Turkey
8 Chiswick Terrace
Acton Lane
London W4 5LY
Tel: 081-747 1011

Skybus Holidays
24a Earls Court Gardens
London SW5 0TA
Tel: 071-373 6055

Sovereign Cities
Astral Towers
Betts Way
Crawley
West Sussex RH10 2GX
Tel: (0293) 599900

Steepwest Holidays
130-132 Wardour Street
London W1V 3AU
Tel: 071-629 2879

Stena Sealink Travel
Charter House
Park Street
Ashford
Kent TN24 8EX
Tel: (0233) 647033

Sunquest Holidays
9 Grand Parade
Green Lanes
London N4 1JX
Tel: 081-800 8030

Sunvil Holidays
Sunvil House
7 & 8 Upper Square
Old Isleworth
Middlesex TW7 4BJ
Tel: 081-568 4499

Taber Holidays
126 Sunbridge Road
Bradford
West Yorkshire BD1 2SX
Tel: (0274) 735611

Thomson City Breaks
Parway House
202-204 Finchley Road
London NW3 6XB
Tel: 071-431 1950

Time Off
Chester Close
Chester Street
London SW1X 7BQ
Tel: 071-235 8070

Travelscene
Travelscene House
11-15 St Ann's Road
Harrow
Middlesex HA1 1AS
Tel: 081-427 4445

Ultimate Holidays
Twyford Business Centre
33 London Road
Bishop's Stortford
Herts CM23 3YT
Tel: (0279) 508889

Unicorn Holidays
Intech House
34 Cam Centre
Wilbury Way
Hitchin
Herts SG4 0RL
Tel: (0462) 422223

Venice Simplon Orient Express
Sea Containers House
20 Upper Ground
London SE1 9PF
Tel: 071-928 6000

VFB Holidays
Normandy House
High Street
Cheltenham
Glos GL50 3HW
Tel: (0242) 526338

Voyages Jules Verne
21 Dorset Square
London NW1 6QG
Tel: 071-486 8080

Wallace Arnold Tours
Gelderd Road
Leeds LS12 6DH
Tel: (0532) 636456

WEATHER STATISTICS

	JAN		FEB		MAR		APR		MAY	
	T	R	T	R	T	R	T	R	T	R
Amsterdam	5	23	4	19	7	16	10	14	14	13
Athens	13	16	14	11	16	11	20	9	25	8
Barcelona	13	5	14	5	16	8	18	9	21	8
Berlin	2	17	3	15	8	12	13	13	19	12
Bruges	5	13	6	12	9	11	11	12	15	11
Budapest	1	13	4	12	10	11	17	11	22	13
Copenhagen	2	17	2	13	5	12	10	13	16	11
Dublin	8	13	8	10	10	10	13	11	15	10
Florence	9	8	11	8	14	8	19	8	23	8
Istanbul	8	18	9	14	11	14	16	9	21	8
Lisbon	14	15	15	12	17	14	20	10	21	10
Madrid	9	8	11	7	15	10	18	9	21	10
Moscow	−9	18	−6	15	0	15	10	13	19	13
Nice	13	9	13	7	15	8	17	9	20	8
Paris	6	17	7	14	12	12	16	13	20	12
Prague	0	13	1	11	7	10	12	11	18	13
Rome	11	8	13	9	15	8	19	6	23	5
St Petersburg	−7	21	−5	17	0	14	8	12	15	13
Salzburg	2	16	4	14	9	13	14	16	19	17
Venice	6	6	8	6	12	7	17	9	21	8
Vienna	1	15	3	14	8	13	15	13	19	13
London	6	15	7	13	10	11	13	12	17	12

T = Average daily maximum temperature °C

R = Average number of rainy days [*] per month

JUNE		JULY		AUG		SEPT		OCT		NOV		DEC	
T	R	T	R	T	R	T	R	T	R	T	R	T	R
18	13	20	17	20	17	18	18	14	22	9	21	6	24
30	4	33	2	33	3	29	4	24	8	19	12	15	15
25	6	28	4	28	6	25	7	21	9	16	6	13	6
22	13	24	14	23	14	20	12	13	14	7	16	3	15
18	10	20	12	20	13	19	10	15	13	10	15	6	16
26	13	28	10	27	9	23	7	16	10	8	14	4	13
19	13	22	14	21	14	18	15	12	16	7	16	4	17
18	11	20	13	19	12	17	12	14	11	10	12	8	14
27	7	30	3	30	4	26	6	20	8	14	10	11	10
25	6	28	4	28	4	24	7	20	11	15	14	11	18
25	5	27	2	28	2	26	6	22	9	17	13	15	15
27	5	31	2	30	3	25	6	19	8	13	9	9	10
21	12	23	15	22	14	16	13	9	15	2	15	−5	23
24	5	27	2	27	4	25	7	21	9	17	9	13	9
23	12	25	12	24	13	21	13	16	13	10	15	7	16
21	12	23	13	22	12	18	10	12	13	5	12	1	13
28	4	30	1	30	2	26	5	22	8	16	11	13	10
20	12	21	13	20	14	15	17	9	18	2	18	−3	22
22	18	24	18	23	17	20	14	14	13	8	14	3	14
25	8	27	7	27	7	24	5	19	7	12	9	8	8
23	14	25	13	24	13	20	10	14	13	7	14	3	15
20	11	22	12	21	11	19	13	14	13	10	15	7	15

[*] Days with 0.1mm or more rain – except Dublin, Florence, Rome and Venice where the figures denote days with 1.00mm or more rain, and London where they denote days with 0.25mm or more rain.

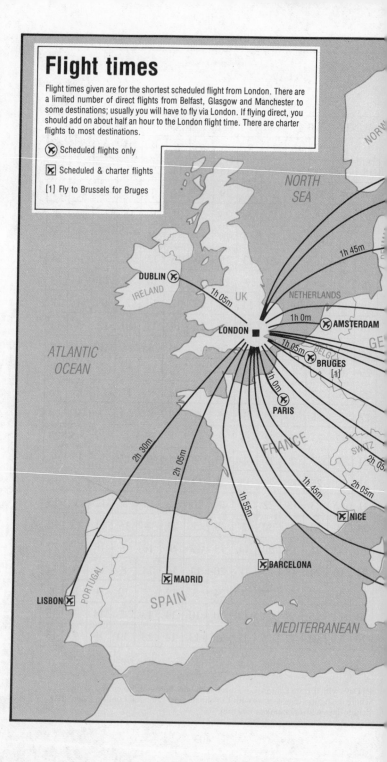

Flight times

Flight times given are for the shortest scheduled flight from London. There are a limited number of direct flights from Belfast, Glasgow and Manchester to some destinations; usually you will have to fly via London. If flying direct, you should add on about half an hour to the London flight time. There are charter flights to most destinations.

(✕) Scheduled flights only

✕ Scheduled & charter flights

[1] Fly to Brussels for Bruges

NORTH SEA

NORW

NETHERLANDS

DUBLIN (✕)
IRELAND

1h 05m UK

LONDON

1h 45m

1h 0m (✕) AMSTERDAM

GE

1h 05m (✕) BRUGES
BELG
[1]

ATLANTIC OCEAN

1h 0m (✕) PARIS

FRANCE

SWITZ 2h 05m

2h 30m

2h 05m

1h 45m

2h 05m

✕ NICE

1h 55m

PORTUGAL

✕ MADRID

✕ BARCELONA

LISBON ✕

SPAIN

MEDITERRANEAN

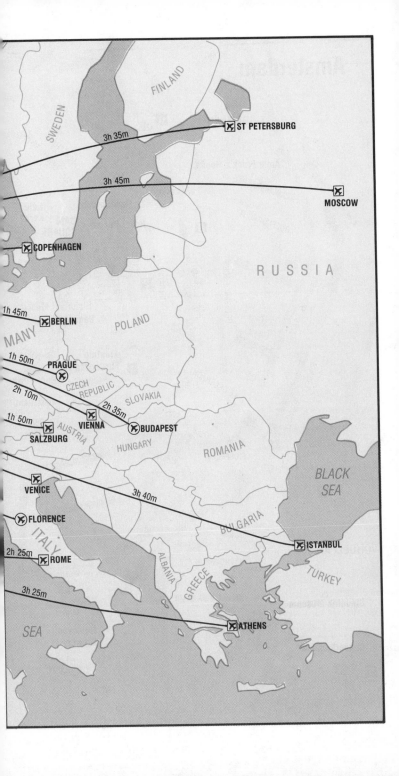

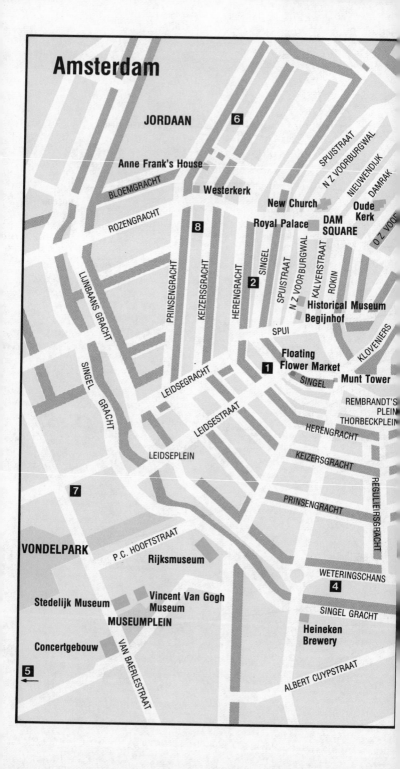

Amsterdam

JORDAAN

6

SPUISTRAAT

N Z VOORBURGWAL

NIEUWENDIJK

DAMRAK

Anne Frank's House

Westerkerk

BLOEMGRACHT

ROZENGRACHT

8

New Church

Royal Palace

DAM SQUARE

Oude Kerk

O Z VOO

PRINSENGRACHT

KEIZERSGRACHT

HERENGRACHT

SINGEL

SPUISTRAAT

N Z VOORBURGWAL

KALVERSTRAAT

ROKIN

2

Historical Museum

Begijnhof

SPUI

KLOVENIERS

LIJNBAANS GRACHT

SINGEL GRACHT

1

Floating Flower Market

Munt Tower

SINGEL

LEIDSEGRACHT

LEIDSESTRAAT

REMBRANDT'S PLEIN

THORBECKPLEIN

HERENGRACHT

LEIDSEPLEIN

KEIZERSGRACHT

REGULIERSGRACHT

7

PRINSENGRACHT

VONDELPARK

P. C. HOOFTSTRAAT

Rijksmuseum

WETERINGSCHANS

4

Stedelijk Museum

Vincent Van Gogh Museum

MUSEUMPLEIN

SINGEL GRACHT

Concertgebouw

VAN BAERLESTRAAT

Heineken Brewery

5

ALBERT CUYPSTRAAT

Centraal Station

🅼 *i*

mstelkring

URGWAL

Z ACHTERBURGWAL

BURG WALL

Waag

🅼 *Nieuwmarkt*

PRINS HENDRIK KADE

Scheepvaart Museum

JODENBREESTRAAT

Flea Market

Rembrandt's House

HOOGTE KADIJK

WATERLOOPLEIN

🅼 *Waterlooplein*

Blue Bridge

PLANTAGE MIDDENLAAN

Zoo

Willet-Holthuysen Museum

NIEUWE KEIZERSGRACHT

PRINSENGRACHT

Skinny Bridge NIEUWE

UTRECHTESTRAAT

AMSTEL

Tropical Museum

SINGEL GRACHT

3

Weesperplein 🅼

Inset map:

NORTH SEA

Enkhuizen

Alkmaar

Edam • Volendam

Monnickendam • Marken

Broek-in-Waterland •

Keukenhof • Aalsmeer

AMSTERDAM

The Hague

Delft • Rotterdam

HOTELS

1   Agora
2   Ambassade
3   Amstel Inter-Continental
4   Asterisk
5   Borgmann
6   The Canal House
7   Owl
8   Pulitzer

🅼   Metro

0   METRES   500
0   YARDS   500

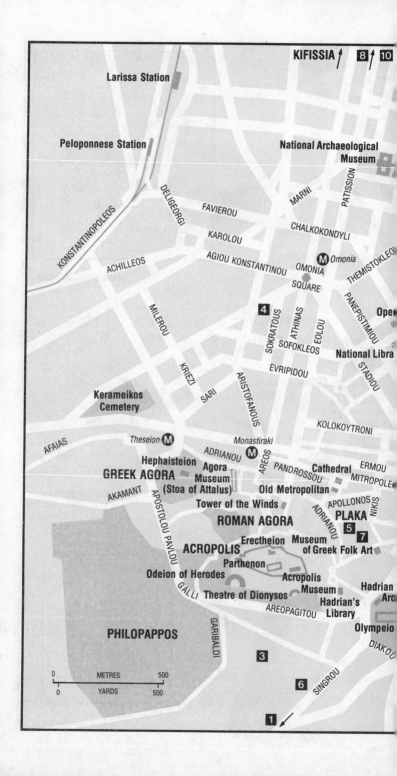

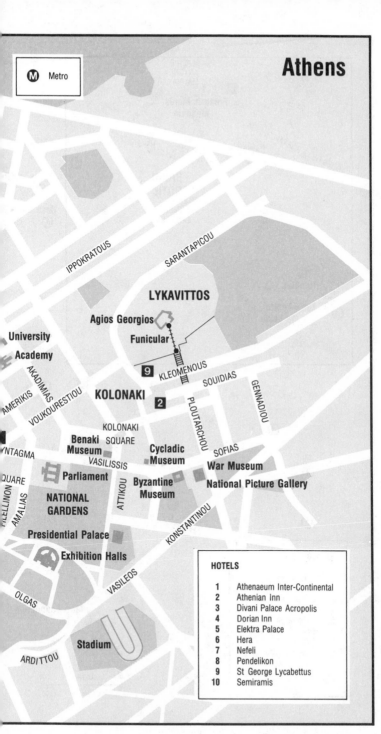

Athens

M Metro

IPPOKRATOUS
SARANTAPICOU

LYKAVITTOS

Agios Georgios
Funicular

University
Academy

AKADIMIAS
AMERIKIS
VOUKOURESTIOU

9 KLEOMENOUS

SOUIDIAS

GENNADIOU

KOLONAKI

2

PLOUTARCHOU

KOLONAKI SQUARE

Benaki
Museum

VASILISSIS

Cycladic
Museum

SOFIAS

NTAGMA

QUARE

PILELLINON
AMALIAS

Parliament

ATTIKOU

Byzantine
Museum

War Museum

National Picture Gallery

NATIONAL
GARDENS

KONSTANTINOU

Presidential Palace

Exhibition Halls

VASILEOS

OLGAS

ARDITTOU

Stadium

HOTELS

1	Athenaeum Inter-Continental
2	Athenian Inn
3	Divani Palace Acropolis
4	Dorian Inn
5	Elektra Palace
6	Hera
7	Nefeli
8	Pendelikon
9	St George Lycabettus
10	Semiramis

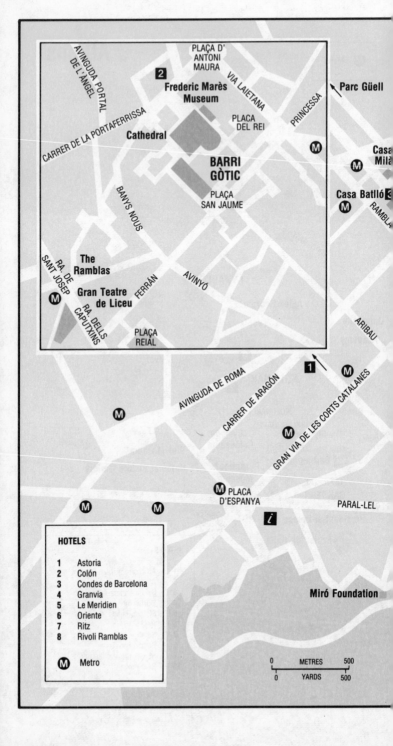

PLAÇA D'ANTONI MAURA

AVINGUDA PORTAL DE L'ÀNGEL

2

Frederic Marès Museum

VIA LAIETANA

PRINCESSA

→ **Parc Güell**

CARRER DE LA PORTAFERRISSA

Cathedral

PLAÇA DEL REI

Ⓜ

Casa Milà

Ⓜ

BARRI GÒTIC

Casa Batlló 3

RAMBLA

BANYS NOUS

PLAÇA SAN JAUME

Ⓜ

RBLA

RA. DE SANT JOSEP

The Ramblas

FERRÁN

AVINYÓ

Ⓜ

Gran Teatre de Liceu

RA. DELS CAPUTXINS

PLAÇA REIAL

ARIBAU

1 →

Ⓜ

AVINGUDA DE ROMA

CARRER DE ARAGÓN

Ⓜ

GRAN VIA DE LES CORTS CATALANES

Ⓜ

Ⓜ

Ⓜ PLAÇA D'ESPANYA

PARAL-LEL

i

Miró Foundation

HOTELS

1 Astoria
2 Colón
3 Condes de Barcelona
4 Granvia
5 Le Meridien
6 Oriente
7 Ritz
8 Rivoli Ramblas

Ⓜ Metro

0 ___ METRES ___ 500
0 ___ YARDS ___ 500

Sagrada Família

DIAGONAL

PASSEIG DE CARLOS I

CARRER DE ARAGÓN

PASSEIG DE SAN JUAN

CORTS CATALANES

Station

PASSEIG DE GRÀCIA

GRAN VIA DE LES

7

4

RONDA DE SANT PERE

DE CATALUNYA

VIA LAIETANA

RONDA DE SANT PERE

Modern Art
Museum

**PARC DE LA
CIUTADELLA**

Zoo

RONDA
UNIVERSITAT

PLAÇA DE
CATALUNYA

RA. DELS ESTUDIS

8

5

Picasso
Museum

Station

RONDA DE SANT ANTONI

BARRI
GÒTIC

PASSEIG ISABEL

BARCELONETA

CARRER DE L'HOSPITAL

SEE INSET

PASSEIG NACIONAL

6

RA. DE SANTA
MONICA

Harbour

Barcelona

MONTJUÏC

Military Museum

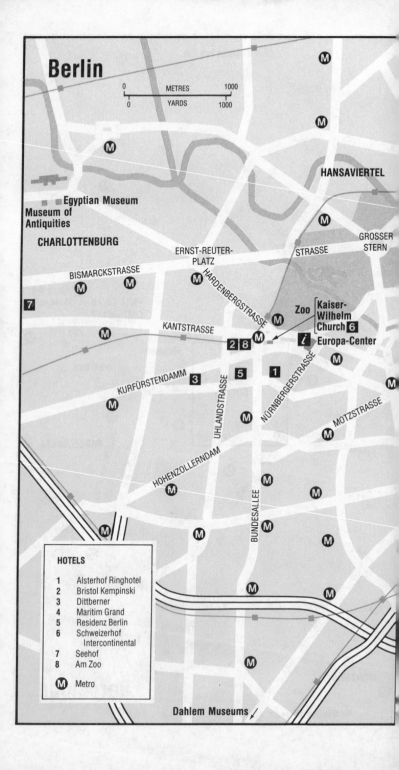

Berlin

METRES 0 — 1000
YARDS 0 — 1000

HANSAVIERTEL

Egyptian Museum
Museum of
Antiquities

CHARLOTTENBURG

GROSSER
STERN

ERNST-REUTER-
PLATZ

STRASSE

BISMARCKSTRASSE

HARDENBERGSTRASSE

Zoo
Kaiser-
Wilhelm
Church **6**

KANTSTRASSE

2 **8**

i Europa-Center

KURFÜRSTENDAMM

3

5

1

NÜRNBERGERSTRASSE

UHLANDSTRASSE

MOTZSTRASSE

HOHENZOLLERNDAM

BUNDESALLEE

HOTELS

1   Alsterhof Ringhotel
2   Bristol Kempinski
3   Dittberner
4   Maritim Grand
5   Residenz Berlin
6   Schweizerhof
     Intercontinental
7   Seehof
8   Am Zoo

Ⓜ   Metro

Dahlem Museums

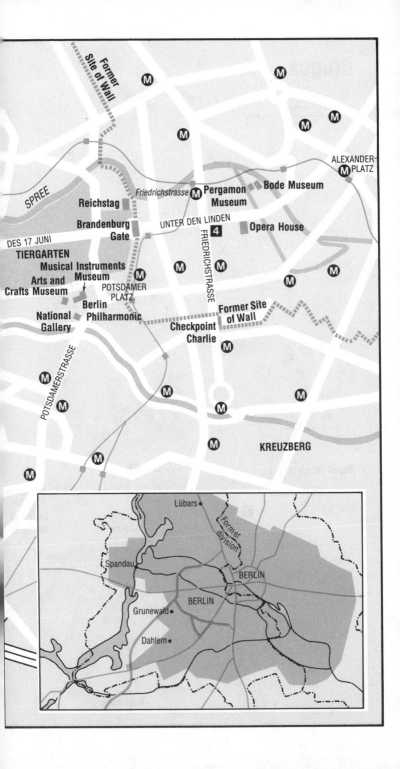

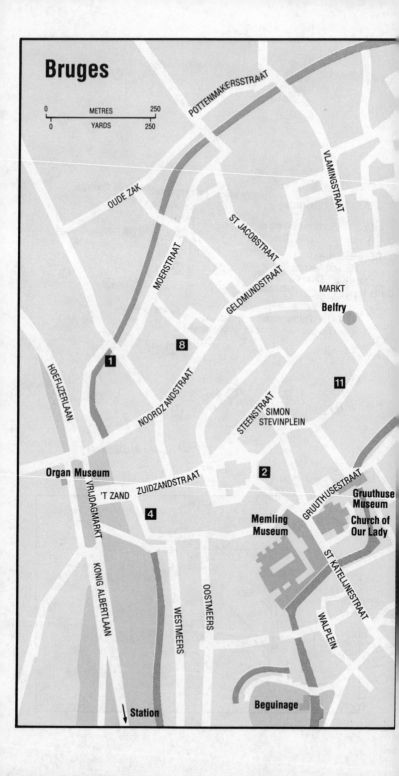

Bruges

0   METRES   250
0   YARDS   250

POTTENMAKERSSTRAAT

VLAMINGSTRAAT

OUDE ZAK

ST JACOBSTRAAT

MOERSTRAAT

GELDMUNDSTRAAT

MARKT

Belfry

8

1

NOORDZANDSTRAAT

HOEFIJZERLAAN

11

STEENSTRAAT

SIMON
STEVINPLEIN

Organ Museum

VRIJDAGMARKT

'T ZAND

ZUIDZANDSTRAAT

2

4

GRUUTHUSESTRAAT

Gruuthuse
Museum

Memling
Museum

Church of
Our Lady

KONIG ALBERTLAAN

OOSTMEERS

WESTMEERS

ST KATELIJNESTRAAT

WALPLEIN

Station

Beguinage

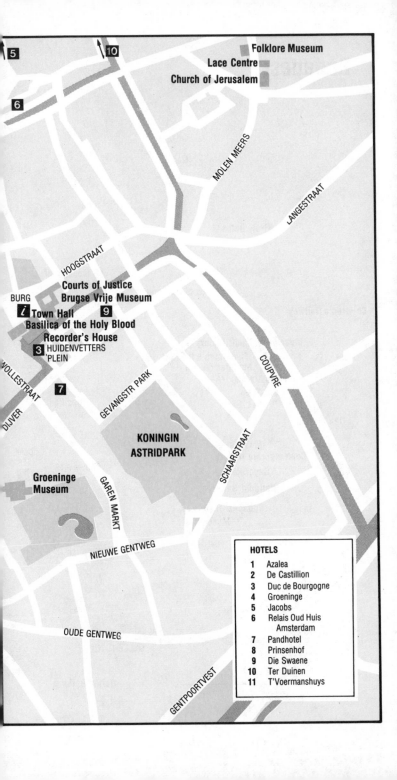

Folklore Museum

Lace Centre

Church of Jerusalem

MOLEN MEERS

LANGESTRAAT

HOOGSTRAAT

Courts of Justice
Brugse Vrije Museum

BURG

Town Hall

Basilica of the Holy Blood

Recorder's House

HUIDENVETTERS
'PLEIN

WOLLESTRAAT

DIJVER

GEVANGSTR PARK

COUPVRE

KONINGIN
ASTRIDPARK

SCHAARSTRAAT

Groeninge
Museum

GAREN MARKT

NIEUWE GENTWEG

OUDE GENTWEG

GENTPOORTVEST

HOTELS

1	Azalea
2	De Castillion
3	Duc de Bourgogne
4	Groeninge
5	Jacobs
6	Relais Oud Huis Amsterdam
7	Pandhotel
8	Prinsenhof
9	Die Swaene
10	Ter Duinen
11	T'Voermanshuys

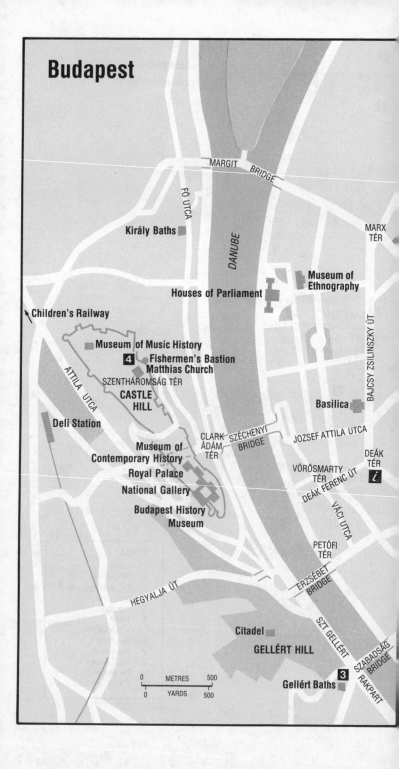

Budapest

MARGIT BRIDGE

FŐ UTCA

MARX TÉR

Király Baths

DANUBE

Museum of Ethnography

Houses of Parliament

Children's Railway

BAJCSY ZSILINSZKY ÚT

Museum of Music History

4 Fishermen's Bastion
Matthias Church

SZENTHÁROMSÁG TÉR

Basilica

CASTLE HILL

ATTILA UTCA

Deli Station

CLARK SZÉCHENYI
ÁDÁM BRIDGE
TÉR

JOZSEF ATTILA UTCA

DEÁK TÉR

Museum of Contemporary History

VÖRÖSMARTY TÉR

DEÁK FERENC ÚT

i

Royal Palace

National Gallery

VÁCI UTCA

Budapest History Museum

PETŐFI TÉR

ERZSÉBET BRIDGE

HEGYALJA ÚT

SZT GELLÉRT

SZABADSÁG BRIDGE

Citadel

GELLÉRT HILL

RAKPART

0   METRES   500
0   YARDS   500

3

Gellért Baths

Széchenyi Baths

Museum of Fine Arts

Museum of
Agriculture

HÖSÖK
TERE

Museum of Transport

PODMANICZKY UTCA

GYÖRGY ÚT

VAROSLIGET

Nyugati Station

ANDRASSY ÚT

AJTÓSI DÜRRER SOR

TERÉZ

6

KÖRÚT

ERZSÉBET KÖRÚT

State Opera
House

Café Hungaria

Keleki Station

Synagogue

DOHÁNY UTCA

RÁKÓCZI ÚT

5

KÖRÚT

1

MÚZEUM KÖRÚT

2

JOZSEF

Hungarian National
Museum

KALVIN TÉR

ÜLLÖI ÚT

Museum of Applied Arts

HOTELS	
1	Astoria
2	Erzsébet
3	Gellért
4	Hilton
5	Nemzeti
6	Radisson Béke

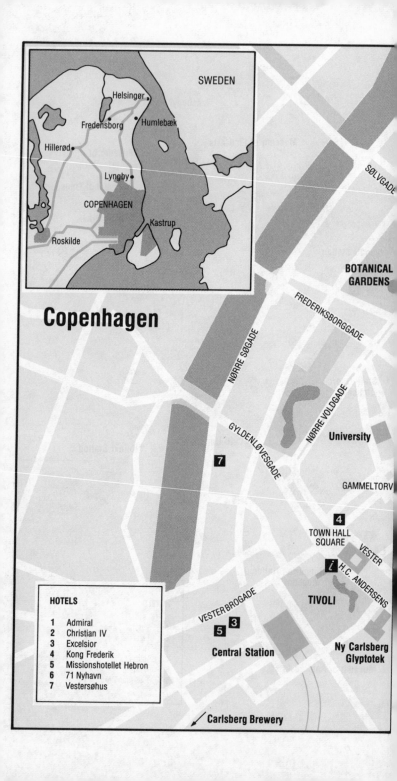

Copenhagen

SWEDEN

Helsingør

Fredensborg • Humlebæk

Hillerød •

Lyngby •

COPENHAGEN

Kastrup

Roskilde

SØLVGADE

BOTANICAL
GARDENS

FREDERIKSBORGGADE

NØRRE SØGADE

NØRRE VOLDGADE

GYLDENLØVESGADE

University

7

GAMMELTORV

4

TOWN HALL
SQUARE

VESTER

i H.C. ANDERSENS

TIVOLI

VESTER BROGADE

5 3

Central Station

Ny Carlsberg
Glyptotek

HOTELS

1 Admiral
2 Christian IV
3 Excelsior
4 Kong Frederik
5 Missionshotellet Hebron
6 71 Nyhavn
7 Vestersøhus

Carlsberg Brewery

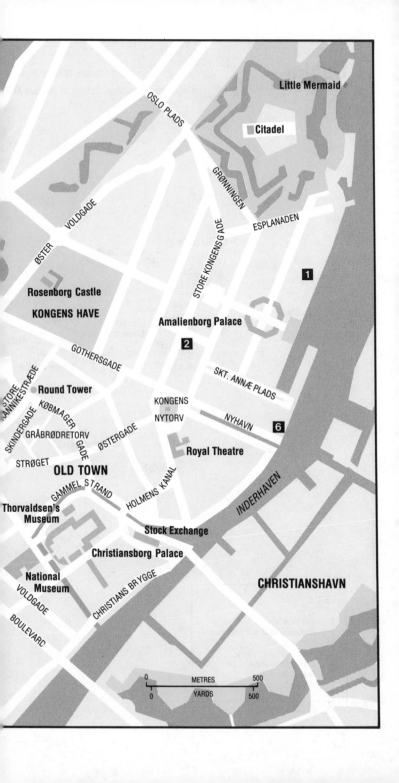

Dublin

Dublin Writers Museum

Hugh Lane Municipal Gallery of Modern Art

PARNELL STREET

MARY STREET

CAPEL STREET

CHURCH STREET

PHOENIX PARK ←

St Michan's

Four Courts

ARRAN QUAY

ORMOND QUAY

INNS QUAY

USHER'S QUAY

BRIDGE ST

MERCHANTS QUAY

WINE TAVERN

WOOD QUAY

WELLINGTON QUAY

Olympia Theatre

Guinness Hop Store Museum

Christ Church Cathedral

LORD EDWARD ST

DAME ST

City Hall

CORNMARKET

HIGH ST

Iveagh Market

FRANCES STREET

PATRICK ST

NICHOLAS ST

Dublin Castle

AUNGIER ST STH

St Patrick's Cathedral

NEW STREET SOUTH

WEXFORD ST

CAMDEN

CLANBRASSIL ST

HARRINGTON ST

RICHMO

GROVE ROAD

HOTELS

1 The Fitzwilliam
2 Georgian House and Ante Room
3 Gresham
4 Jurys Hotel and Towers
5 Leeson Court Hotel
6 Russell Court
7 The Shelbourne

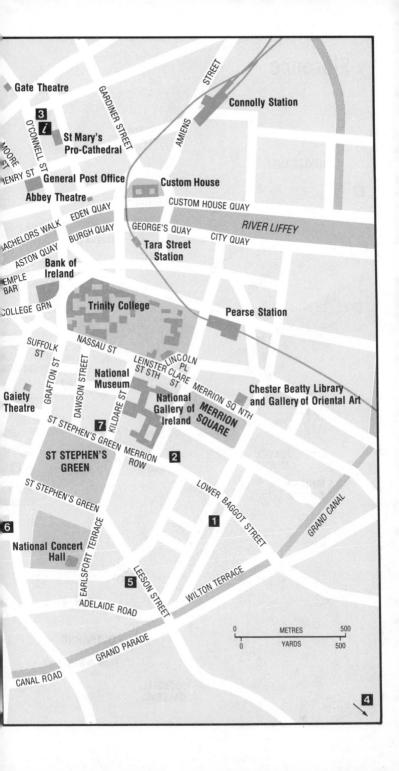

◆ **Gate Theatre**

3 *i*

St Mary's Pro-Cathedral

GARDINER STREET

O'CONNELL ST

MOORE ST

HENRY ST

General Post Office

Abbey Theatre

BACHELORS WALK

EDEN QUAY

BURGH QUAY

ASTON QUAY

TEMPLE BAR

COLLEGE GRN

Bank of Ireland

SUFFOLK ST

NASSAU ST

GRAFTON ST

DAWSON STREET

Gaiety Theatre

National Museum

KILDARE ST

7

ST STEPHEN'S GREEN

ST STEPHEN'S GREEN

ST STEPHEN'S GREEN

MERRION ROW

2

6

National Concert Hall

EARLSFORT TERRACE

LEESON STREET

5

ADELAIDE ROAD

GRAND PARADE

CANAL ROAD

STREET

AMIENS STREET

Connolly Station

Custom House

CUSTOM HOUSE QUAY

GEORGE'S QUAY

CITY QUAY

RIVER LIFFEY

Tara Street Station

Trinity College

Pearse Station

LEINSTER ST STH

LINCOLN PL

CLARE ST

MERRION SQ NTH

National Gallery of Ireland

MERRION SQUARE

Chester Beatty Library and Gallery of Oriental Art

1

LOWER BAGGOT STREET

GRAND CANAL

WILTON TERRACE

| 0 | METRES | 500 |
| 0 | YARDS | 500 |

4

Florence

OGNISSANTI

Station

VIA FAENZA

VIA NAZIONALE

PZA STAZIONE

VIA DELLA SCALA

S Maria Novella

S Lorenzo

VIA DE CERRETANI

2

VIA SOLFERINO

VIA PALAZZUOLO

BORGO OGNISSANTI

VIA MONTEBELLO

Ognissanti

1

VIA DELLA SPADA

VIA DE PECORI

VIA DE TORNABUONI

VIA ROMA

PZA DELLA REPUBBLICA

VIA DEL VIGNA NUOVA

VIA STROZZI

9

7

VIA DEL PARIONE

PONTE A VESPUCCI

PONTE ALLA CARRAIA

CALIMALA

VIA PORTA

BORGO S FREDIANO

LUNGARNO GUICCIARDINI

PONTE S TRINITA

Palazzo Davanzati

VIA POR S MARIA

3

PZA DEL CARMINE

VIA S MONACA

VIA S SPIRITO

BORGO S JACOPO

Ponte Vecchio

S Maria del Cármine

S Spirito

VIA DE SERRAGLI

VIA S AGOSTINO

PZA S SPIRITO

S MAZZETTA

VIA MAGGIO

PZA DEL PITTI

Pitti Palace

VIA ROMANA

OLTRARNO

Forte di Belvedere

BÓBOLI GARDENS

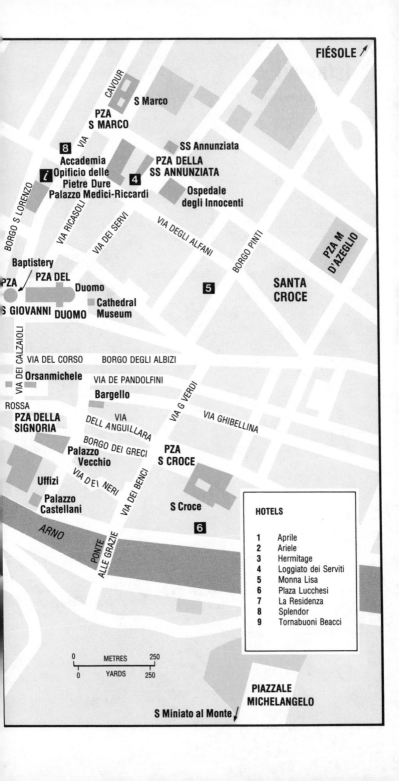

FIÉSOLE ↗

CAVOUR

S Marco

PZA
S MARCO

VIA

8

Accademia
i Opificio delle
Pietre Dure
Palazzo Medici-Riccardi

SS Annunziata

PZA DELLA
SS ANNUNZIATA

4

Ospedale
degli Innocenti

BORGO S LORENZO

VIA RICASOLI

VIA DEI SERVI

VIA DEGLI ALFANI

BORGO PINTI

PZA M
D'AZEGLIO

Baptistery

PZA / PZA DEL

S GIOVANNI DUOMO

Duomo

Cathedral
Museum

5

SANTA
CROCE

VIA DEI CALZAIOLI

VIA DEL CORSO

BORGO DEGLI ALBIZI

VIA DEI

Orsanmichele

VIA DE PANDOLFINI

ROSSA

Bargello

PZA DELLA
SIGNORIA

VIA
DELL'ANGUILLARA

BORGO DEI GRECI

Palazzo
Vecchio

VIA DEI NERI

Uffizi

Palazzo
Castellani

ARNO

VIA G VERDI

VIA GHIBELLINA

PZA
S CROCE

VIA DEI BENCI

S Croce

6

PONTE
ALLE GRAZIE

HOTELS

1   Aprile
2   Ariele
3   Hermitage
4   Loggiato dei Serviti
5   Monna Lisa
6   Plaza Lucchesi
7   La Residenza
8   Splendor
9   Tornabuoni Beacci

0   METRES   250

0   YARDS   250

PIAZZALE
MICHELANGELO

S Miniato al Monte ↓

Istanbul

Eyüp Mosque

FATIH BRIDGE

Kariye Museum

EDIRNEKAPI CADDESI

ABDÜLEZEL PAŞA CADDESI

GOLDEN HORN

ATATÜRK BRIDGE

TOPKAPI

City Walls

FEVZI CADDESI

VATAN

ATATÜRK BULVARI

Süleymaniye Mosque

MILLET CADDESI

CADDESI

6

4

ORDU CADDESI

KENNEDY CADDESI

BELGRATKAPISI DEMIRHANE

KENNEDY CADDESI

0	METRES	1000
0	YARDS	1000

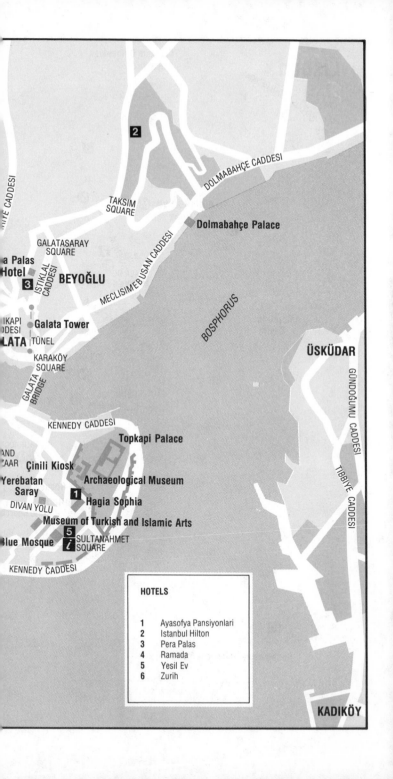

DOLMABAHÇE CADDESI

TAKSIM
SQUARE

Dolmabahçe Palace

GALATASARAY
SQUARE

MECLISIMEBUSAN CADDESI

...DDESI

...a Palas
Hotel

3 ISTIKLAL
CADDESI

BEYOĞLU

BOSPHORUS

ÜSKÜDAR

...IKAPI
...ODESI

Galata Tower

GALATA

TÜNEL

KARAKÖY
SQUARE

GÜNDOĞUMU CADDESI

GALATA
BRIDGE

TIBBIYE CADDESI

KENNEDY CADDESI

...AND
...AAR

Çinili Kiosk

Topkapi Palace

**Yerebatan
Saray**

Archaeological Museum

1

DIVAN YOLU

Hagia Sophia

Museum of Turkish and Islamic Arts

5

Blue Mosque

i

SULTANAHMET
SQUARE

KENNEDY CADDESI

```
HOTELS

1    Ayasofya Pansiyonlari
2    Istanbul Hilton
3    Pera Palas
4    Ramada
5    Yesil Ev
6    Zurih
```

KADIKÖY

Sintra

Queluz

LISBON

Belém

River Tagus

ALMADA

25 Abril Bridge

National Museum of Azulejos

AVENIDA ALMIRANTE REIS

AVENIDA GENERAL ROCADAS

AVENIDA INFANTE D. HENRIQUE

RUA DA PALMA

Ⓜ

Ⓜ

7

CAMPO DE SANTA CLARA

MOURARIA

São Vicente de Fora

Castelo de São Jorge

Ⓜ ROSSIO

SANTA CRUZ

Museum of Decorative Arts

Santa Luzia

RUA DA PRATA

RUA AUGUSTA

RUA DO OURO

BAIXA

ALFAMA

Cathedral

Conceição Velha Church

PRAÇA DO COMERCIO

DAS NAUS

RIVER TAGUS

HOTELS

1	Avenida Palace
2	Capitol
3	Lisboa Plaza
4	Meridien Lisboa
5	Principe Real
6	Rex
7	Albergaria Senhora do Monte
8	Sheraton
9	Tivoli Lisboa
10	York House

Ⓜ Metro

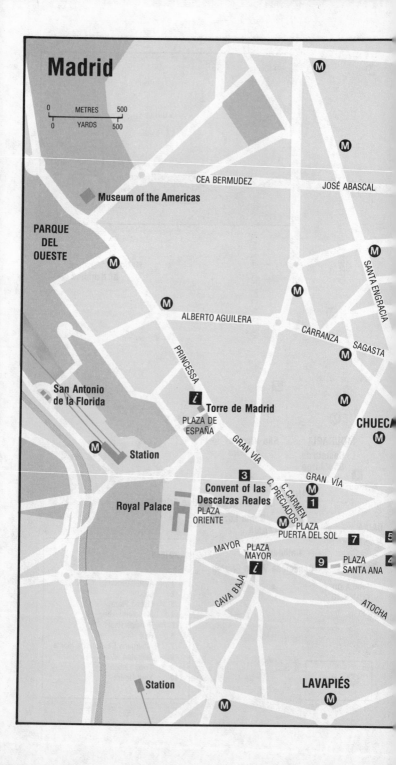

Madrid

METRES 0 — 500

YARDS 0 — 500

Museum of the Americas

PARQUE DEL OUESTE

CEA BERMUDEZ

JOSÉ ABASCAL

SANTA ENGRACIA

ALBERTO AGUILERA

CARRANZA

SAGASTA

PRINCESSA

San Antonio de la Florida

Torre de Madrid

PLAZA DE ESPAÑA

CHUECA

Station

GRAN VÍA

GRAN VÍA

C. CARMEN

C. PRECIADOS

3

1

Convent de las Descalzas Reales

Royal Palace

PLAZA ORIENTE

PLAZA PUERTA DEL SOL

7

5

MAYOR

PLAZA MAYOR

9

PLAZA SANTA ANA

4

CAVA BAJA

ATOCHA

Station

LAVAPIÉS

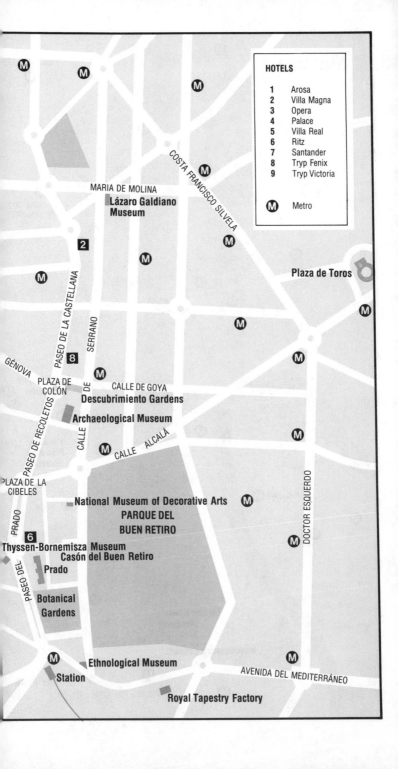

HOTELS

1	Arosa
2	Villa Magna
3	Opera
4	Palace
5	Villa Real
6	Ritz
7	Santander
8	Tryp Fenix
9	Tryp Victoria

Ⓜ Metro

COSTA FRANCISCO SILVELA

MARIA DE MOLINA

Lázaro Galdiano Museum

Plaza de Toros

PASEO DE LA CASTELLANA

SERRANO

GÉNOVA

CALLE DE

CALLE DE GOYA

Descubrimiento Gardens

PLAZA DE COLÓN

Archaeological Museum

PASEO DE RECOLETOS

CALLE

CALLE ALCALÁ

PLAZA DE LA CIBELES

National Museum of Decorative Arts

PARQUE DEL BUEN RETIRO

DOCTOR ESQUERDO

PRADO

Thyssen-Bornemisza Museum

Casón del Buen Retiro

PASEO DEL

Prado

Botanical Gardens

Ethnological Museum

Station

AVENIDA DEL MEDITERRÁNEO

Royal Tapestry Factory

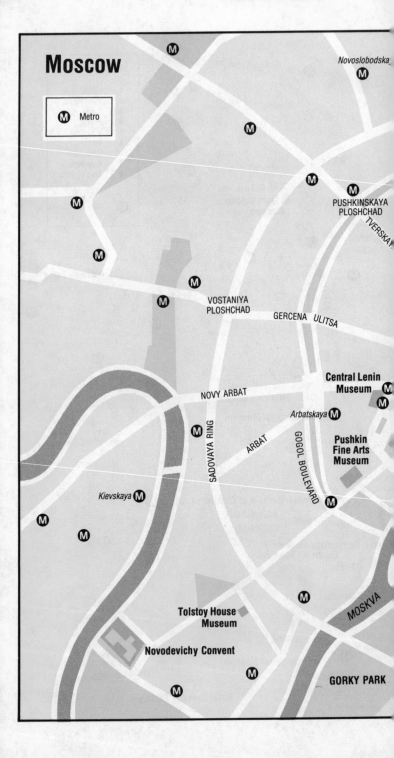

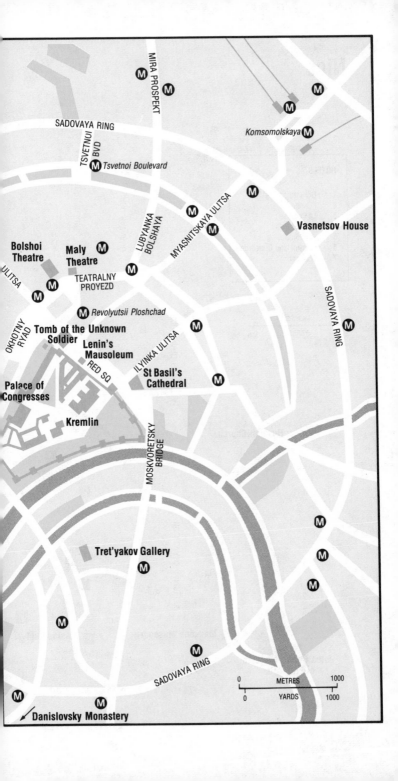

MIRA PROSPEKT

SADOVAYA RING

TSVETNOI BVD

(M) Tsvetnoi Boulevard

Komsomolskaya **(M)**

LUBYANKA BOLSHAYA

MYASNITSKAYA ULITSA

Vasnetsov House

Bolshoi Theatre

Maly Theatre

ULITSA

TEATRALNY PROYEZD

SADOVAYA RING

(M) Revolyutsii Ploshchad

Tomb of the Unknown Soldier

OKHOTNY RYAD

Lenin's Mausoleum

ILYINKA ULITSA

RED SQ

St Basil's Cathedral

Palace of Congresses

Kremlin

MOSKVORETSKY BRIDGE

Tret'yakov Gallery

SADOVAYA RING

| 0 | METRES | 1000 |
| 0 | YARDS | 1000 |

Danislovsky Monastery

Nice

HOTELS

1 Durante
2 l'Oasis
3 La Perouse
4 Le Petit Palais
5 Vendôme
6 Westminster Concorde
7 Windsor

METRES 500
YARDS 500

BD DE GORBELLA

BOULEVARD DE CESSOLE

BOULEVARD RAYNAUD

AVENUE BORRIGLIONE

AVENUE MALAUSSENA

BOULEVARD GAMBETTA

Russian Church

Station

AVENUE THIERS

1

2

BOULEVARD GAMBETTA

AV DES FLEURS

BOULEVARD VICTOR HUGO

RUE DU MARÉCHAL JOFFRE

7

RUE DE FRANCE

i

Masséna Museum

6 Casino Ruhl

Jules Chéret Museum
of Fine Arts

PROMENADE DES ANGLAIS

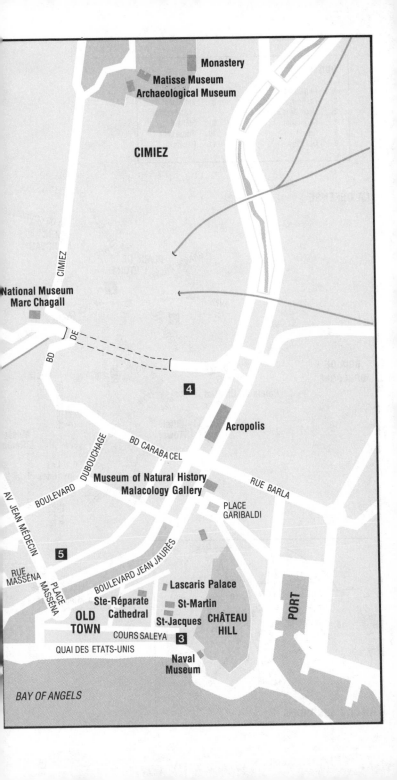

Monastery

Matisse Museum

Archaeological Museum

CIMIEZ

CIMIEZ

National Museum
Marc Chagall

BD DE

4

Acropolis

DUBOUCHAGE

BD CARABACEL

Museum of Natural History
Malacology Gallery

RUE BARLA

BOULEVARD

PLACE
GARIBALDI

AV JEAN MÉDECIN

5

BOULEVARD JEAN JAURÉS

RUE
MASSÉNA

PLACE
MASSÉNA

Lascaris Palace

Ste-Réparate
Cathedral

St-Martin

St-Jacques

CHÂTEAU
HILL

PORT

OLD
TOWN

COURS SALEYA

3

QUAI DES ETATS-UNIS

Naval
Museum

BAY OF ANGELS

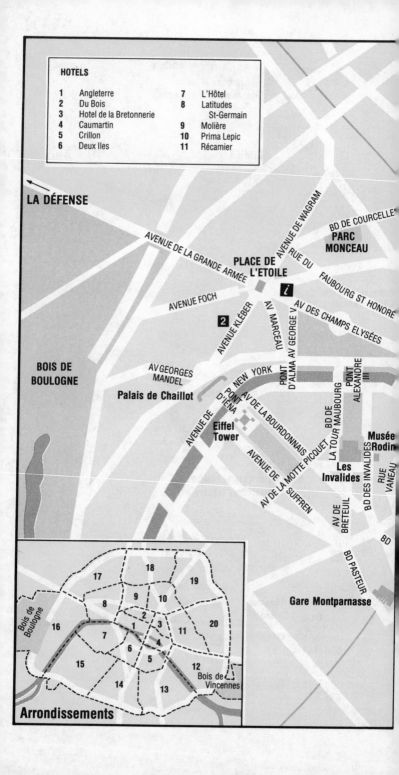

HOTELS

1 Angleterre
2 Du Bois
3 Hotel de la Bretonnerie
4 Caumartin
5 Crillon
6 Deux Iles
7 L'Hôtel
8 Latitudes
  St-Germain
9 Molière
10 Prima Lepic
11 Récamier

LA DÉFENSE

AVENUE DE WAGRAM

BD DE COURCELLE

PARC MONCEAU

AVENUE DE LA GRANDE ARMÉE

PLACE DE L'ETOILE

RUE DU

FAUBOURG ST HONORÉ

AVENUE FOCH

AV MARCEAU

AV DES CHAMPS ELYSÉES

AVENUE KLÉBER

AV GEORGE V

PONT D'ALMA

2

AV GEORGES MANDEL

BOIS DE BOULOGNE

NEW YORK

Palais de Chaillot

PONT D'IÉNA

AV DE LA BOURDONNAIS

PONT ALEXANDRE III

AVENUE DE

Eiffel Tower

BD DE LA TOUR MAUBOURG

Musée Rodin

RUE VANEAU

AVENUE DE LA MOTTE PICQUET

Les Invalides

BD DES INVALIDES

AVENUE DE SUFFREN

AV DE BRETEUIL

BD

BD PASTEUR

Gare Montparnasse

Bois de Boulogne

17
18
19
8
9
10
2
1
3
16
7
11
20
6
5
15
4
12 Bois de Vincennes
14
13

Arrondissements

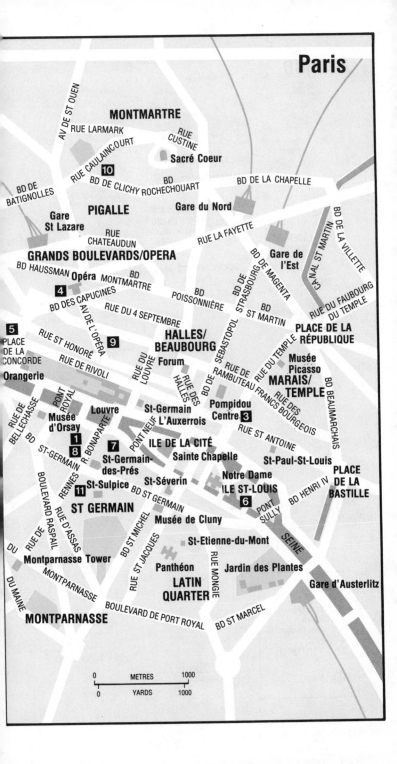

Paris

MONTMARTRE

AV DE ST OUEN

RUE LARMARK

RUE CAULAINCOURT

RUE CUSTINE

Sacré Coeur

10

BD DE CLICHY

BD ROCHECHOUART

BD DE LA CHAPELLE

BD DE BATIGNOLLES

PIGALLE

Gare St Lazare

Gare du Nord

RUE CHATEAUDUN

RUE LA FAYETTE

BD DE LA VILLETTE

BD DE STRASBOURG

CANAL ST MARTIN

GRANDS BOULEVARDS/OPERA

BD HAUSSMAN

Opéra

MONTMARTRE

BD

Gare de l'Est

4

BD POISSONNIÈRE

BD DE MAGENTA

RUE DU FAUBOURG DU TEMPLE

BD DES CAPUCINES

RUE DU 4 SEPTEMBRE

AV DE L'OPERA

BD ST MARTIN

PLACE DE LA RÉPUBLIQUE

5

PLACE DE LA CONCORDE

RUE ST HONORÉ

9

HALLES/ BEAUBOURG

RUE DU LOUVRE

Forum

RUE DE RAMBUTEAU

BD DE SEBASTOPOL

RUE DU TEMPLE

Musée Picasso

MARAIS/ TEMPLE

RUE DE RIVOLI

RUE DES HALLES

BD DE

FRANCS BOURGEOIS

RUE DES

BD BEAUMARCHAIS

Orangerie

PONT ROYAL

RUE DE BELLECHASSE

Louvre

St-Germain L'Auxerrois

Pompidou Centre **3**

RUE ST ANTOINE

Musée d'Orsay

1

R. BONAPARTE

PONT NEUF

ILE DE LA CITÉ

St-Paul-St-Louis

8

BD ST-GERMAIN

7

St-Germain-des-Prés

Sainte Chapelle

Notre Dame

PLACE DE LA BASTILLE

RENNES

11

St-Sulpice

St-Séverin

ILE ST-LOUIS

BD HENRI IV

BD ST GERMAIN

6

PONT SULLY

ST GERMAIN

Musée de Cluny

SEINE

BOULEVARD RASPAIL

RUE D'ASSAS

BD ST MICHEL

St-Etienne-du-Mont

RUE DU MAINE

RUE DE

DU

Montparnasse Tower

MONTPARNASSE

RUE JACQUES

Panthéon

RUE MONGIE

LATIN QUARTER

Jardin des Plantes

Gare d'Austerlitz

MONTPARNASSE

BOULEVARD DE PORT ROYAL

BD ST MARCEL

0   METRES   1000

0   YARDS   1000

Prague

Station

JELENI

MARIÁNSKÉ BRADBY

HRADČANY

U PRAŠNÁEHOMOSTU

Convent of St George

VALDŠTEJNSKÉ NÁMĚSTÍ

Hradčany Castle

Sternberk Palace

HRADČANSKÁE NÁMĚSTÍ

KEPLEROVA

LORETÁNSKÉ NÁMĚSTÍ

St Vitus's Cathedral

TOMÁŠSKÁ

Wallenstein Palace

LORETÁNSKÁ

LORETÁNSKÁ

LETENSKÁ

Schwarrenberg Palace

NERUDOVA MALOSTRANSKÉ NÁMĚSTÍ

POHOŘELEC

MALTÉZSKÉ NÁMĚSTÍ

TRŽIŠTĚ

MOSTECKÁ

5

Strahov Abbey

KARMELITSKÁ

VELKOPŘEVORSKÉ NÁMĚSTÍ

MALÁ STRANA

KAMPA

VŠEHRDOVA

PETRÍSKÉ SADY

ÚJEZD

MOST 1

STŘELECKÝ OSTROV

DÉTSKÝ OSTROV

S. M. KIROVA

HOTELS

1 Esplanade
2 Forum
3 Inter-Continental
4 Paříž
5 U Tří Pštrosů

Ⓜ Metro

LETENSKESADY

VLTAVA

MÁNOSŮV
MOST

PAŘÍŽSKÁ

3

17 LISTOPADU

STARÉ MĚSTO

Josefov
Museum of Applied Arts

REVOLUČNÍ

KARLŮV MOST
(CHARLES BRIDGE)

M

STAROMĚSTSKÉ
NÁMĚSTÍ

TÝNSKÁ

Týn
Church

JAKUBSKÁ

Old
Town
Hall

MAISLOVA

HUSOVA

CELETNÁ

NÁMĚSTÍ
REPUBLIKY

Smetana
Museum

KARLOVA

MALÉ
NÁMĚSTÍ

ŽELEZNÁ

HYBERNSKÁ

Nostitz Theatre

NA PŘÍKOPĚ

PANSKÁ

4

BETLÉMSKÉ
NÁMĚSTÍ

DIVADELNÍ

M

JINDŘIŠSKÁ

VÁCLAVSKÉ NÁMĚSTÍ

MÁJE

NÁRODNI

National Theatre

WASHINGTONOVA

SLOVANSKÝ
OSTROV

KŘEMENCOVA

NOVÉ MĚSTO

VODIČKOVA

1

M

ŠTĚPANSKÁ

0	METRES	500
0	YARDS	500

Dvořák Museum

2 ↓

M

Rome

Villa Giulia

VILL

Santa Maria del Pópolo

PIAZZA
DEL POPOLO

7

VIA DI
RIPETTA

VIA COLA DI RIENZO

VIA DI
BABU

9

VIA DEL

Castel
Sant'
Angelo

VIA CRESCENZIO

PIAZZA
CAVOUR

Ara Pacis
Augustae

CONDOT

VI
CORSO

Vatican
Museums

2

PIAZZA
SAN
PIETRO

VIA DELLE
CONCILIAZIONE

San Luigi
dei Francesi

VIA DELLA SCROFA

St Peter's

10

13

1

PIAZZA
NAVONA

PZA
ROTONDA

CORSO VITTORIO EMANUELE

Pantheon

VIA DELLA

JANICULUM
HILL

CAMPO DEI FIORI

PIAZZA
FARNESE

Santa Maria
sopra Minerva

Ges

TIBER

Corsini
Gallery

Villa
Farnesina

Spada Gallery

PIAZZALE
GARIBALDI

Theatre of
Marcellus

San Pietro di Montorio

TRASTEVERE

VIA DELLA MARMORATA

HOTELS

1	Cesari
2	Columbus
3	Excelsior
4	Forum
5	D'Inghilterra
6	King
7	Locarno
8	Madrid
9	Margutta
10	Portoghesi
11	Regina Baglioni
12	Scalinata di Spagna
13	Sole al Pantheon

St Petersburg

KAMENNOOSTROVSKY PROSPEKT Ⓜ

BOLSHOI PROSPEKT

Ⓜ **LENIN PARK**

Peter the Great's Cabin

Auror Cruise

Summer Palace

Peter and Paul Fortress

SUMMER Field GARDENS of Mars

PUSHKINSKAYA PLOSHCHAD • **Strelka**

Ⓜ

VASILYEVSKY ISLAND

Pushkin's Flat

Hermitage Winter Palace

Temple of the Spilled Blood

Admiralty

Russian Museum

DVORTSOVAYA PLOSHCHAD

Dom Knigi

Maly Theatre Philharmonia

NEVSKY Ⓜ

Gastronom

Ⓜ PROSPEKT

St Isaac's Cathedral

Gostinny Dvor

TEATRAL'NAYA PLOSHCHAD

Mariinsky Theatre

VOZNESENSKY PROSPEKT

SENNAYA Ⓜ PLOSHCHAD

PROSPEKT

SADOVAYA ULITSA

FONTANKA CANAL

ZAGORODNYY Ⓜ **Station**

Ⓜ

| 0 | METRES | 1000 |
| 0 | YARDS | 1000 |

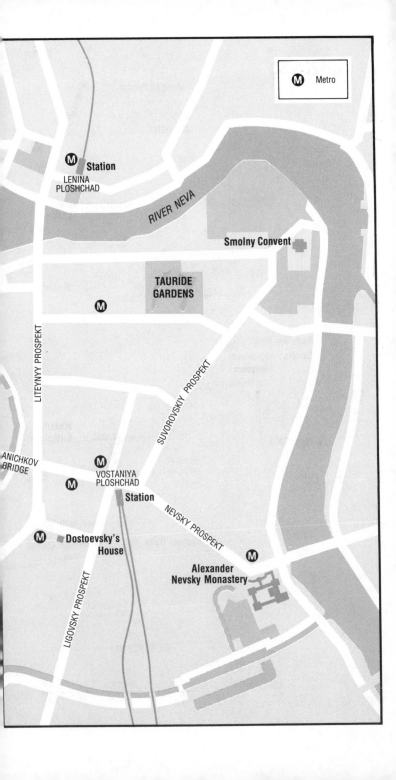

M | Metro

M **Station**
LENINA
PLOSHCHAD

RIVER NEVA

Smolny Convent

**TAURIDE
GARDENS**

M

SUVOROVSKIY PROSPEKT

LITEYNYY PROSPEKT

ANICHKOV
BRIDGE

M
VOSTANIYA
PLOSHCHAD

M

Station

NEVSKY PROSPEKT

M **Dostoevsky's
House**

M

**Alexander
Nevsky Monastery**

LIGOVSKIY PROSPEKT

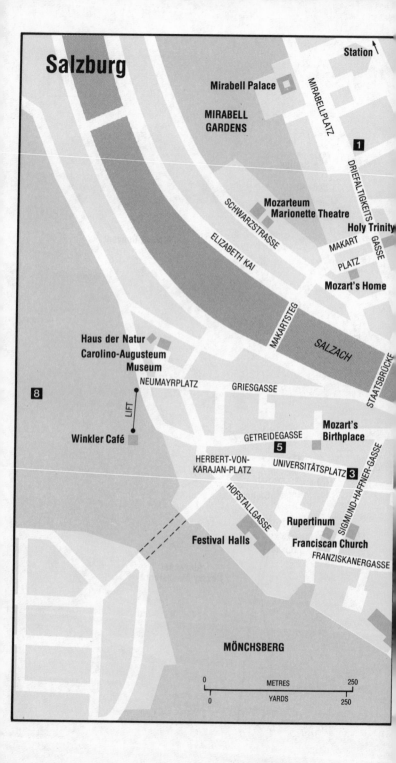

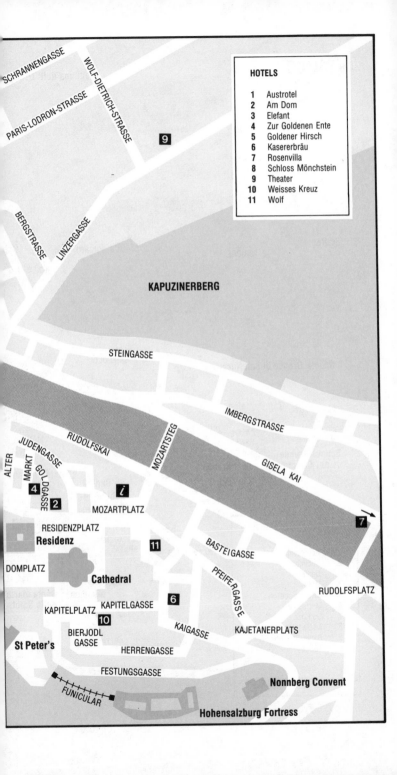

HOTELS

1 Austrotel
2 Am Dom
3 Elefant
4 Zur Goldenen Ente
5 Goldener Hirsch
6 Kasererbräu
7 Rosenvilla
8 Schloss Mönchstein
9 Theater
10 Weisses Kreuz
11 Wolf

SCHRANNENGASSE

WOLF-DIETRICH-STRASSE

PARIS-LODRON-STRASSE

9

BERGSTRASSE

LINZERGASSE

KAPUZINERBERG

STEINGASSE

RUDOLFSKAI

IMBERGSTRASSE

MOZARTSTEG

GISELA KAI

ALTER

JUDENGASSE

MARKT

GOLDGASSE

4

2

i

MOZARTPLATZ

RESIDENZPLATZ

Residenz

11

BASTEIGASSE

7

DOMPLATZ

Cathedral

PFEIFERGASSE

RUDOLFSPLATZ

KAPITELPLATZ

KAPITELGASSE

6

10

KAIGASSE

KAJETANERPLATS

St Peter's

BIERJODL
GASSE

HERRENGASSE

FESTUNGSGASSE

Nonnberg Convent

FUNICULAR

Hohensalzburg Fortress

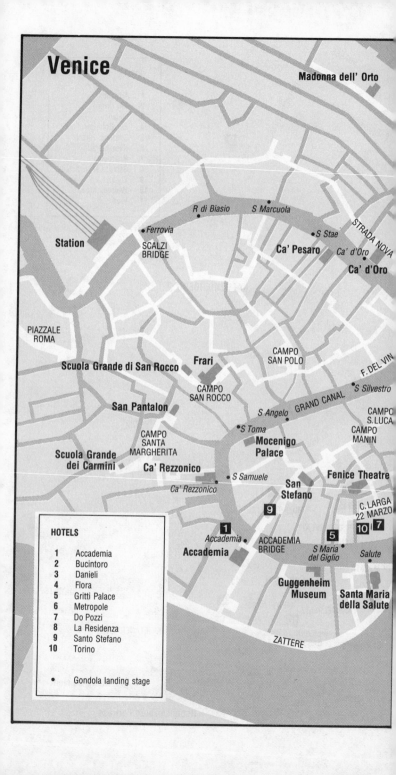

Venice

Madonna dell' Orto

Station

R di Biasio •   • S Marcuola

• Ferrovia   • S Stae

SCALZI BRIDGE

STRADA NOVA

Ca' Pesaro   Ca' d'Oro

Ca' d'Oro

PIAZZALE ROMA

Scuola Grande di San Rocco   Frari

CAMPO SAN POLO

F. DEL VIN

• S Silvestro

CAMPO SAN ROCCO

San Pantalon   S Angelo

GRAND CANAL

CAMPO S.LUCA

CAMPO SANTA MARGHERITA   • S Toma

Mocenigo Palace

CAMPO MANIN

Scuola Grande dei Carmini   Ca' Rezzonico

Ca' Rezzonico   • S Samuele

San Stefano

Fenice Theatre

9

C. LARGA 22 MARZO

1

Accademia •

ACCADEMIA BRIDGE

5

10 **7**

Accademia

S Maria del Giglio

Salute

Guggenheim Museum

Santa Maria della Salute

ZATTERE

HOTELS

1   Accademia
2   Bucintoro
3   Danieli
4   Flora
5   Gritti Palace
6   Metropole
7   Do Pozzi
8   La Residenza
9   Santo Stefano
10   Torino

•   Gondola landing stage

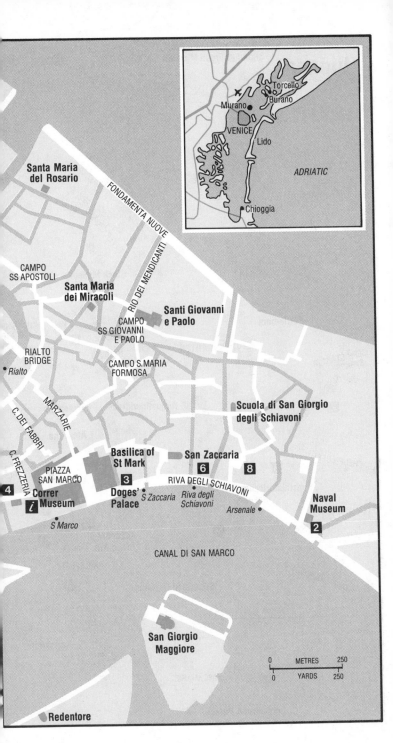

Santa Maria
del Rosario

FONDAMENTA NUOVE

RIO DEI MENDICANTI

CAMPO
SS APOSTOLI

Santa Maria
dei Miracoli

CAMPO
SS GIOVANNI
E PAOLO

Santi Giovanni
e Paolo

RIALTO
BRIDGE

• Rialto

CAMPO S.MARIA
FORMOSA

MARZARIE

C. DEI FABBRI

Scuola di San Giorgio
degli Schiavoni

C.FREZZERIA

PIAZZA
SAN MARCO

Basilica of
St Mark

3

San Zaccaria

6

8

4

Correr
Museum

i

Doges'
Palace

• S Zaccaria

RIVA DEGLI SCHIAVONI

Riva degli
Schiavoni

Naval
Museum

• S Marco

Arsenale •

2

CANAL DI SAN MARCO

San Giorgio
Maggiore

0   METRES   250
0   YARDS   250

Redentore

Torcello

Burano

• Murano

VENICE

Lido

ADRIATIC

• Chioggia

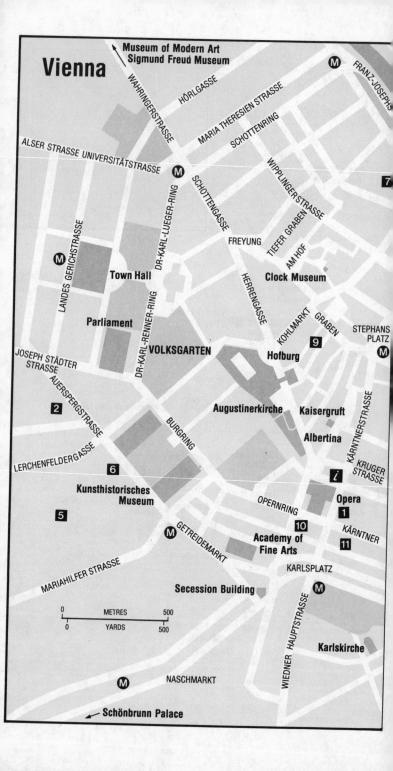

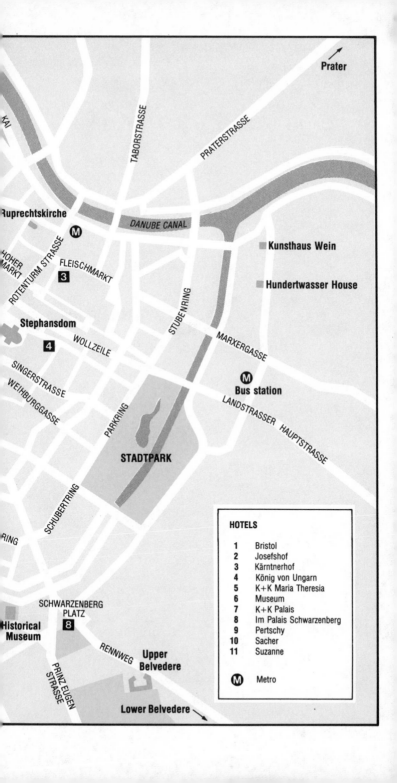

Prater

TABORSTRASSE

PRATERSTRASSE

KAI

Ruprechtskirche

(M)

DANUBE CANAL

HOHER MARKT

ROTENTURM STRASSE

FLEISCHMARKT

3

Stephansdom

4

WOLLZEILE

SINGERSTRASSE

WEIHBURGGASSE

PARKRING

STUBENRING

MARXERGASSE

(M)
Bus station

LANDSTRASSER HAUPTSTRASSE

Kunsthaus Wein

Hundertwasser House

STADTPARK

SCHUBERTRING

RING

SCHWARZENBERG PLATZ

8

Historical Museum

RENNWEG

PRINZ EUGEN STRASSE

Upper Belvedere

Lower Belvedere →

HOTELS

1   Bristol
2   Josefshof
3   Kärntnerhof
4   König von Ungarn
5   K+K Maria Theresia
6   Museum
7   K+K Palais
8   Im Palais Schwarzenberg
9   Pertschy
10 Sacher
11 Suzanne

(M)   Metro